QUEER DATA STUDIES

FEMINIST TECHNOSCIENCES

Rebecca Herzig and Banu Subramaniam, Series Editors

EDITED BY PATRICK KEILTY

QUEER

DATA

STUDIES

University of Washington Press *Seattle*

UNIVERSITY OF WASHINGTON PRESS *uwapress.uw.edu*

Cataloging information is available from the Library of Congress
LIBRARY OF CONGRESS CONTROL NUMBER: 2023946235
ISBN 9780295751962 (hardcover)
ISBN 9780295751979 (paperback)
ISBN *9780295751986 (ebook)*

♾ This paper meets the requirements of ANSI/NISO Z39.48-1992
(Permanence of Paper).

CONTENTS

ACKNOWLEDGMENTS

This volume is indebted in no small part to the personal participation of others. It saw its genesis in the especially conducive environments of the Technoscience Research Unit and Faculty of Information at the University of Toronto. I am especially indebted to the students, faculty, and administrative staff in these units for their support, encouragement, and intellectual generosity. Substantial portions of this volume were read by Melissa Adler, Barbara Brents, Elspeth Brown, Michael Brown, Ryan Conrad, Bianca Dahl, Dustin Friedman, Gregory Leazer, Cait McKinney, Maya Mikdashi, Stephen Molldrem, Eric Mykhalovskiy, Scott Richmond, David Seitz, Benjamin Weil, and Shana Ye. This book owes much to the intellectual and moral support of a number of colleagues, near and far, including Sharla Alegria, Claire Battershill, Jordan Bear, Malayna Bernstein, Kristen Bos, Zach Blas, James Cahill, Joseph Clarke, Beth Coleman, Marika Cifor, Priyank Chandra, Rachel Corbman, Negin Dayha, Robert Diaz, Dan Guadagnolo, Lynne Howarth, Lilly Irani, Selmin Kara, Irina Mihalache, Mireille Miller-Young, Robert Montoya, Michelle Murphy, Tim Murray, David Phillips, Leslie Shade, Rebecka Sheffield, Chris Smith, Olivier St-Cyr, Simon Stern, Siobhan Stevenson, and Bri Watson. My recent doctoral students, A. Hawk, Camille Intson, Maggie MacDonald, Emily Maemura, and Andrew Wiebe, always provide intellectual curiosity and point me in new directions. I discussed early ideas for this book in a media aesthetics writing group, which includes Brooke Belisle, Stephanie Boluk, Kris Cohen, Jacob Gaboury, Jim Hodge, Patrick Jagoda, Patrick LeMieux, and Scott Richmond.

Generous funding for the design of figures in this volume came from Sara Grimes in her role as director of the Knowledge Media Design Institute at the University of Toronto. Special thanks to Kenji Toyooka for his incredible design talent. Chris Dodge provided an excellent index for this volume. I am especially grateful to Banu Subramaniam for suggesting I publish this book as part of the Feminist Technoscience Series at the University of Washington Press. Banu provided initial feedback on this manuscript. I am grateful to all of the anonymous peer reviewers whose comments and suggestions improved the chapters in this volume. I cannot heap enough praise on Larin McLaughlin, the editorial director at UWP, for giving me the time, space, and freedom to develop this book fully. Evangelos Tziallas helped to develop the idea for the book in its infancy. Finally, throughout the writing and editing of this volume, the support of my partner, Matthew Schuman, has been especially meaningful. My short-haired gray cat, Lucy, has been a constant companion and delightful distraction during the time I spent editing the present volume.

QUEER DATA STUDIES

PATRICK KEILTY

Introduction

Queerness is often transmitted covertly. This has everything to do with the fact that leaving too much of a trace has often meant that the queer subject has left herself open for attack. Instead of being clearly available as visible evidence, queerness has instead existed as innuendo, gossip, fleeting moments, and performances that are meant to be interacted with by those within its epistemological sphere—while evaporating at the touch of those who would eliminate queer possibility.
—José Esteban Muñoz, "Ephemera as Evidence"

The loss of stories sharpens the hunger for them.
—Saidiya Hartman, "Venus in Two Acts"

QUEER DATA STUDIES theorizes data from bodies that have not historically assumed autonomy and therefore data sovereignty. What's a queer approach to data when queer bodies could never historically assume safety, privacy, and transparency? What does queer—as in peculiar or irregular—data look like? What might it mean to queer data? Since the publication of Laud Humphreys's *Tearoom Trade: Impersonal Sex in Public Places* in 1975, questions about the ways in which data impact queer subjects have proliferated throughout the subsequent decades and continue to provoke research to this day.[1] Ethical issues abound in Humphreys's methodology: posing as a participating voyeur, he observed men having sex in public toilets, he failed to acquire any form of consent, and he recorded vehicle license plates and used that information to track down participants and interview them under the (dis)guise of researching public health. Humphreys's study remains controversial to this day because the ethical dilemmas and quandaries it raised remain unresolved—how data is collected, with whom it is shared, how its analysis can impact the subject(s) from which it is derived, what qualifies as consent and privacy, and the false dichotomy between public and private.

Meanwhile, the way data politics affects queer subjects has taken on a new sense of urgency in light of a changing digital, health, and administrative landscape, from hostile antisex and antiqueer policies by major technology companies, the security theater of airports, the disproportionate rates of policing of queer people and people of color, digital surveillance in border security, the biopolitics of pharmaceutical companies, online data breaches, and the proliferation of digital health and administrative records, to name only a few. Therefore, this anthology challenges scholars to take up issues related to "queer data" and rethink the ways in which the extraction, circulation, modeling, governance, and use of data impacts queer subjects in a variety of contexts and how the power of data might be harnessed for queer ethics or queer lives. Like Catherine D'Ignazio and Lauren Klein's *Data Feminism*, this book does not conceive of data as numbers alone. Instead, it takes a capacious approach to data, to include archival data, stories, intimacies, sounds, research data, medical data, police data, maps, and algorithmic modeling, to name only a few.

Queer Data Studies is indebted to a rialto of lending, borrowing, and exchange from a wide range of research. It threads together disparate themes, debates, definitions, concepts, contradictions, and histories of queer data. What makes queer data distinct from cognate data studies is its ethical and political ambivalence toward data, the way it pushes us to think data beyond fixed forms, and how it creates an intellectual genealogy for queer studies of data that is not always obvious. The latter isn't a transformation of past research into "data studies." Attuned to data as an organizing intellectual force, the chapters in this volume reveal that much queer writing and thinking is preoccupied with data, even if it is not explicitly conceived as such. This conception of "queer data studies" therefore finds thinking about data in sometimes unlikely places, unencumbered by disciplinarity. Where and how do we locate queer data? Consider the epigraphs to this introduction for the ways in which queer thinking about data can be found in implicit places. José Esteban Muñoz and Saidiya Hartman together help us think about queer data's many paradoxes. Ostensibly, they each call for a very different relationship to data. For his part, Muñoz summons the long history of shared cultural forms, namely everyday performative gestures, that enable queer communities to evade people and institutions that despoil queer lives. Like Simone Browne's *Dark Matters*, Muñoz's work finds power in opacity. Yet he extends our understanding of opacity to recognize the value in gestural, fleeting, or irregular forms of data, accessible only to those within its epistemological sphere. Read as an analysis of data, Muñoz's "Ephemera as Evidence" broadens data to include data transmitted covertly, unfixed, or traceless, as a necessary precondition for queer survival. This isn't simply a way to evade surveillance. Instead, it's an approach to data that signifies only in particular ways, within particular contexts, or for particular people. Perhaps this is why so many queer scholars, including the contributors to this book, have come to embrace affect as a rich site for understanding queer experience; works by Eve Sedgwick, Sianne Ngai, Heather Love, Lauren Berlant, and Sarah Ahmed are among those cited in this volume. This book includes chapters, such as those by Mathew Gagné and Lina Žigelytė, that conceive of data ephemerally, as intimacy or sexual attraction — data that is visible in some contexts and opaque in others. Muñoz also demonstrates that opacity, surveillance, and evasion are not new topics for queer studies. They are part of our everyday experience, even if they're not always explicitly discussed within the context of data. The authors in this book cite several queer scholars who have engaged these topics in the past two decades; they include David Johnson, Jasbir Puar, Nicholas de Villiers, Mel Y. Chen, Toby Beauchamp, Zach Blas, C. Riley Snorton, Gary Kafer and Daniel Grinberg, and Harris Kornstein, to name only a few. Meanwhile, Nikita Shepard's chapter in this volume provides crucial historicization of opacity, surveillance, and evasion within queer contexts throughout much of the period since the mid-1970s. I strongly encourage readers to peruse Shepard's extensive bibliography, which provides a more thorough account of the relevant queer scholarship on surveillance than I can provide here. Reading Shepard's work paired with Gary Kafer's chapter, we can begin to understand a past and future of queer opacity. While each of the above authors is concerned with opacity in different contexts — the "Lavender Scare," figures of post-9/11 terrorism, disability politics, Black and trans identities, contemporary art, and mobile apps — they each suggest that queers have a long, sophisticated relationship to evading data capture. Based on much of this scholarship, one might speculate whether queers are data experts. Yet Harris Kornstein and Ryan Conrad's chapters quickly remind us that while queers are data experts in some respects, especially about the risks of pervasive surveillance and data overreach, we're uncritical of data in other contexts, such as third-party apps, larger data ecosystems, and the politics of data infrastructures.

By contrast, Saidiya Hartman reflects on the deeply personal need to hear and be heard, to be legible and visible, to tell different stories in the absence of archival data. Hartman develops creative methods, such as speculation or fabulation, as a necessary response to archival erasure of Black women. Perhaps no area of queer data studies is richer and more extensive than feminist and queer thinking about archives. While Žigelytė is the only author in this volume to engage archival themes directly, the extent to which many of the authors rely on queer archival scholars reflects the relevance of archives to data studies. At times, it's impossible to know how far to think these two intellectual lineages together or separately. That's perhaps not surprising, since queer archival scholarship engages with many of the same themes as queer data studies, such as ephemerality, absences, access, capture, extraction, circulation, process and protocol, administration, institutionalization, metadata, and the importance of data for telling queer stories. Works by Ann Cvetkovich, Jack Halberstam, Heather Love, Anjali Arondekar, Steven Maynard, K. J. Rawson, Ajamu X et al., Kate Eichorn, Syrus Marcus Ware, Zeb Tortorici, Mireille Miller-Young, Elspeth Brown, Rebecka Sheffield, Harrison Apple, and Marika Cifor pepper the citations within this volume. This list is by no means comprehensive of the field of queer archival scholarship. With a sense of the entanglements of racialized sexuality, historical erasure, and material precarity, these authors conceive of the "archive" broadly to include organizations, communities, oral traditions, embodiment, affect, and the psychic archive. Like Hartman, many of these scholars view an archive as more than a site for historical accumulation and administrative power. Instead, it is also a site of creative irruption that reassembles history to serve as the contestatory ground over race, sexuality, gender, and evidence. Authors in this volume, too, grapple with questions of omission, counterdata, and injurious inclusion. While some authors, such as Žigelytė, Gagné, and Susanna Paasonen and Jenny Sundén, contend with institutional prohibition and omission when data is intimate, Stephen Molldrem and Suisui Wang reveal a desire to liberate data from injurious institutional constraints. This seeming contradiction can be summed up simply: sometimes we want to be counted; sometimes we don't. Put another way, surveillance is cruising, except when it's policing—especially in Samuel Delaney's *Times Square Red, Times Square Blue*. The question "Who counts?" has a double meaning. It asks not only who gets to be legible but also who decides who is legible. At the same time, Muñoz and Hartman reveal the limits of queer data. Its irregularities can constitute both a strategy for evasion and, simultaneously, a threat to storytelling crucial to queer world-making. Chapters in this book demonstrate that simplifying the world enough that it can be captured only with data can mean overlooking queer worlds, often ephemeral as a matter of survival and reliant on data that falls outside the usual modes of legibility. This book makes its intervention within the tensions between queerness and data. Data is both powerful and perilous. Queer data is irregular and limited. It matters both who counts and who is counting. It is partly this ambivalent relationship to data that makes queer data distinct.

This introduction would be remiss not to acknowledge the extent to which this volume's authors engage with feminist and queer scholars of media, science, and technology. I encourage readers to peruse the bibliography from Molldrem's chapter to see the extent of the particular influence of feminist science and technology in a queer data context. The many media, science, and technology scholars cited in this book could be said to provide a foundation for queer data studies, each contending with data's supposed objectivity, rhetorical power, protocols, and administrative control over life. They include Michel Foucault, Donna Haraway, Lorraine Daston and Peter Gailson, Steve Epstein, Michelle Murphy, Kath Browne, Martha Lampland and Susan Leigh Star, Mary Gray, Shaka McGlotten, Kara Keeling, Dean Spade, Fiona Barnett et al., Kane Race, Cyd Cipolla et al., Stephen Molldrem and Mitali Thakor, Jen Jack Gieseking, Jacob Gaboury, Tara McPherson, Trevor Hoppe, Bo Ruberg, and Cait McKinney, to name only a few.

Readers will likely notice multiple citations for scholars of HIV/AIDS. The disease's fatal impact on queer communities continues to haunt queer social organizing and theory decades after its first victims succumbed. Its influence within queer data studies is no exception. Fighting for their survival against antiqueer governments and epidemiological regimes, queer activists reorganized how medical institutions summon and circulate data, with lessons for our current moment.[2] *Queer Data Studies* comes at a time when the phenomenal power of data is never more evident. The COVID-19 pandemic demonstrates just how vulnerable the world can be when we lack good statistics. Surrounded by so much uncertainty, data can seem like a comfort.

At the same time, we are living through renewed awareness of the vast surveillance powers of technology companies and governments that use data as management techniques to preserve an unequal status quo. Look no further than the United States and Canada for the ways in which such power disproportionately affects historically subordinated communities, including Black and brown people, Indigenous people, diasporic communities, migrants and refugees, sex workers, people with health conditions and disabilities, and queer and trans people. In response, there has been a rise in scholarship that wrestles with the politics of the current data context. Black and Indigenous feminist science and technology scholarship (STS) has significantly influenced queer thinking about data. Authors in this book extend Michelle Murphy's analysis of extractive data practices in medical research's necropolitics to examine the contexts of HIV health regimes.[3] For Marissa Duarte, Indigenous communities build communication platforms and networks for themselves, which finds resonance among queer technology communities in this volume.[4] Recent works by Simone Browne, Safiya Noble, and Ruha Benjamin are representative of a vast body of research about the racial bias of computational technologies. Several authors in this volume show that it is perhaps impossible to think about the vast power of computational technologies without these groundbreaking scholars. Meanwhile, Allissa Richardson's scholarship on the impact of citizen journalism documenting police violence against Black people in the United States is a prime example of how the power of data can be turned around and wielded against an oppressor. Those with the direct experience of inequality know better than anyone how best to use data against injustice.

Contributors to *Queer Data Studies* come from a wide range of academic backgrounds, including anthropology, cinema, communications, history, media studies, science and technology studies, and gender studies, and almost all of them are emerging scholars. Five contributions examine queer data outside the context of the United States and Canada (China, Lebanon, Lithuania, and Scandinavia) and across transnational circulations of bodies and capital. Multiple contributions focus on queer data from the standpoint of global trans studies and US-based Black queer studies. This anthology makes contributions to intersectional, decolonial, feminist, queer, and trans research and adds to the ongoing multidisciplinary and transdisciplinary dialogues about data across the social sciences, humanities, and applied sciences. *Queer Data Studies* will be especially relevant to scholars in science and technology studies, information studies, digital humanities, communications and media studies, and queer theory and queer studies.

Yet this book is by no means comprehensive, and any list of absences could only ever be partial. Among other things, it reflects a sometimes uncomfortable alliance between queer theory and trans studies. While there are productive encounters with trans studies in multiple chapters, and while trans people (in terms of specific people, authors, and subject positions) are present within this volume, *Queer Data Studies* nevertheless does not contain a sustained study of trans people's relationships to data. Within this book, a good example of queer theory's relationship with trans studies can be found in Molldrem's contribution (chapter 5). The author takes meaningful care to note the complicated relationships of gender and sexuality as categories within HIV public health data regimes while acknowledging the way trans and intersex subjects are made "queer" within systems that focus on a cis gay male experience. Molldrem's acknowledgment helps us understand the limits of queer data as it relates to trans and intersex subjects. Readers would benefit from reading this book alongside *Trap Door: Trans Cultural Production and the Politics of Visibility*, by Reina Gossett et al., for a richer understanding of the contradictions of accommodating trans bodies and communities only insofar as they cooperate with dominant norms. Rather than being comprehensive, this book is meant to contribute in a small way to a much larger conversation. My hope is that any gaps will be seen as opportunities for additional scholarship and conversation. No scholarship is ever definitive.

Queer Data Studies begins with Shaka McGlotten's chapter, "Black Data," as way to signal that any contemporary queer data studies must take queer of color critique as foundational. Originally published in 2016, "Black Data" considers the historical and contemporary ways Black people are interpolated by big data, by which McGlotten means *technés* of race and racism and the various efforts of states and corporations to capture, predict, and control political and consumer behavior.[5] Bringing Black queer studies into dialogue with critical studies of new technologies and network cultures, McGlotten figures Black data as "Black ops"—secret or encrypted forms of counterknowledge that challenge or refuse some of the demands of contemporary imperial power, especially the demand to be seen. In a new preface to his original article, McGlotten brings their analysis into conversation with more recent Black technology studies. In addition, they consider how Black community organizing, particularly Black Lives Matter, has wielded data to fight back through citizen journalism and the use of mobile technologies.

Following McGlotten, *Queer Data Studies* brings Nikita Shepard's essay "'To Fight for an End to Intrusions into the Sex Lives of Americans'" into conversation with Gary Kafer's essay "Machine Learning and the Queer Technics of

Opacity." Shepard's essay historically contextualizes the changing valences surrounding data and surveillance encountered by gay and lesbian communities. They trace how queers in the United States have historically forged complex relationships with data, research, and privacy, demonstrating how LGBTQ movements have collaborated with or contested different forms of data collection. Shepard offers insight into the shifting relationship between sexual dissidents and the state across the twentieth century, reflecting how deeply the concepts of dignity, democratic inclusion, social justice, scientific rationality, economic security, and political access have become intertwined. Meanwhile, Kafer extends the idea of queer technics in rigorous and valuable ways by articulating a politics of opacity in opposition to big data's regime of transparency when the dominant means through which things become perceptible as data rely on opacity itself. Drawing particularly on Black and queer scholarship, Kafer theorizes opacity as a sociotechnical formation that animates both the operation of big data systems and the impacts of these systems on minoritarian life. Kafer casts into relief how power-knowledge takes shape at the intersections between social and technological life and how embodied difference becomes consolidated with the formal materialism of machine learning algorithms. Finally, Susanna Paasonen and Jenny Sundén's chapter, "Objectionable Nipples," examines Facebook's community standards policies that filter sexually explicit content, thereby demonstrating how US-based sexual politics and histories shape some infrastructures of intimacy online. They argue for the importance of sexuality, sexual agency, and pleasure for mundane sociability and the politics of everyday life.

Following Paasonen and Sundén's chapter, Stephen Molldrem's "HIV Data as Queer Data" provides rich conceptualizations of queerness relative to data with which subsequent scholars will need to contend. Specifically, Molldrem examines how HIV data produces specific deviant sexual subjectivities, forms of queerness, and "biomedical sexualities." Finding his evidence in US HIV/AIDS health policy, LGBTQ health policy, the administration of health information technology, and fieldwork in the metropolitan Atlanta HIV/AIDS and LGBTQ health communities, Molldrem demonstrates how clinical HIV data reimagines the sexualities of people living with HIV, thereby raising questions of consent and redefining the very idea of health and risk. Meanwhile, Ryan Conrad's essay, "Generated Vulnerability," examines how the management of data privacy on third-party for-profit advertising websites geared toward sex workers generates forms of vulnerability for hustlers, hookers, dancers, rent boys, escorts, trade, or just your average university student struggling to figure out how to make ends meet. Focusing on the US federal raid on Rentboy.com and the emergence of Rentmen.com, Conrad demonstrates the ongoing risk to the personal data of sex workers and the asymmetrical power relations between the sex workers and the sites' owners that yield uniquely awful working conditions. Ultimately, Conrad argues that sex workers need to own and operate their own online platforms and set their own data security agenda.

Imagining alternative data futures, Lina Žigelytė's "Not Enough Meaningful Data?" provides a practical toolkit for creative work with data. Focusing on sites of queer intimacy in eastern Europe, Žigelytė examines her own creative work with data: "Queer Routes," an audiovisual digital mapping project committed to documenting Lithuania's queer past. She envisions an engagement with data not as a universal good that disregards current data violence but, instead, as a productive possibility for the celebration of queer lives. In the process, she explores the politics of queer data and mapping queer histories, labor as a form of data, the value of low-fi tools, the need for digital preservation, and the need to rethink collaboration.

Continuing with themes of data intimacy, Mathew Gagné's "Reciprocating Sexy Information" upends prevailing notions of ethics in ethnographic research by examining the ethical quandaries of participating in the socio-sexual lives of men who have sex with men in Beirut, where sodomy remains illegal. He argues for an ethical approach to sex-based ethnographies that challenge our prevailing understandings of ethical relations between ethnographers and their ethnographic subjects. In the process, he explores themes of reciprocity, consent, vulnerability, ambiguity, affect, and the moral challenges of building relations through research.

Harris Kornstein's "Homobiles: Queering Data through Ephemerality and Intimacy" considers San Francisco–based Homobiles as a case study of a low-tech service by and for queer and trans people that demonstrates strategies for queering popular technologies and their collection, storage, and use of data—in contrast to ride-hailing services like Uber and Lyft. Focusing on how Homobiles employs small data practices, which involve collecting little data and eliminating data, Kornstein conceives of Homobiles as a "minor platform" in both offering a unique form of affective engagement with technology as well as complicating teleological understandings of success and failure that differ significantly from Silicon Valley business models rooted in forms of "surveillance capitalism." In the final chapter, "Situated Indications: Queer STS Experiments on Global

Datafication," Suisui Wang critically examines the "LGBTI inclusion index," a calculation of the supposed status of LGBTI people in various life domains, including education, health, personal security and violence, economic well-being, and political and civic participation. Critical of the global "datafication" of queer life, Wang draws on his ethnographic fieldwork in China to argue that these indexes have a way of reimagining the world to generate new topographies. Wang argues for constructing countertopographies that enable scale-jumping and geography-crossing for new political-economic alliances that transcend both place and identity. Ultimately, Wang envisions quantification as a tool to mobilize alternative abstractions for insurgent queer actions.

Taken together, the chapters in this volume are neither exclusively antidata nor prodata. Like Marika Cifor and the other authors of "Feminist Data Manifest-No," the contributions in this collection "refuse harmful data regimes and commit to new data futures." While *Queer Data Studies* is by no means comprehensive, its heterogeneity is one of its strengths, allowing readers to see the ways in which concepts such as "queer" and "data" have been taken up in a variety of different fields with different pressure points and academic standards. This volume may be undisciplined, but it is not unruly. Across these disciplinary differences, several of the authors in this volume enable us to think about the paradoxes of data practices by extending Foucauldian biopolitics to imagine data as more than a tool for administrative regulation. Žigelytė sees the potential to harness data for queer affirmation, survival, and digital storytelling and to imagine different worlds, remember shared histories, and create queer data futures. For Žigelytė's art-based project, data from our lives is a snapshot of the world. Data can describe hidden patterns found in every aspect of our lives, from our digital existence to urban spaces. Similarly, for Gagné, data reflects and enables the creation of shared cultural forms and moments of intimacy as a political act, not just an accumulation for research and "knowledge production." In Gagné's analysis, data represents forms of queer joy and pleasure that sustain community and survival. Meanwhile, Paasonen and Sundén remind us of the immense power and influence of technology companies to censor data that reflects our joy and community. They highlight the precarious nature of queer data as an articulation of the self within corporate and managerial contexts. Kafer, McGlotten, and Wang extend Foucault to include race and colonialism, for which Foucault had little or no analysis. Wang, for example, demonstrates how data's ostensible use as an effective policy tool in international development is often a remapping of colonial civilizing hierarchies. Shepard and Kafer remind us of the historical and contemporary needs to evade data collection practices while simultaneously developing queer cultural forms to enable opacity. Finally, Molldrem, Kornstein, and Conrad reveal the computational and administrative power of data while making us attuned to the ways in which data about us is *our* data. They insist on new kinds of technical infrastructures that center queer autonomy and data sovereignty for drag queens, sex workers, and people with HIV.

Queer people have complex, sometimes contradictory relationships to data. As these authors show, in different contexts we evade or eliminate data for survival, harness data for political action, refuse to comply with data, summon data for evidence, reimagine data to tell different stories, redefine data to expand what counts, create our own data as shared cultural forms, and reveal hidden data to rediscover and remake the world. This relationship to data is distinct from Kevin Guyan's understanding of "queer data," which narrowly examines how incomplete data informs legislation and social services.[6] This narrow approach to data largely takes a positive view of data accumulation. The problem with data, according to Guyan, is its incompleteness. Correlatively, accumulation is the corrective goal of queer data. Instead, as I mentioned above, Kornstein's and Conrad's chapters demonstrate that queers have a much more ambivalent relationship to data. Editing this volume has taught me that queer approaches to data are messy, non-innocent, contradictory, and nevertheless crucial for autonomy, reinvention, survival, and critique of a material-data world. Attentive to the intersectional workings of power and privilege, queer and trans people agitate with and against data as a requirement for survival and existence. These authors center data activism, practices, relationships, and autonomies that foster data justice.

Based on the chapters in this volume, then, what might a queer approach to data look like? First, queer data centers queer and trans people. Inspired by Amy Hamraie and Kelly Fritsch's "Crip Technoscience Manifesto," a queer approach to data might start with an understanding of data not *for* but *by and with*. It recognizes that queer and trans people know best how data both despoils and enables queer lives. Second, queer data focuses on what data *does*. Without the historical assumption of bodily autonomy and data sovereignty, the writings that compose this volume are much more calibrated, as per Muñoz, to meditate on what data *does*—that is, how it acts and is enacted. Focusing on what data does in a queer social and political matrix, these authors demonstrate how data shapes and can be shaped by queer worlds. Third, queer data is capacious. It is necessarily agile and flexible, which ranges from ephemeral cultural forms to new technical infrastructures to data evasion. Fourth, queer data is curious, irregular, and messy because it does not always conform easily to standards, it expands our understanding of what counts, it requires reinvention, it is contradictory, and it is impossible to know in advance what it will do. Fifth, queer data is committed to justice.

While writing from their positions as English-speaking, mostly North American settler scholars, the authors in this volume variously demonstrate commitments to intersectionality, collective action, harm reduction, strategic refusals, and agential, politicized, and transformative relationships to data to make the world a more just place. Finally, queer data struggles for futures in which queer and trans lives are anticipated and welcomed. In a US and Canadian context, this feels particularly urgent, given recent antiqueer and trans legislation in the United States. We see the legislation in Florida that prevents teachers from talking about queer and trans lives. We see the legislation in Texas that outlaws trans care, proclaiming it child abuse. Throughout the United States we see the overturning of privacy rights that protect bodily autonomy and queer intimacy. The authors in this volume understand that data has the power to enable queer and trans people to live and to thrive—or to prevent them from doing so. Data, perilous and powerful, is both a world-making and dismantling force. The chapters collected here provide glimpses into the ways in which data might enable and imagine something different, something more.

NOTES

1. See, for example, Igo, *Known Citizen.*
2. Shilts, *And the Band Played On.*
3. See Murphy, *Economization of Life.*
4. See Duarte, *Network Sovereignty.*
5. McGlotten's "Black Data" was previously published in E. Johnson, *No Tea, No Shade*, 262–86.
6. See Guyan, *Queer Data.*

BIBLIOGRAPHY

Ahmed, Sarah. *The Promise of Happiness.* Durham, NC: Duke University Press, 2012.
Apple, Harrison. "'I Can't Wait for You to Die': A Community Archives Critique." *Archivaria* 92 (November 2021): 110–37.

Arondekar, Anjali. *For the Record: On Sexuality and the Colonial Archive in India.* Durham, NC: Duke University Press, 2009.

Barnett, Fiona, et al. "QueerOS: A User's Manual." In *Debates in the Digital Humanities 2016*, edited by Matthew K. Gold and Lauren Klein, 50–59. Minneapolis: University of Minnesota Press, 2016.

Beauchamp, Toby. *Going Stealth: Transgender Politics and U.S. Surveillance Practices.* Durham, NC: Duke University Press, 2019.

Benjamin, Ruha. *Race after Technology: Abolitionist Tools for the New Jim Code.* Cambridge: Polity, 2019.

Berlant, Lauren. *Cruel Optimism.* Durham, NC: Duke University Press, 2011.

Blas, Zach. "Informatic Opacity." *Journal of Aesthetics and Protest*, no. 9 (Summer 2014). http://www.joaap.org/issue9/zachblas.htm.

——— . "Opacity: An Introduction." *Camera Obscura* 31, no. 2 (September 2016): 149–53.

Brown, Elspeth. "Archival Activism, Symbolic Annihilation, and the LGBT2Q+ Community Archive." *Archivaria* 89 (May 2020): 6–33.

Browne, Kath. "Selling My Queer Soul or Queerying Quantitative Research?" *Sociological Research Online* 13, no. 1 (January 2008): 1–15.

Browne, Simone *Dark Matters: On the Surveillance of Blackness.* Durham, NC: Duke University Press, 2015.

Chen, Mel. Y. "Masked States and the 'Screen' between Security and Disability." *WSQ: Women's Studies Quarterly* 40, no. 1–2 (Spring–Summer 2012): 76–96.

Cifor, Marika. *Viral Cultures: Activist Archiving in the Age of AIDS.* Minneapolis: University of Minnesota Press, 2022.

Cifor, Marika, P. Garcia, T. L. Cowan, J. Rault, T Sutherland, A. Chan, J. Rode, A. L. Hoffmann, N. Salehi, and L. Nakamura. "Feminist Data Manifest-No." 2019. https://www.manifestno.com/.

Cipolla, Cyd, Kristina Gupta, David A. Rubin, and Angela Willey, eds. *Queer Feminist Science Studies: A Reader.* Seattle: University of Washington Press, 2017.

Cvetkovich, Ann. *An Archive of Feelings: Trauma, Sexuality, and Lesbian Public Cultures.* Durham, NC: Duke University Press, 2003.

Daston, Lorraine, and Peter Galison. "The Image of Objectivity." *Representations* 40 (Fall 1992): 81–128.

Delaney, Samuel. *Times Square Red, Times Square Blue.* New York: New York University Press, 1999.

de Villiers, Nicholas. *Opacity and the Closet: Queer Tactics in Foucault, Barthes, and Warhol.* Minneapolis: University of Minnesota Press, 2012.

D'Ignazio, Catherine, and Lauren F. Klein. *Data Feminism.* Cambridge, MA: MIT Press, 2020.

Duarte, Marissa Elena. *Network Sovereignty: Building the Internet across Indian Country*. Seattle: University of Washington Press, 2017.

Eichorn, Kate. *The Archival Turn in Feminism: Outrage in Order*. Philadelphia: Temple University Press, 2013.

Epstein, Steve. *Impure Science: AIDS, Activism, and the Politics of Knowledge*. Berkeley: University of California Press, 1996.

——— . *Inclusion: The Politics of Difference in Medical Research*. Chicago: University of Chicago Press, 2007.

Foucault, Michel. *Discipline and Punish: The Birth of the Prison*. New York: Vintage Books, 1975.

——— . *The History of Sexuality, Vol. 1*. Translated by Robert Hurley. New York: Vintage Books, 1978.

Gaboury, Jacob. "Becoming NULL: Queer Relations in the Excluded Middle." *Women and Performance: A Journal of Feminist Theory* 28, no. 2 (Summer 2018): 143–58.

Gieseking, Jen Jack. "Size Matters to Lesbians, Too: Queer Feminist Interventions into the Scale of Big Data." *Professional Geographer* 70, no. 1 (Summer 2017): 150–56.

Gossett, Reina, Eric A. Stanley, and Johanna Burton. *Trap Door: Trans Cultural Production and the Politics of Visibility*. Cambridge, MA: MIT Press, 2019.

Gray, Mary. *Out in the Country: Youth, Media, and Queer Visibility in Rural America*. New York: New York University Press, 2009.

Guyan, Kevin. *Queer Data: Using Gender, Sex, and Sexuality Data for Action*. London: Bloomsbury, 2022.

Halberstam, Jack. *In a Queer Time and Place: Transgender Bodies, Subcultural Lives*. Durham, NC: Duke University Press, 2005.

Hamraie, Amy, and Kelly Fritsch. "Crip Technoscience Manifesto." *Catalyst: Feminist, Theory, Technoscience* 5, no. 1 (April 2019): 1–34.

Haraway, Donna. "Situated Knowledges: The Science Question in Feminism and the Privilege of Partial Perspective." *Feminist Studies* 14, no. 3 (Fall 1988): 575–99.

Hartman, Saidiya. "Venus in Two Acts." *small axe* 12, no. 2 (Summer 2008): 1–14.

Hoppe, Trevor. *Punishing Disease: HIV and the Criminalization of Sickness*. Oakland: University of California Press, 2018.

Humphreys, Laud. *Tearoom Trade: Impersonal Sex in Public Places*. New York: Routledge, 1975.

Igo, Sara. *The Known Citizen: A History of Privacy in Modern America*. Cambridge, MA: Harvard University Press, 2018.

Johnson, David. *The Lavender Scare: The Cold War Persecution of Gays and Lesbians in the Federal Government*. Chicago: University of Chicago Press, 2004.

Johnson, E. Patrick, ed. *No Tea, No Shade: New Writings in Black Queer Studies*. Durham, NC: Duke University Press, 2016.

Kafer, Gary, and Daniel Grinberg. "Queer Surveillance." *Surveillance and Society* 17, no. 5 (December 2019): 592–601.

Keeling, Kara. "QueerOS." *Cinema Journal* 53, no. 2 (Winter 2014): 152–57.

Kornstein, Harris. "Under Her Eye: Digital Drag as Obfuscation and Countersurveillance." *Surveillance and Society* 17, no. 5 (December 2019): 681–98.

Lampland, Martha, and Susan Leigh Star, eds. *Standards and Their Stories: How Quantifying, Classifying, and Formalizing Practices Shape Everyday Life.* Ithaca: Cornell University Press, 2009.

Love, Heather. *Feeling Backwards: Loss and the Politic of Queer History.* Cambridge, MA: Harvard University Press, 2007.

Maynard, Steven. "Police/Archives." *Archivaria* 68 (Fall 2009): 159–82.

McGlotten, Shaka. "Black Data." In *No Tea, No Shade: New Writings in Black Queer Studies,* edited by E. Patrick Johnson, 262–86. Durham, NC: Duke University Press, 2016.

——— . *Virtual Intimacies: Media, Affect, and Queer Sociality.* Albany: State University of New York Press, 2013.

McKinney, Cait. *Information Activism: A Queer History of Lesbian Media Technologies.* Durham, NC: Duke University Press, 2020.

McPherson, Tara. *Feminist in a Software Lab: Difference + Design.* Cambridge, MA: Harvard University Press, 2018.

Miller-Young, Mireille. "Exotic, Erotic, Ethnopornographic: Black Women, Desire, and Labor in the Photographic Archive." In *Ethnopornography: Sexuality, Colonialism, and Archival Knowledge,* edited by Pete Sigal, Zeb Tortorici, and Neil L. Whitehead, 41–66. Durham, NC: Duke University Press, 2019.

Molldrem, Stephen, and Mitali Thakor. "Genealogies and Futures of Queer STS: Issues in Theory, Method, and Institutionalization." *Catalyst: Feminism, Theory, Technoscience* 3, no. 1 (Fall 2017): 1–15.

Muñoz, José Esteban. "Ephemera as Evidence: Introductory Notes on Queer Acts." *Women and Performance* 8, no. 2 (Summer 1996): 5–16.

Murphy, Michelle. *The Economization of Life.* Durham, NC: Duke University Press, 2017.

——— . *Seizing the Means of Reproduction: Entanglements of Feminism, Health, and Technoscience.* Durham, NC: Duke University Press, 2012.

Ngai, Sianne. *Ugly Feelings.* Cambridge, MA: Harvard University Press, 2005.

Noble, Safiya Umoja. *Algorithms of Oppression: How Search Engines Reinforce Racism.* New York: New York University Press, 2018.

Puar, Jasbir. *Terrorist Assemblages: Homonationalism in Queer Times.* Durham, NC: Duke University Press, 2007.

Race, Kane. *The Gay Science: Intimate Experiments with the Problem of HIV.* New York: Routledge, 2017.

Rawson, K. J. "Accessing Transgender // Desiring Queer(er?) Archival Logics." *Archivaria* 68 (Fall 2009): 123–40.

Richardson, Allissa V. *Bearing Witness While Black: African Americans, Smartphones, and the New Protest #Journalism*. Oxford: Oxford University Press, 2020.

Ruberg, Bo. *Video Games Have Always Been Queer*. New York: New York University Press, 2019.

Ruberg, Bo, and Spencer Ruelos. "Data for Queer Lives: How LGBTQ Gender and Sexual Identities Challenge Norms and Demographics." *Big Data and Society* 7, no. 1 (Winter 2020): 1–12.

Sedgwick, Eve. *Touching, Feeling: Affect, Pedagogy, Performativity*. Durham, NC: Duke University Press, 2003.

Sheffield, Rebecka. *Documenting Rebellions: A Study of Four Gay and Lesbian Archives*. Sacramento, CA: Litwin Books, 2020.

Shilts, Randy. *And the Band Played On: Politics, People, and the AIDS Epidemic*. New York: St. Martin's Griffin, 1987.

Snorton, C. Riley. *Black on Both Sides: A Racial History of Trans Identity*. Minneapolis: University of Minnesota Press, 2014.

Spade, Dean. *Normal Life: Administrative Violence, Critical Trans Politics, and the Limits of Law*. Durham, NC: Duke University Press, 2015.

Tortorici, Zeb. *Sins against Nature: Sex and Archives in Colonial New Spain*. Durham, NC: Duke University Press, 2018.

Ware, Syrus Marcus. "All Power to All People? Black LGBTTI2QQ Activism, Remembrance, and Archiving in Toronto." *TSQ: Transgender Studies Quarterly* 4, no. 2 (May 2017): 170–80.

X., Ajamu, Topher Campbell, and Mary Stevens. "Love and Lubrication in the Archives, or rukus! A Black Queer Archive for the United Kingdom." *Archivaria* 68 (Fall 2009): 271–94.

1 Black Data

BLACK DATA REVISITED: A PREFACE

"Black Data" was originally published in 2016. I conceived of and wrote the essay in 2013 after arriving in Berlin, Germany, for a research fellowship. The result of many years of thinking about race and technology, the essay was initially inspired by then-emergent research about biases inherent in so-called "predictive policing" and the particular dangers facial recognition systems posed for Black and brown people. Then, in June 2013, came the revelations leaked by Edward Snowden that the US government had undertaken a massive domestic surveillance program after 9/11 that sought to capture the data not only of criminals but of everyone. Its motto was "Collect it all." This program expanded globally, supported by the United States' Five Eyes Intelligence partners (Canada, the United Kingdom, Australia, and New Zealand), to include spying on some of our closest allies, including Germany, where the leaks held special historical resonance.

The effects of the Snowden leaks are still felt today, as I write this in the spring of 2022. Indeed, I would argue that they continue to provide an important frame for making sense of ongoing debates about privacy and transparency, as well as the weaponization of big data in the lead-up to Brexit and the 2016 and 2020 US presidential elections, as well as the viral spread of mis- and disinformation across social media and other tech platforms.

Of course, a lot has changed for some of the figures I discussed in "Black Data." After a dramatic cat-and-mouse game with the US government, Edward Snowden is in exile in Russia, although he regularly gives speeches via teleconference. From 2012 until 2019, Julian Assange found refuge in the Ecuadorian embassy in London; after conflicts with the Ecuadorian authorities, he was eventually arrested and imprisoned. A 2021 UK court ruling found Assange could be deported to the United States, where he faces charges of violating the 1917 Espionage Act. Chelsea Manning's thirty-five-year prison sentence was commuted after seven years by former president Barack Obama, in 2017. She was jailed twice again in 2019 after refusing to testify against Assange, before being released in 2020.

Also in 2013, the Black Lives Matter (BLM) movement appeared, although its networked spread and its appeal as a counterpolitics did not begin to gain mainstream visibility until a year later, after the police killings of Eric Garner, Michael Brown, and Tamir Rice.[1] Importantly, the rise of BLM was predicated on previously cultivated technical and organizing skills—by the many ways Black people have learned over decades to leverage media and other technologies to construct, refine, and disseminate political messages.[2] In the internet age, Moya Bailey calls this "digital alchemy."[3]

After the 2020 murder of George Floyd by former police officer Derek Chauvin, tens of millions protested globally, and there have been shifts in policy and across public culture more broadly. As municipalities seek to integrate the insights and demands of this decentralized grassroots movement, corporations are increasingly pressured to adapt to new political sentiments. And while calls to defund the police have not been fully answered, various reforms are underway in policing and across other governmental services. These incipient reforms constitute an acknowledgment of systemic inequities; over the last two years, they have frequently been dubbed a "reckoning." We will see. Corporations, with an eye toward public perception and their bottom line, have also realized that their silence is not an option. Some have withdrawn advertising from particular platforms, while other companies, like Ben & Jerry's, have made forceful denunciations of anti-Black violence.

Much has changed on intellectual and creative fronts as well. There has been an explosion of work—in academia and beyond—addressing themes overlapping those I explore in "Black Data." Simone Browne's *Dark Matters*, for instance, considers the historical relationships between Blackness and surveillance, namely the ways the legal apparatuses of enslavement and its aftermath demanded Black people be legible as laboring bodies and not subjects. Browne also explores the ways racism was subsequently built into the scientific systems of classification like phrenology, an antecedent for today's biometric technologies. She turns to artists such as Mendi + Keith Obadike and Hank Willis Thomas to look at how Blackness is collected and consumed in the digital age.

Safiya Noble's landmark *Algorithms of Oppression*, published in 2018, underscores the ways algorithmic biases do violence to Black people, specifically emphasizing the ways search engines neglect and simultaneously profit from sexualized images of Black girls and women—one iteration of what she dubs "technological redlining," a term that captures the ways algorithmic decision-making processes have differential impacts for marginalized groups.[4] Catherine Knight Steele similarly foregrounds Black women in her *Digital Black Feminism*, where she traces the historical ways Black women developed technical literacies before turning to the Black blogosphere of the 2000s and 2010s, as well as more recent examples of Black digital thinkers. Linking past to present is important because, as she notes, "capturing, publishing, and threading/stitching are three forms of Black feminist praxis that have existed for centuries."[5] Moya Bailey likewise draws on Black feminist praxis in her 2021 book *Misogynoir Transformed*. Bailey coined the term "misogynoir" in the Black blogosphere, and it has since gained international circulation. The term reflects the intersectional nature of Black women's oppression, simultaneously subject to anti-Black and antiwoman stereotypes and policies. "Black women," she writes, "are caught at a vexing crossroads: hypervisible in media through misogynoir and invisible when in need of lifesaving attention. Misogynoir is the visual representation of anti-Black misogyny not only through caricature and false representations of Black women that inform how Black women are treated, but also through the omission of Black women and girls from view altogether."[6] Taking an expansive view of the category "Black women" to include Black nonbinary, agender, and gender variant people, she looks to the digital alchemy they employ to create digital media that serve these communities as "a form of self-preservation and harm reduction that disrupts the onslaught of the problematic images that society perpetuates."[7]

Curiously omitted from my original essay, André Brock's numerous contributions to Black cyberculture studies have since become even more influential. Across his work, he has developed a theoretical and methodological framework for engaging Black technocultures dubbed "critical technocultural discourse analysis (CTDA)."[8] This approach "prioritize[s] the epistemological standpoint of underrepresented groups of technology users . . . to understand how digital practitioners filter their technology use through their cultural identity rather than some preconceived 'neutral' perspective."[9] It is not possible to do full justice to Brock's contribution with such limited space, but one finds his approach expertly mobilized in his and others' discussions of Black Twitter. Black Twitter operates simultaneously as a platform, cultural object, social sphere, and space of transformation.[10] Like the authors I discuss above, Brock emphasizes the forms of expertise necessary to make dynamic and creative use of the platform. Black signifiyin' practices are central to what makes Twitter Twitter, as well as to the emergence of Black Twitter specifically.

Ruha Benjamin's *Captivating Technology* and *Race after Technology* likewise provide valuable metaperspectives on race and technology, extending the work of earlier writers I cite in "Black Data," as well as Simone Browne and André Brock, among others. Benjamin's *Captivating Technology* explores the gaps between narratives of technological progress and a variety of coded inequities she has dubbed the "New Jim Code" through case studies that include "engineered inequity, default discrimination, coded exposure, and technological benevolence."[11] "Race critical code studies" is Benjamin's framework for challenging the anti-Blackness of black boxed technologies.[12]

I have continued the lines of inquiry from "Black Data" in my essays "Streaking," "What's Love Got to Do with It?," and "Life in the Network." In each, I seek to render the complexities of relations, algorithmic and otherwise. This does not necessarily mean decoding the black box of the algorithm or, as in "What's Love," intimacy. Rather, I seek to dwell in the ambivalence of incommensurability, adopting a stance toward opacity that recognizes it as generative and never fully closed off. As Gary Kafer notes in chapter 3 of this volume, "Ultimately, as a queer technics, opacity insists that we peer not inside the black box but across it toward the forms of racialized, gendered, and sexual exclusions that occur at the intersections between the social and the technological."

"Streaking," in particular, looked to artists whose work addresses themes of "algorithmic violence," including Mimi Onuoha, who coined the phrase, as well as responses to absented or evacuated data, by American Artist, Ayo Okunseinde, and Stephanie Dinkins, who each link Blackness to past, present, and future technological innovations. These artists and others, such as An Duplan, Rashaad Newsome, and Jacolby Satterwhite, have all advanced high-profile discussions over the last several years about queerness, race, and technology at, among other sites, respectively, the Center for Afrofuturist Studies, the Park Avenue Armory, and MoMA PS1. The Black Quantum Futurism Collective, composed of Camae Ayewa and Rasheedah Phillips, has also been instrumental in these discussions, publishing short books and engaging in a variety of community-based projects.[13] In 2021, the collective was awarded a CERN Collide award to support research on Afro-diasporic temporalities and quantum physics.[14]

Another part of the developing infrastructure for research on race and technology is the Center for Critical Race and Digital Studies (CR+DS), composed of academics, policy makers, journalists, and others who focus on issues of race, ethnicity, and identity with the aim of making our research publicly accessible. I and many of those I cite here are affiliates of CR+DS.

Research on Black data is part of a literature and network of scholars and creators that is sure to grow as technologies are ever more integrated into all aspects of our personal and social lives, with the violences and possibilities always associated with them.

#HOWBLACKAREYOU

Comedian, geek, and author Baratunde Thurston began his 2009 South by Southwest slideshow *How to Be Black (Online)* with a very brief explanation of why Black people are important: "we look good / history proves black people are the future / e.g., rock n roll / e.g., hip hop / e.g., ass/lip injections."[15] His playful intro led into a more sophisticated, if also still comical, analysis of Black online life. He noted in particular the waning "digital divide." Black people are online as much as whites if both tethered and wireless access are considered, and both groups tend to use the same sites, with a few exceptions.[16] Thurston also noted the persistence of racism on the web, a point also underlined by numerous scholars of race and the internet.[17] Thurston focused specifically on Black use of Twitter, which he links to the call and response game of insults known as "the dozens."[18] Of course, tweeting Black people caused consternation among some whites, such as the one who posted this comment: "wow!! too many negros in the trending topics for me. I may be done with this whole twitter thing."[19]

Thurston's work on race and technology provides a template for my own efforts here. In this essay, I engage in a Black queer call and response with a few key concepts circulating in network theories and cultures.

I use an eclectic group of artifacts—Thurston's slideshow, an interview with Barack Obama in the wake of the NSA surveillance scandal, the artwork of Zach Blas, and a music video about technology and gentrification—to proffer this heuristic: "black data." This heuristic, I suggest, offers some initial analytical and political orientations for Black queer studies to more fully engage with the theories, effects, and affects of network cultures. There are significant bodies of literature in science and technology, as well as cultural and media studies, that grapple with race.[20] In addition, a handful of works address sexuality and new media technologies.[21] Black queer studies is itself still a developing, loosely organized group of scholars and cultural practitioners.[22] As such, it has not generated many analyses of the particular ways Black queer people are interpolated by or employ new media and other technologies.[23] Here, I use black data to think through some of the historical and contemporary ways Black queer people, like other people of African descent and people of color more broadly, are hailed by big data, in which *technés* of race and racism reduce our lives to mere numbers.[24] Reduced to mere numbers, we appear as commodities, revenue streams, statistical deviations, or vectors of risk.[25] Big data also refers to the various efforts of states and corporations to capture, predict, and control political and consumer behavior. Black data is, then, a response to big data's call, and here I offer readings that outline some possible political and affective vectors, some ways to refuse the call or perhaps even to hang up.

Black queer lives are often reduced to forms of accounting that are variously intended to elicit alarm or direct highly circumscribed forms of care. Statistics are used to mobilize people to fight HIV/AIDS—such as the fact that Black people account for 44 percent of new HIV infections.[26] They are used to direct attention to the omnipresence of violence in Black life or to the specific forms of violence directed against Black LGBTQ people, as in the 2012 National Coalition of Anti-Violence Programs' (NCAVP) report, which indicates that LGBTQ people of color were nearly twice as likely to experience physical violence as their white counterparts and that transgender people of color were two and a half times as likely to experience police violence as white cisgender survivors and victims.[27]

Assigning numerical or financial value to Black life, transforming experience into information or data, is nothing new; rather, it is caught up with the history of enslavement and the racist regimes that sought to justify its barbarities. Between the sixteenth and nineteenth centuries, more than twelve and a half million Africans were transported from Africa to the New World. Two million, and likely many more, died during the Middle Passage.[28] A typical slave ship could carry more than three hundred slaves arranged like sardines; the sick and dead would be thrown overboard, their loss claimed for insurance money, as in the infamous *Zong* massacre. Other, more recent data circulate in the wake of the 2008 global recession and the protests against George Zimmerman's exoneration in the killing of seventeen-year-old Trayvon Martin: Black families saw their wealth drop 31 percent between 2007 and 2010.[29] In 2012, 136 unarmed Black men were killed by police and security guards.[30] In the wake of a spate of police violence in 2014 and the failed indictments of the police who killed Michael Brown and Eric Garner, an analysis by the investigative journalism site ProPublica showed that Black males were twenty-one times more likely to be fatally shot than young white males.[31]

It is tempting to ascribe these racialized accountings to the cruel systems of value established by capitalism, which seeks to encode—quantify and order—life and matter into categories of commodity, labor, exchange value, and profit. Indeed, race itself functions as commodity in the era of genomics—a simple oral swab test can help you answer Thurston's question #howblackareyou, and you can watch others' reactions to their results on *Faces of America*, a popular show about genealogical testing. Yet, as Lisa Nakamura, Peter Chow-White, and Wendy Chun observe, race is not merely an effect of capitalism's objectifying systems; rather, race is itself a co-constituting technology that made such forms of accounting possible in the first place.[32] "Race *as* technology," Chun notes, helps us understand "how race functions as the 'as,' how it facilitates comparisons between entities classed as similar or dissimilar."[33] Race is a tool, and it was intrinsic, not anterior, to constructions of capital, as well as to ideas about biology and culture. As Mel Chen puts it, race is an animate hierarchy in which the liveliness and value of some things (whiteness, smart technology) are established via a proximity to other things positioned lower or farther away (blackness, dumb matter).[34] "Wow!! too many negros in the trending topics for me" simply reiterates in the realm of microblogging hierarchical *technés* of racism that see Black people as polluting and therefore as distasteful or dangerous, or that would deny information/technology to the subjects of discrimination.[35]

Of course, the above statistics are familiar, and, while useful, they tell only very partial stories, reducing Black experience to an effect of capitalism (a vulgar Marxism if ever there was one) or to a kind of numerology of bare life.

In what follows I sketch a few different trajectories for black data. I performatively enact black data as a kind of informatics of Black queer life, as reading and throwing shade, to grapple with the NSA surveillance scandal, new biometric technologies, and the tech-fueled gentrification of San Francisco. These readings (actings out?) also help to illustrate the ways Black queer theories, practices, and lives might be made to matter in relation to some of the organizing tensions of contemporary network cultures: privacy, surveillance, capture, and exclusion. Black queers frame what is at stake in these debates inasmuch as we quite literally embody struggles between surveillance and capture, between the seen and unseen. Moreover, we have developed rogue epistemologies, which often rely on an array of technological media, which help us to make ourselves present, and to disappear. In the reads that follow, I also gesture toward the virtual affinities Black queer theoretical or political projects might share with cryptographic and anarchist activisms.

OBAMA'S FACE AND BLACK OPACITIES

Ima read.[36] In this context, my Black queer call and response takes the specific form of reading and shade—critical performative practices wielded by queers of color and made famous in the film *Paris Is Burning*. "Reading" is an artfully delivered insult, while "shade" refers to disrespectful behaviors or gestures, which can be subtly or not so subtly communicated. In *Paris Is Burning*, Dorian Corey describes it this way: "Shade is, 'I don't tell you you're ugly, but I don't have to tell you because you know you're ugly.' And that's shade."[37] Academics know how to be shady, but they usually dress it up in ideology or jargon. Part of my intervention here has to do with how I seek to occasionally sidestep some of these professional niceties.

Obama was raised by white people, not drag queens, but he knows how to give good face. But in the moments before a 2013 interview with PBS's Charlie Rose, Obama's signature smile cracked, revealing instead an ugly mask. This mask held a tense set of ironies. The United States' first Black president defended his unprecedented expansion of the National Security Agency's (NSA) surveillance programs to include the collection of the metadata of millions of Americans' and global citizens' telephone and email correspondence. He accused Edward Snowden, a former NSA contractor turned whistleblower, of spying and called for his arrest, continuing a pattern of aggressively prosecuting leakers of governmental overreach.[38] The racial melodrama is striking: a Black man authorizes the capture and arrest of a young white man, who, by revealing the spying program, directly challenged the hegemony of US imperialism, a project historically and presently tied to the control, domination, torture, and murder of brown and Black people around the world.[39]

Obama's grin is a failed mask, or the slippery gap that hosts the mask before its radiant, populist actualization: "Charlie, let me tell you . . . I want to assure all

FIGURE 1.1. Obama's grin. Screenshot by the author.

Americans. . . . " In another era, and maybe still in this one, Obama's grin might embody the racist fantasy that all Black people are animated by an animalistic desire to please or reassure white people. But here the mask is a more familiar code, a politician's lie—"don't worry, everything's fine, carry on." Although brief, Obama's expression arrested my attention, an attention shared with other queers and people of color, one that is always attuned, through calibrated and diffused looks, speculations, and modes of attention, to "the evidence of felt intuition," to the subtle or not-so-subtle gestures that indicate shared desire or the threat of violence.[40] My cynical intuition—Ima read—collides with nostalgia for a scene of optimism. I cannot help but juxtapose this rictus grin with Shepard Fairey's famous image of Obama gazing hopefully into the distance. To this juxtaposition we can add a meme that emerged in the wake of the NSA scandal—"Yes We Scan."

For Giorgio Agamben and Emmanuel Lévinas, faces condition our ethical encounters with one another. Agamben writes, "Only where I find a face do I encounter an exteriority and does an outside happen to me."[41] In the work of Gilles Deleuze and Félix Guattari, however, the face is something more ambivalent; it is operationalized as a regulating function whose origins lay in racism. "Faciality" determines what faces can be recognized or tolerated.[42] The dozens, and Black queer reading practices in particular, are uncanny inversions of faciality. Rather than serve to hierarchically order bodies into viscous clumps,

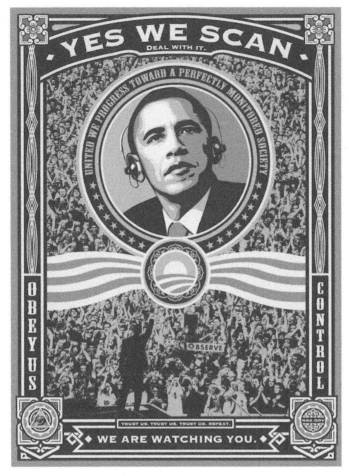

FIGURE 1.2. "Yes We Scan." Courtesy of Rene Walter.

dominating "by comparison to a model or a norm," reading Obama's face in this way might yield a comic finality—"you're so ugly, even Hello Kitty says goodbye" or "your grin is such a lie that not even your white grandmother would believe you."[43] But Obama's grimacing mask is not merely a sign to be decoded, a truth to be unveiled. A read is a punctum that is also always an invitation, a salvo in a call and response.

Edward Snowden unmasked himself in part because he believed that by stepping out from the veil of anonymity, by revealing his identity and giving face, he might effect some degree of control over the representation of his decision to confirm the unprecedented scale of the NSA's programs, as well as to encourage others to come forward.[44] In addition, and unsurprisingly, he believed that his anonymity might endanger him, making him vulnerable to the intimidation, kidnapping, torture, and murder he knew the US government was capable of. By coming forward/out, Snowden curiously mimicked some Black and queer practices, which mix a performative hypervisibility (an awareness of one's difference and visibility) with invisibility or opacity (an indifference or even hostility to the norm or to being read properly). James Baldwin, riffing on Ralph Ellison, expressed it somewhat differently in a 1961 interview in which he linked Black in/visibility to whiteness: "What white people see when they look at you is not visible. What they *do* see when they *do* look at you is what they have invested you with. What they have invested you with is all the agony, and pain, and the danger, and the passion, and the torment—you know, sin, death, and hell—of which everyone in this country is terrified."[45]

Snowden had gone stealth for years, passing as a mild-mannered analyst, keeping his civil libertarian streak on the down-low. Snowden appeared, *carried it*, and then vanished.[46] For years Snowden remained in Russia, which provided him asylum, while the United States continues to bully other nations into denying him egress. (In 2022 he was granted Russian citizenship.) Snowden's face (like that of convicted army whistleblower Chelsea Manning) has appeared on the placards of thousands of protesters around the world. Their faces have become screens and masks, standing in for or projecting a generalizable face—my face, your face, all of our faces. And increasingly, as at a summer 2013 protest in Germany, the faces of these figures are worn as masks, barring access to an individual or specific face, while calling into existence a shared or collective one.[47] These faces/masks make a dual demand: transparency from the government, opacity for the rest of us.

In her study of the transatlantic performances of Black women, historian and performance studies scholar Daphne Brooks uses the concept of "spectacular opacity" to retool colonial tropes of darkness, which have "historically been made to envelop bodies and geographical territories in the shadows of global and hegemonic domination."[48] Like some uses of masks, or going stealth, darkness and opacity have the capacity to resist the violent will-to-know, the will-to-transparency. Martinican critic and poet Édouard Glissant says that "a person has a right to be opaque."[49] This is a point echoed, in different contexts, by cypherpunks like Julian Assange and the hacktivist group Anonymous. For Assange, Anonymous, and others such as the Electronic Frontier Foundation

(EFF), developing cryptographic literacies is essential. This may involve using an anonymizing browser such as TOR, an array of browser add-ons, secure file transfer services, or encrypted chat, among many other techniques.[50] Encryption transforms information into codes that are unreadable by anyone without the appropriate cipher. Learning how to make oneself opaque is a practical necessity and a political tactic in this moment of big data's ascendancy, in which clickstreams, RFID tags, the GPS capacities of our cell phones, CCTV, and new biometric technologies are employed by states and corporations to digitally log our movements and virtually every technologically mediated interaction. Yet states and corporations have made encryption more difficult, describing cryptographic tools as weapons and encrypted communications as threats to national security.[51] How can citizens challenge state and corporate power when those powers demand we accede to total surveillance, while also criminalizing dissent? How do we resist such demands when journalists, whistleblowers, activists, and artists are increasingly labeled as traitors or terrorists?[52]

Network theorist Alexander Galloway provides some conceptual and political starting points in his essay "Black Box, Black Bloc." In the essay, he considers the ways the black bloc, an anarchist tactic of anonymity and massification, and the black box, a technological device for which only inputs and outputs are known, but not the contents, collide in the new millennium.[53] The black box provides a model for the individual and collective black bloc to survive: using an array of technological and political tools, we might turn to black boxing ourselves in order make ourselves illegible to the surveillance state and big data. To resist the hegemony of the transparent, we (a "we" I imagine as loosely comprising people opposed to the unholy marriage of militarism, corporatocracy, manufactured consent, and neoliberal economic voodoo) will need to embrace techniques of becoming dark or opaque in order to better become present, to assert our agency and autonomy, or merely to engage in truly private interactions, without being seen or apprehended. We too can employ masks that lie, but, unlike Obama's mask, these masks might help to produce a sense of camaraderie. In the black bloc, or among the real world protests organized by Anonymous and others, a mask anonymizes while also representing a shared collectivity, as evidenced by the ways the Guy Fawkes mask popularized by Anonymous is being taken up in contexts around the world—in the student protests in Quebec in 2014, as well as in protest movements in Europe and Brazil. In these contexts masks operate as part of a new politics of opacity, a form of black data that helps to make identities or identifying information go dark or disappear while simultaneously hailing an incipient multitude. Such a multitude is also reflected in mobilizations in the wake of George Zimmerman's acquittal in which protesters were arrayed in hoodies that declared, "I am Trayvon Martin."

Reading Obama's mask, or trying to decipher his real character or intentions, invites us to reflect on our own desires for transparency, for knowing or settling on a truth in an era in which transparency is always already staged. In an era of pervasive surveillance—by the NSA, Google, Apple, Microsoft, and Facebook, as well as by our bosses, colleagues, students, parents, friends, lovers—masks can offer a layer of protection rather than hide a real essence. A good mask, one resistant to efforts to decode it, may in fact provide us with a little room to maneuver, a little room outside the grasp of our "control society."

BLACK SKIN, QUEER MASKS

While the collection and interpretation of metadata—data about data—has become increasingly sophisticated, other racial and sexual profiling techniques remain crude. Currently, most of these techniques rely on the visual apprehension of another's difference. "Stop-and-frisk," the New York City Police Department policy that went into effect in 2002 and has resulted in four million stops, nearly 90 percent of them involving Black and Latino people, is one example. The wanton murder of queers of color is another.

Recent work in biometrics and the study of movement presage new technologies for capturing and recording the body. Recent scientific research in facial recognition, for example, provides a basis for a biometrics of queerness. On its surface the research gives credence to the concept of gaydar; a series of studies show that people are able to make very fast, above chance judgments about sexual orientation.[54] How soon might these abilities be coded into facial recognition software? How difficult might passing become?

Christoph Bregler, a professor of computer science at New York University and director of its movement lab, is among the leaders of this research. In an interview with NPR's *On the Media* in the wake of the Boston Marathon bombing, he described the coming technologies. He began by noting his ability to identify other Germans while walking in New York City. This quasi-intuitive form of accounting happens almost automatically. A barely audible snippet of language, a person's gait, and body language all contribute to nearly subliminal processes of identification. He used this personal example to describe problems with identifying the Boston bombing suspects, Tamerlan and Dzhokhar Tsarnaev. Surveillance camera footage demanded that law enforcement spend many hundreds of hours combing through the footage.[55] Bregler believes that this work can, should, and will be automated. His own research teams can already identify national identity with 80 percent accuracy.

Bregler imagines a world in which these technologies are more widely available and automated, making the identification of criminals or terrorists easier for law enforcement. Shoshana Magnet and Simone Browne, however, address some of the many problems with such approaches, emphasizing in particular the ways biometric technologies reproduce social stereotypes and inequalities.[56] Magnet notes the ways biometrics works differently for different groups. Many biometric technologies, for example, rely on false ideas about race, such as the association of particular facial features with racial groups, and these technologies also reproduce the marginalization of transgender people. Browne links contemporary biometrics to a history of identification documents shaping "human mobility, security applications and consumer transactions," as well as to racializing surveillance technologies such as slave passes and patrols, wanted posters, and branding.[57] Details about a person's life, their experience and embodiment, are coded as data that do not strictly speaking belong to them, and which are put to use by states and corporations in ways over which that person may have little control.

Magnet and Browne thereby underscore the ethical dilemmas related to social stratification and intellectual property. They, and others, also describe the ways these technologies represent a desire for unerring precision and control that is not now and can never be achievable. As Wendy Chun notes, this control is first bound, paradoxically, to ideas that technologies will help us to be free.[58] Second, the control represented by automated processes is not infallible; they fail. Magnet's work in particular underscores biometric failures, and she argues that "biometrics do real damage to vulnerable people and groups, to the fabric of democracy, and to the possibility of a better understanding of the bodies and identities these technologies are supposedly intended to protect."[59]

In recent and upcoming projects, artist-theorist Zach Blas offers creative hacks that disrupt new biometric technologies of the face. The collaborative "Facial Weaponization Suite" contests the ideological and technical underpinnings of face-based surveillance. In this community-based project, masks are collectively produced "from the aggregated facial data of participants."[60] His *Fag Face Mask* responds directly to the above studies on sexual orientation and

FIGURE 1.3. Zach Blas, *Fag Face Mask—October 20, 2012, Los Angeles, CA,* from "Facial Weaponization Suite," 2012. Painted, vacuum-formed recycled polyethylene terephthalate. Courtesy of the artist.

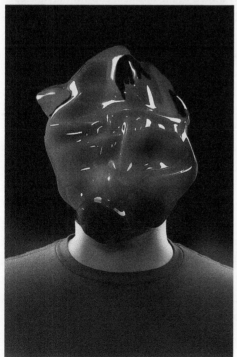

FIGURE 1.4. Zach Blas, *Mask—May 31, 2013, San Diego, CA,* from "Facial Weaponization Suite," 2013. Painted, vacuum-formed recycled polyethylene terephthalate. Courtesy of the artist.

facial cue recognition and offers ways to induce failures in these technologies. *Fag Face Mask* uses facial data from queer men, creating a composite that is then rendered by a 3D printer. The resulting mask is a blob, an unreadable map. Thus far, two masks have been printed, one pink, the other black. In video documentation for the work, which self-consciously echoes the aesthetics of the videos released by Anonymous, a figure wearing the pink mask describes the ways biometric technologies seek to read identity from the body, reproducing in the process the notion that one could have a stable identity at all. A few moments into the video, the mask itself, now a pulsing animation, recounts in a synthetic voice the failures of biometrics: "Biometric technologies rely heavily on stable and normative conceptions of identity and, thus, structural failures are encoded in biometrics that discriminate against race, class, gender, sex, and disability. For example, fingerprint devices often fail to scan the hands of Asian women and iris scans work poorly if an eye has cataracts. Biometric failure exposes the inequalities that emerge when normative categories are forced upon populations." Blas goes on to ask, "What are the tactics and techniques for making our faces non-existent? How do we flee this visibility into the fog of a queerness that refuses to be recognized?"[61]

Fag Face Mask uses masks, aggregated faces of fags, as weapons in order to evade or escape capture. Explicitly linked to the masked, communal figures of the black bloc, the Zapatistas, and Anonymous, Blas's project invites us to share in an air of "deliberate mystery," an opaque queer fog.[62] Yet resisting biometric technologies of the face, or introducing disruptions into this field of surveillance, can also result in yet more extreme approaches among law enforcement. As Blas observes in the video missive, Occupy activists and Afghan civilians alike became the object of biometric data collection, and the NYPD criminalized the wearing of masks in public. The *Washington Post* revealed that more than 120 million people have been unwittingly added to facial recognition databases when, for example, they obtained a driver's license.[63]

Techniques of refusal, such as anonymous massification vis-à-vis masks, are unevenly available. There are some for whom flight may not be possible and/or for whom it may be forced. For example, becoming clandestine or deserting are not really options for populations already subject to spatialized forms of control.[64] The stop-and-frisk policy is administered almost entirely in Black and brown neighborhoods, contexts in which people yearn to escape police harassment and violence but where efforts to evade surveillance or to contest it only result in heightened forms of scrutiny; hoodies and baggy pants, or mascara and glitter, are already sufficient to attract dangerous forms of attention. In these contexts, young Black and brown men and queers might be better served by technologies that could help them to pass, that would make them white—a dark wish encoded in the song I turn to next.

GOOGLE GOOGLE APPS APPS

> Queers, all the queers
> Queers, all the queers
> We're on the move
> Hey girl, where the fuck you moving to?
> Moving to the East Bay
> Living life the broke way

The Black Glitter Collective's 2013 music video "Google Google, Apps Apps" is an angry lament for the death of queer San Francisco. Latina drag queen Persia, together with Collective members DADDIE$ PLA$TIK, work it to an up-tempo beat, but the song itself is pretty depressing.[65] If the previous two sections of this essay are concerned with the relationship between masks and the political possibilities represented by darkness figured as opacity, this section employs the darkness of "black data" in a different way. I focus on the material effects those companies whose business is data have had on the spatialization of dark or unseen people, focusing in particular on the ways queers and people of color have been forced to flee the gentrifying processes effected by San Francisco's most recent tech boom. Here black data takes the form of "black ops."[66] It constitutes an angry, ambivalent, even masochistic queer of color response to the entwined logics of white supremacy and the "values" of the high-tech industry.

Persia wrote the song in response to the stress of her imminent unemployment. She was about to lose her job at SFMOMA, and Esta Noche, the gay Latino bar where she performed in San Francisco, was having trouble paying its bills.[67] In the song, she responds to the most recent wave of tech-fueled gentrification in San Francisco, which has resulted in astronomical increases in the rents—the median rent for a one-bedroom apartment was $2,764 in 2013.[68] Unsurprisingly, these increases have disproportionately impacted already vulnerable populations, like the poor, people of color, underemployed queers, activists, and a host of community organizations and nonprofits.

New technologies seek to transmute the base matter of bodies into code, into digital forms of information that are intended to enhance communication and sociability, as well as, to borrow a category from Apple's apps, to boost "productivity." They thereby also aid in the biopolitical management of populations and for-profit corporations like Google, Apple, Facebook, and Twitter, giants in a region also saturated with other smaller and midsize tech businesses and the venture capitalists who support them. Here we see the results of their success without requiring any complicated decryption algorithms. This is simple addition: they reap record profits, they work with city governments to bring jobs to the region and "develop" city districts, rents go up.

"SF keep your money/Fuck your money!" shouts Persia. The song underscores the material effects the growth of digital technologies and economies has had on real world spaces, in this case the forced exodus of the people and cultures that helped to make San Francisco a political and creative laboratory, that made it home to so many freaks, artists, and sexual adventurers. In a now famous account, Richard Florida noted the appeal of quirky, diverse cities to high-tech companies, forward-looking entrepreneurs, and the "creative class."[69] Florida did not, however, account for the ways the immigration of white-collar creatives and geeks tends to fundamentally alter the very things that made the destination so appealing in the first instance. Persia's resentment, like that of the working class more broadly, does not figure into his analyses.[70] In a discussion about Silicon Valley's recent awkward and usually selfish forays into politics, the *New Yorker*'s George Packer observes, "The technology industry . . . has transformed the Bay Area without being changed by it—in a sense, without getting its hands dirty."[71]

Importantly, the song's refrain links these processes of gentrification and displacement, and the underlying ideologies and practices of neoliberal capitalism, to whiteness. Persia and her crew sing,

> Google Google Apps Apps
> Google Google Apps Apps
> Gringa Gringa Apps Apps
> Gringa Gringa Apps Apps
> I just wanna wanna be white!

The technological giants that aim to connect people everywhere are intimately tied to new surveillance regimes, something the song acknowledges early on, when Persia tells her audience to "Twitter, Twitter me / Facebook,

Facebook me." They are also linked to white privilege and class domination.[72] The new arrivals to San Francisco, these gringos and gringas (terms that refer to English-speaking non-natives), reproduce the violent fantasies of white Manifest Destiny. They are bringing civilization, in the forms of design-savvy gadgets, tweets, instant picture sharing, cat videos, augmented reality, biometric tagging, commercial data mining, and apps for everything, to the unwashed hippies and queers of San Francisco, as well as to billions of needy people around the world. Although they might give the impression of being insensitive—if comments like "adapt or move to Oakland" are any indication—they don't have it out for anyone in particular.[73] They are rational, self-evident social actors, self-evident because their motives are pure and transparent: technological mastery, professional achievement, economic success, white-collar comforts (like living in the Bay Area).

Their privilege is evident as well in the alarm and discomfort they feel in the wake of recent protests against their presence in the Bay Area. In a much-discussed Twitter image, protesters at a May 2013 antigentrification event smashed a piñata of a Google Bus, a papier-mâché avatar of the cushy luxury bus shuttle service Google provides to its San Francisco employees. The buses (also used by other companies) transport workers to the Google offices and are equipped with high-speed Wi-Fi so that they can stay connected 24/7, so that they can optimize their work flows, or gossip, or sleep en route to work without having to mix it up with the masses.

In the video, DADDIE$ PLA$TIK members Tyler Holmes and Vain Hein comically reflect on their own chances of becoming white:

How does one become white?
A little bleach might do the trick
Well I bleach my asshole—
Does that count?

In this instance, the song ties bleached assholes, a trend that involves depigmentation of the skin around the anus, to whiteness more broadly. While this is a satirical jab at perceived white sexual hang-ups, the wish that underlies the chorus "I just wanna wanna be white" is nonetheless powerful and real. Whites want to become whiter (all over), but so too do many people of color. Whatever their political orientation, few queers of color can escape the lure of whiteness. Who doesn't want to be beautiful, rich, and white? Who doesn't want to possess

FIGURE 1.5. Vain Hein and Persia dance in whiteface against a digital backdrop of San Francisco. Screenshot by the author.

technological, financial, and social power? Who doesn't want to control space? Who doesn't want to escape the darkness of violence, poverty, and exclusion? Why wouldn't one opt instead for translucency, transparency, and technological control and power? Venus Xtravaganza was not alone in the wish she expressed in *Paris Is Burning*: "I would like to be a spoiled rich white girl."

The song ambivalently expresses this wish. First, it articulates an erotics of gentrification that mixes sexual desire with domination through the ironic lyrics that link BDSM play to gentrification vis-à-vis an ode to Madonna's "Justify My Love"—"Techies, take the mission / Techies, gentrify me / Gentrify me / Gentrify my love." Second, however, it underscores the grotesquerie that results when the outcasts, the freaks and queers of color, do try to become white. Near the end of the video, Persia and her crew smear white paintstick over their faces and don blond wigs, while Vain Hein adds a Leigh Bowery–style doll mask over his already clownish white face. The chorus now takes on another meaning—one that makes the violence of the wish, and the impossibility of its realization, more palpable. I wanna be white, but obviously I never will be, not if that means having money or the ability to influence the shape of particular technologies or urban spaces rather than be the target consumers of high-tech firms or the chaff cities are trying to cull in their obsequious efforts to please tech companies.

Of course, this critique of the marriage of high tech, gentrification, and whiteness is struck through with ironies. Persia wrote the lyrics to the song on her phone (I wrote most of this essay on a seven-year-old MacBook Pro, if you're wondering). The song and video required considerable technical manipulation—audio engineering and video editing. It appears on YouTube, a Google property, and it has been circulated widely on Facebook and Twitter (where I found it), all in an effort to achieve some traction in network culture in which traction equals attention equals hits equals, Persia hopes, some form of remuneration. Maybe just enough to help her put down a deposit on her new East Bay gigs.

In the comments section of the video, an inevitable troll remarked on some of these ironies: "interesting that the lyrics of this song hostile to the tech industry were written on a phone."[74] To that comment another poster sarcastically replied, "It's interesting how all those blacks wanted out of slavery even though they got free food, and home [sic]."[75]

The desire to become white is a shadow that haunts the lives of queers of color. Perhaps the most common reaction to such a wish is to deny it or to deconstruct it. But, following Jack Halberstam's work on "shadow feminisms," I wonder if the urge to challenge the logic of whiteness in ourselves—the internalized and not-so-internalized violences engendered in us by white settler colonialisms—does not itself reproduce another set of violences, for racial authenticity or purity, for example.[76] Instead, we might embrace those forms of darkness in which identity is obscured or rendered opaque. There are no coherent rational, self-knowing subjects here, just furious refusals. These refusals are a kind of black ops, a form of black data that encrypts without hope of a coherent or positive output. Queers and people of color might tactically redeploy black ops as techniques of masking, secrecy, or evasion. Rather than follow the logic of the "Black Hole," the government contractor Electronic Warfare Associates' wireless traffic intercept tool, black ops imagines a world in which our identities and movement are our own, opaque to the securitized gazes of states and corporations.[77] New black ops technologies might help us all play out our masochistic fantasies of becoming white, becoming animal, becoming other, or just pure, private becoming.

Persia embraces a darkness that responds to the antisociality engendered by the tech giants with an ambivalent queer antisociality in turn. Her face morphs; masked, she affirms, yes, I want to be white like you. Twitter me, Facebook me, gentrify my love. I'll become white, jerky, stumbling, angry, cruel. Her crew's transformation parodies the awkwardness and unsublimated violence of whiteness (and at least some white people). Their black ops is both a refusal and a rearticulation of the stuck frustrations that activists, queers of color, and others feel in the wake of gentrification and neoliberal economic policies more generally. This ambivalence is even present in their name, the Black Glitter Collective: black is for mourning (or encrypting), glitter is for queer fun (it gets *everywhere*).

CONCLUSION

I have sought to enact a form of black data that is different from discussions of Black life that reduce it to lists of bare accountings, which are incomplete and misleadingly suggest that Black queer life must always and only be subtended to historical and contemporary traumas or victimization. Instead, I have used interpretive and performative Black queer practices—reading and throwing shade—to cultivate a notion of black data tied to defacement, opacity, and encryption. Black queer reads can shame a face (in this case Obama's), and they can also articulate an opaque, encrypted point of view, one that resists being fully apprehended or made transparent. Throwing shade, in the context of drag and Kiki balls, for instance, does not require any specific enunciation to deliver an insult; rather, it uses looks, bodily gestures, and tones to deliver a message at once clear ("ratchet") and open-endedly sneaky ("I didn't *say* anything"). I have suggested that such Black queer practices, figured here as "black data," might be usefully brought to bear on discussions about network culture, especially those related to surveillance and the relationship and impact of communication technologies on spaces and mobilities. I have moreover allied the political possibilities of a Black queer conception of black data with the orientations of anarchists and cryptographers. I hope that these perhaps unlikely alliances might yield new, creative, and viable forms of black ops, or encrypted forms of regnant reading and refusal imbued with a dark optimism toward the present, in which political and corporate interests collude to produce an ever-expanding web of ruin.[78] Such a web is a vast system of surveillance and capture that seeks to transform us all into code.

NOTES

ACKNOWLEDGMENTS: I am grateful to E. Patrick Johnson for the invitation to participate in *No Tea, No Shade: New Queer of Color Critique*, where this chapter first appeared, as well as for his thoughtful feedback on earlier versions of this essay. Two anonymous reviewers for Duke University Press also made suggestions that improved my discussion here. Other readers who offered important insights include Hentyle Yapp, Amit Gilutz, and Bill Baskin. This essay was completed in part through the support of a fellowship provided by the Alexander von Humboldt Foundation. My thanks as well to Patrick Keilty and to the reviewers chosen by the University of Washington Press for the opportunity to return to this essay for this book.

1. Jackson et al., *#HashtagActivism*.

2. McIlwain, *Black Software*; Steele, *Digital Black Feminism*.

3. M. Bailey, *Misogynoir Transformed*, 22.

4. Noble, *Algorithms of Oppression*, 1.

5. Steele, *Digital Black Feminism*, 18.

6. M. Bailey, *Misogynoir Transformed*, 6.

7. M. Bailey, *Misogynoir Transformed*, 11.

8. Brock, *Distributed Blackness*, 2.

9. Brock, *Distributed Blackness*, 2.

10. For one among many excellent examples of research on Black Twitter, see Freelon, McIlwain, and Clark, "Quantifying the Power and Consequences of Social Media Protest."

11. Benjamin, *Captivating Technology*, 47.

12. Benjamin, *Captivating Technology*, 34.

13. See, for example, R. Phillips, *Black Quantum Futurism*.

14. CERN, "Black Quantum Futurism Wins This Year's Collide Residency Award," accessed 28 March 2022, https://home.cern/news/news/knowledge-sharing/black -quantum-futurism-wins-years-collide-residency-award.

15. Thurston, *How to Be Black (Online)*.

16. At the time of Thurston's presentation, for example, Black people tended to use Yahoo! and MySpace more than whites. Thurston, *How to Be Black (Online)*.

17. For an extended, but not exhaustive list, see Kolko, Nakamura, and Rodman, *Race in Cyberspace*; Nakamura, *Cybertypes*, and *Digitizing Race*; Nakamura and Chow-White, *Race after the Internet*; C. Bailey, "Virtual Skin"; Hansen, "Digitizing the Racialized Body or the Politics of Universal Address"; González, "Face and the Public"; Gosine, "Brown to Blonde at Gay.com"; and McGlotten, "Ordinary Intersections."

18. For recent treatments of the dozens, see Neff, *Let the World Listen Right*; and Wald, *The Dozens*. For discussions of Black Twitter, see Farhad Manjoo's (in)famous

"How Black People Use Twitter"; and Hilton, "Secret Power of Black Twitter." For an excellent critical account, see Sharma, "Black Twitter?"

19. Twitter post by @Nicholas1136 featured on OMG! Black People!, last updated July 1, 2009, http://omgblackpeople.wordpress.com/.

20. For a few notable examples, see Haraway, *Modest Witness@Second-Millennium. FemaleMan-Meets-OncoMouse*; Foster, *Souls of Cyberfolk*; and Chun, "Introduction: Race and/as Technology," and *Programmed Visions*.

21. See Campbell, *Getting It Online*. See also the essays in O'Riordan and Phillips, *Queer Online*.

22. For recent discussions, see Allen, "Introduction: Black/Queer/Conjuncture at the Current Conjuncture"; and McGlotten and Davis, *Black Genders and Sexualities*. Also see Johnson and Henderson, *Black Queer Studies*.

23. For exceptions, see McBride, *Why I Hate Abercrombie and Fitch*, 88–133; McGlotten, "Ordinary Intersections," and *Virtual Intimacies*; and Herukhuti, *Conjuring Black Funk*.

24. The notion of race as a technology is discussed by Lisa Nakamura and Peter Chow-White, as well as Beth Coleman, among others. Nakamura and Chow-White, for example, discuss the "enforced forgetting" that deprived slaves of information (data) about their pasts: racism is a technology, "a systematic way of doing things that operates by mediating between users and techniques to create specific forms of oppression and discrimination." Nakamura and Chow-White, "Introduction: Race and Digital Technology," 3. Beth Coleman makes the connection to *techné* more explicit (thereby echoing Foucault). For Coleman, *techné* refers to an applied, reproducible skill; race thus emerges as a productive technique of power. See B. Coleman, "Race as Technology." See also Chun, "Introduction: Race and/as Technology."

25. For a discussion of discriminatory social costs that result from data mining, see Danna and Gandy, "All That Glitters Is Not Gold."

26. "New HIV Infections in the United States, 2010," Centers for Disease Control, accessed 15 April 2023, https://www.hivlawandpolicy.org/sites/default/files/New%20 HIV%20Infections%20in%20the%20United%20States%2C%202010%20%28CDC%29 .pdf.

27. "Lesbian, Gay, Bisexual, Transgendered, and HIV-Affected Hate Violence in 2012," National Coalition of Anti-Violence Programs, 4 June 2013, https://avp.org /wp-content/uploads/2017/04/2013_ncavp_hvreport_final.pdf.

28. See the important and rich resources available at the Trans-Atlantic Slave Trade Database, http://www.slavevoyages.org/tast/index.faces.

29. McKernan et al., "Less Than Equal."

30. Eisen, "Operation Ghetto Storm."

31. Gabrielson, Jones, and Sagara, "Deadly Force, in Black and White."

32. Nakamura and Chow-White, "Introduction: Race and Digital Technology"; Chun, "Introduction: Race and/as Technology."

33. Chun, "Introduction: Race and/as Technology," 8.

34. Chen, *Animacies*.

35. Nakamura and Chow-White, "Introduction: Race and Digital Technology," 3.

36. See Katz, *Ima Read*. Black queer rapper Zebra Katz explicitly links his song "Ima Read" to the art of insult developed in the queer Black and Latino Harlem ball scene and popularized in Jennie Livingston's 1990 film, *Paris Is Burning*.

37. Dialogue from Livingston, *Paris Is Burning*.

38. More accurately, the Obama administration aggressively pursued *unauthorized* leakers. The administration, like others before it, itself leaked information to the media in order to influence public opinion. As has been widely reported, Obama's administration leveled charges against seven people, including convicted army private Chelsea Manning, for leaking information to news media; all previous administrations totaled three such prosecutions. As a candidate, Obama had promised to protect leakers and whistleblowers.

39. A long list of historical examples come to mind, from the legal techniques employed to turn Black people into chattel, to Jim Crow, COINTELPRO, the War on Poverty, and the War on Drugs, as well as extrajudicial murder. Terroristic "antiterrorism" programs have a long history of field testing within the United States and across the globe. The drone wars in Afghanistan, Pakistan, and Yemen are simply more recent expressions of these policies.

40. The quoted phrase refers to Phillip Brian Harper's "Evidence of Felt Intuition."

41. Agamben, *Means without End*, 100; and see Lévinas, *Totality and Infinity*. For related discussions, see Saldanha, *Psychedelic White*; and Chen, "Masked States and the 'Screen' between Security and Disability."

42. Deleuze and Guattari, *Thousand Plateaus*.

43. The "comparison to a model" quote is from Watson, "Theorizing European Ethnic Politics with Deleuze and Guattari," 209.

44. Others, including news organizations like *The Guardian* and WikiLeaks, had already gleaned many insights and published information about these programs. As an insider, Snowden was uniquely positioned to confirm them. See Assange, *Cypherpunks*.

45. Baldwin, *Conversations with James Baldwin*, 6.

46. To "carry" is to work it. See the explanation of Leo Gugu, artist, stylist, and performer, "Speaking with Distinction," Open House with Patricia Field, accessed 16 February 2023, http://www.youtube.com/watch?v=UX3BrPe4dxc.

47. Chen, "Masked States and the 'Screen' between Security and Disability," 77. Chen's discussion also underscores the relationship between masks and screens and "securitized, nondisabled whiteness," a compelling reading I nonetheless do not pursue here.

48. Brooks, *Bodies in Dissent*, 8.

49. Quoted in Manthia Diawara, "Conversation with Édouard Glissant aboard the Queen Mary II," August 2009, 6, http://www.liv.ac.uk/media/livacuk/csis-2 /blackatlantic/research/Diawara_text_defined.pdf.

50. For a discussion of these techniques and tips on how to use them, see Schoen, "Technology to Protect against Mass Surveillance (Part I)."

51. See the discussion between Jacob Appelbaum, Andy Müller-Maguhn, and Jérémie Zimmerman in the chapter "The Militarization of Cyberspace," in Assange, *Cypherpunks*, 33–40.

52. See, for example, Greenwald, *No Place to Hide*.

53. For the last few decades, the anarchist "black bloc" has been both hypervisible and absent. Governments and mainstream media have ignored anarchists' emphasis on mutual aid, self-organization, and voluntary association and have instead presented anarchists as terroristic threats to state power. The black bloc is unfailingly represented as hoodlums intent on the wanton destruction of property. But the black bloc's origins lie in the 1970s and 1980s, in social protest movements in Germany, where members sought to protect demonstrators from police violence and arrest. Their black clothing and masks were meant to help other protesters identify them while maintaining their own anonymity, a fact exploited in the 1999 WTO protests, when law enforcement themselves donned similar clothing to infiltrate and discredit the protesters (a technique widely employed since). The black bloc's secondary role, the contours of which are hotly contested in anarchist communities, is to act as the militant direct action wing, which can include precisely the sort of destruction of property with which anarchism is synonymous in mainstream media. For refreshing anarchist indymedia, see "Stim's Last Stand," Sub-Media, accessed 6 March 2023, http://stimulator.tv/.

54. See Rule and Ambady, "Brief Exposures"; and Rule et al., "Found in Translation."

55. Although there was a widespread effort to crowdsource the Boston Marathon bombing suspects, this ultimately proved fruitless, with epic racial profiling fails, as well as ever more shameful missteps by the *New York Post*, which published the images of two Arab-looking men as suspects—they were a local coach and a high school athlete.

56. Magnet, *When Biometrics Fail*; Browne, "Digital Epidermalization."

57. Browne, "Digital Epidermalization," 132.

58. Chun, *Control and Freedom*.

59. Magnet, *When Biometrics Fail*, 3.

60. Blas, "Facial Weaponization Suite."

61. Blas, "Facial Weaponization Suite."

62. Coleman, "Anonymous—From the Lulz to Collective Action."

63. Craig Timburg and Ellen Nakashima, "State Photo-ID Databases Become Troves for Police," *Washington Post*, 16 June 2013.

64. The radical left French journal *Tiqqun* advocates forms of autonomous secession through the creation of an Imaginary politics, clandestinity, and a politics of refusal. For a sympathetic critique, see Cunningham, "Clandestinity and Appearance." Such a politics of secessionist refusal served as part of the rationale for the arrest of the Tarnac Nine, a group of French anarchists who'd taken up in a grocery in a small village. They were accused of sabotaging the French rail network (there were no injuries). One of the rationales provided for their arrest was that the group were "pre-terrorists"—their an-archo-autonomist tendencies were reason enough for suspicion. Then-interior minister Michèle Alliot-Marie said, "They have adopted underground methods. They never use mobile telephones, and they live in areas where it is very difficult for the police to gather information without being spotted. They have managed to have, in the village of Tarnac, friendly relations with people who can warn them of the presence of strangers." Quoted in Alberto Toscano, "Criminalising Dissent," *The Guardian*, 28 January 2009. Toscano goes on to observe that "the very fact of collective living, of rejecting an astoundingly restrictive notion of normality (using a mobile, living in cities, being easily observable by the police) has itself become incriminating." See also "Tarnac Nine," Wikipedia, last modified 13 June 2013, http://en.wikipedia.org/wiki/Tarnac_9.

65. "Persia and DADDIE$ PLA$TIK, Google Google Apps Apps," accessed 16 February 2023, https://www.youtube.com/watch?v=5xyqbc7SQ4w.

66. I am riffing here on Fred Moten's sketch of a fugitive Black imagination in "Black Optimism/Black Operation."

67. Marke B., "Here's Your Gentrification-Eviction-Displacement Electro Theme Song. Let's Dance," *San Francisco Bay Guardian Online*, 29 May 2013, https://sfbgarchive.48hills.org/sfbgarchive/2013/05/29/heres-your-gentrification-theme-song.

68. Kuchar, "Mapping the Average Rental Rate of a One and Two Bedroom in San Francisco."

69. Florida, *Rise of the Creative Class*.

70. For a critique of Florida and an analysis of the effects the creative class can have on urban environments, see Long, *Weird City*.

71. Packer, "Change the World."

72. This statement is complicated, but not undermined, by the fact that half of high-tech workers in California are Asian. Asian Americans hold slightly more jobs in the Bay Area. See Dan Nakaso, "Asian-American Citizens Hold Slight Edge over Non-citizen Asians in Bay Area Tech Jobs," *San Jose Mercury News*, 9 December 2012, https://www.mercurynews.com/2012/12/07/asian-american-citizens-hold-slight-edge-over-non-citizen-asians-in-bay-area-tech-jobs/. The presence of people of color in the tech industry does not fundamentally alter the organizing ideologies of Silicon Valley, inasmuch as the owners, managers, and venture capitalists who shape the industry are overwhelmingly white.

73. See the comment thread in response to the article by Rebecca Bowe, "Vanishing City," *San Francisco Bay Guardian Online*, 21 May 2013, http://www.sfbg.com/2013/05/21/vanishing-city?page=0,0.

74. See the comments section for Persia and DADDIE$ PLA$TIK, "Google Google Apps Apps."

75. Comments at Persia and DADDIE$ PLA$TIK, "Google Google Apps Apps."

76. On "shadow feminisms," see Halberstam, *Queer Art of Failure.*

77. "Black Hole: Wireless Traffic Intercept, Reconstruction and Analysis," EWA Government Systems, accessed 1 July 2013, http://www.ewa-gsi.com/Fact%20Sheets/Black%20Hole%20Fact%20Sheet.pdf (no longer accessible). Electronic Warfare Associates is a leading contractor in the development of new biometric facial recognition technologies.

78. Galloway, "Networks," 283.

BIBLIOGRAPHY

Agamben, Giorgio. *Means without End: Notes on Politics.* Translated by Vincenzo Binetti and Cesare Casarino. Minneapolis: University of Minnesota Press, 2000.

Allen, Jafari S. "Introduction: Black/Queer/Diaspora at the Current Conjuncture." *GLQ: A Journal of Lesbian and Gay Studies* 18, no. 2–3 (2012): 211–48.

Assange, Julian. *Cypherpunks: Freedom and the Future of the Internet.* New York: OR Books, 2012.

Bailey, Cameron. "Virtual Skin: Articulating Race in Cyberspace." In *Immersed in Technology: Art and Virtual Environments*, edited by Mary A. Moser and Douglas MacLeod, 29–49. Cambridge, MA: MIT Press, 1996.

Bailey, Moya. *Misogynoir Transformed: Black Women's Digital Resistance.* New York: New York University Press, 2021.

Baldwin, James. *Conversations with James Baldwin.* Edited by Fred L. Standley and Louis H. Pratt. Jackson: University of Mississippi, 1989.

Benjamin, Ruha, ed. *Captivating Technology: Race, Carceral Technoscience, and Liberatory Imagination in Everyday Life.* Durham, NC: Duke University Press, 2019.

——— . *Race after Technology.* Medford, MA: Polity, 2020.

Blas, Zach. "Facial Weaponization Suite." July 7, 2013. http://www.zachblas.info/projects/facial-weaponization-suite/.

Bonilla, Yarimar, and Jonathan Rosa. "#Ferguson: Digital Protest, Hashtag Ethnography, and the Racial Politics of Social Media in the United States." *American Ethnologist* 42, no. 1 (February 2015): 4–17. https://doi.org/10.1111/amet.12112.

Brock, André, Jr. *Distributed Blackness: African American Cybercultures.* New York: New York University Press, 2020.

Brooks, Daphne. *Bodies in Dissent: Spectacular Performances of Race and Freedom, 1850–1910*. Durham, NC: Duke University Press, 2006.

Browne, Simone. *Dark Matters: On the Surveillance of Blackness*. Durham, NC: Duke University Press, 2015.

———. "Digital Epidermalization: Race, Identity and Biometrics." *Critical Sociology* 36, no. 1 (2010): 131–50.

Campbell, John Edward. *Getting It On Online: Cyberspace, Gay Male Sexuality, and Embodied Identity*. New York: Harrington Park Press, 2004.

Chen, Mel Y. *Animacies: Biopolitics, Racial Mattering, and Queer Affect*. Durham, NC: Duke University Press, 2012.

———. "Masked States and the 'Screen' between Security and Disability." *WSQ: Women's Studies Quarterly* 40, no. 1–2 (2012): 76–96.

Chun, Wendy. *Control and Freedom: Power and Paranoia in the Age of Fiber Optics*. Cambridge, MA: MIT Press, 2006.

———. "Introduction: Race and/as Technology; or, How to Do Things to Race." *Camera Obscura* 24, no. 1 (2009): 7–35.

———. *Programmed Visions: Software and Memory*. Cambridge, MA: MIT Press, 2011.

Coleman, Beth. "Race as Technology." *Camera Obscura* 24, no. 1 (2009): 176–207.

Coleman, Gabriella. "Anonymous—From the Lulz to Collective Action." *The New Significance*, 9 May 2011. http://www.thenewsignificance.com/2011/05/09/gabriella -coleman-anonymous-from-the-lulz-to-collective-action/.

Cunningham, John. "Clandestinity and Appearance." *Mute* 2, no. 16 (2010). http:// www.metamute.org/editorial/articles/clandestinity-and-appearance.

Danna, Anthony, and Oscar H. Gandy Jr. "All That Glitters Is Not Gold: Digging beneath the Surface of Data Mining." *Journal of Business Ethics* 40, no. 4 (2002): 373–86.

Deleuze, Gilles, and Félix Guattari. *A Thousand Plateaus: Capitalism and Schizophrenia*. Minneapolis: University of Minnesota Press, 1987.

Eisen, Arlene. "Operation Ghetto Storm: 2012 Annual Report on the Extrajudicial Killing of 313 Black People." Malcolm X Grassroots Movement, 7 April 2013. Available at *ProudFlesh: New Afrikan Journal of Culture, Politics and Consciousness*, no. 7 (2013). https://www.africaknowledgeproject.org/index.php/proudflesh/article/ view/1758.

Florida, Richard L. *The Rise of the Creative Class*. New York: Basic Books, 2004.

Foster, Thomas. *The Souls of Cyberfolk: Posthumanism as Vernacular Theory*. Minneapolis: University of Minnesota Press, 2005.

Freelon, Deen, Charlton McIlwain, and Meredith Clark. "Quantifying the Power and Consequences of Social Media Protest." *New Media and Society* 20, no. 3 (2018): 990–1011.

Gabrielson, Ryan, Ryann Grochowski Jones, and Eric Sagara. "Deadly Force, in Black and White." ProPublica, 10 October 2014. http://www.propublica.org/article/deadly -force-in-black-and-white#update-note.

Galloway, Alexander. "Black Box, Black Bloc." In *Communization and Its Discontents: Contestation, Critique, and Contemporary Struggles*, edited by Benjamin Noys, 237–49. New York: Minor Compositions, 2011.

——— . "Networks." In *Critical Terms for Media Studies*, edited by W. J. T. Mitchell and Mark B. N. Hansen, 280–96. Chicago: University of Chicago Press, 2010.

González, Jennifer. "The Face and the Public: Race, Secrecy, and Digital Art Practice." *Camera Obscura* 24, no. 1 (2009): 37–65.

Gosine, Andil. "Brown to Blonde at Gay.com: Passing White in Queer Cyberspace." In *Queer Online: Media Technology and Sexuality*, edited by Kate O'Riordan and David Phillips, 139–53. New York: Peter Lang, 2007.

Greenwald, Glenn. *No Place to Hide: Edward Snowden, the NSA, and the U.S. Surveillance State*. New York: Metropolitan Books, 2014.

Halberstam, Judith. *The Queer Art of Failure*. Durham, NC: Duke University Press, 2011.

Hansen, Mark B. N. "Digitizing the Racialized Body or the Politics of Universal Address." *SubStance* 33, no. 2 (2004): 107–33.

Haraway, Donna Jeanne. *Modest Witness@Second-Millennium.FemaleMan-Meets-OncoMouse: Feminism and Technoscience*. New York: Routledge, 1997.

Harper, Phillip Brian. "The Evidence of Felt Intuition: Minority Experience, Everyday Life, and Critical Speculative Knowledge." In *Black Queer Studies: A Critical Anthology*, edited by E. Patrick Johnson and Mae G. Henderson, 106–23. Durham, NC: Duke University Press, 2005.

Herukhuti. *Conjuring Black Funk: Notes on Culture, Sexuality, and Spirituality, Volume 1*. New York: Vintage Equity Press, 2007.

Hilton, Shani. "The Secret Power of Black Twitter." *Buzzfeed*, 16 July 2013. http://www .buzzfeed.com/shani/the-secret-power-of-black-twitter.

Jackson, Sarah J., Moya Bailey, Brooke Foucault Welles, and Genie Lauren. *#HashtagActivism: Networks of Race and Gender Justice*. Illustrated ed. Cambridge, MA: MIT Press, 2020.

Johnson, E. Patrick, and Mae G. Henderson, eds. *Black Queer Studies: A Critical Anthology*. Durham, NC: Duke University Press, 2005.

Katz, Zebra. *Ima Read*. Mad Decent, 2012. Mp3. https://www.youtube.com/watch?v =5a7toRopm1g.

Kolko, Beth E., Lisa Nakamura, and Gilbert B. Rodman, eds. *Race in Cyberspace*. New York: Routledge, 1999.

Kuchar, Sally. "Mapping the Average Rental Rate of a One and Two Bedroom in San Francisco." *Curbed SF*, 23 May 2013. http://sf.curbed.com/archives/2013/05/23

/mapping_the_average_rental_rate_of_a_one_and_two_bedroom_in_san_francisco
.php.

Long, Joshua. *Weird City: A Sense of Place and Creative Resistance in Austin, Texas.*
Austin: University of Texas Press, 2010.

Lévinas, Emmanuel. *Totality and Infinity: An Essay on Exteriority.* Pittsburgh, PA:
Duquesne University Press, 1969.

Livingston, Jennie, dir. *Paris Is Burning.* Miramax Films, 1990.

Magnet, Shoshana. *When Biometrics Fail: Gender, Race, and the Technology of Identity.*
Durham, NC: Duke University Press, 2011.

Manjoo, Farhad. "How Black People Use Twitter." *Slate*, 10 August 2010.

McBride, Dwight. *Why I Hate Abercrombie and Fitch: Essays on Race and Sexuality.*
New York: New York University Press, 2005.

McGlotten, Shaka. "Life in the Network." *Women and Performance: A Journal of Feminist Theory* 28, no. 2 (4 May 2018): 161–69. https://doi.org/10.1080/0740770X.2018
.1477244.

———. "Ordinary Intersections: Speculations on Difference, Justice, and Utopia in
Black Queer Life." *Transforming Anthropology* 20, no. 1 (2012): 123–37.

———. "Streaking." *TDR: The Drama Review* 63, no. 4 (2019): 152–71.

———. *Virtual Intimacies: Media, Affect, and Queer Sociality.* Albany: State University
of New York Press, 2013.

———. "What's Love Got to Do with It?" In *A Networked Self and Love,* edited by Zizi
Paparachessi, 230–52. New York: Routledge, 2018.

McGlotten, Shaka, and Dána-Ain Davis, eds. *Black Genders and Sexualities.* New York:
Palgrave Macmillan, 2012.

McIlwain, Charlton D. *Black Software: The Internet and Racial Justice, from the AfroNet
to Black Lives Matter.* New York: Oxford University Press, 2019.

McKernan, Signe-Mary, Caroline Ratcliffe, C. Eugene Steuerle, and Sisi Zhang. "Less
than Equal: Racial Disparities in Wealth Accumulation." Urban Institute, 26 April
2013. https://www.urban.org/research/publication/less-equal-racial-disparities
-wealth-accumulation.

Moten, Fred. "Black Optimism/Black Operation." Unpublished paper, 2007. http://
lucian.uchicago.edu/blogs/politicalfeeling/files/2007/12/moten-black-optimism
.doc.

Nakamura, Lisa. *Cybertypes: Race, Ethnicity, and Identity on the Internet.* New York:
Routledge, 2002.

———. *Digitizing Race: Visual Cultures of the Internet.* Minneapolis: University of
Minnesota Press, 2008.

Nakamura, Lisa, and Peter Chow-White. "Introduction: Race and Digital Technology;
Code, the Color Line, and the Information Society." In *Race after the Internet,*

edited by Lisa Nakamura and Peter Chow-White, 1–18. New York: Routledge, 2011.

———, eds. *Race after the Internet*. New York: Routledge, 2011.

Neff, Ali Colleen. *Let the World Listen Right: The Mississippi Delta Hip Hop Story*. Jackson: University of Mississippi Press, 2009.

Noble, Safiya Umoja. *Algorithms of Oppression: How Search Engines Reinforce Racism*. New York: New York University Press, 2018.

O'Riordan, Kate, and David Phillips, eds. *Queer Online: Media Technology and Sexuality*. New York: Peter Lang, 2007.

Packer, George. "Change the World." *New Yorker*, 27 May 2013.

Paris Is Burning (documentary). Art Matters, Inc., BBC Television, Edelman Family Fund, 1991.

Phillips, Rasheedah, ed. *Black Quantum Futurism: Theory and Practice*. Vol. 1. Philadelphia: House of Future Sciences Books/AfroFuturist Affair, 2015.

Rule, Nicholas O., and Nalini Ambady. "Brief Exposures: Male Sexual Orientation Is Accurately Perceived at 50 Ms." *Journal of Experimental Social Psychology* 44, no. 4 (2008): 1100–1105.

Rule, Nicholas O., Keiko Ishii, Nalini Ambady, Katherine S. Rosen, and Katherine C. Hallett. "Found in Translation: Cross-Cultural Consensus in the Accurate Categorization of Male Sexual Orientation." *Personality and Social Psychology Bulletin* 37, no. 11 (2011): 1499–1507.

Saldanha, Arun. *Psychedelic White: Goa Trance and the Viscosity of Race*. Minneapolis: University of Minnesota Press, 2007.

Schoen, Seth. "Technology to Protect against Mass Surveillance (Part I)." Electronic Frontier Foundation, 17 July 2013. https://www.eff.org/deeplinks/2013/07 /technology-protect-against-mass-surveillance-part-1.

Sharma, Sangay. "Black Twitter? Racial Hashtags, Networks, and Contagion." *New Formations*, no. 78 (2013): 46–64.

Steele, Catherine Knight. *Digital Black Feminism*. New York: New York University Press, 2021.

Tarnac Nine. "Tarnac Nine." Wikipedia. Wikimedia Foundation, 13 March 2023. https://en.wikipedia.org/wiki/Tarnac_Nine.

Thurston, Baratunde. *How to Be Black (Online)*. 2009. Available at Slideshare.net. http://www.slideshare.net/baratunde/how-to-be-black-online-by-baratunde.

Wald, Elijah. *The Dozens: A History of Rap's Mama*. New York: Oxford University Press, 2012.

Watson, Janell. "Theorizing European Ethnic Politics with Deleuze and Guattari." In *Deleuze and Politics*, edited by Ian Buchanan and Nicholas Thoburn, 196–217. Edinburgh: University of Edinburgh Press, 2008.

NIKITA SHEPARD

2 "To Fight for an End to Intrusions into the Sex Lives of Americans" *Gay and Lesbian Resistance to Sexual Surveillance and Data Collection, 1945–1972*

IN MARCH 2017, the release of a federal report on the upcoming 2020 Census and American Community Survey (ACS) infuriated LGBTQ advocates across the United States. The report omitted prior proposals to add questions that would specifically pertain to LGBTQ communities, despite requests "from more than 75 members of Congress and multiple federal agencies" for the data such questions would produce.[1] As the National LGBTQ Task Force stated in a press release, the exclusion of census and ACS questions on sexual orientation and gender identity constituted "yet another step to deny LGBTQ people freedom, justice, and equity."[2] This advocacy built on previous efforts, such as the Task Force's 2010 "Queer the Census" campaign, which distributed stickers encouraging the agency to collect sexual orientation and gender identity statistics for supporters to affix to the envelopes in which they mailed their completed census forms. An article in *The Nation* labeled the campaign "one of today's great struggles," because since census inclusion indexes democratic citizenship and personhood on a fundamental level, such questions would ensure "that Americans are counted into—not out of—the republic." MSNBC host Rachel Maddow repurposed a familiar chant to sum up the demand: "We're here, we're queer, count us!"[3]

Thus, LGBTQ advocates reacted with outrage when the Census Bureau, under the newly arrived Trump administration, appeared to dismiss this demand. Lambda Legal referred to the decision as "an assault on science as well as on a uniquely vulnerable group of Americans" and called on the administration "to begin collecting sexual orientation and gender identity data on the American Community Survey as soon as possible." The Human Rights Campaign mobilized on Twitter using the hashtag #CantEraseUs. Even Chelsea Clinton weighed in: "This is outrageous. No one should be invisible in America."[4]

The controversy reflected how deeply concepts of dignity, democratic inclusion, social justice, scientific rationality, economic security, and political access have become intertwined with being subjected to quantitative study by the state in the twenty-first-century United States. The plaintive demand "Count us!" plays on the double sense of the verb, in its transitive meaning—to quantitatively tabulate, to add up—as well as its intransitive meaning—to *matter*, to be of value, to hold significance. Critics described the experience of not being counted by state agencies within sexual orientation-specific categories as *erasing* LGBTQ people, as rendering them *invisible*. This cuts to the heart of a movement that has valorized visibility as a central political demand and a necessary practice of resistance.

How strange it must then seem to today's LGBTQ activists that when their predecessors developed the first national gay rights platform more than fifty years ago, one of the key planks centered precisely on the right to *not* be made into data by the state. In February 1972, the National Coalition of Gay Organizations (NCGO) drew up a policy agenda for legislative and executive action, including a demand for "appropriate executive orders, regulations, and legislation banning the compiling, maintenance and dissemination of information on an individual's sexual preference, behavior, and social and political activities for dossiers and data banks."[5]

This was no fringe demand. In fact, within weeks it had been adopted by Democratic presidential candidate George McGovern, who included in his statement on gay rights—the first by a presidential campaign in US history—the proposal that "government and private investigatory agencies should cease to collect data on the sexual preferences of individuals."[6]

Most of the proposed planks in the NCGO's gay rights platform have remained mainstays of LGBTQ advocacy ever since: antidiscrimination laws, decriminalization of private sexual activity between consenting adults, and the right to serve in the armed forces, for example. Yet the provision pushing a ban on government collection of data on the sexual preference of individuals, uniquely among the other demands, has been entirely reversed. Today, many leading activist groups insist that the federal government do precisely that—albeit on their own terms—as a matter of equality and fairness.

Of course, all data is not alike. The collection of information about an individual's sexual behavior by hostile institutions without their consent or knowledge is quite different from voluntarily submitting anonymized, self-reported data to be used in aggregates, as with today's census and ACS. From Alfred Kinsey's famous reports to Laud Humphreys's study published as *Tearoom Trade*, from the FBI's "Sex Deviates" program to debates over HIV/AIDS reporting, queers in the United States have forged complex relationships with data, research, surveillance, and privacy.[7] Government bureaucracies, law enforcement agencies, medical and psychological authorities, and private companies have used sexual surveillance and data for a range of purposes, producing forms of knowledge about homosexuality often deeply harmful to the objects of their investigative gaze and facing creative forms of resistance from the individuals and communities they targeted. Examining how LGBTQ movements have collaborated with or contested different forms of data collection offers insight into the shifting relationship between sexual dissidents and the state across the twentieth century.

The history of how LGBTQ movements have related to data and visibility provides insight into theorizations of the concept of opacity explored by contemporary queer and media theorists. Nicholas de Villiers's discussion of queer strategies of opacity and Jack Halberstam's exploration of darkness within an aesthetic of queer failure have helped to establish a critical relationship to the presumed goal of visibility and legibility for proper LGBTQ subjects.[8] More recently, trans studies scholars such as Toby Beauchamp have argued that "surveillance is a central practice through which the category of transgender is produced, regulated, and contested," proposing a nuanced approach that engages, but does not uncritically valorize, illegibility as a tool to resist gendered surveillance.[9] As the significance of big data grows, these insights increasingly intersect with critical data studies scholarship in the theorizing of new modes of political resistance in the twenty-first century informed by queer and trans strategies of opacity. As Zach Blas suggests, "Informatic opacity might best be understood as a mutated queerness, brought to a global, technical scale, that strives to subvert identification standardization."[10] In the context of US LGBTQ politics, this subversion emerges not only from theoretical insights but also from a distinctive history rooted in decades of gay and lesbian resistance to surveillance and data collection.

This chapter traces how this long-forgotten provision to ban data collection became a key demand of the US gay and lesbian movement in the early 1970s. It begins by examining the network of government and private agencies that investigated homosexuality in the post–World War II period, the consequences of their sexual surveillance on gay and lesbian communities, and how the people they targeted resisted such surveillance.[11] In the aftermath of the Stonewall Rebellion and the rise of gay liberation, the demand to end data collection emerged within New York City's Gay Activists Alliance (GAA), as they documented cases in which companies and government agencies used data on sexual orientation to restrict access to employment, insurance, and other critical services. The GAA brought the demand to the 1972 NCGO conference, from which it proliferated into both gay activist and Democratic Party groupings and from there into McGovern's national platform. However, growing gay and lesbian political clout, national debates over data and privacy, and the emergence of HIV/AIDS shifted the context, leading advocates to alter, drop, and eventually invert this demand over the decades to come. I conclude with reflections on what this plank, and its subsequent disappearance and reversal by later generations of activists, might indicate about queer history, social movements, and data politics today.

SEXUAL SURVEILLANCE
IN THE POSTWAR UNITED STATES

In the years following World War II, government and private surveillance posed a constant threat to same-sex loving men and women in the United States. The war marked a turning point both in the consolidation of gay and lesbian communities across the country and in the proliferation of increasingly intrusive modes of investigating sexual deviance. In the years leading up to the war, as Allan Bérubé explains, psychiatrists had drawn on their expanded authority to institute new screening procedures to detect homosexuals, which in turn "introduced into military policies and procedures the concept of the homosexual as a personality type unfit for military service and combat." Shifting attention from sexual acts to categories of individuals, Bérubé argues, "forced military officials to develop an expanding administrative apparatus for managing homosexual personnel that relied on diagnosis, hospitalization, surveillance, interrogation, discharge, administrative appeal, and mass indoctrination."[12] While these procedures were relaxed during the war itself in response to the urgent demand for higher staffing levels, after 1945 the imperative to identify and exclude homosexuals from the armed services consolidated into a regime of intensive surveillance and repression.

In the emerging Cold War political climate, the association of homosexuality with weakness, deception, and susceptibility to communist influence or black-mail extended through both military and civilian agencies. As David Johnson has documented, the acceleration of antihomosexual investigations in the late 1940s and 1950s constituted a "Lavender Scare," in which the FBI collaborated with the DC vice squad and US Park Police to gather information on thousands of suspected homosexuals, who were then purged from or prevented from obtaining federal government jobs. The establishment of a federal "loyalty/security" program targeting Communists and "sex perverts" swept through bureaucracies in Washington and rippled outward across the country.[13] While this campaign has been most thoroughly documented in the nation's capital, fragmentary evidence suggests that federal antihomosexual purges spread to locales as far-flung as Mountain Home, Idaho (the location of an air force base), Huntsville, Alabama (the rocket division of the federal space program), and Fort McPherson, Georgia (a Women's Army Corps unit).[14]

Beyond the military and federal government agencies, state and municipal authorities initiated their own waves of antihomosexual surveillance and purges in response to regional and local imperatives. Investigations into homosexuality conducted by southern state legislatures, such as the Mississippi Sovereignty Commission and the Florida Legislative Investigation Committee, were mod-eled on federal efforts such as the House Un-American Activities Committee and drew on similar anticommunist discourses. However, these efforts were specifically motivated by racial anxieties and the desire to uphold white su-premacy; these bodies attempted to discredit Black civil rights movements by linking them to political subversion and sexual deviance.[15] Mass arrest cam-paigns against suspected homosexuals in Idaho, Iowa, Ohio, and elsewhere took place during the period in response to sensationalized anxieties over the abuse and murder of children in what George Chauncey has termed the "post-war sex crime panic."[16] Purges of homosexuals at public universities in Wisconsin and Missouri in the late 1940s focused on protecting institutional reputations and did not echo the loyalty/security justifications that would characterize the federal purges.[17] As Timothy Stewart-Winter notes in his study of Chicago, "antigay policing in the 1950s entailed more variation and unevenness than the Lavender Scare framework alone can explain."[18]

Although geographically dispersed and varied in their rationales, antihomosexual investigations during the postwar period were linked in an increasingly dense network of communication through which sexual data, surveillance techniques, and personnel circulated. At the apex sat the Federal Bureau of Investigation, whose "Sex Deviates" program assembled hundreds of thousands of pages of files on suspected homosexuals. While federally driven, investigations by its own agents and those of other federal bureaucracies—most prominently the US Postal Service—provided only part of the data it collected. Its vast scope relied on collaboration with a wide range of public and private agencies, which both requested and supplied information on sexually suspect individuals, supplemented by a network of confidential informants. Local law enforcement and military police officials from San Antonio, Texas, to Oak Park, Michigan, conducted sexual surveillance and exchanged intelligence with the FBI, drawing on federal resources to pursue local goals.[19] The homophile magazine *ONE* reported in November 1954 on a Fort Lauderdale public official who began his "war on perverts" by gathering data on all arrests related to homosexual behavior in Florida after requesting and receiving "bulky files from Dade County and the FBI."[20]

While federal agencies formed a critical node within this network of exchange, the data and techniques they generated drew on the initiative of local law enforcement departments, which pioneered new forms of antihomosexual surveillance in response to local pressures. The small town of Mansfield, Ohio, found itself on the cutting edge in 1962 when, under pressure after the murder of two girls in a public park, it undertook an unprecedented surveillance campaign against men who met for sex in a popular public restroom. The Mansfield Police Department installed a two-way mirror and spent weeks filming sexual activity between men in the restroom and surreptitiously identifying participants after they left. The filming led to the convictions of thirty-seven men on sodomy and other charges, as well as the closing and razing of the restroom building by the local park service. Mansfield police then edited the footage of local men engaged in sexual activity with each other into a film titled *Camera Surveillance*, explaining the surveillance techniques and elaborating on the urgency of firm law enforcement responses to "sex perversion." The film was then circulated through police departments across the country.[21] In the police journal *Law and Order*, W. Cleon Skousen—a former FBI agent who later became chief of police in Salt Lake City and initiated an aggressive campaign to rid the city of "perverts"—reviewed the film favorably, describing the Mansfield police techniques and praising it as "an important contribution to the police education field."[22] The two-way mirror techniques were subsequently adopted by local police in public restrooms around the United States, indicating how sexual surveillance practices evolved through a closely connected network of state, local, and federal officials.

The ferocity of surveillance against gays and lesbians shaped the emergence of the incipient trans public sphere. One of the first major publications for "Transvestites," as editor Virginia Prince termed herself and her subscribers, was *Transvestia*, which launched in 1960 as a platform for connection and information exchange. In a March 1961 issue, Prince noted that the magazine's continuation depended not only on herself and her subscribers but "UNCLE SAM," since "the Post Office believes that a few unscrupulous persons make use of the PERSON TO PERSON section of the magazine to make contacts with others with whom they then exchange obscene mail." Insisting that the magazine was not in any way obscene and distancing herself from any erotic intention for the project, she urges readers to inform on any subscribers who send mail "in any way obscene, pornographic, or questionable." She was familiar with pervasive antigay surveillance; as she noted, "the world confuses transvestism and homosexuality and when there is a campaign against the latter we are caught in the crossfire." As a result, she argued, "WE must keep our own house clean and above reproach"—in other words, devoid of the homoerotic content targeted for sexual surveillance.[23]

This insistence was not motivated merely by a politics of respectability but out of an immediate and deeply personal sense of the risks involved in becoming a target of surveillance for challenging gender or sexual norms. Prince herself had just been investigated by postal inspectors and prosecuted for exchanging letters describing lesbian sexual fantasies. As she was preparing this issue of *Transvestia* in early 1961, she narrowly escaped prison time by accepting a plea deal mandating five years of probation and forbidding her to dress as a woman in public.[24] Despite her efforts to insist on the distinctions between homosexuality and gender nonconformity, antigay surveillance caught a wide range of gender and sexual dissidents in its web, often with severe consequences.

Beyond law enforcement agencies and postal inspectors, a wide range of institutions deployed sexual surveillance and generated data that constrained the lives of gay men and lesbians. For example, insurance and bonding agencies used suspicion of homosexuality as a basis for denying the certification necessary to secure housing or jobs in certain industries. As attorney Kenneth Zwerin remarked at the 1957 convention of the Mattachine Society, a national homophile organization, an otherwise law-abiding man who had been arrested on a homosexual charge and who might later apply for a job selling insurance could be rejected because "his picture is on file in Washington with the FBI. It seems that bonding companies will not take a chance on a man who has even been suspected of being a homosexual."[25] The Household Finance Corporation drew on sexual surveillance data gathered from private investigation firms to deny loans to homosexual applicants.[26] As Clayton Howard has demonstrated in his research on suburban development in California, postwar bureaucrats coded normative heterosexuality into housing policy, resulting in the creation of suburbs inaccessible to gay men, lesbians, and other unmarried people. The Federal Housing Administration's "character" guidelines discouraging lenders from extending mortgages to unmarried people intersected with escalating criminalization of same-sex sexuality and interconnected webs of surveillance to shape the geography and culture of postwar gay life.[27]

Sexual surveillance and data collection proved particularly harmful to postwar gay and lesbian communities in the form of employee screening programs. Such efforts by corporate employers dated back to the use of Pinkerton detectives to spy on suspected labor agitators. However, World War I marked a turning point, as concern over sabotage had prompted increased scrutiny of defense plant employees and the military introduced psychological and intelligence testing for newly enlisted soldiers. The use of surveillance and testing by corporate employers to screen their workforces expanded dramatically in subsequent decades, as the field of "personnel management" emerged. By the late 1940s, Cold War tensions and efforts to check the power of labor had led a growing number of firms across many industries to institute screening programs modeled on the federal government's loyalty/security criteria.[28] Personnel managers at private companies during this period frequently mentioned homosexuality as one of the main traits they hoped to avoid by screening applicants, drawing on a wide range of techniques and data sources to ascertain sexually suspect candidates.[29] In addition to criminal background checks, government records required in the application process could offer clues to identify undesirable applicants. For example, by the 1960s, veterans with discharge papers bearing the designation "SDN514" were identifiable as homosexuals to potential employers, who possessed the key to interpret military codes that the veterans themselves often could not.[30] Personality and psychological tests originally deployed by the military to scan for homosexuality and characteristics considered undesirable in prospective soldiers were adapted by civilian employers, with features such as the Minnesota Multiphasic Personality Inventory's M-F (masculinity and femininity) scale used to identify sexual and gender nonconformity.[31] *The Ladder*, the leading lesbian magazine of the period, reported in 1964 on a Coca-Cola bottling plant in Sacramento, California, that had required applicants to take a "Depth Interview and Polygraph Evaluation," including questions concerning sexuality, as a condition of employment.[32] As the web of public and private surveillance expanded, having one's homosexuality enter into circulation as data collected by any of these overlapping institutions could render an individual virtually unemployable.

The expansion of background and loyalty/security screenings by private employers, landlords, creditors, and insurers created a growing demand for surveillance and investigation services. Beginning in the 1950s, a number of FBI agents left the Bureau to launch careers in the private sector, forming investigation agencies that offered services to companies seeking background information about prospective employees. One such company was Fidelifacts, founded in New York in 1956 by a group of former agents "to bring FBI type background investigations to the corporate sector."[33] These agencies advertised to prospective clients their ability to dredge up information on types of behavior, including homosexuality, that would render individuals unfit for employment. As a writer in the homophile magazine *Mattachine Review* observed, "Not only has the Federal Government expressed its aim to refuse to employ homosexuals for the sake of 'tightening security measures' or 'improving moral standards,' but an increasing number of private businesses are following the Government's lead. . . . Investigative agencies purporting to be miniature FBIs have sprung up. They have acted to meet this demand for employee screening. Listed on the letterhead of one of these (Chicago) agencies are the 'undesirables' this agency specializes in ferreting out and 'Homosexuals' stands out in bold print."[34]

These private investigators played central roles in some of the most dramatic homosexual scandals of the period, as when the investigations by Howard Dice of Gem State Investigation Service into the sex lives of several men in Boise, Idaho, led to three arrests and a public outcry in 1955.[35] In the resulting uproar, the Boise city council hired William Fairchild, a private investigator who had previously worked to identify homosexuals in the State Department and the

US Air Force. Fairchild interviewed over a thousand people, developed a list of hundreds of suspected homosexuals, and helped police ultimately charge sixteen people with crimes against nature and other offenses.[36]

This cadre of professionals, moving fluidly between federal and local police agencies and the private sector, built careers as specialists in investigating homosexuals and promoted their expertise, alongside that of medical and psychological figures, as authoritative in the production of public knowledge about sexual deviance. Fred Otash, a former Venice Beach vice squad officer hired as an investigator for the tabloid *Confidential*, was invited to speak as an authority about homosexuality for a 1958 episode of the Los Angeles television program *Crime Story*, one of the first television programs on the subject.[37] The Florida Legislative Investigation Committee quoted a "veteran investigator of homosexuality" in its official 1964 report to explain how tolerance for same-sex sexuality invariably led to the exploitation of children.[38] As the *Camera Surveillance* film that circulated nationally through police departments declared, "Law enforcement officials agree that practices of sex perversion are acquired patterns of abnormal depravity, and that such practices are in violation of both natural and moral law. Society is bound to be seriously damaged if practices of this kind are condoned."[39] The understandings of homosexuality generated by the investigative gaze at the nexus of state and local governments, law enforcement, and private companies substantially influenced laws, policies, and social attitudes toward gay men and lesbians, while damaging countless individual lives through imprisonment, loss of employment, and social disgrace.

RESISTANCE TO SEXUAL SURVEILLANCE IN THE HOMOPHILE MOVEMENT

Despite the intensity and variability of the regimes of sexual surveillance they faced, gay men and lesbians demonstrated consistent, creative, and at times effective resistance to the institutions gathering data about them throughout the 1950s and 1960s. In addition to the tactics of everyday resistance woven into gay and lesbian culture—the concepts of the "mask" or the "double life," expressed in linguistic codes and social practices tailored to different spatial contexts—they spoke out actively in their publications and in the courts against the net of surveillance that increasingly closed around sexual nonconformists. The emerging homophile public sphere of magazines, novels, conferences, and activist groups provided a platform for gay men and lesbians to document and contest the surveillance they faced and to condemn the weaponization of sexual data against them.

Postwar gay and lesbian communities used literature as a means to circulate knowledge about sexual surveillance techniques. James Barr's *Quatrefoil* (1950), one of the most widely read postwar novels with a sympathetic rendering of homosexual characters, featured a US Navy officer who takes a battery of personality tests: "To his amusement two of the IQ tests had given him the rating of genius. However, there was one dark spot which had shown up in the personality series. On a masculinity-femininity scale he was barely across the border in the right direction. The questions, designed with a time limit, had to be answered reflectively. He supposed that in racing through them, one inadvertently gave a clear picture of his tastes."[40]

Such depictions flagged for homosexual readers a key register within the test battery that could cause them problems. They also normalized gender nonconforming test results (by portraying them as compatible with high intelligence) and provided clearly implied instructions on how to overcome the test's intentions and sidestep sexual suspicion.

Another instructive warning to queer readers appears in *The Price of Salt* (1952), one of the most popular postwar lesbian novels. Its two protagonists are followed by a private investigator, whose recordings of their romantic tryst are used to deny one of the women custody of her children. This story was based on the actual experience of Virginia Kent Catherwood, a former lover of the novel's author, Patricia Highsmith, and served as both a cautionary tale and a critique of the cruel consequences of sexual surveillance.[41] Other gay novels made their didactic countersurveillance intentions even more explicit. In 1961, *ONE Magazine* reviewed *The Case against Colonel Sutton*, by Bruce Cameron, which portrayed an army officer facing allegations of homosexuality. Colonel Sutton finds himself targeted by the army's top "queer chaser," a ruthless investigator named Larry Adams "who uses every dirty trick in the book to try to coerce a confession." Reviewer Hank Richardson urged readers to consult the novel, especially "those in governmental or military service who might just possibly someday find themselves across the table from a Larry Adams."[42] In response to the ongoing threat of sexual surveillance, gay and lesbian writers synthesized their experiences of repression, testing, and interrogation to construct a countersurveillance politics that enabled self-defense, while using literary formats to avoid direct contests with authority that could lead to censorship.

These efforts at community education and self-defense dovetailed with occasional direct challenges to sexual surveillance through community organizing or court cases, as exemplified in homophile responses to surveillance of public restrooms. The Los Angeles Mattachine Society's 1952 "Citizens Campaign to Outlaw Entrapment" challenged the arrest of activist Dale Jennings on charges of lewd vagrancy for being present in a popular gay cruising area, ultimately succeeding in obtaining a hung jury and a dismissed case.[43] Throughout the 1950s and 1960s, writers in homophile publications condemned sexual surveillance in public bathrooms and parks as "Orwellian" and "gestapo tactics," reported on police methods, distributed know-your-rights literature, and fought arrests in the courts. Attorney and homophile advocate Frank C. Wood argued the cases of two men arrested in 1962 in Long Beach on the evidence of vice squad officers who spied on men through the stalls of public restrooms. In a landmark decision, the California Supreme Court ruled unanimously in *Bielicki v. Superior Court* that the convictions were unconstitutional because the police surveillance procedures violated Fourth Amendment protections against unreasonable searches and seizures.[44] In a speech to a homophile meeting in 1963, Wood described the implications of the court's ruling and urged people arrested for lewdness, vagrancy, or other "morals" charges to plead not guilty and to file lawsuits against the city to defend their right to privacy.[45]

However, homophile conceptions of privacy took distinct gendered forms. As Shirley Willer, president of the lesbian organization Daughters of Bilitis (DOB), noted in a 1966 article, the issues that plagued gay men around police harassment and entrapment touched her sisters hardly at all: "the problems of importance to the Lesbian are job security, career advancement, and family relationships."[46] Lesbian women expressed frustration with male homophile activists for emphasizing exclusively male concerns and disregarding their own struggles; as Billye Talmadge, an early member of the DOB, recalled, "There was a lot of animosity and resentment over the fact that it was the gay guys who were creating such havoc with the police—the raids, the indiscriminate sex, their bathroom habits, and everything else."[47] For lesbian women, finding paid work sufficient to sustain an independent life without a husband constituted a substantial struggle. The Student Homophile League at Columbia University noted that for lesbians, since they cannot rely on a husband's income, "employment and salary discrimination hit them harder than any other class of women."[48] Thus, the stakes of maintaining privacy remained especially high, since their frequently already precarious economic independence—as well as, for mothers, custody of their children—depended on preventing disclosure of their sexuality to employers as well as former spouses and courts. While differently positioned within a matrix of gendered power and less concerned over law enforcement and sexual surveillance in public space, lesbians joined gay men in identifying privacy as a critical priority for their shared movement, specifically as it impacted employment and child custody.

Homophile advocates during the period consistently spoke out on issues of surveillance in magazines, novels, public meetings, and the courts, and they drew on civil libertarian, constitutionalist, and antifascist discourses to condemn what they saw as violations of privacy by invasive data collection efforts. According to Robert Self, the homophile movement's dominant ideology before the late 1960s emphasized "sexual privacy as an inviolable component of equal citizenship" and focused on demanding "the right not to be policed, the right to be left alone"—a conception centrally shaped by the centrality of surveillance to gay and lesbian oppression.[49] This set the stage for the significance of resistance to data collection within the gay liberation movement that would soon emerge, even as that movement's new emphasis on visibility would reconfigure concepts of privacy.

THE POLITICS OF DATA IN THE EARLY GAY LIBERATION MOVEMENT

As the homophile movement grew and took on increasingly militant overtones in the late 1960s, resistance to sexual surveillance held an important place on its political agenda. By the time of the Stonewall Rebellion and the emergence of the Gay Liberation Front in New York City in 1969, homophile writers and activists had been publicly critiquing and challenging government and corporate surveillance of their communities for nearly two decades. In the antiwar and countercultural movements with which gay liberation activism overlapped, government surveillance was a prominent concern frequently discussed in the radical press. When the Gay Activists Alliance (GAA) formed in New York City in December 1969 to focus the movement's explosive energy on specific demands and policy objectives, one of the first areas of focus they undertook related to sexual surveillance and data.

The GAA adopted a confrontational, media-savvy style of public actions complemented by a sprawling structure of committees examining the issues impacting the lives of gay New Yorkers. In June 1970, it formed the Fair Employment Committee, focused on documenting employment discrimination against homosexuals and preparing a report for the New York City Commission on Human Rights. Committee member and GAA president Jim Owles wrote to gay and lesbian groups in Washington DC, Philadelphia, Columbus, Los Angeles, San Francisco, and Chicago to solicit information on antigay discrimination in employment. Owles also sent letters to various agencies seeking information about the types of data used to screen employees. He directed letters to Fidelifacts and Pinkerton, Inc., demanding to know how these companies justified their practice of investigating the private sexual behavior of individuals. The feisty missives concluded with a promise "to fight for an end to intrusions into the sex lives of Americans either by private investigatory agencies such as yours, by private industry, or by government."[50]

In July 1970, the Fair Employment Committee consolidated its research and presented its preliminary report, "Employment Discrimination against Homosexuals," to the city's Commission on Human Rights. The report laid out what it considered to be the central issue and the stakes for the new gay liberation movement: "The conspiracy of private industry and government against homosexuals in the area of employment is at the heart of the problem we face today. There are millions upon millions of gay people in America living in daily fear of losing their jobs (or losing their chance to find decent employment) should their personal sex orientation or private love lives become a matter of record to be used against them, indiscriminately. We recognize this type of harassment to be one of the major obstacles to personal liberation and social equality."[51]

What was required, the GAA argued, was assertive government action to prohibit employers from firing or declining to hire employees due to their sexual orientation "and to ban the sale and/or dissemination in any way or form (by governmental agencies and private investigatory agencies) of information concerning the sexual orientation of, and private love lives of, any individual." The authors noted that pending federal legislation, proposed by Senator Sam Ervin and known as the "government employee's Bill of Rights," would prohibit both the questioning of prospective employees regarding their sexual attitudes or conduct and the use of psychological or lie-detector tests to elicit such information. The GAA considered this bill a step in the right direction but still insufficient, due to its focus only on federal employment. The organization proposed to focus on state-level agencies and the private sector, where much of the most egregious discrimination took place, and on the gathering and sale of sexual data by investigatory firms.[52]

The report concluded with recommendations for measures to fight employment discrimination against homosexuals to be enacted by the New York City Council as well as the state legislature. It urged passage of laws prohibiting "dissemination of information, by both city and state governmental agencies and by private investigatory agencies, relating to sexual orientation or private sexual activities of persons with the intent of influencing a decision by any prospective employer to employ or not employ said person."[53] To translate these recommendations into viable policy proposals, GAA's Ad Hoc 1970 Elections Committee set to work devising a questionnaire to send to candidates for public office gauging their stance on questions of gay rights. In September they mailed surveys to all standing candidates, with such questions as, "Would you work to oppose governmental collection of data on the sexual preference of individuals?" and "Would you work for an immediate investigation of the insurance and bonding companies which practice discrimination against homosexuals?" The responses the GAA received from a variety of candidates indicated their success at pushing questions of data collection and sexual surveillance onto the political agenda. Adam Walinsky, a Democratic candidate for New York state attorney general, specifically noted, "I am opposed to the collection of data on the sexual preference of individuals by government agencies." Senate incumbent Charles Goodell elaborated further: "People's private sexual conduct, like their private opinions, should not be the subject of governmental investigation. Information on an individual's private sexual activities should not be a subject on which files are kept or information is stored."[54]

By January 1971, the GAA had established itself as a force to be reckoned with in New York City politics and secured sponsors for what they called a "Fair Employment Bill for Homosexuals," or Intro 475. The bill would become a political lightning rod for years to come, catalyzing many impassioned debates at city hall. It proposed to extend the city's existing human rights law to forbid discrimination against homosexuals in housing, employment, and public accommodations. The GAA reached out to dozens of unions and other labor organizations to canvass their perspectives and solicit support, while building relationships with local politicians in pursuit of the bill's passage.

As a publicity stunt to generate media attention for Intro 475, the GAA took on Fidelifacts, one of the nation's most notorious private investigation firms with a documented record of intrusive sexual surveillance. The company had become a particular target of GAA's ire when Richard Amato, a member of the GAA's Fair Employment Committee, encountered an article titled "The Career Killers" in the June 1970 issue of *Playboy* while conducting research on the role of private investigation agencies in facilitating employment discrimination.[55] The article reported that Fidelifacts president Vincent Gillen, addressing a meeting of the Association of Stock Exchange Brokers, had explained that "establishing that someone is a homosexual is often difficult, but I like to go on the rule of thumb that if one looks like a duck, walks like a duck, associates only with ducks, and quacks like a duck, he is probably a duck."[56]

To promote Intro 475 and raise public awareness of the role of private investigation firms in harmful sexual surveillance, dozens of activists from the GAA and the Daughters of Bilitis converged on Fidelifacts' Times Square headquarters in January 1971. Wielding rubber ducks and signs condemning the company's invasions of privacy and led by an activist dressed in a full-body white duck costume, the group led a campy picket and leafletted passersby.[57] News media followed a group of protesters into the office, where a Fidelifacts employee attacked one of the activists and GAA president Jim Owles explained the harmful consequences of the company's surveillance of private sex lives. Following up on the Times Square action, the Fair Employment Committee next targeted the Household Finance Corporation (HFC), which drew on information garnered from companies like Fidelifacts to deny loans to homosexuals. In March, activists leafletted at HFC offices and converged on the corporation's Park Avenue headquarters to emphasize the need for legislation preventing sexual orientation data collection and protecting gays and lesbians against discrimination.[58] They pushed to keep the issue in the public eye by reaching out to local media. As Richard Amato declared in an April 1971 letter to the *New York Post*, the government was promoting discrimination by "increasing its surveillance of the population and digging up and spreading 'derogatory' data" in collaboration with "private investigatory agencies which are making a financial profit out of digging this information up and selling it to employers!"[59]

THE NATIONAL CONFERENCE OF GAY
ORGANIZATIONS AND THE MCGOVERN CAMPAIGN

After the New York City Council narrowly voted to reject Intro 475 in December 1971, the GAA turned its sights toward a national mobilization. Having corresponded with other gay liberation groups across the country during its research on employment discrimination, the organization felt well positioned to use the coming election year to catalyze broader gay political coordination. Bruce Voeller, the chair of the GAA's State and Federal Committee, worked with activists from the Chicago Gay Alliance to plan a nationwide strategy session for the rapidly growing movement, inviting hundreds of organizations to come together to discuss goals and prepare "a gay stance for the 1972 elections."[60] Around two hundred delegates representing over eighty organizations converged in Chicago on a chilly February weekend, dubbed themselves the National Coalition of Gay Organizations, and set to work crafting the country's first comprehensive national gay rights platform.

The meeting opened with discussion of the current political situation, debates over the relative merits of different candidates, and an appearance by Dr. Benjamin Spock from the radical antiwar People's Party. The delegates agreed not to endorse specific candidates but designated a committee to propose guidelines for candidate endorsement and to draft a gay rights platform with federal- and state-level demands. By the following morning, the platform was prepared, and much of the second day was spent refining it and debating its merits. Drawing on the GAA's campaign against the collection of data on sexual orientation, the first draft included "appropriate executive orders, regulations, and legislation banning the compiling, maintenance and dissemination of information on an individual's sexual preference and behavior for dossiers and data banks" as the platform's seventh demand for federal action and reprised it in the state-level demands. This plank was unanimously adopted, though a proposal from the floor to strengthen it added the phrase "and ordering the immediate destruction of all such existing data." At the urging of the radical caucus, the phrase "social and political activities" was added to the list of information the group wanted expunged from dossiers and data banks. The platform received the assent of the majority of the delegates, and it quickly became the template for gay rights demands across the country.[61]

These demands would soon cross the desk of George McGovern, the aspiring Democratic presidential front-runner. The South Dakota senator had courted gay votes as early as late 1971, when he had sent an assistant to New York's city hall to read a statement of support during deliberations on Intro 475.[62] The GAA had forged ties with the New Democratic Coalition and other Democratic Party organizations since 1970 in an effort to establish themselves as a viable constituency whose demands had to be taken seriously. Thus, when the GAA attended the NCGO, the McGovern campaign took note, sending a box of campaign literature and a telegram to the assembled delegates.[63]

In the aftermath of the Chicago conference, returning activists quickly mobilized to share the platform among supporters and worked to make inroads into Democratic Party organizations through which it might make an impact on national politics. The following week, New York gay activists distributed copies of the newly minted platform to delegates of the state's Democratic Party. Shortly thereafter, the northeastern section of the New Democratic Coalition—described by the *New York Times* as the party's liberal/reform wing, boasting eighteen thousand members in the state of New York—discussed the platform and agreed to endorse most of it, including the data collection provisions.[64] The approval of the influential New York state NDC branch, whose endorsement had helped George McGovern secure his position as the "liberal candidate" in the upcoming primary elections, lent legitimacy to the gay rights platform. Meanwhile, the northern California chapter of Americans for Democratic Action, a leading progressive organization with strong ties to the Democratic Party, adopted a gay rights resolution based on the platform and forwarded it to that group's national convention. Together, these initiatives inserted the NCGO platform into some of the most dynamic and progressive segments of Democratic Party—precisely the constituencies the South Dakota senator hoped to mobilize in his race to win the primary elections.

McGovern took notice—and took action. Within weeks, his campaign had devised a series of positions on gay rights that reflected the NCGO platform nearly verbatim. Phrased in the form of seven proposals, which he promised to back with "the full moral and legal authority of his presidency," the McGovern campaign made the first direct appeal to gay rights by a major party presidential candidate in US history. Third on the list was the proposal that "government and private investigatory agencies should cease to collect data on the sexual preferences of individuals." An April 1972 campaign letter declared "McGovern Supports Civil Rights and Civil Liberties for Homosexuals" and listed the candidate's proposals for gay rights.[65] McGovern's gay supporters quickly mobilized to spread the word, with a group of wealthy Democrats coming together to form the Gay Citizens for McGovern Committee. The new group sponsored a full-page ad in the Los Angeles magazine *Lesbian Tide* that reproduced the text of the mailer in full, introducing lesbian readers across the country to the candidate's platform and to the anti–data collection plank.[66] McGovern went on to win the nomination, in part due to assertive campaigning by the gay community during the primaries in California and other states.[67] Some activists who had attended the February NCGO conference made plans to go to the Democratic National Convention, where they would stage protests outside the venue in Miami Beach to support the work of delegates inside as they lobbied for adoption of the gay rights platform.

As gay activists prepared to travel down to Florida to advocate for an agenda that included an end to sexual surveillance by government agencies and private companies, those same forces were conducting extensive surveillance operations on the activists themselves. A declassified memo from the FBI's Chicago field office dated 5 July 1972 reported on information sharing between the bureau, local police departments, and "a representative of a local agency that conducts security type investigations in the Miami, Florida area." This private investigator had provided the FBI with a list of gay delegates planning to attend the convention, including four activists from Chicago, whose names and addresses were listed in the memo. Another security investigator based in Chicago affirmed that they had no information on file about the activists in question, apart from a record of a letter sent by one of them to the Chicago superintendent of police protesting harassment of homosexuals—indicating intimate linkages and flows of data between law enforcement and private agencies. The memo documents the existence of an extensive network of information gathering and sharing linking the FBI, Chicago and Miami police, confidential informants close to gay and radical movements, credit agencies, and private investigation firms.[68] It was precisely this nexus of hostile surveillance by an opaque, interlinked network of public and private agencies that the GAA and the NCGO hoped to rein in and disarm through legislation prohibiting collection of sexual orientation data.

Despite lobbying inside and protests outside, the Democratic National Convention declined to adopt the gay rights platform. However, after continued pressure from the GAA, McGovern's campaign drafted a white paper on civil liberties emphasizing his commitment to gay rights alongside the rights of other marginalized groups and sent copies to major media outlets.[69] The white paper accused President Nixon of complicity with discrimination, specifically criticizing how "data on sexual orientation of individuals has been collected by government and private investigator agencies."[70] Beyond its significance as the first statement of support for gay rights by a major presidential candidate in US history, this statement and McGovern's proposals are remarkable for their trenchant antisurveillance politics. Given the salience of data and information gathering to contemporary relations of power—indeed, McGovern's campaign itself drew on data banks of gay voters and consumers for its targeted mailings—as well as the formidable power of the law enforcement establishment and the overlapping private investigation sector, the candidate's willingness to call for a ban on amassing sexual data demonstrated the effectiveness of gay political advocacy. By conducting research, soliciting experiences from within their communities, and developing discourses that resonated with concerns over privacy, labor rights, and civil liberties, the GAA drew on a long legacy of queer resistance to data collection stretching back two decades to forge a powerful critique of sexual surveillance that gained considerable political traction on local and national levels.

THE CHANGING MEANINGS OF SEXUAL PRIVACY

Ironically, just as national scrutiny over data and privacy peaked in the mid-1970s, the expanding mainstream gay political movement began to shift its focus away from issues of data collection and surveillance. Richard Nixon won a landslide victory in the 1972 election, and some Democratic critics cited Mc-Govern's flirtation with the politics of homosexuality as a factor in his defeat; the NCGO demands would not be featured in Democratic platforms in the coming years. Although Nixon emerged from the election triumphant, his subsequent impeachment, combined with revelations of the extent of the FBI's domestic surveillance of social movements and marginalized communities, accentuated widespread anxiety about surveillance. The Watergate scandal, Senator Frank Church's committee investigating allegations of government spying, and the passage of new federal privacy legislation shifted the conversation among activists and within American culture at large around data and surveillance.

Within this broader social debate, anxieties about sexual privacy, as well as the concerns of homosexuals specifically, had become more visible. As a 1972 report from the National Academy of Sciences Project on Computer Databanks indicated, the American public was increasingly insisting that "information about the exercise of lawful political dissent, cultural nonconformity, and homosexual preferences should no longer be used to bar otherwise qualified individuals from basic opportunities and rights."[71] A Roper Organization survey in 1974 had found that most Americans opposed the collection of data on sexuality: only 24 percent approved of the FBI collecting sexual histories, and just 5 percent approved of private credit agencies doing so.[72] That same year, Aryeh Neier, executive director of the American Civil Liberties Union, authored *Dossier: The Files They Keep on You*, documenting the devastating consequences for marginalized groups of government and private information banks that collected data on all aspects of citizens' lives. The book praised the efforts of homosexuals and other stigmatized populations to organize against their imprisonment within the "paper cage" of data.[73] Such examples reflected how a mainstream heterosexual public concerned with privacy, regardless of their opinions on homosexuality more generally, viewed the particular data-driven vulnerabilities of gay men and lesbians with sympathy. The legislative successes of a broader movement for privacy protections addressed some of the data collection concerns gay activists had previously raised, freeing their energies to focus on specific antidiscrimination efforts. The NCGO platform's demand for a ban on sexual data collection last appeared in 1976, on the agenda of a small New York–based organization called the National Coalition of Gay Activists. Thereafter, it disappears from the archives of the movement.[74]

Meanwhile, the emergence of professionalized, mainstream political advocacy through the National Gay Task Force (NGTF) and the Gay Rights National Lobby mirrored an overall shift in the character of the movement toward accommodation with and integration into structures of government, professional, and corporate authority. As "queer clout" in some cities increased, local antidiscrimination ordinances began to appear and overt police harassment directed toward (at least certain more privileged segments of) the LGBTQ community attenuated, the relationship between gay men, lesbians, and the state slowly began to shift. While Bruce Voeller, co-founder of NGTF, had taken part in crafting the NCGO platform in 1972, his turn away from street activism toward the political mainstream was reflected in the demands the new organization adopted and those—such as the call to end sexual data collection—it dropped. Activists of the mid- to late 1970s, eschewing antagonism with the state and business in favor of inclusion and insider politics, were revising their conceptions of privacy in anticipation of broader inclusion in the institutions of American life. They faced the dilemma of how, in a decreasingly private society that demanded considerable transparency as a condition for full participation in social, political, and economic life, the traditional concern of gays and lesbians with sexual privacy could be reconciled with the movement's widening aspirations for inclusion in the state.

As with the earlier homophile movement, this dilemma continued to unfold differently along gendered lines. For many lesbian women, the burgeoning feminist movement provided language for their frustrations with gay men's sexism and disregard for women's issues, leading them to refocus on women's organizing. Del Martin, co-founder of the Daughters of Bilitis, famously bid good-bye to the male-dominated gay movement in a searing 1970 essay in *The Ladder*, declaring, "I have been forced to the realization that I have no brothers in the homophile movement. . . . They neither speak for us nor to us."[75] Feminist activists in the early 1970s working to secure reproductive freedom found that the legal concept of sexual privacy, a "penumbral" right affirmed by the Supreme Court in *Griswold v. Connecticut* (1965), provided a successful constitutional rationale for the legalization of abortion in *Roe v. Wade* (1973).[76] Thus, as the male-dominated gay movement began to recalculate the balance between privacy and visibility within its advocacy, the women's movement, and its many lesbian adherents, found renewed importance in privacy—not so much in terms of preventing surveillance or data collection but as a framework for defending control over one's own body and reproductive capacity. This constitutional right to privacy became increasingly important as a rationale in custody cases for lesbian parents, a key focus of legal activism from the 1970s forward.[77] The Supreme Court's decision in *Bowers v. Hardwick* (1986), however, upheld the constitutionality of state sodomy laws by rejecting the argument that prior rulings upholding domestic or sexual privacy should apply to homosexuals, renewing the threat posed to lesbians and gay men alike by exposure of information on their sexuality.[78]

The emergence of the AIDS epidemic in the 1980s further raised the stakes around the politics of data, as sexual stigma intersected with fear of contagious disease, resulting in devastating impacts on gay communities. The vulnerabilities facing people with HIV/AIDS in a climate of homophobic hostility led activists to intervene forcefully in debates over health data collection. A sign held by a protestor at a 1989 ACT UP demonstration encapsulated the contradictions and the stakes of data and privacy for the gay community during this era. When New York City commissioner of health Steven Joseph proposed to institute name-based reporting of AIDS cases over community objections, outraged activists warned, "First You Don't Exist, Now You're on Joseph's List."[79] The protest sign highlighted the double bind of the gay and lesbian relationship to data collection: while *not* being counted meant invisibility and denial of social recognition and urgently needed services, *being* counted without protections against discrimination could be life-threatening. In the 1980s, with the specters of backlash, quarantine, loss of child custody, and criminalization striking terror into gay and lesbian communities, activists reflected ruefully on the double-edged sword of sexual visibility in relation to the state.

Yet the type of privacy demanded by AIDS activists was not the same as the ban on sexual data collection sought by a previous generation of gay liberationists. Rather than preventing data from being gathered—indeed, central to ACT UP's demands were more research and studies on sexuality and disease transmission designed to devise urgently needed sexual health protocols and treatment options—these activists demanded control over how such data was tabulated, stored, and shared. While historians of disease surveillance have noted that activist responses to AIDS "revealed the profound anxiety of gay men over government surveillance activities," LGBTQ engagements with public health and government officials across the 1980s and 1990s led to an unprecedented democratization of the concept of medical privacy.[80] Whereas the gay radicals of the early 1970s aimed to keep the state and private companies from collecting data on sexuality altogether, the activist generation forged in the crucible of the AIDS epidemic sought to renegotiate the terms by which these institutions engaged with sexual information and LGBTQ lives. Privacy persisted as a goal and a discourse; for instance, the rechristened National Gay and Lesbian Task Force launched its Privacy Project after *Bowers* to fight against sodomy laws state by state. But in the aftermath of AIDS, the movement increasingly aimed to manage, not abolish, data and to redirect government and corporate power, not contest it.

This renegotiated relationship between privacy, data, sexuality, business, and the state shaped the contours of LGBTQ politics into the twenty-first century. While the widely condemned "Don't Ask, Don't Tell" military policy exposed the contradictions between privacy and inclusion, the Supreme Court's *Lawrence v. Texas* (2003) decision overturned state sodomy laws, simultaneously affirming the legal principle of sexual privacy while obviating a major reason for LGBTQ communities to rely on it out of fear of criminalization. The increasing visibility of upwardly mobile gays and lesbians as distinct markets incentivized the gathering of data on sexual orientation by businesses—not to exclude but to target LGBTQ consumers.[81] Yet the data-driven reimagining of community in consumer terms—focusing on affluent white gay men and to a lesser extent lesbians—has had consequences ranging from depoliticizing Pride to shifting the priorities of LGBTQ activism to marginalizing queer and trans youth of color through gentrification and criminalization.[82]

The emergence of a central focus on legal recognition for same-sex couples within LGBTQ movements in the early twenty-first century epitomized these shifts, particularly around the politics of privacy. Whereas most activists of the early gay liberation era sought to prevent government agencies from gathering data that could identify individuals as homosexual, campaigns to win the right to marry reflected the assumption that most gays and lesbians had more to gain than to lose by being listed in government records as a member of a same-sex partnership. For many partnered LGBTQ people, the prospect of accessing hundreds of state and federal benefits outweighed the risks entailed by making their sexual/gender identities visible, thus rendering them vulnerable to hostility or discrimination. But the political focus on marriage rights, imagined within a domestic sphere of sexual privacy now protected by the courts, came at the expense of a more racially and economically inclusive agenda; assaults on the privacy of LGBTQ welfare recipients, sex workers, prisoners, homeless youth, and other marginalized groups attracted less attention.

Thus, by the twenty-first century, mainstream LGBTQ movements no longer assumed that collecting data on sexual orientation constituted a threat to the livelihoods of the communities they claimed to represent. On the contrary, as an interest group competing for patronage, statistical tabulation presented an opportunity for economic enrichment and political access—as epitomized by the campaign to "Queer the Census." The success of these movements in positioning themselves as brokers between mobilized constituencies of voters and shoppers and the resources commanded by various public and private agencies reconfigured the importance of visibility. While concerns over sexual privacy continue to surface, the days when the prevention of sexual data collection seemed like a critical objective for the gay and lesbian movement appear to have permanently passed.

CONCLUSION: THE HISTORY AND FUTURE OF QUEER DATA POLITICS

But might the brief window of mobilization and coalition organizing to halt sexual data collection offer any lessons for the data-driven political and economic moment in which we now live? As Kathryn Conrad notes, although "gender and sexuality have largely been invisible in surveillance studies, women and queers—that is, those whose bodies, sexual desires, practices and/or identities fall outside of the perceived heterosexual and gender-normative mainstream— have not been invisible to contemporary surveillance technologies."[83] Activists today are grappling with the accelerating impacts of digital platforms, social media, big data, and automated decision-making systems on all aspects of our lives. Debates have erupted over data and surveillance-related issues such as the use of smartphone apps by police to track and repress sexual minorities, claims by a controversial 2017 study that facial recognition software could accurately predict sexual orientation, and social media platforms' use of online behavior data to categorize sexuality-based advertising markets.[84] As LGBTQ communities reflect on how these emerging systems are impacting sexual and political cultures, this history may offer a cautionary tale about the frighteningly repressive and unexpectedly productive effects of sexual surveillance and data gathering.

Attending to this forgotten legacy of queer critiques of data collection may also offer ways to reconceptualize the subjects of pre-Stonewall queer history. Reconceived through the lens of surveillance and countersurveillance, homosexual practices such as anonymous sex and public cruising during the 1950s and 1960s (and beyond) may be interpreted not as expressions of fear and self-hatred but as strategies designed to maximize pleasure and minimize risk through opacity to state and private institutions. The paradigm of the closet offers one template for interpreting queer practices of challenging the visibility of same-sex sexual behavior, one that has proved politically useful in the years since Stonewall. However, as Martin Meeker's discussion of "the mask" as an alternative to the metanarrative of the closet indicates, there are other ways we might make sense of identity and sexuality during the homophile era, especially when paying closer attention to dynamics of surveillance and strategic (in)visibility.[85]

The radicalism of the liberationists of the late 1960s and early 1970s in contrast to that of their homophile predecessors has been framed by historians as a shift in emphasis from insisting on the right to keep one's intimate life *out of* the public sphere toward bringing gay sexuality and identity *into* the public sphere. Against the liberal lens through which sexuality has traditionally been conceived as "beyond the purview of state action in a domain of 'privacy,'" gay and lesbian activists of the 1970s challenged not only specific government policies and practices but the very notion of what constituted politics and the types of power relations appropriate to the public sphere.[86] As Robert Self concludes, "The sexual privacy demands, which had dominated homophile politics, remained, but there was no question that even those demands more than ever required a public gay presence."[87] Similarly, Sarah Igo notes that for this new generation of gay and lesbian activists, "privacy and liberation seemed to be at loggerheads"; the political imperative to come out served not only as "a disavowal of stigma" but equally as "a repudiation of a particular kind of privacy."[88]

Yet the central presence of a demand to end collection of data on sexual preference at the height of the gay liberation movement in 1972 complicates this narrative about the tension between privacy and visibility. Contesting sexual surveillance and data collection did not index merely a residual desire to preserve privacy against an intrusive public sphere but a demand for the autonomy to explore sexual identities and meanings outside of the discursive power of institutions that claimed the authority to determine the boundaries and meaning of homosexuality. Here, for a brief moment, the strategic opacity of the homophiles intersected with the defiant visibility of the gay and lesbian militants: while insisting on making non-normative sexuality visible in the fields of social life defined by the state as public, these activists also defied the state's imperative to govern through the imposition and administration of sexual categories, which they believed only constrained the possibilities for liberation.

In the heady atmosphere of early gay liberation, conventional framings of homosexuals as a minority group seeking civil rights coexisted with nonidentitarian conceptions of queer being and becoming. Some framed the lesbian as "the rage of all women condensed to the point of explosion," while another activist defined gay liberation not "as an oppressed minority fighting for rights but more the process of [creating] a society in which people can come out and be all that it's possible to be" while rejecting "the false categories of homosexuality and heterosexuality."[89] The gay liberationist call to resist being captured in matrices of data, then, was not merely an aspiration to privacy but a refusal of the power of police, bureaucrats, psychologists, and corporations to define the terms of sexual identity. By subverting the investigative gaze of government and corporate data collection, these activists sought to prevent authorities from enclosing the commons of erotic power/knowledge that the new feminist, gay, and sexual liberation movements were exploring as they struggled to transcend the constraints of "Straight Amerika."[90]

This vision surfaced at the 1972 NCGO conference in Chicago, where the demand for a ban on sexual data collection would crystallize and surge to national prominence. A young activist named Morty Manford distributed a statement on behalf of his student organization, Gay People at Columbia, which declared that "implicit in our presence at this conference" was "the recognition that our future must be determined by ourselves: 'Gay is what we make it.'"[91] This radically indeterminate and self-determined sense of sexual identity emerged from an environment in which gay activists were insisting on the right for people to live their sexual lives without surveillance, without their desires and practices being made into data.

As activists reformat queer politics for the digital age, we might pause to consider alternatives that appeared in past iterations of liberation movements. The articulation, however brief and abortive, of a sexual politics *against data* could gesture toward alternative visions of liberation that stand in critical opposition to many contemporary formulations. These resonate with Gary Kafer's contemporary reflections on opacity as a "queer technics" that can contain "alternative modes of embodiment and visions of the future that are otherwise expelled from capitalist, colonial, and imperial structures."[92] Engaging with this history of the politics of queer opacity may illuminate some of the limitations of notions of liberation designed around the paradigm of the closet and "coming out." It urges a rethinking of LGBTQ integration into notions of citizenship increasingly anchored in a biopolitics of administrative categories, in which institutional power is exerted through the compilation of statistics and the selective extension of life, within a regime of compulsory panoptic transparency. In an era when our very constitution as social, political, economic, legal, and indeed sexual subjects is saturated with processes of datafication, the 1972 platform demanding an end to sexual data collection may prove not just a curious anachronism but a strikingly visionary path not taken.

NOTES

ACKNOWLEDGMENTS: I am grateful to Elspeth Brown, George Chauncey, Dan Ewert, Sarah Igo, Camille Robcis, and other friends and colleagues for improving this chapter with their thoughtful feedback.

1. Hansi Lo Wang, "Collecting LGBT Census Data Is 'Essential' to Federal Agency, Document Shows," NPR, 20 June 2017, https://www.npr.org/2017/06/20/533542014/collecting-lgbt-census-data-is-essential-to-federal-agency-document-shows.

2. "BREAKING: Trump Administration Omits LGBTQ People from 2020 Census and American Community Survey," National LGBTQ Task Force, 28 March 2017, http://www.thetaskforce.org/breaking-trump-administration-omits-lgbtq-people-from-2020-census-and-american-community-survey/.

3. Maddow quoted in John Nichols, "Queer the Census," *The Nation*, 1 April 2010, https://www.thenation.com/article/archive/queer-census/.

4. Nick Visser, "The U.S. Won't Tally LGBT People in 2020 Census," *Huffington*

Post, 29 March 2017, https://www.huffingtonpost.com/entry/us-census-lgbt-americans _us_58db3894e4b0cb23e65c6cd9.

5. "1972 Gay Rights Platform," February 1972, Box 29, Subject Files: National Coalition of Gay Activists, National Conference, 1972, MS Morty Manford Papers, Manuscripts and Archives Division, New York Public Library.

6. "McGovern Supports Civil Rights and Civil Liberties for Homosexuals," undated letter, postmarked 20 April 1972, Folder 1, Subject Vertical Files: Sexual Freedom—Political Activities, Joseph A. Labadie Collection, University of Michigan Library, Ann Arbor.

7. Henry Minton, *Departing from Deviance: A History of Homosexual Rights and Emancipatory Science in America* (Chicago: University of Chicago Press, 2001); Randall Sell, "Defining and Measuring Sexual Orientation: A Review," *Archives of Sexual Behavior* 26, no. 6 (1997): 643–57.

8. Jack Halberstam, *The Queer Art of Failure* (Durham, NC: Duke University Press, 2011); Nicholas de Villiers, *Opacity and the Closet: Queer Tactics in Foucault, Barthes, and Warhol* (Minneapolis: University of Minnesota Press, 2012).

9. Toby Beauchamp, *Going Stealth: Transgender Politics and U.S. Surveillance Practices* (Durham, NC: Duke University Press, 2019), 2.

10. Zach Blas, "Informatic Opacity," *Journal of Aesthetics and Protest*, no. 9 (2014), https://www.joaap.org/issue9/zachblas.htm.

11. This chapter focuses on sexual surveillance targeting individuals and communities that most commonly identified themselves as homophiles, gay men, and lesbians during this period. While individuals who sexually desired both men and women formed part of these communities, the term "bisexual" was infrequently used and did not form a locus of extensive political mobilization until the 1980s, and thus I do not include it except when describing later periods. I briefly address trans experiences in the 1960s, using the term "transvestite" as it was used by the community in question, but my research did not identify surveillance and data collection as significant priorities among the early trans organizations that emerged in the 1960s and 1970s. I use the contemporary acronym LGBTQ (lesbian, gay, bisexual, trans, and queer) to describe a political coalition of non-normative sexual and gender identities in the twenty-first century and the term "queer" more loosely, both as a general term for diverse sexual and gender dissidents across time and as a political and theoretical term for challenges to fixed gender/sexual norms.

12. Allan Bérubé, *Coming Out under Fire: The History of Gay Men and Women in World War II* (New York: Free Press, 1990), 2.

13. David Johnson, *The Lavender Scare: The Cold War Persecution of Gays and Lesbians in the Federal Government* (Chicago: University of Chicago Press, 2004).

14. On Mountain Home, see John Gerassi, *The Boys of Boise: Furor, Vice, and Folly*

in an American City (New York: Macmillan, 1966): 22–23; on Huntsville, "On Security Firings, the FBI, etc.," *ONE* 9, no. 12 (December 1961), 11–12; and on Fort McPherson, Margot Canaday, *The Straight State: Sexuality and Citizenship in Twentieth-Century America* (Princeton: Princeton University Press, 2009), 174–213.

15. On the Mississippi Sovereignty Commission, see John Howard, *Men Like That: A Southern Queer History* (Chicago: University of Chicago Press, 1999). On the Florida Legislative Investigation Committee, see James A. Schnur, "Closet Crusaders: The Johns Committee and Homophobia, 1956–1965," in *Carryin' On in the Lesbian and Gay South*, ed. John Howard (New York: New York University Press, 1997), 132–63; and Stacey Braukman, *Communists and Perverts under the Palms: The Johns Committee in Florida* (Gainesville: University Press of Florida, 2013).

16. George Chauncey, "The Post-War Sex Crime Panic," in *True Stories from the American Past*, ed. William Graebner (New York: McGraw-Hill, 1993), 160–78. On Iowa, see Neil Miller, *Sex-Crime Panic: A Journey to the Paranoid Heart of the 1950s* (Los Angeles: Alyson Books, 2002); on Boise, see Gerassi, *Boys of Boise*; on Ohio, see William E. Jones, *Tearoom* (Los Angeles: 2nd Cannons, 2008).

17. Margaret A. Nash and Jennifer A. R. Silverman, "'An Indelible Mark': Gay Purges in Higher Education in the 1940s," *History of Education Quarterly* 55, no. 4 (November 2015): 441–59.

18. Timothy Stewart-Winter, *Queer Clout: Chicago and the Rise of Gay Politics* (Philadelphia: University of Pennsylvania Press, 2016), 16.

19. Douglas M. Charles, *Hoover's War on Gays: Exposing the FBI's "Sex Deviates" Program* (Lawrence: University Press of Kansas, 2015), 72.

20. Lynn Pedersen, "Miami Hurricane," *ONE* 2, no. 9 (November 1954): 8.

21. Jones, *Tearoom*.

22. *Law and Order* 11, no. 11 (November 1963), cited in Jones, *Tearoom*, 11.

23. Charles [Virginia] Prince, "The Question," *Transvestia* 2, no. 8 (March 1961).

24. Susan Stryker, *Transgender History* (Berkeley, CA: Seal Press, 2008), 50–54.

25. Sten Russell, "Mattachine Society Convention," *ONE* 5, no. 8 (October–November 1957): 26.

26. Toby Marotta, *The Politics of Homosexuality* (Boston: Houghton Mifflin, 1981), 204–5.

27. Clayton Howard, "Building a 'Family-Friendly' Metropolis: Sexuality, the State, and Postwar Housing Policy," *Journal of Urban History* 39, no. 5 (September 2013): 933–55.

28. Aryeh Neier, *Dossier: The Secret Files They Keep on You* (New York: Stein and Day, 1974), 141–42.

29. Myron Brenton, *The Privacy Invaders* (New York: Coward-McCann, 1964), 65.

30. Neier, *Dossier*, 78.

31. The M-F scale originated in Lewis Terman and Catherine Cox Miles's 1936 "Attitude Interest Analysis Survey," developed through research on homosexual psychiatric patients and inmates. See Jennifer Terry, *An American Obsession: Science, Medicine, and Homosexuality in Modern Society* (Chicago: University of Chicago Press, 1999), 165–74.

32. *The Ladder* 8, no. 4 (January 1964): 8.

33. "About Us," Fidelifacts, 4 June 2020, https://fidelifacts.com/about-new-york -background-check/.

34. Robert Kirk, "Fair Employment Practices and the Homosexual," *Mattachine Review* 2, no. 2 (April 1956): 41–42.

35. *ONE* 4, no. 1 (January 1956): 12.

36. Gerassi, *Boys of Boise.*

37. Dal McIntyre, "News and Views," *ONE* 6, no. 8 (August 1958): 15; *ONE* 11, no. 6 (June 1963): 15; Sten Russell, "Crime Story," *ONE* 6, no. 9 (September 1958): 27–8.

38. *Homosexuality and Citizenship in Florida: A Report of the Florida Legislative Investigation Committee* (Tallahassee: Florida Legislative Investigation Committee, 1964).

39. "*Camera Surveillance*: A Transcript of the Film's Soundtrack," cited in Jones, *Tearoom,* 9.

40. James Barr, Quatrefoil (1950; Boston: Alyson, 1982), 130.

41. Claire Morgan [Patricia Highsmith], *The Price of Salt* (New York: Coward-Mc-Cann, 1952).

42. Hank Richardson, review of *The Case against Colonel Sutton*, by Bruce Cameron, *ONE* 9, no. 11 (November 1961): 17–18.

43. C. Todd White, *Pre-Gay L.A.: A Social History of the Movement for Homosexual Rights* (Chicago: University of Illinois Press, 2009).

44. Bielicki v. Superior Court, 371 P.2d 288, 292 (Cal. 1962).

45. Frank C. Wood, "The Right to Be Free from Unreasonable Search & Seizure," *ONE* 11, no 4 (April 1963): 21–24.

46. Shirley Willer, "What Concrete Steps Can Be Taken to Further the Homophile Movement?," *The Ladder* 11, no. 2 (November 1966): 17–18.

47. Quoted in Marcia Gallo, *Different Daughters: A History of the Daughters of Bilitis and the Rise of the Lesbian Rights Movement* (New York: Carroll and Graf, 2006), 16.

48. Student Homophile League, "Student Homophile League Statement on the Lesbian," reprinted in *The Ladder* 13, no. 9–10 (June–July 1969): 17.

49. Robert Self, *All in the Family: The Realignment of American Democracy since the 1960s* (New York: Hill and Wang, 2012), 78.

50. Jim Owles, letters to Vincent Gillen and to Pinkerton, Inc., 19 June 1970, Folder 2: Committee Files, Fair Employment, 16 June 1970–8 December 1983, Box 16, MS Gay Activists Alliance, New York Public Library.

51. Gay Activists Alliance, "Employment Discrimination against Homosexuals," report to New York City Human Rights Commission, 10 July 1970, 20, Folder 1, Box 16, MS Gay Activists Alliance.

52. Gay Activists Alliance, "Employment Discrimination against Homosexuals," 30.

53. Gay Activists Alliance, "Employment Discrimination against Homosexuals," 32.

54. All quotes from Donn Teal, *The Gay Militants* (New York: Stein and Day, 1971), 254–58.

55. Toby Marotta, *The Politics of Homosexuality* (Boston: Houghton Mifflin, 1981), 204.

56. Gillen was no stranger to controversy, or to sexual surveillance. His company had been in the news the previous year when General Motors paid out $425,000 to settle an invasion of privacy lawsuit brought by consumer activist Ralph Nader. According to the suit, Nader claimed that GM had hired Gillen and his firm to investigate him, by following him around, subjecting him to harassing phone calls, interrogating his associates, and hiring attractive women to attempt to seduce him into compromising situations. When this failed, they attempted to dig up information on possible homosexual tendencies; as Gillen stated to the *New York Times*, "Well, we have to inquire about these things. I've seen him on TV and he certainly doesn't look like . . . but we want to know about such matters." Alan Westin, "The Career Killers," *Playboy* 17 (June 1970): 233; Craig R. Whitney, "G.M. Settles Nader Suit on Privacy for $425,000," *New York Times*, 14 August 1970; Walter Rugaber, "Critic of Auto Industry's Safety Standards Says He Was Trailed and Harassed," *New York Times*, 6 March 1966.

57. Coincidentally, the production crew filming the opening credits sequence to the movie *Shaft* happened to be filming in Times Square on the same day as the GAA picket against Fidelifacts. Just over two minutes into the film, protagonist John Shaft (played by Richard Roundtree) can be seen walking through the picket, his normally unflappable persona dissolving into astonishment as he surveys the gay activist spectacle.

58. David Eisenbach, *Gay Power: An American Revolution* (New York: Carroll and Graf, 2006), 164–65; Marotta, *Politics of Homosexuality*, 204–5.

59. Richard Aunateau [Richard Amato], letter to the editor, *New York Post*, 30 April 1971, Folder 1: 154, Box 16, MS Gay Activists Alliance.

60. Laud Humphreys, *Out of the Closets: The Sociology of Homosexual Liberation* (Englewood Cliffs, NJ: Prentice-Hall, 1972), 162.

61. The account of the NCGO conference is drawn from meeting notes and other documents in Box 29, MS Morty Manford Papers.

62. Barbara Trecker, "McGovern Backs Gay Bill: Applause Halts Hall," *New York Post*, 17 December 1971.

63. "National Gay Conference, Chicago 1972," tape 7 of 7 (no. 02841), MS Morty Manford Papers.

64. Thomas P. Ronan, "M'Govern Gains Coalition's Vote," *New York Times*, 30 January 1972. The NDC insisted upon excising the original NCGO platform's controversial provisions advocating abolition of age of consent laws and legalization of same-sex and multiple-partner marriages, which, as a critic noted, "could not gain popular support even among liberal politicians." Humphreys, *Out of the Closets*, 168.

65. "McGovern Supports Civil Rights and Civil Liberties for Homosexuals," undated letter, postmarked 20 April 1972.

66. *Lesbian Tide* 1, no. 8 (March 1972): 15.

67. Linda Hirschman, *Victory: The Triumphant Gay Revolution* (New York: Harper, 2012), 198–99; Dudley Cleninden and Adam Nagourney, *Out for Good: The Struggle to Build a Gay Rights Movement in America* (New York: Simon and Schuster, 1999), 132–36.

68. "Gay Activists Alliance (GAA): Demonstrations at Democratic and Republican National Conventions, July and August 1972, Miami Beach, Florida," memo, 5 July 1972, File CG 100-49116, Gay Activist Alliance, part 1, 64–67, FBI Records: The Vault, https://vault.fbi.gov/gay-activist-alliance-part-01-of-02/gay-activist-alliance-part-01 -of-02/view.

69. Eisenbach, *Gay Power*, 175–79.

70. Ron Gold, "McGovern Backs Gay Rights," press release, 12 October 1972, Folder 9, Box 16, MS Gay Activist Alliance Papers.

71. Alan F. Westin and Michael A. Baker, *Databanks in a Free Society: Computers, Record-Keeping, and Privacy* (New York: Quadrangle Books, 1972), 343.

72. Neier, *Dossier*, 191.

73. Neier, *Dossier*, 169–70.

74. Former GAA president Morty Manford, who had attended the 1972 NCGO meeting in Chicago, resuscitated the group as the National Coalition of Gay Activists in 1975, revisited the 1972 platform in discussions with the new group's members, and promoted it as representing the movement's demands during the 1976 presidential race, circulating copies at a NCGA-organized protest outside the Democratic National Convention in New York City. The group appears to have been inactive from 1977 onward, and no evidence suggests that other groups engaged the 1972 NCGO platform or its data demand afterward. Folders 1–12, Box 29–30, Subject Files: National Coalition of Gay Activists, MS Morty Manford Papers.

75. Del Martin, "If That's All There Is," *The Ladder* 15, no. 3–4 (December–January 1970–71): 4.

76. David J. Garrow, *Liberty and Sexuality: The Right to Privacy and the Making of Roe v. Wade* (Berkeley: University of California Press, 1998). David Minto has provoca-

tively argued that the origin of the infamous "penumbra" in *Griswold* lies in the trans-atlantic context of the Wolfenden Report (1957) in Britain and the US Supreme Court's unspoken anxieties over the place of homosexuality within legal claims to privacy; in this light, "the protection of gay sex can indeed appear to be a precursor to, as well as a result of, other kinds of privacy claims." David Minto, "Perversion by Penumbras: Wolfenden, *Griswold*, and the Transatlantic Trajectory of Sexual Privacy," *American Historical Review* 123, no. 4 (October 2018): 1096.

77. Benna F. Armanno, "The Lesbian Mother: Her Right to Child Custody," *Golden Gate University Law Review* 4, no. 1 (Fall 1973): 15; Daniel Winunwe Rivers, *Radical Relations: Lesbian Mothers, Gay Fathers, and Their Children in the United States since World War II* (Chapel Hill: University of North Carolina Press, 2013).

78. Bowers v. Hardwick, 478 U.S. 186 (1986); Rivers, *Radical Relations*, 78. The high court's 5–4 majority was countered by Justice Harry Blackmun's dissent, which argued that the sodomy law in question "interferes with constitutionally protected interests in privacy and freedom of intimate association." The case, Blackmun maintained, "impli-cates both the decisional and the spatial aspects of the right to privacy"; in his view, the majority's ruling reflected the court's "overall refusal to consider the broad principles that have informed our treatment of privacy in specific cases." Thus, the ruling, while refuting lesbian and gay activist claims to a legal right to sexual privacy, simultaneously preserved hope that the discourse of privacy might still offer a basis for decriminal-izing same-sex sexual behavior in the future. Blackmun later acknowledged that his dissent was primarily authored by his openly lesbian clerk, Pamela Karlan.

79. *ACT UP Reports* 4 (June 1989): 1.

80. Amy Fairchild, Ronald Bayer, and James Colgrove, *Searching Eyes: Privacy, the State, and Disease Surveillance in America* (Berkeley: University of California Press, 2007), 176.

81. Kathleen Sender, *Business, Not Politics: The Making of the Gay Market* (New York: Columbia University Press, 2004).

82. Christina Hanhardt, *Safe Space: Gay Neighborhood History and the Politics of Violence* (Durham, NC: Duke University Press, 2013); *Gay, Inc.: The Nonprofitization of Queer Politics* (Minneapolis: University of Minnesota Press, 2018).

83. Kathryn Conrad, "Surveillance, Gender and the Virtual Body in the Information Age," *Surveillance and Society* 6, no. 4 (2009): 380.

84. Kara Gronborg, "Dating Apps Pose Security Threats to LGBTQ Users," World-Aware, 3 October 2019, https://www.worldaware.com/resources/blog/dating-apps-pose-security-threats-lgbtq-users; Yilun Wang and Michal Kosinski. "Deep Neural Net-works Are More Accurate than Humans at Detecting Sexual Orientation from Facial Images," *PsyArXiv*, 7 September 2017, https://psyarxiv.com/hv28a.

85. Martin Meeker, "Behind the Mask of Respectability: Reconsidering the Mat-tachine Society and the Male Homophile Practice, 1950s and 1960s," *Journal of the*

History of Sexuality 10, no. 1 (January 2011): 78–116.

86. Mark Blasius, *Sexual Identities: Queer Politics* (Princeton: Princeton University Press, 2001), 7.

87. Self, *All in the Family*, 225.

88. Sarah Igo, *The Known Citizen: A History of Privacy in Modern America* (Cambridge, MA: Harvard University Press, 2018), 295.

89. Radicalesbians, "The Woman-Identified Woman," in *The Second Wave: A Reader in Feminist Theory*, ed. Linda Nicholson (New York: Routledge, 1997), 153–57; Kiyoshi Kuromiya quoted in Marc Stein, *City of Brotherly and Sisterly Loves: Lesbian and Gay Philadelphia, 1945–72* (Chicago: University of Chicago Press, 2000), 334.

90. Fag Rag Collective, "About FAG RAG," *Fag Rag* 2 (Fall 1971): 2.

91. "Statement from Gay People at Columbia," Box 29, Subject Files: National Coalition of Gay Activists, National Conference, 1972, MS Morty Manford Papers.

92. Gary Kafer, "Machine Learning and the Queer Technics of Opacity" (chapter 3, this volume).

GARY KAFER

3 Machine Learning and the Queer Technics of Opacity

BIG DATA TRADES IN AN ECONOMY OF TRANSPARENCY: stock markets, climate modeling, border security, and predictive policing all profess to render the world visible within an ever-expanding array of modular digital networks. Indeed, given the unending expansion of data-driven technologies to illuminate all that remains unknown, transparency might in fact appear to be big data's modus operandi. And yet, just as modernity's panoptic architectures of "pure visibility . . . proved impossible to achieve either in theory or practice," more recent scholarship in digital media studies has demonstrated how computational systems in fact accommodate a certain degree of opacity even as they aim for total transparency.[1] This is exceedingly the case, for example, when algorithms yield predictions that assign identities based on likelihood scores produced from a set of indeterminate and shifting data relations.[2] Furthermore, what becomes visible or knowable is often contingent upon proxy correlations, not causative models. As Wendy Chun remarks, "The light of big data creates big shadows."[3]

In this chapter, I ask the following question: how might we articulate a politics of opacity in relation to big data's regime of transparency when the means through which things become perceptible as data is through the conditions of opacity itself? Part of the ambition behind this question is to bring into conversation two very different understandings of opacity within big data studies in order to think more critically about its political stakes in relation to contemporary sociopolitical and technological realities. On the one hand, some strands of big data studies have turned to Édouard Glissant's concept of the "right to opacity" to theorize forms of resistance against data-driven surveillance. On the other hand, other strands locate opacity as a key technical form through which machine learning systems construct predictive models. By assessing how opacity might traffic across disciplinary domains, I recognize the incongruities that emerge when attending to its specific contextual formulations. In the former, opacity is conceived as an ethico-poetic imperative for maneuvering an antiracist struggle within capitalist, colonial, and imperial power. In the latter, opacity describes how power is maintained through specific technological processes of computational abstraction. It seems, then, that the conceptual specificity of opacity repels any sort of universalizing project, perhaps itself a reflection of the occasionally uneasy relationship between cultural studies and media studies.[4] And yet, at a very base level, we might say that opacity emerges as a dynamically inconsistent heuristic that describes a range of contradictory political relations within and against normative frameworks of visibility in computational media. In this way, opacity dwells among a number of other concepts—like potentiality, speculation, imagination, fabulation, and futurity—that sit uncomfortably at the intersection of contemporary modes of techno-capitalist power and various Black, Indigenous, trans, queer, feminist, and decolonial liberation projects.

In what follows, I take this conceptual friction as a productive problem to consider how we might theorize opacity as a sociotechnical formation that animates both the operation of big data systems and the impacts of these systems on minoritarian life. To do so, I locate opacity as what Jacob Gaboury calls a "queer technics" that "looks to engage with the historical and technical specificity of these captive apparatuses in order to identify explicitly queer modes of being within computational systems."[5] Importantly, as Gaboury notes, a queer technics does not obviate the specificity of LGBTQIA2S+ experiences under big data's regime of transparency. Rather, it troubles the notion that queerness in the context of big data must always describe a stable identity that purportedly precedes algorithmic mediation and instead attends to the conditions of visibility through which the subject emerges within computational media. In line with Gaboury, I consider how opacity, as a queer technics, casts into relief how power-knowledge takes shape at the intersection between the social and the technological and, more specifically, how sociopolitical difference becomes consolidated within the formal materialism of machine learning.

This chapter begins with a review of the critical uptake of opacity as a resistive rejoinder to big data. Taking stock of the limitations posed by discourses of invisibility, I locate an alternative framework of opacity through a reading of Glissant via Black studies that centers on a relational dynamic that I call (*in*)*commensurability*. Here, opacity is not a simple negativity but instead is both generative of and in excess to transparency and its hegemonic schema of classification. Adopting this particular model, I next turn my attention to the technical operation of opacity in machine learning. I specifically examine the *k*-nearest neighbor (*k*-NN) algorithm to consider a machinic form of opacity that both conditions and exceeds the processes of commensuration that shape predictive analytics. Finally, I argue that what is queer about this machinic opacity is how it functions as an animating difference that adjudicates how the subject emerges within the processes of computational abstraction central to machine learning. As a queer technics, opacity contracts how minoritarian life is abstracted and reconstructed within algorithmic modes of governance at the same time that it reveals how forms of racialized, gendered, and sexualized exclusion exceed predictive logics. I conclude by returning to the spirit of resistance in Glissant's writing in order to speculate how a queer technics of opacity allows us to explore new orientations to the political that limn the idiosyncratic processes of commensuration in machine learning systems within capitalist, colonial, and imperial regimes of transparency.

AN OPAQUE POLITICS

More recently, scholars in big data studies have turned to the concept of opacity to theorize modes of resistance against data-driven surveillance.[6] In opposition to transparency, opacity appears as a technological and aesthetic tactic for interfering with the epistemological project of big data through forms of obfuscation, camouflage, and concealment. Across his scholarly and artistic work, Zach Blas, for example, proposes "informatic opacity" as a political tactic that refuses the total transparency demanded by global surveillance systems, like those disclosed in Edward Snowden's leak of national security intelligence in 2013. As Blas writes, informatic opacity aims "to maintain obscurity, to not impose rubrics of categorization and measurement, which always enact a politics of reduction and exclusion."[7] Based on "a practice of anti-standardization at the global, technical scale," informatic opacity attends to the unique ways that machines render the world visible through specific perceptual operations.[8] In this case, opacity might materialize through a range of performative practices (masks, code-switching, and camouflage) or technical exploits (cell signal jammers, online encryption, biometric-resistant clothing) that operate by, as Clare Birchall argues, "obscuring one's digital shadow" in order to dodge formations of state and corporate surveillance and their ideological trappings of visibility, rights, and citizenship.[9]

Key among such debates is the writing of Martinican poet and theorist Édouard Glissant, in particular his invocation of a "right to opacity." As he states in his oft-cited definition, opacity is the "right to remain illegible to other groups or otherwise imperceptible according to the dominant terms through which things become perceptible."[10] Writing in the wake of transnational settler-colonial circuits of chattel slavery, genocide, and resource extraction, especially as it took hold in the Caribbean, Glissant considers opacity as an anti-imperial and antiracist ethics that seeks a world beyond Western ideals of subjectivity and knowledge. In contrast to transparency's attempt to account for the subject within juridical technologies of measurement and perceptibility, opacity refutes the inexhaustible violences that accumulate under colonial and capitalist technics of calculation, or what Katherine McKittrick calls the "mathematics of the unliving" through which the Black subject is brought into existence.[11] Ultimately, as Glissant argues, by refusing the power differentials of the colonial encounter, we might work toward a "going-on-and-with" that imagines futures for collective solidarities beyond racializing systems of classification and legibility.[12]

In line with critiques in big data studies, I maintain that Glissant's theorization of opacity offers a fertile resource for conceptualizing antiracist and anti-imperial resistances to data-driven surveillance. This is especially the case, as Blas notes, for oppressed groups (such as trans people of color and undocumented persons) that are most often targeted by classification and identification systems.[13] However, in doing so, I argue that we must be careful not to overstate opacity as a form of invisibility, obscurity, or anonymity that exists in a negative opposition to transparency. To be sure, Glissant maintains that "the opaque is not the obscure, though it is possible for it to be so and be accepted as such." Rather, as a key dynamic within his broader ethico-poetic philosophy of Relation, opacity is "that which cannot be reduced, which is the most perennial guarantee of participation and confluence."[14] As that which cannot be reduced, opacity insists upon the illegibility or unrecognizability of a person or group of people within Western ideals of identity and difference. In this framework, opacity might be more precisely defined as a mode of incommensurability: not being proportionate to or aligning with dominant standards of classification. Stated differently, if transparency is the demand for commensuration (the reduction of difference within the racializing grammar of identity), then opacity is the recognition of the incommensurability of existence beyond the regimes of signification proper to the modern political category of Man. Opacity exists now, in this world, in the nontransferable elements of experience that have not yet been assigned and that always elude efforts that might fix them in place.

The distinction between invisibility and incommensurability is important for two reasons. First, even as an oppositional absence, invisibility often operates as a technology of transparency. As scholars in Black studies have repeatedly shown, within the Manichaean deadlock of colonial visuality, invisibility is marked as a racialized, fragmented entity that is incorporated as a hyper-visibility within dominant systems of representation affixed to a hegemonic whiteness. As Fred Moten argues, "To be invisible is to be seen, instantly and fascinatingly recognized as the unrecognizable, as the abject, as the absence of individual self-consciousness, as a transparent vessel of meanings wholly independent of any influence of the vessel itself."[15] Moreover, invisibility can also eclipse forms of strategic visibility that minoritarian subjects might require in specific contexts, such as trans and disabled persons who must continually make their experiences legible within certain diagnostic criteria to gain access to vital medical care. As such, while invisibility might function as a tactical form of resistance in some cases through practices of digital encryption or obfuscation, as a broader conceptual and discursive formation it falls short of acknowledging the racialized, gendered, and sexualized forms of exclusion that operationalize surveillance optics. It is perhaps more useful then to grasp invisibility as but one specific modulation of opacity that functions primarily upon incommensurability rather than absence.

Second, when understood as a mode of incommensurability rather than invisibility, opacity emerges less as immediately oppositional to transparency and instead evinces a more oblique relational dynamic that is simultaneously within and beyond dominant systems of commensuration. It is in this context that I use the term "(in)commensurable" to signal the way that opacity is figured as simultaneously generative of but nonetheless in excess of hegemonic regimes of classification. To be sure, Glissant signals this relational dynamic when he qualifies opacity as "penetrable," allowing for "subsistence within an irreducible singularity" rather than an "enclosure within an impenetrable autarchy."[16] To quote him at length from his critique of those who presume the universality of the French language, "An attentive observer will notice that such windbags are anxiously intent on confining themselves to the *false* transparency of a world they used to run; they do not want to enter into the *penetrable* opacity of a world in which one exists, or agrees to exist, within and among others. In the history of the language the claim that the conciseness of French is consecutive and noncontradictory is the veil obscuring and justifying this refusal."[17] On the one hand, penetrability indexes how some aspect of an oppressed person or population is always at risk of being made commensurate within hegemonic technologies of computation, thus threatening the singularity of one's existence. But as Glissant suggests, penetrability is not something to be feared but is instead an important element of Relation wherein one exists "within and among others" as a recognizable but irreducible entity. A penetrable opacity thus entails a kind of perception of the other without reduction, a joining rather than a merging. On the other hand, then, even as much as opacity is partially penetrable, there is always something that remains unaccounted, a "reflected density" that lies beyond dominant systems of classification.[18] Ultimately, this dual movement in opacity reveals transparency to be "false" insofar as falseness is not the failure to make things visible but is instead the "veil" of total commensurability in the face of a profound and proliferating excess.

To be clear, I don't intend to suggest through (in)commensurability that opacity is merely sublimated into transparency, defanged in its opposition to Western ideals of legibility and recognition. Rather, in tracking how opacity maneuvers a relational dynamic within and in excess of transparency, I aim to describe how a political project of refusal regarding big data might take other forms besides an outside opposition or a negative absence, perhaps one that instead dwells within the very architectures of transparency as a layered or indeterminate density. Indeed, such an understanding of opacity has long been advanced by Black feminist scholars who see opacity as a performative mode of insurgency and freedom by which racialized, gendered, and sexualized subjects negotiate a palimpsest of representations within dominant systems of commensuration.[19] In the context of predigital and digital systems of surveillance, concepts like "dark sousveillance" from Simone Browne and "black data" from Shaka McGlotten (chapter 1, this volume) index how opacity configures a mode of datafied insurgency that confounds colonial, imperial, and capital regimes of measurement by enabling one to be at once both present and absent—partially legible, but never completely so.[20] In C. Riley Snorton's words, such demands for opacity proliferate in the subterranean ground of a false transparency, a repertoire of "submerged forms of relationalities that need not be visible to have effects."[21]

In what follows, I ask how we might extend this relational dynamic of opacity to critiques of machine learning systems in the literature of big data studies. In doing so, I locate an (in)commensurable opacity within the technical conditions of abstraction that both generate and exceed the classification processes central to algorithmic modes of governance. Importantly, such an understanding of opacity is not meant to evacuate the sociopolitical moorings so crucial for Glissant's project. Rather, I consider how opacity in machine learning brackets the political forms of minoritarian experience in the realms of both the social and the technological. I consider this to be a key vector through which queerness comes to bear in big data, a point to which I return in the subsequent section.

OPACITY IN THE MACHINE

For the most part, scholars in big data studies tend to critique opacity as a technical condition within two major categories: scale and secrecy.[22] Scale refers to the epistemological difficulty in apprehending the mathematical sublime of big data, its vast archives, and its barriers to literacy. By contrast, secrecy refers to the range of governmental and corporate data practices that strategically conceal information from the public. Harris Kornstein (chapter 9, this volume), for example, tracks how this latter form of opacity is expressed within Silicon Valley's approach to information collection, storage, and processing and how queer communities might conceive alternative possibilities for data management rooted in safety, intimacy, and improvisation.

While these frameworks for opacity are no doubt central to the formations of state and corporate power that inflict violences on marginalized communities, my analysis centers a third definition that I argue is better suited for considering opacity as an (in)commensurability within machine learning. In what follows, I understand opacity as emerging from the conditions of computational abstraction central to algorithmic processes. Computational abstraction refers to the reduction, translation, and instrumentalization of material and social realities into generalizable mathematical forms that can be processed as data. For some scholars, this might index the discrepancy between the way a computer learns and builds classification systems and how humans might do so with their own styles of semantic interpretation.[23] For others, it registers how algorithms entail processes of selective forgetting in order to fit data into fixed parameters, which might in turn "generate ballooningly complex sets of machine states."[24] In either case, computational abstraction acknowledges an inherent uncertainty that is not simply incidental but necessary in data-driven technologies. In the following analysis, I understand opacity as a complex of indeterminacy that works within high-dimensional feature space, enabling machine learners to produce stable boundaries for predictive modeling.

In order to explore the technical conditions of opacity that subtend machine learning, I now bring into focus the k-nearest neighbor (k-NN) algorithm. The k-NN algorithm is a kind of machine learner, which as a general class of algorithms uses methods of data analysis to produce computational models based on perceived patterns in a dataset in order to automate decision-making processes, such as classification. My interest in k-NN algorithms is twofold. First, k-NN algorithms are considered by the machine learning community to be one of the most fundamental of classification methods, often used as a benchmark for comprehending more complex systems like support-vector machines, decision trees, and convolutional neural networks. I thus treat k-NN algorithms as a representative and expository case for scaling down the technical aspects of opacity caused by computational abstraction that more broadly characterize machine learning as a genre of computational aesthetics. Indeed, other scholars have already explored how opacity inheres within learners like neural nets due to the occlusion of computation within hidden layers of analysis.[25] I take this to suggest that while opacity is not specific to a kind of machine learner, each algorithm is designed to negotiate opacity through unique formal strategies of classification and modeling. Second, k-NN algorithms are nonparametric, which means that they do not assume in advance a functional form of the problem being solved but instead learn that form from the training data. This quality of k-NN algorithms makes them one of the best performers for addressing real-world problems even when compared to more powerful classifiers. In research and industry applications, k-NN algorithms have been used for economic forecasting, gene function prediction, and distress detection in speech, as well as for identifying photographs of people on Facebook and recommending movies to Netflix users.

A k-NN algorithm is an example of a supervised machine learning model used for classification and regression analysis.[26] It specifically can predict the class membership of an unknown data object based on how similar it is to other data objects in a training set. The training set is the group of data objects for which classification is already known in advance based on a set of chosen features. The corresponding figure here presents a kind of problem for which a k-NN algorithm might be used. In this example, we find a training dataset that contains twenty-three objects (fruit) that belong to four different classes (banana, lemon, pineapple, and blueberry). The training set is distributed in a feature space according to the content's relative measurement along the x-axis and y-axis. Here the feature space is characterized by two dimensions based on the two features (sweetness and size) used for classification. The learner uses this distribution of training data to predict the class of an unknown object (the question mark), which is placed in the feature space according to its relative measurement along the two axes. Like many machine learning classifiers, k-NN algorithms assume that similarity among data objects can be determined by their relative proximity. Such an analytic is predicated on a "regime of between-ness" where classification is subject to the geometry of the feature space and the distribution of data in the training set.[27] For the k-NN algorithm, the class of the unknown object is determined by a "vote" among the closest neighbors in the feature space. Whichever class is represented by the majority of the nearest neighbors determines the final classification output. For example, if the majority of the nearest neighbors are classed as blueberries, then the unknown object will be classed similarly. The parameter k defines the number of neighbors that will be involved in the vote. Importantly, different values of k often result in different classification outputs depending on the distribution of training data in the feature space. Ultimately, by testing different values of k upon the training set, the learner can produce a predictive model with boundaries defining neighborhoods in the feature space that enable it to classify new data objects.[28]

It's imperative to note that the figure shown here (fig. 3.1) productively misrepresents how machine learners like k-NN algorithms predict classification and model neighborhoods. On the one hand, data objects should not be understood as discrete points on a plot but as vectors, or arrays of numbers that encode length and distance. As a geometric analogy, vectors can be used to visualize the distance between data objects. However, vectors are useful more broadly for transforming data of varying types (e.g., quantitative, ordinal, or categorical) into new additive and scalar relations that smooth over inconsistencies in the dataset, thus allowing data to be manipulated and modeled. On the other hand, the figure depicts a narrow array of classes, a small training set, and limited features. In reality, things are never this simple. In most applica-

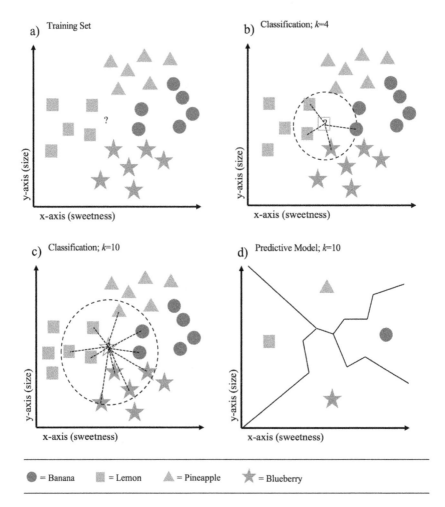

a) Training Set

b) Classification; *k*=4

c) Classification; *k*=10

d) Predictive Model; *k*=10

y-axis (size)

x-axis (sweetness)

● = Banana ▪ = Lemon ▲ = Pineapple ★ = Blueberry

FIGURE 3.1. A graphical representation depicting how a *k*-NN algorithm is used to classify a new data object between four classes. In this example, the learner is asked to classify the new object (?) among four kinds of fruit (banana, lemon, pineapple, or blueberry) based on the two features of sweetness (*x*-axis) and size (*y*-axis). (a) The training set data is represented by four distinct shapes mapped onto a feature space defined by the two classification features (sweetness and size). When the classification query is initialized, the learner uses the parameter *k* to determine how many of the closest data objects in the feature space surrounding the new data object will be used in the vote for class membership. (b) When *k* = 4, the new object is classified as a lemon. (c) When *k* = 10, it is classified as a blueberry. (d) The learner produces a predictive model using *k* = 10 to determine boundaries among the training data by drawing vectors that have the maximum distance between datasets of different classes. Any new data object that falls within a neighborhood is automatically assigned to the corresponding class. Schematic by the author.

tions, datasets are exceedingly large and the number of features describing each observation recorded in the dataset (e.g., the shape, texture, and color of fruit) can typically reach into the thousands, if not millions or more. In computer vision applications, for example, a feature could be defined as a unique line in an image or even an individual pixel. Importantly, each new feature used for classification increases the dimensionality of the plot, thus making it more difficult to visualize in a simple two-dimensional graph. If the classification of a new object requires that we correlate the interactions among multiple variables, then our machine learner must be able to determine distances and boundaries within n-dimensions (n being the number of features necessary for classification).

As dimensions of the feature space increase in number, machine learners begin to exhibit a range of behaviors that make classification and predictive modeling more difficult. Key among these is the curse of dimensionality, first described by Richard Bellman in 1961.[29] With each new dimension, the volume of the feature space increases exponentially, but the amount of data included in the training set usually does not. This means that data that might appear close together in low dimensions can suddenly be sparsely distributed in high dimensions. Nearest neighbor classifiers like k-NN algorithms are especially susceptible to dimensional expansion since they measure similarity through proximal distance. In addition, too many features can overwhelm nearest neighbor classifiers since they will no longer be able to determine meaningful similarity among those features most salient for categorization. To contend with these issues, computer scientists have developed techniques—including principal component analysis, multidimensional scaling, and Isomap—to reduce the dimensionality of datasets and thus make them more manageable for machine learning.[30] However, while such techniques might enable nearest neighbor classifiers like k-NN algorithms to better process proximal distance, they ultimately gesture to a multidimensional complexity that in many ways remains computationally recalcitrant, whether due to limitations of the algorithm itself or because of the high cost of data processing. As such, low-dimensional plots like that shown in figure 3.1 merely disclose a limited, partial, and incomplete perspective on a much more complicated web of vectoral relations within high-dimensional space. Adrian Mackenzie describes this aspect of machine learning as an "endemic partiality," which implies "the existence of a hidden, occluded, or internal space that cannot be seen in a data table and cannot be brought to light even in the more complex geometry of a plot."[31] Within this high-dimensional space, machine learners must negotiate a "meta(s)table volume" of n-dimensional relations that defies visualization within two-dimensional and three-dimensional models.[32]

In line with scholars in big data studies, I consider how this endemic partiality expresses a fundamental opacity within machine learning systems. However, in concert with my reading of Glissant, I understand this machinic opacity more specifically as a form of (in)commensurability that is both generative within and in excess of machine learning classification and modeling. I take my cue here from Mackenzie, who succinctly remarks that "opacity—'no direct measure of success'—is generative in machine learning."[33] Central here is the conceit that what is most optimal for machine learners is the most accurate. That is, machine learners are able to produce a predictive output because they actively generate their own probabilistic thresholds for articulating their success, thus circumventing the possibility that their output could ever be wrong. Indeed, the goal of machine learners like k-NN algorithms is to optimize classification modeling by organizing the vectoral relations describing various data objects into classification neighborhoods that take into account expected loss of accuracy.[34] However, distilled within that optimal output are layers of indeterminate relations in high-dimensional space that are reduced to conform to predefined parameters of similarity. In this case, the multidimensional complexity that results from computational abstraction does not prevent machine learners from producing predictive outputs but is instead the very basis by which such prediction is possible. As Louise Amoore explains, "machine learning algorithms generate their outputs through the opaque relations of selves to selves, and selves to others, and . . . these outputs then annul and disavow the opacity of their underlying relations in the name of a crystalline clarity of the output."[35] Opacity thus is simultaneously enumerated and resolved as a relational dynamic that adjudicates the boundaries of predictability subtending algorithmic modes of governance.

Returning to our case study, we can witness how opacity is both enumerated and resolved to produce a single output in k-NN algorithms. Through various values of k, k-NN algorithms transform vector space to generate predictive models that organize data based on their relative proximities. However, as the number of features increases, k-NN algorithms generate an expanding array of nonlinear relations of varying proximity that result from the vectorization of data in high-dimensional space. This inevitably produces a "topological instability" in the predictive model, wherein even very small changes in local neighborhoods within high-dimensional space can yield indeterminate and fluctuating boundaries in low-dimensional space that can't be easily resolved by simply optimizing for k.[36] Thus, while the task of the k-NN algorithm is to organize these indeterminate vectorized shapes into legible classification neighborhoods, there always remain occluded relations in high-dimensional space that exceed what appears in the predictive output. And yet, while such opaque conditions might destabilize any sense of comparative proximity in the feature space, they are nonetheless productive in machine learning insofar as they are consolidated to perceive patterns among data. Opacity thus does not disrupt machine learning; instead, machine learners work through it to produce boundaries for classification, however unstable they might be. Indeed, such instability is precisely an indication of the fundamental indeterminacy that is accommodated in predictive analytics.

Importantly, opacity is not synonymous with errors in misclassification. Any optimal predictive model will inevitably result in various casualties of classification—those data points that are incorrectly located outside of their respective classification neighborhood. In the above figure, it may be the case, for example, that the predictive model produced from $k = 10$ constructs boundaries in the feature space that include bananas in the blueberry neighborhood, or vice versa. However, insofar as misclassifications only appear on the tail end of prediction, such error simply attests to the multidimensional complex of vectoral relations that are accommodated in machine learning prior to the output. In this case, misclassification is perhaps better understood as an epiphenomenon of computational abstraction that indexes the existence of a technical opacity submerged within machine learning.

If opacity emerges as an (in)commensurability within machine learning, then we might also characterize transparency as "false" (via Glissant) insofar as what appears in the optimal predictive output is simply the guise of commensurability. To be sure, transparency is merely the name we give to the consolidation of indeterminacy through various formal strategies of machine learning algorithms used to perceive relations among data objects in n-dimensional space. Transparency then is perhaps less an immediate technical outcome of predictive analytics than the achievement of a system of formalization intended to make opacity align with preexistent classification schema. Whatever crystalline clarity of an output might result from the various computational layers of machine learning is thus but a pretense to commensuration maneuvered upon an irreducible indeterminacy that always lies in excess. In this case, transparency isn't simply concerned with illuminating the unknown but about making the opaque conform to the status quo as the point of departure for predictive conjecture, even if that prediction is unstable and incomplete.

ON A QUEER TECHNICS

Through a reading of Glissant in relation to big data studies, I propose that we might encounter an (in)commensurable opacity that proliferates within and in excess of machine learners like k-NN algorithms. However, in doing so I acknowledge that we risk a potential misreading of Glissant that not only appropriates opacity as a technical feature that manifests within the very structures of transparency at the crosshairs of his critique but also evacuates the coordinates of racial, colonial, and capitalist power that animate opacity as a form of marginalized struggle. And yet, I remain committed to the notion that the technological conditions of machine learning cannot be thought outside its social, political, and historical contexts. To be sure, racial, gendered, and classed modes of discrimination are very often coded into algorithmic architectures.[37] Emerging out of US military research in the 1940s and '50s, k-NN algorithms are no different.[38] As James Dobson documents, the nearest-neighbor rule that forms the basis of this algorithm is the "product of a particular constellation of ideologies" that trafficked across Cold War logistical planning and mid-twentieth-century ideas of segregation, partitioning, and democratization.[39] Complicit here too is a much longer history that sees the logic of homophily (i.e., similarity breeds connection) in k-NN algorithms as a specific cultural and historical trope of racial cohesion rooted in eugenicist thinking even prior to the advent of digital and networked technologies.[40] In this sense, I consider how opacity not only is an artifact of the formal processes of computational abstraction but also emerges as a sociotechnical formation that attests to the ways that computational media like machine learning refract broader systems of control, violence, and dispossession that impact minoritarian life.

In order to examine opacity as a sociotechnical formation, I turn to queer theory. My investment in queerness stems from its vexed relationship to fixed ontological categories, instead materializing as an excessive alterity that surges through bodies, machines, discourses, and practices. Rather than being tethered to a kind of gender or sexuality, queerness for many theorists often takes the form of an illegibility, refusal, or failure that confounds recognition within normative formations of identity and citizenship.[41] Importantly, queerness here should not be interpreted as a simple negativity or as an anti-identitarian project that resists cultural logics of power. Rather, as phrased by Tavia Nyong'o, queerness is perhaps most politically efficacious when articulated as a "problem-space" where we can more fully account for "how norms and normativity actually intersect with power-knowledge."[42] Taken together, I understand queerness as working obtusely within the social order to mediate how sociopolitical processes are made to signify as material, embodied, or affective differences within dominant modes of signification—not the least of which are big data and other systems of surveillance.[43]

By evoking queerness in the context of this argument, I argue that opacity stages a queer politic insofar as it adjudicates how the sociopolitical formation of the subject becomes legible within algorithmic modes of governance like those installed by machine learning. In doing so, I offer opacity as an example of what Jacob Gaboury calls a "queer technics." A queer technics considers how queer forms of relationality are embedded in computational media as an "excessive illegibility" that is "explicitly situated within the logic of information systems but refuses this gesture of capture and extraction."[44] For Gaboury, the NULL marker in relational database management systems is one such example of a queer technics insofar as it marks an indeterminacy that lies both inside and outside the normative logics of the database form. In like manner, I argue that opacity, as an (in)commensurability in machine learning, indexes a queer technics insofar as it is both generative within and in excess of predictive classification. However, as Gaboury cautions, a queer technics is not simply a logical abstraction but instead consolidates the forms of negotiated visibility that Black and queer life typically endures within systems of power. In much the same way, what makes opacity in machine learning available as a queer technics is how it contracts the mode of experience intensive to minoritarian livelihood within the realm of the social—an experience that Kara Keeling articulates as a "structuring antagonism" that is both generative of and excessive to the hegemonic order of racial capitalism.[45] Put differently, opacity gathers around those marked as "queer" who are both violently enumerated in, but nonetheless elude, the unrelenting drive of datafication. To be sure, as a cultural logic, opacity has historically coincided with certain tropes of sociopolitical difference that prop up the white political subject as the privileged center of visibility.

As a queer technics, opacity evinces how minoritarian life is abstracted and elaborated within the problem-space of machine learning. As argued above, when information about the world is captured and processed within training datasets, the dimensionality of that data must be reduced to enable machine learners like k-NN algorithms to construct quasi-stable boundaries for classification and modeling. Within this process, the messiness of the world is consolidated into a set of discrete features that purport to represent the most prominent vectors of variance in the dataset. New data objects are then transformed and made commensurate with those features based on the shape of their shared vectoral relations. And yet, very often such features relate only indirectly to a given person or population, such as in predictive policing software that uses historical crime data to forecast criminal activity rather than explicit categories of racial difference. This latter point is central to the postracial imaginary of big data wherein algorithms are said to be objective and neutral mediators of social reality at the same time that these very same features often implicitly encode for sociopolitical difference. Indeed, within classifiers like k-NN algorithms, the social itself is materially absent, known only through the relative proximity of partial and incomplete feature vectors in n-dimensional space. This is no doubt precisely the appeal of k-NN algorithms insofar as they "claim a supposedly subjectless decision-making capability, one in which data points are imagined as casting free and independent 'votes' for the membership and classification of new data."[46]

However, whether or not machine learners explicitly encode social difference is not the point. Rather, as a queer technics, opacity adjudicates how the subject becomes legible within the racializing grammar of identity that forms the basis of algorithmic modes of governance. As machine learners like k-NN algorithms consolidate high-dimensional data into key feature vectors, they ultimately yield a single predictive classification output through voting mechanisms. This predictive output is in turn the ideological site through which the subject of algorithmic governance emerges as an occasion for power. This subject has many names, often highlighted in media scandals concerning biased AI and "racist algorithms": a Black man prematurely accused of recidivism, a young immigrant woman denied social services, or a trans or gender nonconforming person incorrectly identified by a facial recognition system.[47] Here, sociopolitical difference serves as the exceptional grounds by which opacity becomes generative in machine learning. In order to resolve and stabilize high-dimensional opacity into a single predictive output, machine learners graft onto dominant formations of identity that are oriented around the symbolic dimensions of whiteness as the mediator of optimality.[48] In this case, conditions of racialized, gendered, and sexualized alterity operate as what

Mackenzie calls an "enunciative modality, a way of describing, locating, and perceiving differences in which differences of degree and kind are remapped."[49] While Mackenzie's understanding of enunciative modality is admittedly technical—reserved to describe processes like the nearest neighbor rule—I argue that vectors of sociopolitical difference likewise emerge as animating differences that enable the consolidation of opacity into perceived patterns that ultimately become legible as a single predictive output within dominant grammars of identity. Put differently, the way that machine learners consolidate the indeterminacies that enter high-dimensional space through unique features, parameters, and weightings is predicated upon the negotiated visibilities of minoritarian subjects in systems of algorithmic governance. To repeat, this is neither to suggest that opacity is indexical to sociopolitical difference nor that minoritarian life is somehow represented in those indeterminate relations of data in high-dimensional space. Rather, opacity reveals how the technical limits of machine learning are bracketed by the way that sociopolitical difference is made legible within computational systems of classification.

And yet, even as machine learning attempts to consolidate information about the world into existing categories of knowledge-power, there always remain certain nontransferable elements of experience that lie beyond the single predictive output. These excess elements both disturb dominant categories of comparison and gesture to the uncertainties of relationality submerged in the layers of computational abstraction. Through opacity, we thus acknowledge that the epistemological project of transparency is false insofar as it always already fails to apprehend the social within dominant logics of commensurability. And in that failure we discover the queer temporalities of a raced and gendered embodiment unaccounted within the control diagrams of capitalist and colonial power. Writing in the anticipatory wake of contemporary machine learning systems, Glissant knew as much to be true: "the marginal and the deviant sense in advance the shock of cultures; they live its future excess."[50]

IN THE WILDS

To conclude, I gesture back to the radical spirit that animates Glissant's philosophy of Relation to interrogate how opacity in machine learning may unsettle big data's regime of transparency. Importantly, such a political project might not necessarily bear much resemblance to models of opacity that respond to big data through performative and tactical modes of refusal, nor does it simply offer the possibility of a technological fix that will make computational media more equitable. Rather, I follow Keeling, who proposes in her reading of Glissant that "an insistence on opacity gives queer time for the conceptions of the world sedimented or . . . accumulated within existing relations to appear now."[51] Likewise, I consider how opacity shores up the sediments of relation enumerated within computational abstraction, ultimately reinvesting in this world's embodied differences, which are continually reduced within the edges and nodes of a networked ontology. Such a model of opacity ultimately assumes a queer politic that opens up a utopic imaginary for fostering what José Muñoz envisions as a "collectivity with and through the incommensurable": a commons grounded upon the very conditions of incalculability that proliferate in excess of the insulating logics of racial capitalism and its technologies of signification.[52]

To help contour the political stakes of opacity as a queer technics, I offer three propositions. First, the type of machine learner matters. As evidenced by the above analysis of k-NN algorithms, machine learners construct predictive models based on an array of specific technical parameters, as well as on a prior set of political and ideological frameworks, in turn producing unique accounts of commensurability. For example, the predictive policing software PredPol and HunchLab make use of two different machine learning algorithms—an epidemic-type aftershock model and a stochastic gradient boosting machine, respectively. Even if these algorithms were to use the same dataset of criminal activity in a given city, they would nonetheless abstract and consolidate information about the world in singular ways, thus producing distinct predictive models of racial state violence.[53] As such, we must account for the historically contingent processes of difference-making that structure predictive analytics and whatever we understand to be the architecture of transparency common to our critique.

Second, attending to the queerness of opacity need not be preoccupied with simply exhuming or correcting the misclassifications that accumulate in machine learning systems. Indeed, from the perspective of the machine learner, there simply is no error, only a palimpsest of opaque speculations that both generate and exceed the final predictive output. A politics of opacity should instead attend to those submerged incomputable relations that never show up as error but nonetheless structure the processes of commensuration in algorithmic modes of governance. To echo Amoore, "Rather than contribute to the cacophony of calls for greater transparency, this ethical demand dwells with the vertiginous moment of dazzlement and darkness, with clouded action and opacity, so that the violences of an algorithm cannot simply be mistakes or errors in the algorithm's otherwise logical rationality."[54] Ultimately, as a queer technics, opacity insists that we peer not inside the black box but across it toward the forms of racialized, gendered, and sexual exclusions that occur at the intersections between the social and the technological.

Finally, I argue that a politics of opacity gestures toward the wilds of machine learning. By wilds, I refer at once to the act of implementing machine learners in real-world contexts (when the algorithm is said to "enter the wild"), as well as to the wilds of theory that name, as Jack Halberstam and Tavia Nyong'o write, "while rendering partially opaque, what hegemonic systems would interdict or push to the margins."[55] In the context of a politics of opacity, the wilds index all that remains within or is excluded from dominant systems of commensuration. This is particularly the case for those forms of life that sit at the intersection of multiple marginalized identities and thus don't easily conform to the classificatory models demanded by a machine learner implemented in our lived social reality. As a queer technics, opacity contains alternative modes of embodiment and visions of the future that are otherwise expelled from capitalist, colonial, and imperial structures. Inasmuch as opacity is generative in machine learning for reproducing discriminatory forms of violence upon the social, it also reveals every prediction to be incomplete and partial and thus open to revision. To be in the wilds is thus to be out of network, to hold in abeyance new patterns of the opaque that teem with the potential of what could have been and might still be with other implementations, other speculations. What friction might we find in the wilds of machine learning? And how might such friction still gather around the queer, those rendered (in)commensurable in big data's demand for transparency?

NOTES

1. Mirzoeff, "Ghostwriting," 241.

2. Cheney-Lippold, *We Are Data*.

3. Chun, "On Hypo-Real Models of Global Climate Change," 697.

4. See the discussion of the difficulties that attend examining the design of technological systems alongside the history of sociocultural formations in McPherson, *Feminist in a Software Lab*.

5. Gaboury, "Becoming NULL," para. 6.

6. See, for example, De Vries and Schinkel, "Algorithmic Anxiety"; and Birchall, "Shareveillance."

7. Blas, "Informatic Opacity" (in *JOAAP*). See also Blas, "Opacities."

8. Blas, "Informatic Opacity" (in *Posthuman Glossary*), 199.

9. Birchall, "Managing Secrecy," 159.

10. Glissant, *Poetics of Relation*, 191.

11. McKittrick, "Mathematics Black Life," 17.

12. Glissant, *Poetics of Relation*, 194.

13. Blas, "Informatic Opacity" (in *JOAAP*).

14. Glissant, *Poetics of Relation*, 191, 190, respectively.

15. Moten, *In the Break*, 68.

16. Glissant, *Poetics of Relation*, 190. Nicole Simek similarly observes how Glissant phrases opacity as "a stubborn density, of something layered, something partially pene-trable but with a mind of its own." Simek, "Stubborn Shadows," 372. For Simek, a pene-trable opacity is not an immediately resistive positionality that defies interpretation but instead a mode of relation that shifts attention to the always already unknowability of a given heuristic and its criteria of evaluation.

17. Glissant, *Poetics of Relation*, 114 (emphasis added).

18. Glissant, *Poetics of Relation*, 195.

19. As Daphne Brooks writes, opacity is not simply a representational absence but instead indexes "the insurgent power of imaging cultural identity in grand and polyvalent terms which might outsize the narrow representational frames bestowed on them." Brooks, *Bodies in Dissent*, 8. On opacity as a performative mode of resistance in excess of legibility, see also Hartman, *Scenes of Subjection*.

20. Browne, *Dark Matters*, 21.

21. Snorton, *Black on Both Sides*, 10.

22. For discussions of these two concepts of opacity, see Ananny and Crawford, "Seeing without Knowing"; and Pasquale, *Black Box Society*.

23. Burrell, "How the Machine 'Thinks,'" 2.

24. Fuller and Goffey, *Evil Media*, 29.

25. See Burrell, "How the Machine 'Thinks'"; and Amoore, *Cloud Ethics*.

26. As a general class of learners, a supervised model is one that predicts the corre-sponding output (y) of a given input (x) based on a dataset of training observations (x, y). Other examples of supervised learning algorithms include linear regression, logistic regression, and random forests. An unsupervised learner is one that attempts to model the underlying structure or distribution of a dataset. The goal here is not to produce an output (like a classification label in a k-NN algorithm) but instead to learn more about the input.

27. Aradau and Blanke, "Politics of Prediction," 380.

28. As opposed to most machine learning systems that create a predictive model during a distinct training phase, a k-NN algorithm instead operates through a series of

iterative experimentations in which the training data are continually reanalyzed with new values of k to produce a predictive model. Here a programmer might manually select values of k to determine which one is the most optimal for predicting the class of new objects. This is a subtle reminder that machine learning is not simply an automated technical process but often involves human oversight.

29. Bellman, *Adaptive Control Processes*.

30. Tenenbaum, De Silva, and Langford, "Global Geometric Framework for Nonlinear Dimensionality Reduction."

31. Mackenzie, *Machine Learners*, 100, 62, respectively.

32. Mackenzie, *Machine Learners*, 73.

33. Mackenzie, *Machine Learners*, 81.

34. The optimal predictive model is identified by determining the validation error of each k value. The validation error is the percentage of mistaken predictions in relation to the total number of cases. A low validation error indicates that the model fits well to the training data and can be used to predict the class of unknown objects.

35. Amoore, *Cloud Ethics*, 166.

36. Mackenzie, *Machine Learners*, 174.

37. O'Neil, *Weapons of Math Destruction*; Noble, *Algorithms of Oppression*; Benjamin, *Race after Technology*.

38. The first paper to propose a nonparametric model for discriminant analysis (the basis for the k-NN learner) was an unpublished technical report written in 1951 by Evelyn Fix and Joseph L. Hodges, two statisticians under contract with the US Air Force School who had both long been involved in conducting research for air force operations. Fix and Hodges, *Discriminatory Analysis—Nonparametric Discrimination*. Following this, the military continued to contract research on nearest neighbor discrimination, as evidenced in a 1967 study that proposed the "k_n-nearest neighbor rule." Cover and Hart, "Nearest Neighbor Pattern Classification."

39. Dobson, *Critical Digital Humanities*, 126. See also McPherson, *Feminist in a Software Lab*, for a similar analysis of the way that social and racial formations in the United States in the 1960s and 1970s informed the development of concepts like modularity in the early computing program UNIX.

40. Chun, *Discriminating Data*.

41. See, for example, Edelman, *No Future*; and Halberstam, *Queer Art of Failure*.

42. Nyong'o, *Afro-Fabulations*, 158.

43. Kafer and Grinberg. "Queer Surveillance."

44. Gaboury, "Becoming NULL," para. 6.

45. Keeling, *Queer Times, Black Futures*, 17.

46. Dobson, *Critical Digital Humanities*, 128.

47. Sandvig et al., "When the Algorithm Itself Is a Racist."

48. Simone Browne, for example, calls this a "prototypical whiteness," describing how biometric systems privilege whiteness or light skin when sensing and enrolling bodies for measurement and recognition. Browne, *Dark Matters*, 110.

49. Mackenzie, *Machine Learners*, 126.

50. Glissant, *Poetics of Relation*, 156.

51. Keeling, *Queer Times, Black Futures*, 32.

52. Muñoz, *Sense of Brown*, 7.

53. For a comparison of the predictive policing software PredPol and HunchLab and how they purport to predict crime as a function of racial state violence, see Scannell, "This Is Not *Minority Report*."

54. Amoore, *Cloud Ethics*, 117.

55. Halberstam and Nyong'o, "Introduction: Theory in the Wild," 453.

BIBLIOGRAPHY

Amoore, Louise. *Cloud Ethics: Algorithms and the Attributes of Ourselves and Others.* Durham, NC: Duke University Press, 2020.

Ananny, Mike, and Kate Crawford. "Seeing without Knowing: Limitations of the Transparency Ideal and Its Application to Algorithmic Accountability." *New Media and Society* 1, no. 17 (2016): 1–17.

Aradau, Claudia, and Tobias Blanke. "Politics of Prediction: Security and the Time/Space of Governmentality in the Age of Big Data." *European Journal of Social Theory* 20, no. 3 (2017): 373–91.

Bellman, Richard. *Adaptive Control Processes: A Guided Tour.* Princeton: Princeton University Press, 1961.

Benjamin, Ruha. *Race after Technology: Abolitionist Tools for the New Jim Code.* Medford, MA: Polity, 2019.

Birchall, Clare. "Managing Secrecy." *International Journal of Communication* 10 (2016): 152–63.

——— . "Shareveillance: Subjectivity between Open and Closed Data." *Big Data and Society* 3, no. 2 (2016): 1–12. https://doi.org/10.1177/2053951716663965.

Blas, Zach. "Informatic Opacity." *Journal of Aesthetics and Protest*, no. 9 (2014). https://www.joaap.org/issue9/zachblas.htm.

——— . "Informatic Opacity." In *Posthuman Glossary*, edited by Rosi Braidotti and Maria Hlavajova, 198–99. London: Bloomsbury Academic, 2018.

——— . "Opacities: An Introduction." *Camera Obscura* 31, no. 2 (2016): 151–53.

Brooks, Daphne. *Bodies in Dissent: Spectacular Performances of Race and Freedom, 1850–1910.* Durham, NC: Duke University Press, 2006.

Browne, Simone. *Dark Matters: On the Surveillance of Blackness*. Durham, NC: Duke University Press, 2015.

Burrell, Jenna. "How the Machine 'Thinks': Understanding Opacity in Machine Learning Algorithms." *Big Data and Society* 3, no. 1 (2016): 1–12.

Cheney-Lippold, John. *We Are Data: Algorithms and the Making of Our Digital Selves*. New York: New York University Press, 2017.

Chun, Wendy. *Discriminating Data: Correlation, Neighborhoods, and the New Politics of Recognition*. Cambridge, MA: MIT Press, 2021.

——— . "On Hypo-Real Models of Global Climate Change: A Challenge for the Humanities." *Critical Inquiry* 41, no. 3 (Spring 2015): 675–703.

Cover, Thomas, and Peter Hart. "Nearest Neighbor Pattern Classification." *IEEE Transactions on Information Theory* 13, no. 1 (1967): 21–27.

de Vries, Patricia, and Willem Schinkel. "Algorithmic Anxiety: Masks and Camouflage in Artistic Imaginaries of Facial Recognition Algorithms." *Big Data and Society* 6, no. 1 (2019): 1–12.

Dobson, James. *Critical Digital Humanities: The Search for a Methodology*. Urbana: University of Illinois Press, 2019.

Edelman, Lee. *No Future: Queer Theory and the Death Drive*. Durham, NC: Duke University Press, 2004.

Fix, Evelyn, and J. L. Hodges. *Discriminatory Analysis—Nonparametric Discrimination: Consistency Properties*. Report No. 4, Project No. 21-49-004. Randolph Field, TX: USAF School of Aviation Medicine, 1951.

Fuller, Matthew, and Andrew Goffey. *Evil Media*. Cambridge, MA: MIT Press, 2012.

Gaboury, Jacob. "Becoming NULL: Queer Relations in the Excluded Middle." *Women and Performance* 28, no. 2 (2018). https://www.womenandperformance.org/bonus-articles-1/jacob-gaboury-28-2.

Glissant, Édouard. *Poetics of Relation*. Translated by Betsy Wing. Ann Arbor: University of Michigan Press, 1997.

Halberstam, Jack. *The Queer Art of Failure*. Durham, NC: Duke University Press, 2011.

Halberstam, Jack, and Tavia Nyong'o. "Introduction: Theory in the Wild." *South Atlantic Quarterly* 117, no. 3 (2018): 453–64.

Hartman, Saidiya. *Scenes of Subjection: Terror, Slavery, and Self-Making in Nineteenth-Century America*. New York: Oxford University Press, 1997.

Kafer, Gary, and Daniel Grinberg. "Queer Surveillance." *Surveillance and Society* 17, no. 5 (2019): 592–601.

Keeling, Kara. *Queer Times, Black Futures*. New York: New York University Press, 2019.

Mackenzie, Adrian. *Machine Learners: Archaeology of a Data Practice*. Cambridge, MA: MIT Press, 2017.

McKittrick, Katherine. "Mathematics Black Life." *Black Scholar: Journal of Black Studies and Research* 44, no. 2 (2014): 16–28.

McPherson, Tara. *Feminist in a Software Lab: Difference + Design*. Cambridge, MA: Harvard University Press, 2018.

Mirzoeff, Nicholas. "Ghostwriting: Working Out Visual Culture." *Journal of Visual Culture* 1, no. 2 (2002): 239–54.

Moten, Fred. *In the Break: The Aesthetics of the Black Radical Tradition*. Minneapolis: University of Minnesota Press, 2003.

Muñoz, José Esteban. *The Sense of Brown*. Edited by Joshua Chambers-Letson and Tavia Nyong'o. Durham, NC: Duke University Press, 2020.

Noble, Safiya. *Algorithms of Oppression: How Search Engines Reinforce Racism*. New York: New York University Press, 2018.

Nyong'o, Tavia. *Afro-Fabulations: The Queer Drama of Black Life*. New York: New York University Press, 2019.

O'Neil, Cathy. *Weapons of Math Destruction: How Big Data Increases Inequality and Threatens Democracy*. New York: Crown, 2016.

Pasquale, Frank. *The Black Box Society: The Secret Algorithms That Control Money and Information*. Cambridge, MA: Harvard University Press, 2015.

Sandvig, Christian, Kevin Hamilton, Karrie Karahalios, and Cedric Langbort. "When the Algorithm Itself Is a Racist: Diagnosing Ethical Harm in the Basic Components of Software." *International Journal of Communication* 10 (October 2016): 4972–90.

Scannell, R. Joshua. "This Is Not *Minority Report*: Predictive Policing and Population Racism." In *Captivating Technology: Race, Carceral Technoscience, and Liberatory Imagination in Everyday Life*, edited by Ruha Benjamin, 107–29. Durham, NC: Duke University Press, 2019.

Simek, Nicole. "Stubborn Shadows." *symplokē* 23, no. 1–2 (2015): 363–73.

Snorton, C. Riley. *Black on Both Sides: A Racial History of Trans Identity*. Minneapolis: University of Minnesota Press, 2017.

Tenenbaum, Joshua, Vin de Silva, and John Langford. "A Global Geometric Framework for Nonlinear Dimensionality Reduction." *Science* 290, no. 5500 (2000): 2319–23.

SUSANNA PAASONEN & JENNY SUNDÉN

4 Objectionable Nipples *Puritan Data Politics and Sexual Agency in Social Media*

ALONGSIDE CONTENT CONSIDERED VIOLENT AND CRUEL, social media content policies broadly govern displays of nudity and sexual activity. In the community standards of the market leader Facebook, for example, nudity and sexual display are listed alongside hate speech, bullying, and self-harm as "objectionable content," which is restricted "because some people in our community may be sensitive to this type of content."[1] The notion of community standards has been used in the United States in judging the obscenity of cultural objects since the 1957 court ruling *Roth v. United States*, which dealt with "whether to the average person, applying contemporary community standards, the dominant theme taken as a whole appeals to the prurient interest."[2] Community standards are by necessity culturally (and hence regionally) specific, whereas social media platforms are used by billions of people globally; Facebook alone has almost three billion active monthly users. The "some people" identified in the company's community standards are then by necessity fictitious figures whose presumed puritanical sensibilities are presented as a common, neutral norm of proper behavior.

To argue that the visibility of sexual content is restricted due to being offensive to "some people" obscures rather blunt data politics within which sexual content signifies risk and harm.[3] Social media content policies are certainly coined with user safety in mind—consider, for example, rules pertaining to terrorism and hate speech—but they are also designed to support the platforms' corporate brands and to appeal to advertisers and other commercial partners necessary for their operating. It then follows that Facebook filters out sexual content expansively in order to avoid unnecessary risk—not merely the risk of user disgruntlement but also the risk of advertisers discontinuing their plans and campaigns if their commercial messages are placed next to unpalatable content, as well as the risk of Facebook parent company Meta's stock value suffering due to perceived pornographic stigma.

There is nothing surprising in advertising platforms such as Facebook adopting conservative stances toward content shared by users for the sake of financial gain.[4] At the same time, the staggering volume of visitors frequenting social media platforms and the degrees to which those platforms are used as public goods of sorts by institutions, NGOs, and commercial actors speak of their power to govern forms of networked sociability. In much of the Global North, social media have become not merely an instrumental, mediating factor or "the channel" for intimate attachments but part of their sociotechnical infrastructure.[5] Community standards give shape to such infrastructures of intimacy by disallowing certain exchanges (such as sexual displays) and encouraging others (such as updates on relationship status). As infrastructural, largely automated operations, content moderation delimits available posts, giving social media sociality certain shape in the process.

Exploring the content governance practices of Meta in particular, and zooming in on feminist contestations concerning nipple pics, this chapter inquires after the visibilities and invisibilities of sexual content in social media. The issue, we suggest, concerns culturally specific attitudes toward sexuality and bodily display, which, filtered through the American tradition of puritanism into variations of prudishness, are catered as common standards. As sexual exchanges are expansively labeled as objectionable and banned, news feeds grow Disneyfied—that is, "family friendly" and markedly sexless—through content deemed acceptable to all users. In contrast, we argue for the crucial importance of sexuality, sexual agency, and pleasure for mundane sociality.

PURITAN ECHOES

On the one hand, sex—like racist hate speech equally prohibited in social media community standards—is good for social media business as sticky content gaining the attention of users, driving them to engage, and fueling the flows of data through comments and shares.[6] On the other hand, contra the commonsensical notion that "sex sells," social media platforms find it hard to monetize sexual content, as it does not mesh well with the interests of targeted advertising and sponsored content. Following this line of thought, Meta's Facebook and Instagram promote sociability stripped of sex, implying that sexuality itself lacks importance and value: being difficult to monetize, it is also perceived as lacking in social value, as something best excluded except for acceptable displays of "sexiness." At the same time, even as corporate brands may be unwilling to place their ads next to images of violence and gore, moderation practices concerning these are laxer than those pertaining to nudity.[7] We propose that the conflation of sex with risk and danger, as well as its ousting from platforms, speaks of persistent puritan residual structures of feeling. In other words, the weeding out of sexual exchanges is an issue of puritan social media politics.

This puritanism is devoid of the reformist rigor of centuries past, yet it operates as more than a mere accent. Following Raymond Williams, puritanism can be understood as a residual structure of feeling that orients "impulse, restraint, and tone; specifically affective elements of consciousness and relationships."[8] Residual structures of feeling linger on, possibly unnoticed, while nevertheless giving shape to the social in the here and now: "the residual, by definition, has been effectively formed in the past, but it is still active in the cultural process, not only and often not at all as an element of the past, but as an effective element of the present."[9] As a historical ideology and practice, puritanism is detached from contemporary neoliberal capitalism, of which Meta forms a part, while nevertheless remaining present in it through "reinterpretation, dilution, projection, discriminating inclusion and exclusion."[10] This, we suggest, is the case with the puritan echoes of social media community standards.[11]

With the exception of Chinese services (from WeChat to TikTok), the globally leading social media platforms are of American origin and, more specifically, products of Silicon Valley. Writing on 1990s tech culture, Richard Barbrook and Andy Cameron identify a "loose alliance of writers, hackers, capitalists and artists from the West Coast of the USA" as having "succeeded in defining a heterogeneous orthodoxy for the coming information age: the Californian Ideology," which balances "the free-wheeling spirit of the hippies and the entrepreneurial zeal of the yuppies."[12] As Fred Turner has shown, the history of personal computing, as well as that of the internet, is deeply embedded in the histories of West Coast counterculture, from ways of imagining cybernetic extensions of consciousness to alternative networks of information exchange, community organization, libertarianism, and start-up capitalism.[13] More recently, this outlook has been defined in terms of casualness, individualism, and straight male dominance.[14]

Our proposal is simple: while mapping out crucial sets of values and paradoxes within the Silicon Valley tech sector, these analyses have not extended to the residual puritanism of US culture—not merely as something that hippies turned away from in celebrations of free love but as something that remains manifest in how the boundaries of acceptable sociality are drawn in social media. Stubbornly lingering residual puritanism is then a means of explaining why sexual content is horizontally weeded out in the name of safety and the common good.

NO SEX, PLEASE, WE'RE FACEBOOK

In 2016, a user inquired after rules about sending naked pictures through chat or Messenger on Facebook's Help Center question forum. Another user replied with, "Public nudity is totally prohibited on Facebook, but it's not that bad as long as you keep it on private message and someone do not report it to Facebook." This view did not find support, as other users shared their experiences of accounts being permanently or temporarily disabled: "Some days ago I tried to send a picture to my wife in a private message and after some seconds I got my account disabled. I contacted the Facebook team and unfortunately, yesterday I got that message: 'We've determined that you are ineligible to use Facebook. To learn more about Facebook's policies, please review the Facebook Statement of Rights and Responsibilities. . . . Unfortunately, for safety and security reasons, we cannot provide additional information as to why your account was disabled. We appreciate your understanding, as this decision is final.'"

Like all Facebook traffic, Messenger exchanges generate user data to be harvested, stored, analyzed, and sold in ways impossible for users to influence or control. Within social media architecture, these back channels add increased granularity to the user data mined and aggregated. On the level of content policy, back channels are governed in a manner similar to all other Facebook exchanges, even as they are used for the kinds of sexual exchanges of the kind mentioned above due to their perceived privacy. Facebook CEO Mark Zuckerberg noted as much in 2018, pointing out that Messenger conversations, links, and pictures are screened for their compatibility with community standards.

Clickbait and news sites reacted with dramatic headlines, such as "Facebook confirms it spies on your Messenger conversations"; "Facebook admits spying on Messenger, 'scanning' private photos"; "When you send something on Messenger, Facebook takes a look at it first"; "Zuckerberg admits Facebook scans all your private messages."[15] Evoking the figure of corporate actors—both algorithmic and human—spying on users' intimate affairs, the headlines complained about lost privacy that had, in fact, never existed in the first place.

Despite content screening, the governance of back-channel messaging is less rigorous than that concerning public posts, allowing for exchanges deviating from community standards to take place on Messenger and in Instagram's, TikTok's, and Twitter's direct messages, from flirtations to sexting sprees and unsolicited dick pics.[16] As Gary Kafer (chapter 3, this volume) points out in his discussion of queer studies of big data, computational systems allow for a certain degree of opacity, even as they aim for transparency. Social media back channeling may provide such concealedness as a cover from more open forms of surveillance and control. At the same time, since the practices of platform governance connected to all this are also opaque, unpredictable, and contingent, a dick pic sent to a partner can get one's account disabled. Alternatively, sending an unsolicited dick pic to a random stranger may have no consequences whatsoever.

The (perceived) degrees of privacy, if not necessarily anonymity, in direct messaging feed the circulation of dick pics as networked flashing and trolling, just as they support exchanges based on mutual desire as the playful testing out of boundaries, means of remaining in contact, and turning one another on. Although the multiplicity of their deployments is seldom appreciated, dick pics are used for a range of purposes: as instruments of visual harassment in organized trolling campaigns and misogynistic personal attacks, as advertisements of corporeal assets displayed on dating apps, and as means of humor, diversion, self-exploration, or social commentary.[17]

Social media content policies are horizontal and blind to context in framing offensiveness in terms of pictorial properties (such as a dick) and not the context of exchange (reciprocal play versus unwanted harassment). Sexual content and communication are structurally zoned off so that there is no option to opt in so as to express consent to accessing it—this being the practice on Twitter, as it was on Tumblr before their "porn ban" went into effect in December 2018.[18] Automated flagging and banning is premised on categorical, context-independent, and hence highly abstract notions of offensiveness, risk, and safety that by design fail to accommodate the variety of sexual lives, desires, or titillations that drive people and shape their mutual bonds.

WHAT CONSENT?

Meta's community standards make no distinction between consensual and nonconsensual image sharing in community standards classifying sexual content as broadly objectionable:

> *As noted in Section 8 of our Community Standards, people use Facebook to discuss and draw attention to sexual violence and exploitation. We recognize the importance of and allow for this discussion. *We draw the line, however, when content facilitates, encourages or coordinates sexual encounters . . . between adults.* . . . We also restrict sexually-explicit language that may lead to sexual solicitation because some audiences within our global community may be sensitive to this type of content, and it may impede the ability for people to connect with their friends and the broader community. . . .
>
> Do not post: . . .
>
> Explicit sexual solicitation by, including but not limited to the following . . .
>
> Offering or asking for sex or sexual partners (including partners who share fetish or sexual interests).
>
> Sex chat or conversations.
>
> Nude photos/videos/imagery/sexual/fetish items.
>
> Sexual slang terms.[19]

In addition to banning sexually explicit imagery, community standards govern "suggestive elements," from mentions "or depictions of sexual activity such as sexual roles, sex positions, fetish scenarios, state of arousal, act of sexual intercourse or activity (e.g., sexual penetration or self-pleasuring), commonly sexual emojis" to "poses" left without additional clarification. This rather complex wording owes partly to regionally specific legal constraints such as the 2018 FOSTA-SESTA federal laws, which, while arguably targeting trafficking, have effectively kept sex work and sex workers off social media platforms.[20] As Ryan Conrad (chapter 6, this volume) argues in the context of third-party platforms used by male sex workers, these laws have a severe impact on the ability of sex workers to advertise their services, making the question of vulnerability, risk, and safety largely a question of data security. While these legal ramifications are particularly tangible within communities of sex workers, this has also led to limited possibilities for sexual communication for everyone. Discussions on sexual violence and exploitation are acceptable, even encouraged, in Meta's community standards, whereas exchanges connected to sexual pleasure and hooking up are out of bounds. A line is drawn at messages aiming to communicate sexual availability and arousal—even if this happens in roundabout ways through eggplant or peach emojis (also banned in the community standards).

Social media platforms basically aim to optimize contact and communication between users—be these close friends or strangers—as this increases the flows of user data to be monetized. Those desiring higher degrees of privacy have to adjust the default settings accordingly. In practice, Facebook content posted by users is visible to their friends and potential followers but rarely visible to the platform's other users, unless one opts for "public" status. In framing its service as a global community, Meta assumes the opposite, namely publicness as the norm. This is why, in accordance with community standards, what some users, somewhere, may find offensive is removed from the sight of all, even if the offended ones could not even access it. Specific focus is given to the screening out of sex, while racist and otherwise hateful content begs the question of freedom of speech and, in instances of complaint, is considered on contextual terms of the kind not applied to sexual content.

Consent does not factor into community standards, primarily since it is cumbersome to prove and document: "yes," in this context, is not recognized as a yes. As "suggestive elements," from nude drawings to content hinting at fetish scenarios and masturbation, are removed from the palette of acceptable exchanges, user agency, self-expression, the visibility of sexual cultures, and forms of sexual organizing are all truncated. The baroque wording of community standards nevertheless equally speaks of the vernacular creativity involved in circumventing them, as well as of the increasingly meticulous efforts at platform governance.

*Do not post:

Imagery of real nude adults, if it depicts:

Visible genitalia except in the context of birth giving and after-birth moments or if there is medical or health context situations (for example, gender confirmation surgery, examination for cancer or disease prevention/assessment).

Visible anus and/or fully nude close-ups of buttocks unless photoshopped on a public figure.

Uncovered female nipples except in the context of breastfeeding, birth giving and after-birth moments, medical or health context (for example, post-mastectomy, breast cancer awareness or gender confirmation surgery) or an act of protest. . . .

**Other sexual activities, except in cases of medical or health context, advertisements, and recognized fictional images or with indicators of fiction, including but not limited to:

Erections.

Presence of by-products of sexual activity.

Sex toys placed upon or inserted into mouth.

Stimulation of naked human nipples.

Squeezing female breasts, defined as a grabbing motion with curved fingers that shows both marks and clear shape change of the breasts. We allow squeezing in breastfeeding contexts.[21]

Dependent on targeted advertising and optimized flows of data, social media services operate within an economy of "peek-a-boo," where sexual content is, on the one hand, fully accepted as a titillating, attention-grabbing accent when applied according to corporate guidelines. On the other hand, displays of nudity are liberally conflated with obscenity and pornography, which cannot be posted, shared, or viewed. Community standards grow more detailed over time so as to accommodate mentions of anuses photoshopped on public figures. These revisions also arose in response to protests against previous practices of weeding out images of both breastfeeding and mastectomy as objectionable content; as a result, female breasts are, after a series of complaints, now acceptable on

Facebook in the context of cancer, breastfeeding, or social protest—instances that apparently save these body parts from their inherent obscenity.

The boundaries of appropriateness involved in this are far from clear, while the tools deployed in this involve algorithmic bias of their own. Robert W. Gehl, Lucas Moyer-Horner, and Sara K. Yeo, for example, argue that automatic patrols conducted via computer vision-based pornography filtering (CVPF) techniques operate with a highly limited set of assumptions: "that pornography is limited to images of naked women; that sexuality is largely comprised of men looking at naked women; and that pornographic bodies comport to specific, predictable shapes, textures, and sizes. . . . Judging from their published works and conference articles, computer scientists appear to be training computers to see the narrow form of pornography described above while dismissing a heterogeneous array of other forms of pornography (gay, queer, trans*, hardcore, fat, bondage, hairy, and so much more) as 'noise.'"[22]

The algorithms used for detecting objectionable content have long been primed to recognize white, young female bodies as pornographic objects of straight male desire, with this narrow conception of pornography resulting from gender and sexual inequalities within the tech sector more broadly: "when a field is dominated by straight men, those actors will likely inscribe . . . the shared assumptions and values of that dominant population into their technical output."[23] In this setting, female bodies remain the markers of sex, or objects of sexual desire, as well as symbols of obscenity, whereas "CVPF researchers are not teaching computers how to see penises. Although a lot of attention is paid to skin, some to nipples and breasts, and a smaller amount is paid to female genitals, the word 'penis' does not appear in the 102 articles" that Gehl, Moyer-Horner, and Yeo analyzed for their study.[24] Algorithms have been developed since that research was published, and penises are now indeed automatically filtered out from Facebook, Tumblr, and Instagram alike, and queer pornographies are astutely policed. At the same time, it remains the case that differently gendered bodies occupy structurally different positions as markers of sex.

To add further nuance to the algorithmic governance of images of undress, the newsletter *Salty* reported in 2019 that the Facebook and Instagram ad policy document pertaining to underwear and swimwear was "created in alignment with a Victoria's Secret's [sic] advertising campaign," explaining "in twenty-two bullet points the way models can sit, dress, arch their backs, pose, interact with props, how see-through their underwear can be, how the images can be cropped and where their ads can link to." The document only addressed the bodies of women, "referred to, exclusively, as 'girls.'"[25] As a mainstream marker of acceptable heterosexual sexiness (as well as a brand critiqued for sexism), Victoria's Secret becomes a marker in drawing lines between the acceptable and the unacceptable. In *Salty*'s analysis, this leads to direct discrimination against queer, women-run, body positive, and gender nonconforming content on the structural level of community standards.[26] In addition, these types of content are more easily flagged by other users as offensive or otherwise disturbing in violating gendered norms pertaining to body size, style, and aesthetic, as well as in conflicting with heterosexist notions of desirability.

The issue is, then, manifold. Following a general and strikingly affective puritan logic, sex and nudity become conflated and marked as offensive, even as ample room is left for displays of sexiness on Facebook and Instagram alike. In borderline cases between that which is "cheeky" yet acceptable and that which is not, bodies fitting the commercial template of Victoria's Secret form the norm. Such narrowly defined sexiness holds value for the platforms; more diverse sexual practices, exchanges, and cultures do not. It does not require a sensitive analytical eye to note heteronormative standards of acceptability and desirability as being at play in content policies that flatten out that which bodies can do, want, and be, as well as how their desires, shapes, and interactions can be communicated.

FREE THE NIPPLE!

Perhaps paradoxically, the visual logic of white, young female bodies is also prominent in feminist social media initiatives reacting to content policies on "female nipples." Disallowed in Facebook's, Instagram's, TikTok's, and Tumblr's community standards (Tumblr banning "female-presenting nipples" in a 2018 gesture of gender sensitivity), the visibility of women's nipples results in a range of visual products—from classic paintings to selfies and photos of archaeological objects such as the Willendorf Venus—being algorithmically flagged for violating community standards. At the same time, these platforms continue to host a wealth of artistic and humoristic strategies that play with censorship and nudity.

Activist resistance to Facebook's policies on nudity has been more than a decade in the making and has ranged from petitions to humorous memes and street protests.[27] The most visible and viral of these initiatives involves the tactical use of the hashtag #freethenipple. The launch of the Free the Nipple social media campaign is often credited to Lina Esco—a model, actor, film-maker, and activist—during pre-production for a 2014 comedy drama with the same title. Using the hashtag #freethenipple, in 2012 Esco posted on Facebook teaser clips that showed her running topless in New York. These clips were subsequently removed for violating community standards, and a number of celebrities, including Miley Cyrus, Rhianna, Chelsea Handler, Chrissy Teigen, and Lena Dunham posted nipple pics in support. These were also removed.

While being a networked social media cause for years, Free the Nipple seems very timely in times of increasingly tight social media content moderation. In a *New York Times* article aptly headlined "Will Instagram Ever 'Free the Nipple'?," Julia Jacobs is not too optimistic and observes how during these years "artists have put pressure on Facebook and Instagram to treat female and male nipples equally, but such a change may be too radical for Silicon Valley."[28]

With roots in the feminist movements of the 1960s and 1970s and campaigns for bodily integrity and equal rights, as well as the relaxed swimwear politics of sporting only bikini bottoms extending well into the 1980s, topless activism is a response to both puritanism and heterosexist sexualization of women's bodies. Free the Nipple revolves around gender equality and women's rights to choose how to display their bodies without the threat of violence. Toplessness then comes to serve as an interface and a means of protesting against how, in accordance with a firmly binary gender logic, both physical spaces (such as city streets) and social media platforms (such as Facebook and Instagram) allow men but not women to show off their nipples. Despite Facebook allowing users to define their gender beyond the default options of female and male, there is little that is nonbinary about how bodies and body parts are recognized on gendered terms.

Toplessness within Free the Nipple is further a means of confronting the views according to which female nudity is a source of shame and naked fe-male bodies are sexual by default. In the US context, within which we need to understand much of Meta's content regulation, about one-third of all state laws are either ambiguous vis-à-vis public toplessness or define it as illegal (e.g., Utah, Tennessee, and Indiana). And even in the majority of states where being topless in public is legal, such activities may lead to police involvement, given their contentious nature.

Celebrating nudity as a means of calling out gender inequality makes perfect sense since all bodies should enjoy the same kinds of freedoms. The rhetoric of top freedom movements such as Free the Nipple is nevertheless overde-termined by particular understandings of gender, sexuality and, above all, sexualization. If or when the nipple is freed, the argument goes, it is not merely let loose from the confines of clothing and underwear: the nipple is equally freed from male heterosexist domination and social norms delimiting the vis-ibility of unclad female bodies to cultural realms such as art or pornography, where these bodies become markers of beauty, desire, and obscenity, as well as a range of things beyond, and are valued accordingly. As Esco argues with respect to body shame and shaming, "the shaming of the female nipple is a direct reflection of how unevolved this puritanical country is. You can pay to see women topless in porn videos and strip clubs, but the moment a woman owns her body, it's shameful."[29] Following this line of argumentation, straight men control women's bodies by rendering them sexual objects of visual pleasure so that de-sexualizing female nipples becomes a logical and necessary step in and for female emancipation. Insofar as the nipple is set free, it does not get to signify sex. The nipple is then set free within a nonsexual social framework void of desires and viewing pleasures.

On the one hand, it remains necessary to argue for naked bodies not to be automatically sexual or sexualized, or for nudity to be simply conflated with pornography, as happens in community standards devoid of contextual nuance. Naked bodies, after all, do not signify just one thing. On the other hand, much is lost indeed if sexuality is simply done away with in the context of freed nip-ples and otherwise exposed bodies and not treated as an issue of importance, complexity, and gravity. Sexuality is not something that can simply be either present or absent in human bodies and visual depictions thereof; rather, it is something that underpins, drives, and orients these bodies in their encounters with the world as a contingent dynamic.

Free the Nipple is then not simply or perhaps even primarily about nipples. In an interview with *Time* magazine, Esco argues that "being topless is what we had to do [to] start a real dialogue about equality."[30] Female nipples become poster objects that in fact signify something else, as if nipples in and of themselves were not worthy of our attention. However, given that the campaign is also about reclaiming women's bodies and sexuality, nipples may have an import-ant role to play. We are then presented with a paradox. How can a campaign be about reclaiming women's sexuality when the overall argument is about de-sexualization? The easy answer seems to be that if the nipple can be sexually discharged, it can also be sexually recharged in women's self-shooting practices.

SEXUAL AGENCY AND QUEER VISUAL PLEASURES

In photographic self-shooting practices, the bare nipple becomes part of agentic processes of subject-making as a particular kind of sexual actor. This attempt to perform a shift from sexual objecthood, shame, and stigma to sexual subjecthood, agency, and pride is of course a familiar and established feminist tactic.[31] At the same time, the notion of objectification underpinning it remains simplified and problematic. Rather than understanding sexual objects and subjects as mutually exclusive categories in the binary vein of either/or, they can be more productively seen as simultaneous dynamics of relating. Sexual agency does not foreclose sexual objecthood, or vice versa: it is not only entirely possible but common to enjoy both looking and being seen, fetishizing someone and being fetishized, as well as to take pleasure in sexually desiring being recognized as desirable.[32] Blanket critiques of objectification do little to account for the kinds of relational agencies that underpin mundane sexual sociality.

In and through this shift, the Free the Nipple movement does not challenge slut shaming by firmly siding with the slut or with women proudly baring their flesh in contexts of commercial sex, for example. For who gets to feel bodily pride? Whose breasts and nipples get to be proudly visible and thus legitimate? And whose nipples are still bound by shame or are viewed as objectionable, offensive, or obscene? In a *Buzzsaw* article on Free the Nipple, Lizzy Ring wonders, "So where are the old women, women who aren't completely able-bodied, women of color, transgender women? I think that if an old lady were to 'free her nipple,' everyone might be like, 'Whoa . . . um, maybe we should repress the nipple a little bit.'"[33]

Free the Nipple has been applauded for tackling body shame and objectification, as well as critiqued for focusing on particular kinds of women and breasts, so that the movement may end up fueling rather than subverting the normative mechanisms that it criticizes.[34] To be sure, there is diversity to the social media archives brought together under the #freethenipple hashtag since 2012. But more than anything else, this is also privileged nipple feminism in the making, one building on photographic work dominated by white, cis, straight, and able female bodies and conforming to a range of heteronormative bodily norms that govern desirability and visibility in social media.[35]

It can then be argued that Free the Nipple extends Victoria's Secret templates of bodily display to the contested terrain of topless nudity in an antipuritan gesture while still conforming to the visual logics and body politics of the platforms on which it operates. Gretchen Faust argues that while #freethenipple sets to oppose objectification and censorship, its inner lack of diversity perpetuates the problem.[36] Different bodies may certainly be fetishized or sexualized differently, and thus it is far from clear that the freedom of one nipple means freedom for all. The female nipple, in its varying degrees of freedom and confinement, then becomes a contentious algorithmic object and a dividing line between profitable, conventionally attractive sexy bodies and those considered less lucrative, risky, and queer.

The Free the Nipple movement, while being clearly based on cisgender female anatomy, has to some extent come to include trans bodies and, consequently, a delinking of nipples and gender identifications. In October 2019, Facebook's downtown New York office hosted a meeting with artists and anticensorship activists about their policing of nudity. The meeting, according to those present, had unclear outcomes, if any. Some attendees put pressure on Facebook and other tech companies on behalf of transgender and nonbinary users: What counts as a female nipple? What if the person does not identify as female? Or if their nipples were previously anatomically male, while now part of a trans woman's body?[37] Or indeed, we might add, what if the nipples belong to bodies that cannot be understood with reference to gender binaries at all? Tumblr's attempt to "get it right" by consulting LGBTQ+ communities on appropriate terminology, which resulted in their not entirely successful phrasing "female-presenting nipples," did not help the cause. When algorithms and human commercial content moderators have done their job, it comes down to singling out the nipples that are considered offensive and, above all, inherently sexual.

What if we could imagine a decidedly more queer brand of nipple activism that does not aim to de-sexualize female-identified nipples but rather makes room for pleasures, desires, and fascinations so that these nipples are, in fact, seen as sexual? The question of pleasure does not surface in discussions around Free the Nipple, even as pleasure can indeed be key to nipple self-shooting practices and the sharing of, browsing through, looking at, and admiring of the resulting nipple shots. There is surprisingly little indication in the Free the Nipple movement that breasts and nipples hold sexual appeal among many women and other non-men.

The campaign embraces the feminist claim to every woman's right to be a sexual subject and to give and take pleasure freely and according to "her" own liking. So far so good. But what about the pleasures involved when "she" chooses to be a sexual object for the viewing pleasures of "herself" and others—the pleasure of seeing oneself and being seen in intimate pictorial registers? There is, obviously, a range of ways of looking and taking visual pleasure that have little to do with the notion of the straight male gaze, as operationalized in feminist critiques of objectification since the 1970s. The dynamics of looking and being seen are constantly bent, played with, or simply disrupted, not least in queer contexts where nipple pleasures are shared and devoured among people of diverse genders. What seems to be missing from many contemporary feminist social media initiatives is the conviction that in order to survive in networked contexts governed by puritan data politics, we need critically sex-positive, queer brands of feminism that embrace a wide variety of bodies, genders, sexual expressions, orientations, desires, and pleasures. In witnessing how social media sociality grows all the more devoid of sex, we argue for the value in re-sexualizing, or sexualizing anew, in ways respectful of consent, pleasure, and the diverse shapes that desires take.

CONSENSUAL SEXUAL DATA POLITICS

In a striking move in 2017, Facebook asked for users to send their nude selfies to the company in their campaign against so-called "revenge porn" (aka image-based sexual abuse). According to Antigone Davis, the company's head of international safety, "As part of our continued efforts to better detect and remove content that violates our community standards, we're using image matching technology to prevent nonconsensual intimate images from being shared on Facebook, Instagram, Facebook Groups and Messenger."[38] *The Independent* explained that "Facebook will create a digital fingerprint of a nude picture you flag up to it through Messenger, and automatically block anyone from uploading the same image to the site at a later date."[39]

While the details of the initiative were not always evident in the broad news coverage that it gained, this was an experimental Australian pilot endeavor. Involving both human and nonhuman actors—operations analysts and algorithms alike—the initiative, in something of a leap of faith, asked users to place more trust in Facebook than in their communication partners. Female users in particular were asked to upload and flag their own nudes in the name of safety. This points to the ubiquity of naked image sharing through Facebook back channels while also positioning the platform as premediator and preventer of nonconsensual image sharing—not by filtering out images through automated means but by teaching algorithms to recognize and remove them if flagged.

Since nudes—whether shared with consent or not—are horizontally banned to start with, the experiment further speaks of hesitance in terms of the efficacy of automated content moderation.

All in all, examinations of social media content policies shift attention away from the intentions and experiences of individual users and toward the infrastructures that make certain exchanges possible by design while automatically blocking others. As argued above, the algorithmic governance involved comes steeped in puritan politics and predictably sexist overtones focusing on female bodies as sites of visual risk—and framing women horizontally as potential victims of sexual harassment and abuse. The removal of sexual content and communication from social media pays no heed to distinctions between wanted and unwanted, solicited and unsolicited exchanges. Importantly, these data policies narrow sexual agency and pleasure within networked sociality.

Consent in relation to what Twitter terms "sensitive content" is an imperfect but doubtlessly more productive route in terms of agentic, pleasurable data politics than the horizontal policing of sex practiced by Meta. Reconciling the contractual functions of consent implicit in already ticked boxes (of "yes" and "no") with the subjective and elusive qualities of sexual desire and pleasure is, of course, a difficult task. Indeed, as Joseph Fischel argues, such reconciliation may be impossible within the legal bounds of consent, as consent in the affirmative shuts down or excludes more pleasure-driven, queer, and feminist sexual politics.[40] Consent in this rudimentary, contractual form nevertheless provides an opening for a broader range of networked exchanges respectful of sexual agency. For us, the question of consent as it intersects with both sex and data on social media platforms is crucial. As a starting point, consent offers a springboard for conversations about pleasure-fueled data politics that are less focused on the formal properties of content that "some people in our community may be sensitive to" and more concerned with desired—and in this sense safe—sexual sociality.

The female nipple is where Meta (along with many other platforms) draws the line in terms of appropriate content. While seemingly clear-cut, the policy is, in practice, fuzzy: areolas, for example, are allowed, and artistic value plays a part in what imagery passes muster, or not. In our reading, the contested nipples of social media speak of puritan data politics targeting sex and, more specifically, female bodies as sites of obscenity and risk, so as to effectively limit the ways in which these bodies can be seen and experienced. Feminist tactics aiming to recuperate nipples banned from platforms through nonsexualization, while aiming to expand the visual exchanges that nude photos can enter, easily reproduce the logic in which sex is seen as the terrain of potential harm to be countered in the ephemeral name of user safety: they equally downplay the role of pleasures involved in self-shooting, sexting, and visual displays. In a context where nudity is grouped together with hate speech, terrorism, and suicide as objectionable content, we need transformative politics that not only claim to treat all bodies equally but also speak to the value of sexual agency, desire, and pleasure in personal and social lives as they are both lived on and off social media platforms.

NOTES

ACKNOWLEDGMENTS: Research for this chapter has been supported by the Foundation for Baltic and East European Studies (Östersjöstiftelsen, grant no. 1035-3.1.1-2019), Strategic Research Council at the Academy of Finland (grant no. 327391), and SSSHARC, University of Sydney.

1. Meta, "Facebook Community Standards: Adult Nudity and Sexual Activity."

2. Hudson, "Obscenity and Pornography."

3. Paasonen, Jarrett, and Light, *Not Safe for Work*.

4. Gillespie, *Custodians of the Internet*, 35; Roberts, "Digital Detritus"; Srnicek, *Platform Capitalism*.

5. Paasonen, "Infrastructures of Intimacy"; Sundén, "Networked Intimacies."

6. For a discussion of platformed racist hate speech, see McPherson, "Digital Platforms and Hate Speech."

7. Paasonen, Jarrett, and Light, *Not Safe for Work*, 49–50.

8. Williams, *Marxism and Literature*, 132–33.

9. Williams, *Marxism and Literature*, 122.

10. Williams, *Marxism and Literature*, 123.

11. See Paasonen, Jarrett, and Light, *Not Safe for Work*, 169.

12. Barbrook and Cameron, "Californian Ideology."

13. Turner, *From Counterculture to Cyberculture*.

14. Marwick, *Status Update*.

15. *TNW*, 5 April 2018, https://thenextweb.com/news/facebook-confirms-it-spies-on-your-messenger-conversations; *Breitbart*, 5 April 2018, https://www.breitbart.com/tech/2018/04/04/report-facebook-messenger-analyzes-what-you-send-to-friends-family/; *News Tribune* (Tacoma, WA), 4 April 2018; *NZ Herald*, 5 April 2018, https://www.nzherald.co.nz/technology/zuckerberg-admits-facebook-scans-all-your-private-messenger-texts/W4A3X5LR5P4C2LPH66WYNCYYAI/.

16. Tiidenberg and van der Nagel, *Sex and Social Media*.

17. See, for example, Paasonen, Light, and Jarrett, *Not Safe for Work*; Tiidenberg and Gómez Cruz, "Selfies, Image and the Re-making of the Body"; and Waling and Pym, "'C'mon, No One Wants a Dick Pic.'"

18. Tiidenberg, "Playground in Memoriam"; Pilipets and Paasonen, "Nipples, Memes, and Algorithmic Failure."

19. Meta, "Facebook Community Standards: Sexual Solicitation" (emphasis added).

20. Blunt and Wolf, *Erased*.

21. Meta, "Facebook Community Standards: Adult Nudity and Sexual Activity."

22. Gehl, Moyer-Horner, and Yeo, "Training Computers to See Internet Pornography," 530.

23. Gehl, Moyer-Horner, and Yeo, "Training Computers to See Internet Pornography," 542.

24. Gehl, Moyer-Horner, and Yeo, "Training Computers to See Internet Pornography," 536.

25. Salty, "Exclusive: Victoria's Secret Influence on Instagram's Censorship Policies."

26. See also Are and Paasonen, "Sex in the Shadows of Celebrity," 415.

27. West, "Raging against the Machine."

28. Jacobs, "Will Instagram Ever 'Free the Nipple'?"

29. Esco, "'Free the Nipple' Is Not about Seeing Breasts."

30. Bussel, "Free the Nipple!"

31. Rúdolfsdóttir and Jóhannsdóttir, "Fuck Patriarchy!"

32. Paasonen et al., *Objectification*.

33. Ring, "Flaws of Free the Nipple."

34. Matich, Ashman, and Parsons, "#freethenipple."

35. Faust, "Hair, Blood and the Nipple"; Matich, Ashman, and Parsons, "#freethenipple"; West, "Raging against the Machine."

36. Faust, "Hair, Blood and the Nipple."

37. Jacobs, "Will Instagram Ever 'Free the Nipple'?"

38. See, for example, *Mashable*, 1 November 2017.

39. *The Independent* (UK), 8 November 2017.

40. Fischel, *Screw Consent*, 2–4. See also Sundén, "Play, Secrecy, and Consent."

BIBLIOGRAPHY

Are, Carolina, and Susanna Paasonen. "Sex in the Shadows of Celebrity." *Porn Studies* 8, no. 4 (2021): 411–19. https://doi.org/10.1080/23268743.2021.1974311.

Barbrook, Richard, and Andy Cameron. "The Californian Ideology." *Science as Culture* 6, no. 1 (1996): 44–72. https://doi.org/10.1080/09505439609526455.

Blunt, Danielle, and Ariel Wolf. *Erased: The Impact of FOSTA-SESTA and the Removal of Backpage*. Hacking/Hustling, 2020. https://hackinghustling.org/erased-the -impact-of-fosta-sesta-2020/.

Bussel, Rachel Kramer. "Free the Nipple! The Problem with How We Think about Breasts." *Time*, 12 December 2014. https://time.com/3631924/free-the-nipple-breasts -sex-symbol/.

Esco, Lina. "'Free the Nipple' Is Not about Seeing Breasts." *Time*, 11 September 2015. https://time.com/collection-post/4029632/lina-esco-should-we-freethenipple/.

Faust, Gretchen. "Hair, Blood and the Nipple: Instagram Censorship and the Female Body." In *Digital Environments: Ethnographic Perspectives across Global Online and Offline Spaces*, edited by Urte Undine Frömming, Steffen Köhn, Samantha Fox, and Mike Terry, 159–70. Bielefeld, Germany: Transcript, 2017.

Fischel, Joseph J. *Screw Consent: A Better Politics of Sexual Justice*. Oakland: University of California Press, 2019.

Gehl, Robert W., Lucas Moyer-Horner, and Sara K. Yeo. "Training Computers to See Internet Pornography: Gender and Sexual Discrimination in Computer Vision Science." *Television and New Media* 19, no. 6 (2017): 529–47. https://doi.org /10.1177/1527476416680453.

Gillespie, Tarleton. *Custodians of the Internet: Platforms, Content Moderation and the Hidden Decisions That Shape Social Media*. New Haven: Yale University Press, 2018.

Hudson, David L., Jr. "Obscenity and Pornography." *The First Amendment Encyclopedia*, 2009. https://mtsu.edu/first-amendment/article/1004/obscenity -and-pornography.

Jacobs, Julia. "Will Instagram Ever 'Free the Nipple'?" *New York Times*, 22 November 2019.

Marwick, Alice E. *Status Update: Celebrity, Publicity, and Branding in the Social Media Age*. New Haven: Yale University Press, 2013.

Matich, Margaret, Rachel Ashman, and Elizabeth Parsons. "#freethenipple: Digital Activism and Embodiment in the Contemporary Feminist Movement." *Consumption Markets and Culture* 22, no. 4 (2019): 337–62. https://doi.org/10.1080/10253866 .2018.1512240.

McPherson, Tara. "Digital Platforms and Hate Speech." Paper presented at the annual conference of the Society for Cinema and Media Studies, Toronto, 2018.

Meta. "Facebook Community Standards: Adult Nudity and Sexual Activity." Accessed 7 December 2022. https://transparency.fb.com/en-gb/policies/community -standards/adult-nudity-sexual-activity/.

——— . "Facebook Community Standards: Sexual Solicitation." Accessed 7 December 2022. https://transparency.fb.com/en-gb/policies/community-standards/sexual -solicitation.

Paasonen, Susanna. "Infrastructures of Intimacy." In *Mediated Intimacies: Connectivities, Relationalities and Proximities*, edited by Rikke Andreassen, Michael Nebeling Petersen, Katherine Harrison, and Tobias Raun, 103–16. London: Routledge, 2018.

Paasonen, Susanna, Feona Attwood, Alan McKee, John Mercer, and Clarissa Smith. *Objectification: On the Difference of Sex and Sexism*. London: Routledge, 2020.

Paasonen, Susanna, Kylie Jarrett, and Ben Light. *Not Safe for Work: Sex, Humor, and Risk in Social Media*. Cambridge, MA: MIT Press, 2019.

Paasonen, Susanna, Ben Light, and Kylie Jarrett. "The Dick Pic: Harassment, Curation, and Desire." *Social Media + Society* 5, no. 2 (2019). https://journals.sagepub.com/doi/full/10.1177/2056305119826126.

Pilipets, Elena, and Susanna Paasonen. "Nipples, Memes, and Algorithmic Failure: NSFW Critique of Tumblr Censorship." *New Media and Society* 24, no. 6 (2020): 1459–80. https://doi.org/10.1177/1461444820979280.

Ring, Lizzy. "The Flaws of Free the Nipple." *Buzzsaw*, 9 November 2016. http://www.buzzsawmag.org/2016/11/09/the-flaws-of-free-the-nipple/.

Roberts, Sarah T. "Digital Detritus: 'Error' and the Logic of Opacity in Social Media Content Moderation." *First Monday* 23, no. 3 (2018). https://journals.uic.edu/ojs/index.php/fm/article/view/8283/6649.

Rúdolfsdóttir, Annadís G., and Ásta Jóhannsdóttir. "Fuck Patriarchy! An Analysis of Digital Mainstream Media Discussion of the #freethenipple Activities in Iceland in March 2015." *Feminism and Psychology* 28, no. 1 (2018): 133–51. https://doi.org/10.1177/0959353517715876.

Salty. "Exclusive: Victoria's Secret Influence on Instagram's Censorship Policies." *Salty*, 22 November 2019. https://saltyworld.net/exclusive-victorias-secret-influence-on-instagrams-censorship-policies/.

Srnicek, Nick. *Platform Capitalism*. Cambridge: Polity, 2018.

Sundén, Jenny. "Networked Intimacies: Pandemic Dis/connections between Anxiety, Joy, and Laughter." In *Disentangling: The Geographies of Digital Disconnection*, edited by André Jansson and Paul Adams, 273–94. Oxford: Oxford University Press, 2021.

——— . "Play, Secrecy, and Consent: Theorizing Privacy Breaches and Sensitive Data in the World of Networked Sex Toys." *Sexualities*, 2020. https://journals.sagepub.com/doi/full/10.1177/1363460720957578.

Tiidenberg, Katrin. "Playground in Memoriam: Missing the Pleasures of NSFW Tumblr." *Porn Studies* 6, no. 3 (2019): 363–71. https://doi.org/10.1080/23268743.2019.1667048.

Tiidenberg, Katrin, and Edgar Gómez Cruz. "Selfies, Image and the Re-making of the Body." *Body and Society* 21, no. 4 (2015): 77–102. https://doi.org/10.1177/1357034X15592465.

Tiidenberg, Katrin, and Emily van der Nagel. *Sex and Social Media*. Bingley, UK: Emerald, 2020.

Turner, Fred. *From Counterculture to Cyberculture: Stewart Brand, the Whole Earth Network, and the Rise of Digital Utopianism*. Chicago: University of Chicago Press, 2010.

Waling, Andrea, and Tinonee Pym. "'C'mon, No One Wants a Dick Pic': Exploring the Cultural Framings of the 'Dick Pic' in Contemporary Online Publics." *Journal of Gender Studies* 28, no. 1 (2019): 70–85. https://doi.org/10.1080/09589236.2017.1394821.

West, Sarah Myers. "Raging against the Machine: Network Gatekeeping and Collective Action on Social Media Platforms." *Media and Communication* 5, no. 3 (2017): 28–36. https://doi.org/10.17645/mac.v5i3.989.

Williams, Raymond. *Marxism and Literature*. Oxford: Oxford University Press, 1977.

5 HIV Data as Queer Data *Biomedical Sexualities, Treatment-as-Prevention, and the New Sex Hierarchy for People Living with HIV*

The head of the clinic was soon able to determine the nature of Muzil's illness from the results of these tests, but to safeguard the reputation of his patient and colleague, he took steps to keep the truth from leaking out by monitoring the medical records and lab results linking that famous name to this new disease, by falsifying and censoring this paper trail so that Muzil could retain a free hand with his work until his death, unencumbered by troublesome rumors. He made the unusual decision not to tell even Muzil's companion, Stéphane, whom he knew slightly, so as to keep this terrible specter from haunting their friendship, but he did inform Muzil's assistant, so that he would devote himself more than ever to his employer's wishes and help him with his final projects.

—Hervé Guibert, *To the Friend Who Did Not Save My Life*

THE FRENCH NOVELIST HERVÉ GUIBERT wrote the above passage during the end of his life, in the late 1980s, as he sought treatment for his HIV.[1] The semiautobiographical novel *To the Friend Who Did Not Save My Life* recounts a series of unfulfilled promises about treatments-soon-to-come from the main character's well-connected friends. The secondary Muzil character is a literary evocation of Michel Foucault, who had been Guibert's friend and neighbor in Paris.[2] Foucault famously died of AIDS-related complications in 1984, several years before Guibert himself succumbed to the illness in 1991. The scene in the epigraph above, which describes how the Muzil character received his diagnosis, contains a notable trope in representations of HIV and AIDS: clinicians or health-care workers going out of their way to conceal a patient's diagnosis—or potential diagnosis—on medical records. This literary device functions as a kind of parable to illustrate the very real sensitivity of clinical HIV data, of the potential for an HIV diagnosis to alter the trajectory of a person's life and subjectivity, and of the danger of recording information about an HIV diagnosis even in ostensibly private medical records.

Consider the Roy Cohn character in Tony Kushner's play *Angels in America: A Gay Fantasia on National Themes*, which was first staged in 1991. When Kushner's fictionalized version of Cohn, the famous anticommunist attorney, is given his AIDS diagnosis, he demands that his physician falsify his medical records by reporting his condition as liver cancer. Cohn orders his doctor to do this on the premise that AIDS is a disease that homosexuals get, and Cohn is no homosexual. "Homosexuals are not men who sleep with other men," Cohn says. "Homosexuals are men who in fifteen years of trying cannot get a pissant antidiscrimination bill through City Council. Homosexuals are men who know nobody and who nobody knows. Who have zero clout." Following this diatribe, the doctor relents, while advising Cohn to seek treatment for AIDS by calling in favors from his powerful friends.[3]

A 1990 episode of the television show *The Golden Girls* titled "72 Hours" offers a different, slightly more lighthearted, example. In the episode, the Rose Nylund character (played by Betty White) receives an HIV test following news that she may have been exposed during a blood transfusion. A front desk worker at the clinic tells Nylund that she can opt to have an anonymous test or even provide a fictitious name. The punchline is that the name Nylund provides is that of her pal and confidante Dorothy Zbornak (played by Bea Arthur), who is standing next to Nylund during this moment of levity in an otherwise serious episode. Later in the episode, Nylund ends up testing negative.[4]

These three textual moments reproduce a narrative trope regarding HIV diagnosis that is bound together by two distinctive elements. The first is proactive work by medical professionals to falsify or obscure a patient's records in light of an actual or potential HIV diagnosis. The second is that each scene produces or invokes specific forms of deviant sexual subjectivity that are often generated by an actual or potential HIV diagnosis. These forms of sexual deviance are not necessarily functions of the characters' sexual orientations. Rather, the queer threat in these narratives stems primarily from the fact that the characters knew that they would be made to appear more sexually risky, as well as dangerous—*queer*—via confirmation that they have (or may have) HIV *and that information about their diagnosis could be written down and attached to a medical record.* When read in this way, the queerness produced in these scenes is structured as much by the fact of data collection about HIV as it is by the pathogen itself, its pathways of transmission, associated illnesses, or HIV stigma. Seen in this light, these representations of the potential for HIV data to produce queer subjectivities express some key underlying dynamics related to HIV data, its use by medical and public health authorities, and the role of HIV data in the production of deviant subject-positions.

In what follows, I describe how HIV data functions as a class of data that produces specific deviant sexual subjectivities, forms of queerness, and what I call "biomedical sexualities": *sexualities as they become constituted as objects of knowledge or intervention in health contexts.* I focus on how, during the 2010s in the United States, routinely collected clinical HIV data came to function as key vectors through which the sexualities of people living with HIV were reimagined and acted upon by state, biomedical, and public health actors. I describe how this was made possible through the implementation of universal names-based HIV case reporting since 2008, the reporting of data from routine HIV-related bloodwork to public health surveillance systems operated by state departments of public health since 2013, and the reuse of these data in surveillance and prevention investigations by health departments since 2014.[5]

I draw on health policy analysis research focused on US HIV/AIDS, LGBTQ health, and health information technology (IT) policy covering the period from 2009 to 2020, as well as over two years of fieldwork in the metropolitan Atlanta HIV/AIDS and LGBTQ health communities that I undertook from 2016 to 2019. I chiefly discuss how reuses of individuals' routine clinical HIV data by state and local departments of public health create new sexual hierarchies organized around an HIV disease management paradigm called "treatment-as-prevention."

HIV public health programs built around the HIV treatment-as-prevention paradigm are structured around knowledge that people living with HIV who are adherent to regimens of antiretroviral medications and who become "virally suppressed" or "undetectable" (registering a viral load of under 200 copies/milliliter of blood plasma) cannot pass the virus on to another person via sexual routes.[6] People living with HIV who are found to be out of HIV-related medical care or who are identified as posing an elevated transmission risk can be investigated and contacted by health department staff on this basis. States and localities implement these programs using guidelines from the Centers for Disease Control and Prevention (CDC), reusing people's routine clinical HIV data to enact what CDC refers to as enhanced forms of public health surveillance and outreach.[7]

Because this data collection, analysis, and investigatory work is conducted under public health law, it is done without the consent of people living with HIV.[8] Programs built to support treatment-as-prevention use routine HIV care data to make proactive determinations about presumed dangers that individuals pose based on whether they are retained in care and are thus biomedically compliant patient-subjects according to criteria defined by the state and enforced through federal guidelines implemented by states, municipalities, medical providers, and ultimately people living with HIV themselves. In this chapter, by explaining revolutions in US domestic HIV care, surveillance, and prevention in the era of treatment-as-prevention, I elaborate a theory of HIV data as queer data: a class of data that tends to generate forms of social, legal, and biomedical deviance in relation to individuals' sexual subjectivity.

NEW FORMS OF HIV DATA EXCEPTIONALISM IN THE ERA OF TREATMENT-AS-PREVENTION

The three fictional scenes that I discuss at the beginning of this chapter were first published, staged, or aired between 1990 and 1991, about six years before effective antiretroviral treatments for HIV became available to those with access to health care in high-income countries.[9] In the United States, before effective treatments were widely available, HIV data were treated as an "exceptional" class of health information that was subject to many restrictions on its collection, storage, exchange, and reuse.[10] However, as scholars such as Trevor Hoppe, Ronald Bayer, Amy Fairchild, Anthony K J Smith, and myself have documented, after effective HIV treatments became available, the way that HIV data were regulated and used changed rather dramatically.[11] Since that time, CDC-led initiatives such as the full rollout of mandatory names-based HIV case reporting by 2008, the active discouragement of anonymous HIV testing as part of "high-impact prevention," and the emergence of public health programs that reuse patients' data in public health investigations in order to support treatment-as-prevention goals have made the sort of privacy assurances offered to the Muzil, Cohn, and Nylund characters by their health-care providers in the 1980s and 1990s quite impossible to give in the contemporary moment.[12]

In my work, I document the emergence of new forms of HIV data exceptionalism in the United States that are specific to the era of treatment-as-prevention and that are defined by an expanded range of *mandatory reuses of routine HIV care data* that have been key to US HIV programs during the 2010s rather than the *restrictions on reuses of these data* that marked the 1980s to 2000s.[13] Since 2013, CDC has required laboratories to electronically report individuals' routine clinical HIV bloodwork data to jurisdictional departments of public health in order to track rates of engagement and retention in care among people living with HIV.[14] The classes of routinely collected clinical HIV bloodwork data include viral load (a marker of disease progression and infectiousness), CD4-T cell count (a marker of immune health), and HIV genetic sequence data (often called "drug resistance" data or "molecular" data).[15]

These routine clinical HIV data are also no longer used only for epidemiological surveillance but also for direct prevention outreach aimed at individuals and groups of people living with HIV who are identified as out of care or otherwise posing an elevated transmission risk.[16] During investigations, state and local departments of public health regularly exchange and/or cross-match individuals' HIV data with other sources of information held by government agencies, health-care systems, and private services such as LexisNexis.[17] This work is done without individuals' consent, and people living with HIV are generally not informed that their data are used in this manner.[18]

Therefore, whereas in the 1980s and 1990s HIV data were an exceptional class of health information with many restrictions governing their exchange, reuse, and disclosure, since the 2010s clinical HIV data have become increasingly exceptional in the reverse. Following mandates from CDC, state and local public health agencies are now required to reuse patients' clinical HIV data in enhanced surveillance and prevention programs that are aimed at modifying the care-seeking behaviors of people living with HIV. In the era of HIV treatment-as-prevention, HIV data that are collected from people living with HIV during routine testing and care are no longer merely barometers used by clinicians to measure individual health. These data are also transmitted to and reused by public health agencies in ways that mark people who are living with HIV but not retained in consistent HIV-related medical care as sexually dangerous, deviant, risky, and queer, while rewarding those who are able to remain in care and virally suppressed.[19]

HIV DATA AS QUEER DATA: PRODUCING
DEVIANT BIOMEDICAL SEXUALITIES

In my usage, *data are queer when they come to bear on the sexual subjectivity of a data subject, thus marking them as deviant according to the terms of the contemporary sexual system.* Said otherwise, queer data is information — generally recorded and stored in a manner that renders it retrievable and usable at a future point in time by actors in the health system — that indicates something about a person that suggests that the individual in question (the "data subject") might be out of compliance with the terms of heteronormativity. Queer data are the means through which sexually marginalized people and groups can be turned into *queer data subjects* who can subsequently be interpreted, acted upon, or shaped by uses of those data and/or resistances to those uses.

My use of "data subject" is informed by three separate conceptual genealogies. The first is in regulatory and policy discourse, as in the "data subject" referred to in the European Union's General Data Protection Regulation (GDPR): a person about whom data is recorded.[20] The second is the language of research ethics, as in the "human subject" of biomedical, behavioral, or survey research: subjectivity abstracted from the person and recorded as information to facilitate systematic analysis. The third is the language of poststructuralist theories of subjectivity in relation to technologies of social control and systems of classification: the subject-positions created through what Michel Foucault described as the "specification of individuals" in volume 1 of *The History of Sexuality* or through practices of datafication that produce what Gilles Deleuze described as "dividuals" in his "Postscript on the Societies of Control."[21] In each framework, data function as a kind of socio-technical engine for generating subjectivities. In my usage, when data bear on the sexuality of a data subject and denote sexual abnormality, deviance, or risk, those data can be characterized as queer data.[22]

HIV data are exemplary queer data. Through their reuse by health-care providers and public health agencies in programs that target noncompliant HIV data subjects for enhanced scrutiny, HIV data create new kinds of queer data subjects whose deviance is continuously monitored in health data infrastructures and then acted upon by state and biomedical actors. The aim of programs in this area is to bring people living with HIV into care in order to improve their health while also mitigating the risk that they will transmit HIV.

Confirmation that antiretroviral treatments for HIV are essentially totally effective in preventing sexual transmission has placed an extreme onus on people living with HIV to comply with treatment regimens. Remaining in treatment for HIV is now not only framed as a way to enable people living with HIV to live a normal lifespan; treatment-as-prevention has also turned the bodies of people living with HIV and their health-seeking behaviors into a kind of living prophylaxis.

So, HIV data are queer because they deeply shape the contemporary politics of sexuality, particularly for groups that are disproportionately affected by HIV/AIDS. Indeed, for many queer subpopulations, such as gay and bisexual men, transgender persons, and sex workers, information about one's own HIV serostatus and the serostatus of others (including information about viral suppression) provides an array of coordinates that help to choreograph an elaborate set of techniques that inform sexual practice in relation to HIV transmission risk.[23]

In this chapter, I am interested in the biomedical sexualities that are produced through new reuses of data about HIV that mark some people living with HIV as compliant and others as deviant. These biomedical sexualities are created by (and produce new forms of) what Martin French and Gavin Smith call "'health' surveillance," which are practices operationalized across domains through direct interventions that are enacted by providers, public health agencies, people living with HIV themselves, and a potentially unlimited range of other actors who can become "enrolled" in various public health and care-related activities (to borrow an idiom from actor-network theory).[24] These biomedical sexualities produce new "sexual realities," a term that I lift from classicist Robert Padgug's essay "Sexual Matters" to refer to the ways in which sexuality gives form to everyday life through and beyond sexual acts.[25]

This conceptualization of biomedical sexualities is in dialogue with, but distinct from, what sociologist of sexuality and science Steven Epstein discusses under the rubric of "biosexual citizenship."[26] Epstein draws on the work of sociologist Aaron T. Norton as well as literatures about "sexual citizenship" and "biocitizenship" to describe how sexual health policies can play a role in reshaping individual and group conduct. In contrast, my framework of biomedical sexualities bears specifically on how person-level biomarkers such as HIV status or viral suppression are generated in clinical settings, transmitted to and stored in data infrastructures to facilitate systematic reuses, and then are used to act upon specific people at particular moments in time based on the continuous monitoring of their health status in order to affect their sexual risk profile. Regarding biosexual citizenship, Epstein and Norton are primarily

concerned with forms of disciplinary power and modes of governing populations that are most commonly associated with the work of Michel Foucault and
normative public health frameworks that aim to improve population health
outcomes.[27] With biomedical sexualities, I aim to elucidate forms of power
that are rooted in inducing ongoing forms of behavioral modulation that are
aimed at individual people, a project more closely associated with the work of
Gilles Deleuze on the "societies of control" and emergent uses of public health
data that are primarily intended to improve the health outcomes of individual
people, with an overall public benefit as a potential secondary effect.[28]

QUEER: DEVIANT SEXUAL SUBJECTIVITY

My use of the term "queer" draws from three distinct tendencies in writing on
sexual politics and HIV/AIDS. I use it to refer to specific groups—queerness as
an attribute connoting sexual marginalization—and as shorthand for "sexual
and gender minorities and people living with HIV."

My primary analytical orientation vis-à-vis "queer" comes from sexuality
studies. This use of the term takes nonheterosexuality, nonheteronormative
modes of life, and forms of embodied, felt, or perceived sexual deviance as its
key definitional axis. Queerness refers to sexual categories, subjectivities, power
structures, or acts that do not fit within the parameters of normative acceptability, progression toward domestic familial life, or sexual tendencies lying in
a narrow range allowed in what anthropologist Gayle Rubin characterizes as
"the charmed circle" of "Good, Normal, Natural, Blessed Sexuality" deemed
acceptable by straight society.[29] Like Rubin, I understand sexuality as a system
of power with "its own internal politics, inequities, and modes of oppression."[30]
Sexuality is thus not reducible to the effects of other systems that structure and
order society, such as gender, race, class, and (dis)ability. Sexuality can therefore
be described independently of other systems of power, "if only for analytical
purposes," to quote sexuality studies scholar Rostom Mesli.[31]

My secondary use of "queer" stems from the first: an umbrella term for
sexual and gender minorities, LGBTQ people, or the sexually marginalized.
"Queer," here, is what David M. Halperin calls "an identity without an essence
. . . available to anyone who is or who feels marginalized because of his or her
sexual practices."[32] Notably, this use of "queer" marks transgender and gender
nonconforming individuals as queer. However, it does so not through a kind
of lumping in of noncisgender subjects with other sexual minorities, such as

lesbians, gay and bisexual men, fetishists, or sex workers. Rather, queerness in this mode marks gender minorities as queer using the logics of the first definitional axis: as positioned on the lower rungs of the sex hierarchy due to gender non-normativity's many associations with sexual deviance in cisheteronormative societies.

Taking cues from political scientist Cathy Cohen, this second use of "queer" frames people as queer who—while perhaps not technically sexual minorities—do not conform to other normativities in ways that mark them as being sexually deviant or abnormal.[33] This queer marking occurs much in the same way for gender minorities as it might for heterosexuals who remain uncoupled and are queer because of their noncohabitation with sexual-romantic partners, or in the ways that certain classes of Black women are framed as sexually excessive, or in the manner that many disabled and elderly people who cannot have normative sex are rendered queer.[34]

These subjects are queer not because of their gender, race, age, or ability but as an effect of their subjectivities not fitting into the charmed circle sustained by the sexual system. It would be a serious analytical error to say that queerness in this second mode is an effect of gender, race, class, disability, or even sexual orientation (in the case of the long-term uncoupled heterosexual).[35] Rather, these forms of queer (i.e., sexually deviant) subjectivity are outcomes of the ways in which the modern sexual system positions certain subjects *within its own hierarchies*, which are specific to the politics of sex and which become overlaid and entangled with other vectors of oppression in intersectional assemblages or what the sociologist of sexuality Jay Orne calls the "intersectional knot."[36]

The third tendency that informs my use of "queer" bears specifically upon the ways that HIV produces forms of queerness (i.e., sexual deviance). It stems directly from Cindy Patton's usage of the "queer paradigm" in her 1985 text *Sex and Germs* and her elaboration of this in her 1990 book *Inventing AIDS*.[37] This use of "queer" is about how deviant sexual practices were deemed more so when associated with AIDS. Patton's "queer paradigm" refers to the so-called "4-H paradigm," meaning homosexuals, hemophiliacs, heroin addicts, and Haitians, who were most commonly associated with AIDS in US epidemiological and media discourse in the mid- to late 1980s.[38] When I use "queerness" in this third mode, it is as an extension of the first and second: queer as sexually deviant because of a characteristic that is not (per se) about sexuality (HIV serostatus) but that marks people as aberrant within the logics of the sexual system owing to associations with sexual danger and risk. This association becomes further reinforced when this information is written down and reused, becoming part of the everyday labor of what sociologist Martin French calls "informatic practice" in public health.[39]

My use of "queer" thus encompasses all people living with HIV. This is because HIV-positive serostatus marks people living with HIV as queer, owing to HIV's association with deviant sexuality and risk, and because people living with HIV are subjected to exceptional forms of continuous public health surveillance, investigation, and direct intervention if they are found to be nonadherent; it is a literal and a figurative marking.[40] And, in the treatment-as-prevention paradigm, certain classes of people living with HIV have been marked as being queerer than others. People living with continuously suppressed HIV are less biomedically and sexually deviant than are, on the other extreme, people with untreated HIV who fetishize its transmission. There are infinite degrees between these two poles, neither of which have set limits.

HIV DATA PRODUCING QUEER SUBJECTIVITIES

In this section, I discuss three brief cases that show how different classes of routinely collected HIV care data that are reported to health departments in the United States produce forms of queerness. I first show how data about HIV viral load and CD4-T cell count create queer data subjectivities that are organized around *temporality and compliance* with medication regimens and long-term retention in continuous HIV-related medical care.[41] Second, I describe HIV genetic sequence data that are reported to health departments and are used to model "molecular transmission clusters" of people with genetically similar strains of HIV. HIV molecular cluster detection and response programs generate new forms of *biosocial relationality* among people living with HIV that are structured by the genetic content of the strain(s) of virus in their bodies.[42] In the third brief case, I discuss the state of North Carolina's HIV Control Measures, which were revised in 2018 to allow people living with HIV who are retained in care and have received a viral load test demonstrating suppression during the previous six months to not use condoms or disclose their HIV-positive serostatus to sexual partners. The North Carolina example shows how treatment-as-prevention policies create new *hierarchies of disclosure* organized by viral load and retention in care that are enforced through policy.

The HIV Care Continuum: Queerness
in Relation to Temporality and Compliance

The HIV Care Continuum is a framework for managing HIV at the individual and population levels that has become dominant in the United States since 2013. Adoption of the care continuum accelerated following the launch of the HIV Care Continuum Initiative by presidential executive order in 2013.[43] Since that time, federal, state, and local HIV programs have been expanded or built to manage HIV using the care continuum as their grounding model. The care continuum produces forms of queerness structured by *temporality and compliance* in relation to retention in HIV-related medical care and reaching viral suppression. If a state or local health department stops receiving routine bloodwork for specific people living with HIV, they can be put on HIV "out of care" or "not in care" lists; these lists are also sometimes called "out of care watch lists," as was the case in Georgia during my ethnographic fieldwork with the HIV public health safety net in the Atlanta metro area.[44] By utilizing a policy framework and set of tools developed by CDC called "Data to Care," state and local health departments can investigate and reach out to people on these lists and target them for re-linkage.[45]

The HIV Care Continuum is a narrative in five stages. Stage 1, "Diagnosed with HIV," means that an individual has received an HIV-positive diagnosis. Stage 2, "Linked to Care," means that the individual has scheduled their first medical appointment. Stage 3, "Engaged or Retained in Care," means that the individual has reported HIV-related bloodwork following a medical visit. Stage 4, "Prescribed Antiretroviral Therapy," means that a person living with HIV has started a regimen of antiretroviral medications designed to reduce their viral load. Stage 5, "Achieved Viral Suppression" means that the last viral load count for that person was under 200 copies/milliliter of blood plasma (i.e., suppressed), a level at which they are noninfectious via sexual routes.[46] The goal of the HIV Care Continuum is both to provide a narrative to frame HIV treatment and to support treatment-as-prevention by linking this narrative to public health work.

HIV Molecular Cluster Detection and Response:
New Queer Biosocial Relations

In 2018, CDC began requiring all state and local HIV surveillance jurisdictions to begin collecting and using HIV genetic sequence data, which is also sometimes called molecular HIV data, drug resistance data, or HIV genotype data.[47] HIV genetic sequence data are sent to HIV surveillance systems by testing laboratories when a clinician orders a test for a patient living with HIV to determine if a person's HIV is resistant to specific medications. These tests are usually ordered when an individual initiates treatment or reengages in care.

At the population level, tracking genetic mutations in individuals' HIV allows researchers and surveillance personnel at departments of public health to identify clusters of people with strains of HIV in their bodies that are closely related at the genetic level; this is an indicator of potential recent transmission and that individuals are in a shared transmission network.[48] Close genetic relationships among strains can be used to identify "HIV transmission clusters" — groupings of people whose strains of HIV suggest that they are in a network of people where transmission has recently taken place.[49] In 2019, "HIV molecular cluster detection and response" programs that require health departments to use HIV genetic sequence data to model transmission clusters and then to conduct enhanced investigations aimed at them became the "fourth pillar" of the federal Ending the HIV Epidemic initiative.[50]

HIV molecular cluster detection and response programs use HIV genetic sequence data along with data gathered during investigations to create new forms of *biosocial relationality* among people living with HIV and HIV-negative people who are identified as contacts.[51] These forms of molecular relationality in an HIV transmission network place people living with HIV in material relation to each other, first within CDC-supported and jurisdictional data management platforms and, second, through public health investigations that are aimed at people who are identified in clusters based on the genetic profile of their HIV in relation to others' HIV along with other epidemiological information.[52] Through public health investigations that involve the notification of sexual partners and various other forms of health department personnel reaching out to people living with HIV and potentially their medical providers, these modes of relationality extend beyond these public health data platforms and into daily life.

North Carolina's Modernized HIV Control Measures: New Hierarchies of Sexual Deviance

Advocates and scholars have noted that treatment-as-prevention discourses create new hierarchies of value that can restigmatize people living with HIV who are not retained in care and consistently taking antiretroviral medications.[53] While most people living with HIV can become virally suppressed through medication adherence, some are physiologically unable to do so.[54] Far more persons with HIV experience structural barriers to remaining in consistent medical care, particularly in the United States.[55] For people living with HIV who can remain virally suppressed, treatment-as-prevention has been transformational because of the assurance that they cannot transmit HIV via sexual routes.[56] People who cannot sustain viral suppression are unable to reap these benefits.[57]

Actions by the state of North Carolina demonstrate how the creation of new sexual hierarchies structured around treatment-as-prevention has happened in concrete terms. In 2018, North Carolina "modernized" the section of its public health code called "HIV Control Measures," restructuring them around treatment-as-prevention.[58] The HIV Control Measures are set by the administrative arm of the state government and govern when people living with HIV are legally obligated to disclose their status to sexual and needle-sharing partners. The revised control measures create a hierarchy that valorizes viral suppression and creates clear legal and biomedical divisions between people living with HIV who are not virally suppressed and those who are. Verification of viral suppression hinges upon whether individuals (1) are in care, (2) are following their care plan, and (3) have a viral load test documenting suppression within the last six months. People living with HIV who meet all three conditions do not have to use a condom or disclose their HIV-positive serostatus to sexual partners.[59]

A technical assistance letter from the HIV and STD director of the North Carolina Division of Public Health that was sent to local health departments and HIV care providers in 2018 describes the revised HIV Control Measures. Beyond the three criteria for sexual nondisclosure, the letter contains various instructions, including that "all [people living with HIV], whether virally suppressed or not, must NOT . . . [s]hare needles, syringes, or other injection drug related equipment" or donate blood, tissue, or organs unless as part of a study.[60] Therefore, changes to parameters around disclosure in the state's HIV Control Measures are not generalizable to all potential transmission routes but are specific to sexual pathways. The "modernized" measures for the control of HIV specifically restructure how arms of the state manage the sexualities of people living with HIV on biomedical terms. The implementation of the policy also requires collaboration between public health agencies, health-care providers, changing standards of care, and potentially the criminal justice system if an individual is found to be in violation of the disclosure requirements.[61] The letter also directs clinicians to communicate the new control measures to their patients who are living with HIV.

THE NEW SEX HIERARCHY
FOR PEOPLE LIVING WITH HIV

At the very end of 1983, when Muzil was back coughing worse than ever[,] . . .
I said to him, "Actually, you hope you have AIDS." He shot me back a look, one
that brooked no appeal.

—Hervé Guibert, *To the Friend Who Did Not Save My Life*

The brief case studies in the previous section show how HIV data produce
deviant sexual subject-positions in the era of treatment-as-prevention through
three key vectors: (1) *temporality and compliance* around treatment plans,
(2) *biosocial relationality with other people living with HIV* through the measurement of genetic similarity between individuals' strains of HIV, and (3) the
creation of new hierarchies of acceptability and deviance for people living with
HIV regarding their disclosure to sexual partners. These three vectors together
produce an "intensification" to help support what I call the *new sex hierarchy
for people living with HIV*: a set of logics for understanding and addressing HIV
transmission that are mainly produced by public health institutions and are
specific to the era of HIV treatment-as-prevention.[62]

The new sex hierarchy for people living with HIV is constructed around the
interpretation and enforcement of various regimes of HIV data subjectivity
by biomedical, public health, and other actors using clinical HIV data, other
sources of data gathered during investigations, and forms of self-surveillance
by people living with HIV in relation to transmission risk that are structured
by contemporary medication adherence and care regimens.[63]

Here, I present a diagram of the new sex hierarchy for people living with HIV
(fig. 5.1). The vertical line on the far left indicates degrees of goodness versus
badness of an individual person living with HIV according to the terms of the
contemporary sexual system. The full diagram is further divided into three
shaded horizontal blocks arranged in descending order of "goodness." On the
right side of the vertical line, in circles within each block, I note dominant
framings, public health activities, and other actions that can be taken against
people living with HIV in the current historical moment. Farther to the right, in
hexagons within each block, I note the various deviance-defining data elements
and behaviors of people living with HIV that define the hierarchy.

People living with HIV who are consistently retained in care with a suppressed viral load are situated at the top of the new sex hierarchy for people

The New Sex Hierarchy
for People Living
with HIV

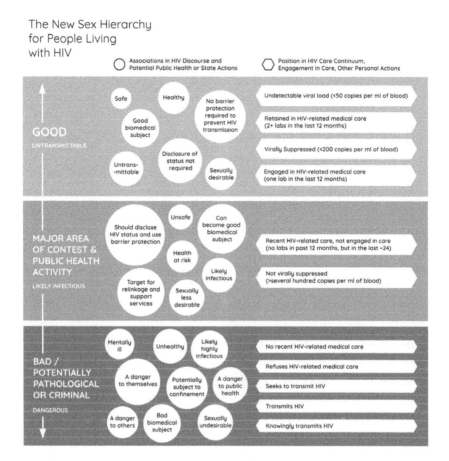

FIGURE 5.1. The new sex hierarchy for people living with HIV.

living with HIV. They are not made objects of enhanced forms of public health investigation owing to their compliance with treatment regimens. The middle section is what I call—drawing from Rubin's framing of the "sex hierarchy" in her essay "Thinking Sex"—the "major area of contest" and public health activity that gives structure and form to the hierarchy.[64] This area encompasses policies, programs, clinical guidelines, public health investigations, and other forces designed to identify and bring uncompliant or nonadherent people living with HIV back into treatment, thus leading to viral suppression and noninfectiousness.

On the bottom of the hierarchy, people who eroticize seroconversion emerge as a kind of unthinkable HIV data subject or as an HIV data subject interpreted by the logics of public health as being so dangerous that they must be managed using very extreme measures. The person who eroticizes seroconversion appears as the sort of individual with whom the health system has no other way to deal than by calling them criminals or as being so deviant that they ought to be subjected to prosecution or enhanced public health measures that resemble criminal enforcement, such as confinement or court-ordered treatment.[65] These abject HIV data subjects are cut out of the imagined constituency of efforts to reform HIV laws, with so-called "malicious infectors" often being discussed as exactly the sort of person whom HIV criminalization reform packages are designed *not* to protect.[66] People who transmit HIV are often discussed without attention to context, such as whether a person living with unsuppressed virus was engaged in acts of sex in exchange for money, housing, food, or another circumstance that might lead an individual not to disclose their HIV-positive serostatus or to transmit HIV.[67]

CONCLUSION: BUILDING
CRITICAL HIV DATA STUDIES

The day after Muzil died, I had lunch with Stéphane in a pizzeria near
his place. He told me that Muzil's illness had been AIDS, and that he'd known
nothing about this until the previous evening, when he'd gone with Muzil's sister
to the hospital registrar's office and they'd both seen the entry in the registrar at
the same moment: "Cause of death: AIDS." The sister had demanded that they
cross this out, that they blacken it completely, or scratch it out if they had to,
or even better, tear out the page and redo it, for while these records are
of course confidential, still, you never know, perhaps in ten or twenty years
some muckraking biographer will come and Xerox the entry, or X-ray the
impression still faintly legible on the page.
—Hervé Guibert, *To the Friend Who Did Not Save My Life*

HIV data are queer data because HIV data are central to the production of the sexual subjectivities of people living with and affected by HIV. HIV data produce valorized and deviant biomedical sexualities and sexual realities that generate queer subject-positions, identities, modes of life, and even potentially political programs or regimes of public health action. Biomedical and state actors work to control and shape the actions of people living with HIV through reuses of HIV data that are aimed at bringing them into compliance with medication treatment regimens, thus acting to move them higher up on the new sex hierarchy for people living with HIV. If people living with HIV fail—or are unable—to comply with these regimes of compliance, they are subjected to additional forms of control: public health investigations and relinkage-to-care processes, which generate more data about them.[68]

The creation of public health programs designed to do this work has been facilitated by new digital health infrastructures that enable exchanges of HIV data between clinicians, laboratories, health-care systems, public health agencies, researchers, and other institutions that play a role in keeping people living with HIV retained in care.[69] In closing, I draw from papers in the currently disaggregated and emergent field of what might be called "critical HIV data studies" to offer a framework for conceptualizing how HIV data produce different forms of queerness as scientific understandings of the illness change.[70] I do so with an eye toward the next phase of HIV prevention programs—for whatever era may come after treatment-as-prevention—and in the spirit of fostering what I have elsewhere described, with Anthony K J Smith, as "HIV data justice," which "draws on the collective resources of the HIV/AIDS movement to build new alliances aimed at providing affected individuals and communities with greater control over how their data are utilized in the healthcare system, with the paired aim of providing them with greater access to better services on terms of their own choosing."[71]

In "Organizing for Ontological Change: The Kernel of an AIDS Research Infrastructure," science and technology studies scholars David Ribes and Jessica Polk describe the research apparatus of the long-term Multicenter AIDS Cohort Study (MACS), the core infrastructure of which is built around current knowledge about HIV/AIDS and the need to anticipate shifts in basic HIV science.[72] New paradigms that I have examined here show that this logic of being "organiz[ed] for ontological change" also extends to the practice of managing HIV by public health institutions and the form of the data infrastructures and epistemic frameworks that are used to manage HIV epidemics and individual people living with HIV. Periodically, some combination of advances precipitates a revolution in the general approach to managing HIV, as has most recently occurred with treatment-as-prevention.[73] The response to new innovations is built upon older infrastructures that have been structured to be responsive to these shifting conditions.

To reflect this underlying reality, critical studies of HIV data should be similarly organized to anticipate ontological changes in our object(s) of analysis. Critical HIV data studies should operate in the modality that anthropologist Tom Boellstorff calls "prolepsis," or rhetorical anticipation, in his article "But Do Not Identify as Gay: A Proleptic Genealogy of the MSM Category."[74] That essay is a reflection on the emergence of the "men who have sex with men" (MSM) classification in HIV prevention and its purported uptake as a category of self-identification rather than exclusively of epidemiological classification. Critical HIV data studies scholars should look to the future of HIV data, always working to be one step ahead of biomedicine and public health, even as health professionals innovate new practices that will likely not become accessible until after they have been deployed. Critical HIV data studies ought to be a simultaneously empirical and speculative practice, working alongside activists, practitioners, and people living with HIV to imagine a variety of futures. Further, the field ought to focus not only on these issues in the Global North but also on using transnational frameworks to understand the digitization of HIV public health data and the effects of HIV treatment-as-prevention paradigms in the Global South.[75]

Critical HIV data studies can conceptualize HIV data and HIV data practices as objects of inquiry to be constantly subjected to analytical procedures of critique. By paying ruthlessly close attention to the trajectory of uses of HIV data as a scholarly practice of the self, critical HIV data scholars can develop forms of academic subjectivity and methodology that work at articulating what Foucault characterized as the "historical ontology of ourselves" or a force "seeking to give new impetus, as far and wide as possible, to the undefined work of freedom"—a mode of self-styling that emerges from the limits of the sayable.[76] Further, through the translation of the findings of critical HIV data studies into political struggles, critical HIV scholars can potentially assist in unmaking the various and myriad injustices that structure the contemporary governance of HIV.

NOTES

ACKNOWLEDGMENTS: I thank my ethnographic interlocutors. I also thank people who read or provided feedback on various iterations of this work; they include Alexandra Minna Stern, Tom Boellstorff, David M. Halperin, Gayle S. Rubin, John Cheney-Lippold, Anthony K J Smith, and Alexander McClelland. The "Producing Transformations: Drugs, Bodies, and Experimentation" open panel at the 2018 meeting of the

Society for Social Studies of Science, held in Sydney, provided an opportunity to present an early version of this chapter; I thank Kane Race, Kiran Pienaar, and Dean Murphy for organizing that session. I also thank the four anonymous reviewers, all of whom engaged with the substance of my arguments and improved the chapter. I also thank Sara Grimes, Kenji Toyooka, and the Knowledge Media Design Institute (KMDI) at the University of Toronto for assistance in preparing figure 5.1. Finally, I extend my deep appreciation to Patrick Keilty for envisioning and editing *Queer Data Studies* and for being a mentor and supportive colleague for many years. Funding for a portion of this research was provided by the Rackham Graduate School at the University of Michigan.

1. Hervé Guibert, *To the Friend Who Did Not Save My Life*, trans. Linda Coverdale (1990; New York: High Risk Books, 1991), 37.

2. Tom Roach, "Impersonal Friends: Foucault, Guibert, and an Ethics of Discomfort," *New Formations: A Journal of Theory/Culture/Politics*, no. 55 (2005): 54–72.

3. Tony Kushner, *Angels in America: A Gay Fantasia on National Themes* (1991; New York: Theatre Communications Group, 2013), 45–47.

4. *The Golden Girls*, season 5, episode 19, "72 Hours," directed by Terry Hughes, aired 17 February 1990 on NBC.

5. Stephen Molldrem, "How to Build an HIV Out of Care Watch List: Remaking HIV Surveillance in the Era of Treatment as Prevention," *First Monday* 25, no. 10 (2020), https://doi.org/10.5210/fm.v25i10.10295; Stephen Molldrem and Anthony K J Smith, "Reassessing the Ethics of Molecular HIV Surveillance in the Era of Cluster Detection and Response: Toward HIV Data Justice," *American Journal of Bioethics* 20, no. 10 (2020): 10–23, https://doi.org/10.1080/15265161.2020.1806373; Patricia Sweeney, Lytt I. Gardner, Kate Buchacz, Pamela Morse Garland, Michael J. Mugavero, Jeffrey T. Bosshart, R Luke Shouse, and Jeanne Bertolli, "Shifting the Paradigm: Using HIV Surveillance Data as a Foundation for Improving HIV Care and Preventing HIV Infection," *Milbank Quarterly* 91, no. 3 (September 2013): 558–603, https://doi.org/10.1111/milq.12018.

6. Alison J. Rodger, Valentina Cambiano, Tina Bruun, Pietro Vernazza, Simon Collins, Olaf Degen, et al., "Risk of HIV Transmission through Condomless Sex in Serodifferent Gay Couples with the HIV-Positive Partner Taking Suppressive Antiretroviral Therapy (PARTNER): Final Results of a Multicentre, Prospective, Observational Study," *The Lancet* 393, no. 10189 (June 2019): 2428–38, https://doi.org/10.1016/S0140-6736(19)30418-0.

7. CDC, "Detecting and Responding to HIV Transmission Clusters: A Guide for Health Departments," June 2018, https://www.cdc.gov/hiv/pdf/funding/announcements/ps18-1802/CDC-HIV-PS18-1802-AttachmentE-Detecting-Investigating-and-Responding-to-HIV-Transmission-Clusters.pdf; CDC, "Data to Care Program Guid-

ance: Using HIV Surveillance Data to Support the HIV Care Continuum (the 'Data to Care Toolkit')," 2017, https://www.cdc.gov/hiv/pdf/funding/announcements/ps18-1802 /CDC-HIV-PS18-1802-AttachmentJ-Data-to-Care-Program-Guidance.pdf .

8. Liza Dawson, Nanette Benbow, Faith E. Fletcher, Seble Kassaye, Amy Killelea, Stephen R. Latham, Lisa M. Lee, et al., "Addressing Ethical Challenges in US-Based HIV Phylogenetic Research," *Journal of Infectious Diseases*, 11 June 2020, 3, https://doi .org/10.1093/infdis/jiaa107; Sweeney et al., "Shifting the Paradigm."

9. Ronald Bayer, "Public Health Policy and the AIDS Epidemic: An End to HIV Exceptionalism?," *New England Journal of Medicine* 324, no. 21 (23 May 1991): 1500–1504, https://doi.org/10.1056/NEJM199105233242111.

10. Gerald M. Oppenheimer and Ronald Bayer, "The Rise and Fall of AIDS Exceptionalism," *AMA Journal of Ethics* 11, no. 12 (1 December 2009): 988–92, https://doi.org /10.1001/virtualmentor.2009.11.12.mhst1-0912.

11. Trevor Hoppe, *Punishing Disease: HIV and the Criminalization of Sickness* (Oakland: University of California Press, 2018), 69–73; Amy L. Fairchild and Ronald Bayer, "HIV Surveillance, Public Health, and Clinical Medicine: Will the Walls Come Tumbling Down?," *New England Journal of Medicine* 365, no. 8 (25 August 2011): 685–87, https://doi.org/10.1056/NEJMp1107294; Molldrem, "How to Build an HIV Out of Care Watch List"; Molldrem and Smith, "Reassessing the Ethics of Molecular HIV Surveillance in the Era of Cluster Detection and Response"; Stephen Molldrem, Anthony K J Smith, and Alexander McClelland, "Predictive Analytics in HIV Surveillance Require New Approaches to Data Ethics, Rights, and Regulation in Public Health," *Critical Public Health* 33, no. 3 (May 27, 2023): 275–81, https://doi.org/10.1080/09581596.2022.2113035.

12. Fieldwork interview with two HIV testing managers in Atlanta, 7 July 2017; CDC, *HIV Surveillance Report, 2011*, vol. 23, February 2013, 5, https://www.cdc.gov/hiv /pdf/library/reports/surveillance/cdc-hiv-surveillance-report-2011-vol-23.pdf.

13. Molldrem, "How to Build an HIV Out of Care Watch List"; Molldrem and Smith, "Reassessing the Ethics of Molecular HIV Surveillance in the Era of Cluster Detection and Response"; CDC, "Data to Care"; CDC, "Detecting and Responding to HIV Transmission Clusters."

14. Kenneth Castro and Amy Lansky, "'Dear Colleague' Letter Announcing New Guidelines for Electronic Laboratory Reporting Data," US Department of Health and Human Services, 21 November 2013, https://www.cdc.gov/hiv/pdf/statistics_Lab _reporting_DCL_final.pdf.

15. Molldrem, "How to Build an HIV Out of Care Watch List"; Molldrem and Smith, "Reassessing the Ethics of Molecular HIV Surveillance in the Era of Cluster Detection and Response"; Alexander McClelland, Adrian Guta, and Marilou Gagnon, "The Rise of Molecular HIV Surveillance: Implications on Consent and Criminalization," *Critical Public Health*, 20 February 2019, 1–7, https://doi.org/10.1080/09581596.2019.1582755.

16. Project Inform Staff, "Using Surveillance and Other Data to Improve HIV Care Linkage and Retention," University of Rochester Center for Community Practice, 7 June 2012, https://www.urccp.org/Images_Content/Site1/Files/Pages/Think_Tank _Report-_Surv_Data_for_LTC.pdf; Don Evans and Nanette Dior Benbow, "Ethical Considerations for a Public Health Response Using Molecular HIV Surveillance Data," Project Inform and Northwestern University, February 2018, https://digitalhub.north western.edu/files/1bff6ec0-af92-48dd-a8e2-d17e4ac4f1ec.

17. Molldrem, "How to Build an HIV Out of Care Watchlist"; CDC, "Data to Care"; CDC, "Detecting and Responding to HIV Transmission Clusters"; fieldnotes and interviews with personnel in Atlanta involved in HIV surveillance and prevention.

18. Cecilia Chung, Naina Khanna, Barb Cardell, Andrew Spieldenner, Sean Strub, Alexander McClelland, Martin French, Marilou Gagnon, and Adrian Guta, "Consent and Criminalisation Concerns over Phylogenetic Analysis of Surveillance Data," *The Lancet/HIV* 6, no. 7 (July 2019): e420, https://doi.org/10.1016/S2352-3018(19)30138-9; McClelland, Guta, and Gagnon, "Rise of Molecular HIV Surveillance."

19. Karen C. Lloyd, "Centring 'Being Undetectable' as the New Face of HIV: Transforming Subjectivities via the Discursive Practices of HIV Treatment as Prevention," *BioSocieties* 13, no. 2 (June 2018): 470–93, https://doi.org/10.1057/s41292-017 -0080-1; Chelsea Cormier McSwiggin, "Moral Adherence: HIV Treatment, Undetectability, and Stigmatized Viral Loads among Haitians in South Florida," *Medical Anthropology* 36, no. 8 (17 November 2017): 714–28, https://doi.org/10.1080/01459740 .2017.1361946.

20. "General Data Protection Regulation (GDPR), Article 4. Definitions," 2016, https://gdpr-info.eu/art-4-gdpr/.

21. Michel Foucault, *The History of Sexuality: Volume 1; An Introduction*, trans. Robert Hurley (New York: Vintage Books, 1978), 42–44; Gilles Deleuze, "Postscript on the Societies of Control," *October* 59 (Winter 1992): 3–7.

22. This is a different definition of "queer data" than the one used by Kevin Guyan in *Queer Data: Using Gender, Sex and Sexuality Data for Action* (London: Bloomsbury Academic, 2022). Guyan's book focuses on the role of data collection in LGBTQ politics and was published during the composition of this edited volume.

23. Douglas Crimp, "How to Have Promiscuity in an Epidemic," *October* 43 (Winter 1987): 237–71; Limin Mao, June M. Crawford, Harm J. Hospers, Garrett P. Prestage, Andrew E. Grulich, John M. Kaldor, and Susan C. Kippax, "'Serosorting' in Casual Anal Sex of HIV-Negative Gay Men Is Noteworthy and Is Increasing in Sydney, Australia," *AIDS* 20, no. 8 (May 2006): 1204–6, https://doi.org/10.1097/01.aids.0000226964.17966 .75; Michael E. Newcomb, Melissa C. Mongrella, Benjamin Weis, Samuel J. McMillen, and Brian Mustanski, "Partner Disclosure of PrEP Use and Undetectable Viral Load on

Geosocial Networking Apps: Frequency of Disclosure and Decisions about Condomless Sex," *JAIDS: Journal of Acquired Immune Deficiency Syndromes* 71, no. 2 (February 2016): 200–206, https://doi.org/10.1097/QAI.0000000000000819; Lisa Jean Moore, "'It's Like You Use Pots and Pans to Cook. It's the Tool': The Technologies of Safer Sex," *Science, Technology, and Human Values* 22, no. 4 (October 1997): 434–71, https://doi.org /10.1177/016224399702200402.

24. Martin French and Gavin Smith, "'Health' Surveillance: New Modes of Monitoring Bodies, Populations, and Polities," *Critical Public Health* 23, no. 4 (December 2013): 383–92, https://doi.org/10.1080/09581596.2013.838210; Michel Callon and John Law, "On Interests and Their Transformation: Enrolment and Counter-Enrolment," *Social Studies of Science* 12, no. 4 (November 1982): 615–25, https://doi.org/10.1177 /030631282012004006.

25. Robert A. Padgug, "Sexual Matters: On Conceptualizing Sexuality in History," *Radical History Review* 1979, no. 20 (1 April 1979): 10, https://doi.org/10.1215/01636545 -1979-20-3.

26. See Steven Epstein, "Governing Sexual Health: Bridging Biocitizenship and Sexual Citizenship," in *Biocitizenship: The Politics of Bodies, Governance, and Power*, ed. Kelly E. Happe, Jenell Johnson, and Marina Levina (New York: New York University Press, 2018), 21–50.

27. Michel Foucault, *Discipline and Punish: The Birth of the Prison*, 2nd ed. (New York: Vintage Books, 1975), 170–230.

28. Deleuze, "Postscript on the Societies of Control." For an analysis of how big data practices are shifting the aims of some public health programs from improving population-level health to improving individuals' health, see Molldrem, Smith, and McClelland, "Predictive Analytics in HIV Surveillance Require New Approaches to Data Ethics, Rights, and Regulation in Public Health."

29. Gayle Rubin, "Thinking Sex: Notes for a Radical Theory of the Politics of Sexuality," in *Deviations: A Gayle Rubin Reader* (Durham, NC: Duke University Press, 2011), 152–53.

30. Rubin, "Thinking Sex," 138.

31. Rostom Mesli, "Gayle Rubin's Concept of 'Benign Sexual Variation': A Critical Concept for a Radical Theory of the Politics of Sexuality," *South Atlantic Quarterly* 114, no. 4 (October 2015): 804, 823, https://doi.org/10.1215/00382876-3157144.

32. David M. Halperin, *Saint Foucault: Towards a Gay Hagiography* (Oxford: Oxford University Press, 1995), 62.

33. Cathy J. Cohen, "Punks, Bulldaggers, and Welfare Queens: The Radical Potential of Queer Politics?," *GLQ: A Journal of Lesbian and Gay Studies* 3, no. 4 (1 January 1997): 437–65, https://doi.org/10.1215/10642684-3-4-437.

34. See also Shaka McGlotten, "Black Data" (chapter 1, this volume).

35. Halperin, *Saint Foucault*, 62.

36. Rubin, "Thinking Sex," 149–54; Jay Orne, *Boystown: Sex and Community in Chicago* (Chicago: University of Chicago Press, 2017), 11, 62–78.

37. Cindy Patton, *Sex and Germs: The Politics of AIDS* (Boston: South End Press, 1985), 10–12; Cindy Patton, *Inventing AIDS* (New York: Routledge, 1990), 117. See also Adam M. Geary, *Antiblack Racism and the AIDS Epidemic: State Intimacies* (New York: Palgrave Macmillan, 2014), 9–29.

38. Patton, *Sex and Germs*, 10–12; Patton, *Inventing AIDS*, 117; Geary, *Antiblack Racism and the AIDS Epidemic*, 9–29.

39. Martin French, "Gaps in the Gaze: Informatic Practice and the Work of Public Health Surveillance," *Surveillance and Society* 12, no. 2 (2014): 227, https://doi .org/10.24908/ss.v12i2.4750.

40. CDC, "Data to Care"; Molldrem, "How to Build an HIV Out of Care Watchlist."

41. See especially Kane Race, *Pleasure Consuming Medicine: The Queer Politics of Drugs* (Durham, NC: Duke University Press, 2009), 106–63.

42. CDC, "Detecting and Responding to HIV Transmission Clusters." On HIV and biosocial relationality, see Gabriel Girard, San Patten, Marc-André LeBlanc, Barry D. Adam, and Edward Jackson, "Is HIV Prevention Creating New Biosocialities among Gay Men? Treatment as Prevention and Pre-Exposure Prophylaxis in Canada," *Sociology of Health and Illness*, 18 November 2018, https://doi.org/10.1111/1467-9566.12826.

43. The White House, "Executive Order—HIV Care Continuum Initiative," 15 July 2013, https://obamawhitehouse.archives.gov/the-press-office/2013/07/15/executive -order-hiv-care-continuum-initiative.

44. CDC, "Data to Care"; Molldrem, "How to Build an HIV Out of Care Watchlist."

45. Julia C. Dombrowski, Joanna Bove, James C. Roscoe, Jessica Harvill, Caislin L. Firth, Shireen Khormooji, Jason Carr, et al., "'Out of Care' HIV Case Investigations: A Collaborative Analysis across 6 States in the Northwest US," *JAIDS: Journal of Acquired Immune Deficiency Syndromes* 74 (February 2017): S81–87, https://doi.org/10.1097/QAI .0000000000001237.

46. Eugene McCray and Jonathan Mermin, "'Dear Colleague' Letter announcing CDC's Position That 'People Who Take ART Daily as Prescribed and Achieve and Maintain an Undetectable Viral Load Have Effectively No Risk of Sexually Transmitting the Virus to an HIV-Negative Partner,'" Dear Colleague Letters, 27 September 2017, https://www.cdc.gov/nchhstp/dear_colleague/2017/dcl-092717-National-Gay -Mens-HIV-AIDS-Awareness-Day.html; Victoria Mobley, "Guidance Letter: Modernization of North Carolina's HIV Control Measures," 13 March 2018, https://www .mecknc.gov/HealthDepartment/CDControl/ForProviders/Health%20Advisory%20 Documents/Updated%20NC%20HIV%20Control%20Measures.pdf.

47. Evans and Benbow, "Ethical Considerations for a Public Health Response Using

Molecular HIV Surveillance Data"; McClelland, Guta, and Gagnon, "Rise of Molecular HIV Surveillance;" Molldrem and Smith, "Reassessing the Ethics of Molecular HIV Surveillance in the Era of Cluster Detection and Response."

48. Alexandra M. Oster, Anne Marie France, and Jonathan Mermin, "Molecular Epidemiology and the Transformation of HIV Prevention," *JAMA* 319, no. 16 (24 April 2018): 1657, https://doi.org/10.1001/jama.2018.1513.

49. Edwin J. Bernard, Barb Cardell, Cecilia Chung, Marco Castro-Bojorquez, Martin French, Devin Hursey, Naina Khanna, et al., "We Are People, Not Clusters!," *American Journal of Bioethics* 20, no. 10 (2 October 2020): 1–4, https://doi.org/10.1080 /15265161.2020.1809550.

50. Department of Health and Human Services (HHS), "Ending the HIV Epidemic: A Plan for America," 7 February 2019, https://www.hhs.gov/sites/default/files/ending -the-hiv-epidemic-fact-sheet.pdf; Anthony S. Fauci, Robert R. Redfield, George Sigounas, Michael D. Weahkee, and Brett P. Giroir, "Ending the HIV Epidemic: A Plan for the United States," *JAMA* 321, no. 9 (5 March 2019): 844, https://doi.org/10.1001 /jama.2019.1343.

51. On biosociality, see Paul Rabinow, "Artificiality and Enlightenment: From Sociobiology to Biosociality," in *Essays on the Anthropology of Reason* (Princeton: Princeton University Press, 1996), 91–111. On biosocialities and molecular HIV data, see Johanna T. Crane, "Viral Cartographies: Mapping the Molecular Politics of Global HIV," *BioSocieties* 6, no. 2 (June 2011): 142–66, https://doi.org/10.1057/biosoc.2010.37; and Tony Sandset, "The Ethical and Epistemological Pitfalls of Translating Phylogenetic HIV Testing: From Patient-Centered Care to Surveillance," *Humanities and Social Sciences Communications* 7, no. 1 (December 2020), https://doi.org/10.1057/s41599-020 -0522-4.

52. CDC, "Detecting and Responding to HIV Transmission Clusters."

53. Lloyd, "Centring 'Being Undetectable' as the New Face of HIV"; Susan Kippax and Niamh Stephenson, *Socialising the Biomedical Turn in HIV Prevention* (London: Anthem, 2016), 96; Center for HIV Law and Policy, "Consensus Statement on HIV 'Treatment as Prevention' in Criminal Law Reform (2017)," 13 July 2017, https://www .hivtaspcrimlaw.org/the-consensus-statement.

54. Francis Kiweewa, Allahna Esber, Ezra Musingye, Domonique Reed, Trevor A. Crowell, Fatim Cham, Michael Semwogerere, et al., "HIV Virologic Failure and Its Predictors among HIV-Infected Adults on Antiretroviral Therapy in the African Cohort Study," ed. Luis Menéndez-Arias, *PLoS ONE* 14, no. 2 (5 February 2019): e0211344, https://doi.org/10.1371/journal.pone.0211344.

55. Kaiser Family Foundation, "HIV Viral Suppression Rate in U.S. Lowest among Comparable High-Income Countries," 3 June 2022, https://www.kff.org/hivaids/slide /hiv-viral-suppression-rate-in-u-s-lowest-among-comparable-high-income-countries/.

56. This was evident in the discourse among my interlocutors during the duration of my fieldwork beginning in 2016 and was particularly pronounced during immersive fieldwork at the 2018 International AIDS Conference, where many attendees walked around the conference with stickers attached to their shirts that stated, "Can't Pass It On." See also Lloyd, "Centring 'Being Undetectable' as the New Face of HIV." For a somewhat different perspective, see Andrew R. Spieldenner, "Infectious Sex? An Autoethnographic Exploration of HIV Prevention," *QED: A Journal in GLBTQ World-making* 4, no. 1 (2017): 121, https://doi.org/10.14321/qed.4.1.0121.

57. McSwiggin, "Moral Adherence."

58. State of North Carolina, "Control Measures—HIV," 10A NCAC 41A .0202 § (2018), http://reports.oah.state.nc.us/ncac/title%2010a%20-%20health%20and %20human%20services/chapter%2041%20-%20epidemiology%20health/subchapter %20a/10a%20ncac%2041a%20.0202.html.

59. Mobley, "Guidance Letter."

60. Mobley, "Guidance Letter."

61. Center for HIV Law and Policy, "North Carolina," in *HIV Criminalization in the United States: A Sourcebook on State and Federal HIV Criminal Law and Practice* (New York, 2018), 1–15, https://www.hivlawandpolicy.org/sourcebook.

62. On "intensification," see Gilles Deleuze and Félix Guattari, *A Thousand Plateaus: Capitalism and Schizophrenia*, trans. Brian Massumi (Minneapolis: University of Minnesota Press, 1987), 232–309. See also Orne, *Boystown*, 145–49.

63. Race, *Pleasure Consuming Medicine*, 106–63; Spieldenner, "Infectious Sex?"

64. Rubin, "Thinking Sex," 153.

65. Hoppe, *Punishing Disease*, 68–98; Alexander McClelland, "'Lock This Whore Up': Legal Violence and Flows of Information Precipitating Personal Violence against People Criminalised for HIV-Related Crimes in Canada," *European Journal of Risk Regulation* 10, no. 1 (March 2019): 132–47, https://doi.org/10.1017/err.2019.20; NSW Health, "Policy Directive—Management of People with HIV Who Risk Infecting Others," 17 January 2019, https://www1.health.nsw.gov.au/pds/ActivePDSDocuments /PD2019_004.pdf; Adrian Guta, Marilou Gagnon, and Morgan M. Philbin, "Ethical Convergence and Ethical Possibilities: The Implications of New Materialism for Understanding the Molecular Turn in HIV, the Response to COVID-19, and the Future of Bioethics," *American Journal of Bioethics* 20, no. 10 (2 October 2020): 26–29, https:// doi.org/10.1080/15265161.2020.1806400; Alexander McClelland, Martin French, Eric Mykhalovskiy, Marilou Gagnon, Eli Manning, Ryan Peck, Chad Clarke, and Tim Mc-Caskell, "The Harms of HIV Criminalization: Responding to the 'Association of HIV Diagnosis Rates and Laws Criminalizing HIV Exposure in the United States,'" *AIDS* 31, no. 13 (August 2017): 1899–1900, https://doi.org/10.1097/QAD.0000000000001570.

66. Ryan Grimes, "Expert: Michigan's HIV Disclosure Law 'Inappropriate,' De-

signed to Chase 'Boogeyman,'" Michigan Radio, 5 April 2016, https://www.michigan radio.org/post/expert-michigans-hiv-disclosure-law-inappropriate-designed-chase -boogeyman.

67. Interview with a longtime HIV prevention professional, Atlanta, GA, January 2017. See also Tim Dean, *Unlimited Intimacy: Reflections on the Subculture of Bare-backing* (Chicago: University of Chicago Press, 2009); Hugh Klein, "Generationing, Stealthing, and Gift Giving: The Intentional Transmission of HIV by HIV-Positive Men to Their HIV-Negative Sex Partners," *Health Psychology Research* 2, no. 3 (22 October 2014), https://doi.org/10.4081/hpr.2014.1582.

68. For a discussion about how data that are collected during HIV surveillance activities are then used to inform future surveillance work, with implications for queer subjectivities, see Martin Holt, "Enacting and Imagining Gay Men: The Looping Effects of Behavioural HIV Surveillance in Australia," *Critical Public Health* 23, no. 4 (December 2013): 404–17, https://doi.org/10.1080/09581596.2013.796038.

69. Guta, Gagnon, and Philbin, "Ethical Convergence and Ethical Possibilities"; Molldrem, "How to Build an HIV Out of Care Watchlist"; Molldrem and Smith, "Re-assessing the Ethics of Molecular HIV Surveillance in the Era of Cluster Detection and Response."

70. Critical HIV data studies would emerge from, or alongside, the existing subfield of critical HIV studies. See Eric Mykhalovskiy and Viviane Namaste, eds., *Thinking Differently about HIV/AIDS: Contributions from Critical Social Science* (Vancouver, BC: UBC Press, 2020); and Jih-Fei Cheng, Alexandra Juhasz, and Nishant Shahani, eds., *AIDS and the Distribution of Crises* (Durham, NC: Duke University Press, 2020).

71. Molldrem and Smith, "Reassessing the Ethics of Molecular HIV Surveillance in the Era of Cluster Detection and Response," 13.

72. David Ribes and Jessica Beth Polk, "Organizing for Ontological Change: The Kernel of an AIDS Research Infrastructure," *Social Studies of Science* 45, no. 2 (April 2015): 214–41, https://doi.org/10.1177/0306312714558136.

73. Kippax and Stephenson, *Socialising the Biomedical Turn in HIV Prevention*, 96.

74. Tom Boellstorff, "But Do Not Identify as Gay: A Proleptic Genealogy of the MSM Category," *Cultural Anthropology* 26, no. 2 (May 2011): 287–90, https://doi.org/10 .1111/j.1548-1360.2011.01100.x. See also Richard Parker, Peter Aggleton, and Amaya G. Perez-Brumer, eds., "Double Special Issue: The Trouble with 'Categories': Rethinking Men Who Have Sex with Men, Transgender and Their Equivalents in HIV Prevention and Health Promotion," *Global Public Health* 11, no. 7–8 (13 September 2016): 819–23, https://doi.org/10.1080/17441692.2016.1185138.

75. In a parallel vein regarding queer forms of resistance to datafication in the Global South, see Suisui Wang, "Situated Indications: Queer STS Experiments on Global Datafication" (chapter 10, this volume).

76. Michel Foucault, "What Is Enlightenment?," in *The Essential Foucault: Selections from Essential Works of Foucault, 1954–1984*, ed. Paul Rabinow and Nikolas S. Rose (1984; New York: New Press, 2003), 54. See also Karl Marx, "For a Ruthless Criticism of Everything Existing (Letter to A. Ruge)," in *The Marx-Engels Reader*, ed. Robert C. Tucker and Friedrich Engels, 2nd ed. (New York: Norton, 1978), 12–15.

RYAN CONRAD

6 Generated Vulnerability *Male Sex Workers,*
Third-Party Platforms, and Data Security

HUSTLERS, HOOKERS, DANCERS, RENT BOYS, ESCORTS, TRADE, or just your average university student struggling to figure out how to make ends meet— guys who sell sexual services are everywhere. While popular culture and law enforcement are preoccupied with human trafficking and while media stereotypes of destitute women prowling seedy back alleys are omnipresent, men who sell sex are largely absent from view. This is in spite of the fact that men are estimated to account for nearly a quarter of the commercial sex industry in North America and Europe.[1] They account for an estimated $1 billion market in the United States alone.[2]

Many thousands of men across the world have used Rentboy.com to advertise their services since the site launched in 1997.[3] The homes of Easyrent Systems, Inc., staff and the New York City office of Easyrent Systems, Inc., the company that owned and operated Rentboy.com, were simultaneously raided by federal agents, including those for the Department of Homeland Security and Immigration and Customs Enforcement (ICE), in 2015. This abruptly ended Rentboy.com's near twenty-year run operating in public view. Staff were arrested and computers containing digital records—legal names, credit card numbers, government-issued identification documents—for many thousands of guys who had purchased advertising space on the platform were seized. After a year of protests by gay and sex worker activists against the raid and the shuttering of Rentboy, only the chief executive officer, Jeffrey Hurant, was charged. He pleaded guilty to "promoting prostitution" and "money laundering conspiracy" in an arranged plea agreement and served a six-month prison sentence.[4] What remains of the sensitive personal data collected by Rentboy, now in the hands of US federal law enforcement, and how it has been used is unknown. In Rentboy's absence, other third-party advertising platforms have risen to prominence, most notably the Bulgarian-based Rent.men that dominates the third-party advertising industry for guys who sell sex, with an average of nearly 1.5 million site views per month.[5]

Researchers have noted that little scholarly attention has been paid to third parties involved in various aspects of the commercial sex industry.[6] Businesses like Rentboy.com or Rent.men that are neither the client nor the service provider are but two obvious examples of the many possible third parties involved in facilitating smooth transactions between clients and sex workers for a fee. Unfortunately, the few studies on third parties that do exist focus exclusively on women, whose perceived gendered vulnerability to so-called pimps, procurers, and traffickers makes them a more likely research subject.[7] Scholarship that does focus on advertisements placed by guys who sell sex on third-party websites tends toward in-depth content analysis while either ignoring or treating online third-party advertising platforms as benign.[8] Even the much anticipated *Routledge Handbook of Male Sex Work, Culture, and Society* (2021) features an entire section on internet-based sex work, yet none of the chapters in that section offer any critical analysis of third-party advertising platforms themselves. Conversely, this chapter takes up these very platforms as its object of study.

The following pages reflect on how data privacy on third-party for-profit advertising websites geared toward sex workers is managed and which types of vulnerabilities are generated through this corporate model. This chapter begins with the documented and possible further harms of the Rentboy.com data breach as a result of the raid in 2015 and investigates the strategies, or lack thereof, put in place by the owners of Rent.men to prevent similar data breaches, as detailed in their "Privacy Policy" and "Terms of Service" statements. Lastly, this chapter turns to the data privacy strategies of online advertising platforms created and managed by sex worker–owned cooperatives like Ottawa Independent Companions (OIC) in Canada. Through an in-person interview with a founding member of the organization, a comparison can be made between the risk mitigation strategies of OIC's hyperlocal, democratic, collaborative, and demonstrably more secure data privacy model and the faceless, revenue-hungry transnational corporations making millions off sex workers with little accountability to the very people they claim to be serving and supporting.

THE FALL OF RENTBOY.COM

On Tuesday morning, 25 August 2015, news websites and broadcast news channels in the United States showed viewers images of numerous federal agents from Homeland Security and ICE carrying computer towers and bank boxes marked "evidence" to a white police van. These items were removed from the Manhattan office of Easyrent Systems, Inc., and would be the material evidence used to prosecute Jeffrey Hurant. These computer towers and paper records likely held sensitive information of all sorts, including detailed personal information of the men who purchased advertising space on Rentboy's popular website. This would include legal names, credit card information, and copies of government-issued identification documents—all materials required by the company to place advertisements. While in the end only the CEO of the company was prosecuted, the extent of the surveillance on individual advertisers utilizing the website, and which records of theirs were kept, remains an unanswered question eight years after the raid. The whereabouts of this seized evidence today are unknown; however, it likely remains in the custody of federal law enforcement.

The raid on Rentboy took place among a constellation of other high-profile raids, as well as the quotidian harassment, intimidation, and arrest of sex workers in the United States and Canada—particularly of working-class, racialized, and/or transgender women who sell sex. The raid of San Francisco–based myRedBook.com, a website primarily used by women in the commercial sex industry, was raided by agents from the Federal Bureau of Investigation (FBI) almost exactly one year before the raid of Rentboy.[9] In 2012, the Canadian government introduced legislation to ban temporary foreign workers from the legal commercial sex industry, and, in 2014, it criminalized the purchasing of sexual services for the first time in Canadian history. In the aftermath of the Rentboy raid, the targeting of sex workers online continued with the decision by American Express, Visa, and MasterCard in 2015 to block the use of their credit cards to pay for individual ads on sex worker–friendly websites like Backpage.com.[10] Then, in 2017, Backpage.com ended its "adult services" section on US pages under a threat of federal prosecution for sex trafficking.[11] This was followed by the FBI seizure of Backpage.com and seven sex trafficking-related indictments against Backpage.com employees in 2018.[12]

The raid on Rentboy and these other targeted raids on sex worker–friendly third-party websites has elicited largely divergent responses. As Samantha Majic has documented, the gendered difference between men and women who sell sex on these online platforms has largely defined how the media has responded to and represented the raids on Rentboy and myRedBook.[13] While most media reports made the claim that shutting down these two websites would increase sex workers' economic vulnerability, "public responses to these [raids] reflected and reinforced gendered notions of women's vulnerability and men's agency in the sex industry."[14] Furthermore, many public responses to the Rentboy raid in the media stressed the implied homophobia of such federal actions targeting gay male sexual expression and activity.[15] What's particularly notable in the gay community's rallying around and defending of Rentboy, whether issuing statements, organizing protests, or penning many of the editorials that appeared online, is the lack of criticism of Rentboy.com's staff and CEO for irresponsibly and insecurely managing the data of sex workers advertising on their site while brazenly flouting the law and making millions of dollars off what are essentially precarious service industry gig workers.[16]

A lone voice from within the queer community publicly questioned this unwavering support for Rentboy.com. Self-identified sex worker Ty Mitchell took to Tumblr to air his grievances:

> It is more important than ever to now ask where Rentboy fits into our visions of justice for sex work. As much as I am pained by the arrests of Rentboy's staff, I'm reluctant to glorify the website as having really been unproblematically good for sex workers as a whole. After all, Rentboy is a private company, and it's a company that has made millions off of the labor of sex workers, even as it facilitates and promotes safer engagement in the sex trades. It works closely with Hook-online, a not-for-profit website that shares vital skills for sex workers, and it clearly cares about asserting the agency and legitimacy of sex workers. It's not a heartless company by any means, but it's also a company that wields a lot of power over its advertisers, and one that we as sex workers have never really held all that accountable.[17]

This careful description of the situation at the time holds open a nuanced position that allows for condemnation of the federal government's raid on Rentboy. com's office and the initial arrest of numerous Rentboy staff, while still wanting to think critically about Rentboy's economic exploitation of guys who do sex work. The ICE news release that was published the day of the raids indicated that Rentboy had made an estimated $10 million between 2010 and 2015 and that warrants had been issued to seize more than $1.4 million held in affiliated bank accounts. This would become all the more ironic when the dispossessed millionaire CEO of Rentboy.com turned to a crowdsourcing platform to pay his legal fees after his many assets were seized during the raid.[18]

Mitchell goes on to describe how he felt betrayed by Rentboy management, explicitly asking, "Why weren't you protecting us better?"[19] Mitchell notes that while sex worker activists were busy working toward the decriminalization of sex work through direct action activism or in collaboration with human rights organizations like Amnesty International, Rentboy was entirely absent from this type of work, despite the many platitudes the Rentboy CEO had offered about making sex work safer for guys who do it. Furthermore, Mitchell suggests Rentboy's only goal seemed to be in the realm of public relations, essentially making male sex work seem normal and fun—goals that align better with increased business and profit-making rather than political or legal change. It wouldn't be until 2017, when a sentencing memorandum was made public by Hurant's legal counsel, that the company acknowledged "Rentboy.com had a policy of always cooperating with law enforcement."[20] In fact, according to this document, Rentboy.com regularly collaborated with law enforcement by turning over users' credit card information, IP addresses, and transcripts of messages sent through the site. This betrayal of sex workers' private data and general safety in return for years of law enforcement looking the other way allowed Hurant to accumulate wealth unattainable to even the most diligent sex workers.

While the harm inflicted on sex workers by Rentboy's admitted collaboration with the police warrants more detailed investigation, there is also a question of ongoing harm as a result of digital and paper records confiscated during the Rentboy raid. Where is the evidence that was taken from Hurant's home and the Rentboy office stored? Who still has access to it? To which types of advertisers' information did Homeland Security and ICE gain access? How has this information been used or stored and with which law enforcement agencies in the United States and abroad has it been shared?

THE RISE OF RENT.MEN

In the vacuum created after Rentboy's demise, numerous websites jostled to absorb the advertisers now left without a popular and globally recognized platform. Rentmen.com, along with the affiliated domains of Rentmen.eu, Rent.men, and dozens of Rentmen-dot-country-code-abbreviation quickly rose to prominence. Aside from the ownership and branding differences, the platform, layout, interface, and individual advertisements look nearly the same. Six guys who were using Rentboy before the raid were interviewed by *New York Magazine* a month after the raid, and half of them reported already having advertisements up on Rentmen.[21] Similar stories of guys who do sex work making the switch to Rentmen after the raid appeared in the British press as well.[22] Like many of these men, I too made the switch in order to continue to afford my graduate studies with limited time to work poorly paid service industry jobs in a Canadian province where I did not yet speak the official language fluently.

While Rentboy operated in public view with Manhattan offices, sponsored floats in New York City's annual Pride Parade, launched the popular gay porn awards called the "Hookies," and cohosted HustlaBall, the massive international circuit party featuring gay porn actors and escorts, Rentmen has remained far more discreet. In fact, it is quite difficult to discern who owns Rentmen or where Rentmen's offices and servers are located. Whois data for Rentmen.com points to a registrant named Daniel Savago in the United Kingdom.[23] Rentmen Ltd. is also a company registered to Savago but is based in Sofia, Bulgaria.[24] The company RentM Media Ltd. has an expired trademark for Rentmen.com registered in the United States through infamous First Amendment law firm the Walters Law Group but again with a business address in Sofia.[25] RentM Media Ltd. also has a current European trademark for Rentmen.com's logo through a German law firm but once again with a business address in Sofia.[26] According to Whois data, both Rent.men and Rentmen.com appear to use the San Francisco–based company Cloudflare, Inc., to direct site traffic through a secure proxy server in order to obscure the location of their own web-hosting provider. Whois data shows Rent.men's ownership information as RM Media B.V., while Rentmen.com's ownership information is private.[27] RM Media B.V. is a registered company in Amsterdam.[28]

The listed address for RentM Media Ltd. in Bulgaria points to a residential neighborhood on the outskirts of Sofia, near the airport—hardly a typical or recognizable business address. RentM Media Ltd. maintains a professional-appearing English-language website, rentmmedia.com, that promotes itself as having "customer service solutions for your entertainment and media business." While the website lists a matching Sofia address, the background skyline image on the website is clearly Lower Manhattan in New York City. Whois data show that RentM Media's website is registered privately, like Rentmen.com's, but both use San Francisco–based Cloudflare's proxy servers to obscure the location of their own web-hosting provider on their respective sites.[29]

RM Media GMBH is a Hamburg, Germany–based business listed as the owner/operator of Rent.men in the introduction to its website's "Terms of Service." A simple online business directory search lists Filippo Salvatore Fascella as managing director of the corporation.[30] Basic Google searches turn up a pair of Palermo-based Mafia-involved brothers, Filippo and Salvatore Fascella, who have been arrested for illegal gambling and drug trafficking in the past.[31] RM Media GMBH's business website rentm.media appears strikingly similar in its design to RentM Media's site, and while the Whois data for this site is also protected privately, this site once again utilizes Cloudflare's US proxy servers to obscure the location of their web-hosting provider.[32]

This amateur internet sleuthing using freely available online tools for searching through public business registration information has not clarified specifically who is now raking in the millions generated by guys who do sex work—money that once went into the pockets of Jeffrey Hurant. Indeed, this jumbled list of companies with similar names but varying addresses, representative law firms, and affiliated owners is more confusing than enlightening. This search has clarified, however, that the previous crackdown on Rentboy has elicited more caution and secretiveness among those who own and operate online third-party platforms for advertising men's sexual services. In 2020 I contacted both Daniel Savago and Rentmen.com's website administrators at the email addresses listed for both in public business registration records. Each time, I used my academic institutional email address and identified myself as an academic interested in discussing their "Data Privacy" and "Terms of Use Statements" on the Rentmen.com website. Neither has ever responded. These emails were sent after receiving no response from Rentmen.com through my user profile as someone who has previously advertised on the site, despite the fact that the "Terms of Service" on Rentmen's website conclude with, "Please contact us if you have any questions concerning these Terms of Service."[33] A similar experience of receiving no response when contacting Rentmen was described by Jeff Kingsley, a former volunteer outreach worker at the sex worker–led organization Maggie's. When organizing a drop-in for guys who do sex work in the Greater Toronto area in mid-2018, he contacted Rent.men, where he also advertises, about getting the word out about the new drop-in program. Similarly, he received no response.[34]

The "Privacy Policy" on Rent.men's website includes the caveat that they share any and all users' personal information when ordered to do so by state authorities, and such personal data could include "physical identity, names, passport details, address, phone number and personal identification numbers, date of birth, personal preferences, GPS position, IP addresses, information about device used."[35] This is done without consent or notification of the user. The "Terms of Service" statement reads like a laundry list of legal caveats that attempt to offload criminal liability onto individual sex workers who advertise on the site and thus not on the site itself. Section 8, "Member Content," reads like a joke to anyone has ever looked at Rentmen's website; it is without a doubt designed to facilitate prostitution, and every single user's advertisement is full of content technically prohibited in the "Terms of Use—Member Content":

> Restrictions on Advertiser Content—Under no circumstances may Your Advertiser Content include any of the following: Actual or simulated sexual activity; Defamatory, obscene, child pornography, harassing, illegal, or otherwise objectionable material (determination of which is in Our sole discretion); Code, slang, and/or acronyms referencing sexual acts, prostitution and escorting, drug use, violence, or other illegal activity; . . . Communications suggesting, soliciting, or implying the unlawful exchange of funds for sexual activity (including, but not limited to prostitution-related services).

For-profit third-party businesses like the defunct Rentboy and the ongoing Rentmen operation are set up to make as much money as possible while trying to walk a fine legal line in regard to prostitution. This model offers no protection to the sex workers advertising on these third-party sites and subjects them to further possible harms when their personal data is shared with state authorities as site owners attempt to save themselves from incrimination and prosecution. Furthermore, while Rentmen.com's owners may be set up in Europe and thus beyond the reach of the overzealous and puritanical US legal apparatus, the site's proxy servers appear to be operating through the US-based company Cloudflare, Inc., and remain vulnerable to search and seizure.

A SEX WORKER COOPERATIVE

The federal raid of Rentboy, as well as the mysterious and disturbing operating procedures at Rentmen, demonstrates the ongoing risk to the personal data of sex workers when advertising sexual services online through third-party websites. The asymmetrical power relations between the sex workers who advertise on these sites and the sites' owners is a glaring equity issue. Sex workers who advertise on Rent.men have no idea who owns and operates it, how secure their personal data is, and if their personal data is shared with various law enforcement agencies—from municipal police forces to federal border agents. When third-party website administrators are contacted by sex workers advertising on the site, they often never respond. Worse, sex workers are set up to compete against one another for clients while profits accumulate in the pockets of faceless site owners who will happily sell sex workers out to law enforcement in order to save themselves. These working conditions, once detailed in such explicit terms, illuminate the need for sex workers to own and operate their own online platforms and set their own data security agenda.

In the spring of 2020, I interviewed Nathalie Lefebvre, a founding member of the all-gender-inclusive sex worker collective Ottawa Independent Companions (OIC). Through her I learned the origin story of OIC, how the collective is structured and operationalized, and which strategies this sex worker collective uses to protect the personal data of its members. While the membership of the organization is open to people of all gender identities and expressions, women dominate much of the advertising space in the same way they make up the majority of the workers in commercial sex industries at large. Nonetheless, guys are members of OIC and utilize its online advertising platform alongside the organization's many women and transgender members.

OIC emerged after an April 2017 social gathering of queer women sex workers in Ottawa just days after the US House of Representatives introduced a bill that would later become the controversial Fight Online Sex Trafficking Act—Stop Enabling Sex Traffickers Act (FOSTA-SESTA) in 2018. These Canadian-based sex workers foresaw how this bill would negatively impact the ability of sex workers to advertise their services via third-party websites because under this new legal framework third parties would now be held criminally responsible for any advertisements on their sites that offer sexual services. Furthermore, this group of sex workers had already become increasingly frustrated with the for-profit third-party online advertising platforms and client-oriented sex worker review boards such as theeroticreview.com. As Lefebvre notes, "The origin [of OIC] is directly related to data and security and this idea that there were so many third-party advertising platforms where we don't know who the third parties are, we don't know where they are located, there's no accountability process. Their goal is solely to profit and benefit off the labour of sex workers."[36]

OIC was also inspired by and formed shortly after a similar collective came together in Montreal under the name Indy Companion.

In conversation, Lefebvre made clear that while OIC may appear to outsiders as simply a website that advertises the sexual services of its members, the collective is much more than that. She stressed that the sex worker–owned and operated online advertising platform itself was secondary to the goal of building a supportive community of sex workers who could in turn build up one another. To this end, Lefebvre further emphasized that OIC is not an activist organization but a workers' organization. Some OIC members have had bad experiences in the sex workers' rights movement in Canada, where activist call-out culture and bullying are not uncommon. OIC is political of course, but at its core it has a focus on building up all sex workers regardless of where they are in terms of education, politicization, or involvement in the global movement to decriminalize sex work.

OIC is a member-based organization with monthly dues, a bank account, a members-only internal website, and four paid staff elected from the membership every two years. It utilizes a consensus-based decision-making model and functions somewhat like a union. OIC offers members subsidized psychotherapy and an emergency relief fund for workers experiencing economic hardship. It also set out to implement a professional development fund to aid the transition out of sex work for members who wish to do so. The members who are in paid staff positions complete day-to-day tasks and implement the ideas and proposals that come through the general membership. They are not considered the leaders of OIC, as the organization maintains a horizontal operating structure.

Unlike Rent.men, OIC does not keep legal identification documents or banking/credit card information on file, in print or digital. Members have varying options to pay their monthly dues, from going in person with cash, to Lefebvre's shared in-call space or a local feminist sex shop that has partnered with OIC, to online bank transfers or PayPal. OIC utilizes ProtonMail, a highly secure encrypted email service with servers based in Switzerland, to conduct online financial business, thereby adding a layer of protection for those who choose to pay their dues online. The largest risk is taken by Lefebvre herself, who, in recognizing the many privileges she has, opened the community bank account with her legal name and address at one of Canada's major banks. Her legal name and address were also used to purchase web-hosting space, private domain registration, and web design services with three separate companies in order to spread risk across multiple companies instead of it being centralized within one. As Lefebvre explained, she took on the risk as someone who is white, university educated, well connected, home-owning, married to a high-ranking federal civil servant, and a high-income earner because she wants to protect members of the community that could not take such risks themselves. Furthermore, she explained that OIC is exactly the kind of organization the Supreme Court decision in *Canada v. Bedford* made way for when striking down Canada's anti–sex work laws in 2013.[37] If at any point the federal government of Canada tries to shut OIC down, or goes after her in particular, the government would have a huge fight on its hands. Additionally, in terms of optics, it would be difficult to portray OIC as nefarious traffickers and pimps because of its horizontal membership structure that essentially organizes them as a local union of sex workers.

OIC's online advertising platform, while secondary to the group's emphasis on community building, is a draw for many of its members who do not have their own websites. Unlike Rent.men and many other third-party platforms, OIC members have full control over how much or how little they share. Each member's advertisement is unique, some with links to personal websites hosted elsewhere and others with full contact information and explicit details about what services are offered. There is no requirement to use coded language or pretend that you are selling your time and companionship as opposed to sexual services. This allows for members to clearly state limits and negotiate services with clients in a clear, direct manner.[38]

OIC also treats all members' advertisements equally. Ads with amateur photos, lower rates, and no link to a personal website appear alongside ads with professional photo sets, higher rates, and links to professional personal websites. When anyone views the OIC website, member ads also appear randomly in a grid each time the page is refreshed. There's no option to pay extra to maintain a top-of-the-page ad, unlike Rent.men, where sex workers pay extra to place VIP ads at the top of the page. This race to the top gives sex workers with more disposable income greater visibility while also raising the average advertising rate for everyone else who is trying to compete for clients. OIC members can have their ads edited or removed at any time with an email to the paid staff member responsible for maintaining the website. Lefebvre noted that only about half of OIC's members have an active ad on the organization's website, but a member's lack of advertising does not necessarily indicate a lack of engagement with the organization.

Website traffic data and analytics for individual members' advertisements are shared with members upon request. This individual data is never shared by way of comparison to other members' data. The only comparative data shared with the membership lets anyone who advertises on the website know which categories or tags are most popular with site visitors. Such data allow members to make better business decisions. For example, the category "incall available" remains the most popular tag on individual advertisements on the site and signals to members that maybe they do want to rent the shared incall space with other members that they saw discussed on the internal members-only site in order to increase their client base. Other tags with comparative analytic data include "available to couples," "available to women," "disability friendly," "fetish friendly," "trans friendly," "francophone," and "outcall available."

Membership at OIC also gives sex workers access to the group's members-only internal website that uses the Microsoft Slack communication platform. Access to the platform is by invitation only, and members each use their own work name and email to register on the platform. Upon registering, new members receive a welcome message that encourages managed risk by only using their work email and not posting personal details on Slack unless they feel comfortable doing so. Members on the platform also agree to a confidentiality policy that requires them to maintain the privacy and security of all members' posted content. While Lefebvre admits there have been occasional breaches of confidentiality, they were not major incidents and no members were suspended or removed from the group. When confidentiality issues arose, her emphasis was on educating members on why maintaining confidentiality is so important and openly discussing the possible harms of breaking this confidentiality as opposed to more punitive measures like kicking people out of the group. Again, building people up remains the central goal of OIC's operation.

This internal, members-only website fosters community and breaks down isolation by giving members a relatively secure place to share information about clients, collectively manage a bad date list, share tips of the trade, access health and safety information, find members to share rented workspaces, organize professional photo shoots together, and meet the more ephemeral needs of just being able to connect with like-minded people and vent frustrations about work with other sex workers. The internal website even gives workers an option to use a check-in mechanism to let others know when and where they are meeting clients to ensure that if something happens to them there is a record of their last known whereabouts and which client they saw last. These online interactions on OIC's internal members' website also have real world counterparts, from members-only social events to self-defense classes and various workshops to improve their business. In this way, OIC is exceptionally different from the average third-party advertising platform, where workers are merely competing against one another for clients and largely working in isolation from one another.

The only major drawback of the Slack platform used for the internal members' website is that there is no way to ensure the security of the Microsoft servers that host each registered Slack site. Strategies to maintain privacy while using these kinds of communication tools hosted in the so-called cloud include using a work-only email address on a secure server like ProtonMail and using only a work name upon registration. Members could also utilize a virtual private network (VPN) tool to shield one's IP address from being recorded when logging in or posting content to Slack. OIC decided to use Slack simply because Indy Companion, a collective of independent adult service providers in Montreal, was already using this communication tool for its internal members-only site and it seemed easy and functional. OIC has considered moving to a more secure Slack-like software platform called Discord, which is utilized by the gaming community, but had not made the switch as of this writing. As Lefebvre explained, the membership has gotten used to Slack, and there is concern that switching over would mean less technologically savvy members would have to relearn how to use a whole new internal site.

NO MORE SHIT!

The much-admired Canadian lesbian activist Chris Bearchell (1952–2007) is credited with shouting "No more shit!" at a February 1981 rally in the aftermath of the largest anti–gay bathhouse raid in Toronto, an effort called Operation Soap.[39] "No More Shit!" would become the gay and lesbian community's rallying cry, and these raids would lead to the creation of the Right to Privacy Committee (RTPC) to defend the rights of gays and lesbians against police encroachment. The "bawdy house" laws under which authorities raided gay bathhouses were the same laws being used to raid indoor sex workers in Canada in the 1980s.[40] Recently arrested sex worker Peggy Miller attended an early RTPC meeting to figure out how sex workers like her and gays and lesbians could work together to fight injustices stemming from the same legal provisions that legitimized state-led attacks on sex workers and queers alike.[41] This meeting of sex worker and gay and lesbian activists would lead to the creation of the

Canadian Organization of the Rights of Prostitutes (CORP) in the living room of Bearchell's home that she shared with gay sex worker Danny Cockerline in 1983.[42] Bearchell would go on to play a supporting role in CORP, as well as to help start Maggie's—the Toronto Prostitutes' Community Service Project (in 1986), while Cockerline would continue to be a central member of CORP and go on to start the Prostitutes' Safe Sex Project (in 1986) as well as co-found the Sex Workers' Alliance of Toronto (in 1992).[43]

The Ottawa Independent Companions organization, much like its aforementioned predecessors, demonstrates what is possible when sex workers draw a line in the sand and proclaim "No More Shit!" Their work demonstrates how queer data practices can and should foreground mutualism, shared power, and collective care. By seizing power and creating their own online platforms, OIC members can not only advertise their services more securely but build a resilient and well-connected community of sex workers who watch out for one another. For-profit third-party websites, whether they focus on advertising, worker reviews, content distribution, or some combination thereof, will never have the best interest of sex workers in mind, regardless of claims otherwise.

NOTES

1. Allman, *M Is for Mutual*, 9; Minichiello and Scott, "Research Shows Distribution of Online Male Escorts, by Nation."

2. Logan, *Economics, Sexuality, and Male Sex Work*, 5.

3. Callander and Scott, "Rise and Fall of Rentboy.com."

4. Michael Tremonte and Noam Biale, "Sentencing Memorandum of Easy Rent Systems, Inc. and Jeffrey Hurant," 28 April 2017, https://storage.courtlistener.com/recap/gov.uscourts.nyed.380763.117.0.pdf.

5. "Rent.Men Traffic Statistics," SimilarWeb.com, accessed 15 August 2020. https://www.similarweb.com/website/rent.men/.

6. Bruckert and Parent, *Getting Past "the Pimp."*

7. Bruckert and Parent, *Getting Past "the Pimp."*

8. Tyler, "Advertising Male Sexual Services"; Logan, "Economic Analysis of Male Sex Work"; Phua and Caras, "Personal Brand in Online Advertisements"; Walby, *Touching Encounters.*

9. Eric Steuer, "The Rise and Fall of RedBook, the Site That Sex Workers Couldn't Live Without," *Wired*, 24 February 2015, https://www.wired.com/2015/02/redbook/.

10. Aamer Madhani, "Visa Follows MasterCard, Cuts Off Business with Backpage.com," *USA Today*, 1 July 2015.

11. Derek Hawkins, "Backpage.com Shuts Down Adult Services Ads after Relentless Pressure from Authorities," *Washington Post*, 10 January 2017.

12. Dell Cameron, "Backpage Has Been Seized by the FBI—Case Sealed by Judge," Gizmodo, 7 April 2018, https://gizmodo.com/backpage-has-been-seized-by-the-fbi-1825057539.

13. Sex work is a highly gendered form of labor that requires workers to perform gendered fantasies revolving around the gender binary. How sex workers engage the gender binary, or how their own sex and gender align or disalign with the fantasies of gender they perform while working, is beyond the scope of this chapter. This chapter purposefully uses terms related to gender, not assigned sex, to reflect the gendered reality of the sexual marketplace and the reality that most trans people's genders align within the gender binary. See Namaste, "Transsexual, Transgender, and Queer."

14. Majic, "Same Same but Different?," 82.

15. Majic, "Same Same but Different?," 91–92.

16. Hayley Gorenberg, "Raiding Rentboy.com Threatens Our Safety," *Lambda Legal*, 27 August 2015, https://www.lambdalegal.org/blog/20150827_raiding-rentboy-threatens-our-safety; David-Elijah Nahmod, "Sex Workers Protest Rentboy Raid," *Bay Area Reporter*, 9 September 2015, https://www.ebar.com/news///245607.

17. Ty Mitchell, "The Rentboy Raid: A Fucking Think Piece," Tumbex, 2015, https://www.tumbex.com/androphilia.tumblr/post/127799973840.

18. "Rentboy.com Legal Defense Fund," 31 August 2015, https://web.archive.org/web/20151116014926/http://rentboyfund.org/.

19. Mitchell, "Rentboy Raid."

20. Tremonte and Biale, "Sentencing Memorandum of Easy Rent Systems, Inc. and Jeffrey Hurant," 8.

21. Tim Murphy, "What Did Busting Rentboy.com Do to the Hustler Economy? 6 Rentboys Tell All," *New York Magazine*, 25 September 2015, https://nymag.com/intelligencer/2015/09/six-rentboys-on-hustling-after-rentboycom.html.

22. Catharine Townsend, "'I Had Sex to Pay Back My Student Loans': Real-Life Hustlers Lift the Lid on the Financial Hardships They Face Now That the Popular Male Escort Site Rentboy Has Shut Down," *Daily Mail*, (UK), 25 September 2015, https://www.dailymail.co.uk/femail/article-3249539/I-started-having-sex-pay-student-loans-Six-escorts-lift-lid-lives-Rentboy-com-shut-down.html.

23. "Rentmen Ltd (Daniel Savago)," Website Informer, accessed 15 August 2020, https://website.informer.com/Daniel+Savago+RentMen+LTD.html.

24. "Company: Rentmen Ltd (Daniel Savago)," Informer Technologies, Inc.,

accessed 15 August 2020, https://website.informer.com/Daniel+Savago+RentMen
+LTD.html.

25. "Rentmen.com Trademark Information," Trademarkia, accessed 15 August 2020,
https://trademark.trademarkia.com/rentmencom-77424339.html.

26. "Rentmen—European Union Trademark Information," TradeMarkers, accessed
15 August 2020, https://trademarkers.com/EUIPO/016504061/trademark-RENTMEN
-granted-to-RentM-Media-LTD-EOD-Bulgaria.

27. "www.rent.men," Informer Technologies, Inc., accessed 15 August 2020, https://
website.informer.com/rent.men; "www.rentmen.com," Informer Technologies, Inc.,
accessed 15 August 2020, https://website.informer.com/rentmen.com.

28. "RM Media BV," Drimble, accessed 15 August 2020, https://drimble.nl/bedrijf
/amsterdam/41457366/rm-media-bv.html.

29. "Whois Record for RentMmeDia.com," DomainTools, accessed 15 August 2020,
https://whois.domaintools.com/rentmmedia.com.

30. "RM Media GmbH," Dun & Bradstreet, Inc., accessed 15 August 2020, https://
www.dnb.com/business-directory/company-profiles.rm_media_gmbh.faf9b53a86591
abc43276100a944514f.html.

31. Editorial Board, "Mafia and Drugs, 'Come and Go' Operation: The Names
of Those Arrested" [in Italian], *Palermo Today*, 21 October 2014, https://www.paler
motoday.it/cronaca/mafia/droga-arresti-21-ottobre-2014.html; Alessandro Bisconti,
"Mafia and Clandestine Gambling, the Betting Lady Appears: 'This Makes a Lot of
Money'" [in Italian], *Palermo Today*, 26 November 2017, https://www.palermotoday.it
/cronaca/mafia/scommesse-clandestine-santa-maria-gesu-arresti-retroscena.html.

32. "www.rentm.media," Informer Technologies, Inc., accessed 15 August 2020,
https://website.informer.com/rentm.media.

33. "Terms of Service," Rent.men, 1 August 2017, https://rent.men/about/terms/.

34. Jeff Kingsley, email to Ryan Conrad, 20 August 2020.

35. "Privacy Policy," Rent.men, 24 May 2018, https://rent.men/about/privacy/.

36. Nathalie Lefebvre, interview regarding OIC by Ryan Conrad, March 2020.

37. Canada v. Bedford (2013), SCC 72, [2013] 3 SCR 1101, https://scc-csc.lexum.com
/scc-csc/scc-csc/en/item/13389/index.do.

38. For further evidence of the harms of coded language in sex worker advertisements, see Sterling, "New Risk-Spaces, New Spaces of Harm."

39. Annie Smith, "Goodbye to a Queer Pioneer," *Xtra! West*, no. 353 (1 March 2007):
11, available at https://walnet.org/csis/news/vancouver_2007/xtrawest-070301.html.

40. Khan, "Homosexuality and Prostitution," 291; Ross, "Whoreganizers and Gay
Activists."

41. Chris Bearchell, "Danny Cockerline," *Walnet*, 7 May 1996, available at https://
walnet.org/97_walnut/danny_cockerline/c_bearchell.html.

42. Bearchell, "Danny Cockerline."

43. Andrew Sorfleet, "A Brief History of Sex Worker Activism in Toronto," *Walnet*, 1995, https://walnet.org/csis/groups/swat/torontohistory.html.

BIBLIOGRAPHY

Allman, Dan. *M Is for Mutual, A Is for Acts: Male Sex Work and AIDS in Canada.* Ottawa: Health Canada, 1999.

Bruckert, Chris, and Colette Parent, eds. *Getting Past the "Pimp": Management in the Sex Industry.* Toronto: University of Toronto Press, 2017.

Callander, Denton, and John Scott. "The Rise and Fall of Rentboy.com." *The Conversation*, 28 August 2015. https://theconversation.com/the-rise-and-fall-of-rentboy -com-46677.

Khan, Ummni. "Homosexuality and Prostitution: A Tale of Two Deviancies." *University of Toronto Law Journal* 70, no. 3 (2020): 283–305. https://doi.org/10.3138/utlj .2019-0082.

Logan, Trevon D. "Economic Analysis of Male Sex Work." In *Male Sex Work and Society*, edited by Victor Minichiello and John Scott, 106–49. New York: Harrington Park, 2014.

——— . *Economics, Sexuality, and Male Sex Work.* New York: Cambridge University Press, 2017.

Majic, Samantha. "Same Same but Different? Gender, Sex Work, and Respectability Politics in the MyRedBook and Rentboy Closures." *Anti-Trafficking Review*, no. 14 (2020): 82–98. https://doi.org/10.14197/atr.201220146.

Minichiello, Victor, and John Scott. "Research Shows Distribution of Online Male Escorts, by Nation." Me, Us & Male Escorting (Queensland University of Technology), 23 November 2017. https://research.qut.edu.au/aboutmaleescorting/2017/11/01 /number-of-online-male-escorts-by-nation-2/.

Namaste, Viviane. "Transsexual, Transgender, and Queer." In *Introducing the New Sexuality Studies: Original Essays and Interviews*, edited by Steven Seidman, Nancy Fischer, and Chet Meeks, 140–47. London: Routledge, 2012.

Phua, Voon Chin, and Allison Caras. "Personal Brand in Online Advertisements: Comparing White and Brazilian Male Sex Workers." *Sociological Focus* 41, no. 3 (2008): 238–55. https://doi.org/10.1080/00380237.2008.10571333.

Ross, Becki L. "Whoreganizers and Gay Activists: Histories of Convergence, Contemporary Currents of Divergence, and the Promise of Non-Normative Futures." In *Red Light Labour: Sex Work Regulation, Agency, and Resistance*, edited by Elya M. Durisin, Emily Van der Meulen, and Chris Bruckert, 256–71. Vancouver, BC: UBC Press, 2018.

Scott, John Geoffrey, Christian Grov, and Victor Minichiello, eds. *The Routledge Handbook of Male Sex Work, Culture, and Society*. New York City: Routledge, 2021.

Sterling, Andrea. "New Risk-Spaces, New Spaces of Harm: The Effects of the Advertising Offence on Independent Escorts." In *Red Light Labour: Sex Work Regulation, Agency, and Resistance*, edited by Elya M. Durisin, Emily van der Meulen, and Chris Bruckert, 94–103. Vancouver, BC: UBC Press, 2018.

Tyler, Allan. "Advertising Male Sexual Services." In *Male Sex Work and Society*, edited by Victor Minichiello and John Scott, 82–105. New York: Harrington Park, 2014.

Walby, Kevin. *Touching Encounters: Sex, Work, and Male-for-Male Internet Escorting*. Chicago: University of Chicago Press, 2012.

LINA ŽIGELYTĖ

7 Not Enough Meaningful Data?
Lessons from Eastern Europe

*The location discussed in this chapter is Vilnius, Lithuania. To me, this eastern
European city is more than a research case or an area of my expertise. I was born
in that city and lived there until my early twenties, when I emigrated. The bulk of
the queer organizing I have been a part of also took place in Vilnius. This organizing
offered me a way of learning about local queer people and a way of unlearning my
belonging in my country of birth—in the history of this country and the stories
that local queer people tell today and will be able to tell tomorrow. So, in this
chapter, I situate myself first as a participant implicated in discussed contexts and
then as someone directly impacted by work with the queer data that I describe.
Throughout this chapter, I summarize some local historical contexts in broad strokes.
I acknowledge that this approach may obscure nuance and details. Where possible,
I include references to additional resources on the complexity of the region described.*

THIS CHAPTER SHOULD BE USED AS A PRACTICAL TOOLKIT for creative work
with data.[1] As a practice-based researcher, I believe that hands-on engagement
with queer data, broadly understood here as data on various particularities of
lives that do not fit within the cisheteronormative constellation, can illuminate
the richness of such lives.[2] This chapter discusses some of the directions for
such work by focusing on the eastern European region and, more specifically,
on one city—Vilnius, the capital of my native Lithuania. I posit that creative
work with data is not a universal good that disregards ongoing data violence
but rather a productive possibility for the documentation of queer lives.

As Sara Ahmed argues, "kits" are important for activists and organizers because we employ practical tools in teaching, writing, brainstorming, and work on projects that speak to wider audiences.³ Our decision to share our tools with each other is a pedagogical gesture. It can empower our collaboration and the communities we serve. In terms of work with data, critical data scholars and media researchers argue that today, data work is mostly possible for those with specialized skills or technological resources.⁴ In order to imagine alternatives to the "data industrial complex," it may be radical to find ways for activists, organizers, educators, scholars, and artists to learn from each other's data kits.⁵

Recently, misuse of data on queer lives has resulted in privacy breaches, surveillance, and violence against the most vulnerable populations—incarcerated individuals, trans people, the homeless, youth, and HIV-positive individuals. This chapter makes an argument for a set of simple creative strategies that can be employed in data-driven work to imagine alternative uses of queer data. My discussion of these strategies stems from the experiences I acquired while working on an ongoing mapping project called "Queer Routes" (in Lithuanian, "Linkmės"). As a queer migrant now based in the United States, I started this digital project in 2012 to document spaces across Vilnius that local queer individuals named as significant to their lives. This chapter outlines the journey of this project: the contexts that currently shape queer data collection in eastern Europe, my engagement with queer history as a form of work with data, and several data lessons I learned over almost a decade of labor on this mapping project.

The lessons I offer here are meant, first and foremost, as an invitation to educators, artists, and scholars to try out data as a medium that could amplify queer perspectives and voices in new ways. These lessons should be approached not as a solution to the ongoing data problems but as a speculative framework for imagining something akin to "reparative" data work, to borrow Eve Kosofsky Sedgwick's term.⁶ It is important to remember that when, in the late 1980s, the dissident energy of queer thinking spread across Anglo-American activist, academic, and artist networks, that moment gave rise to the active production of tangible queer counterculture.⁷ This resulted in programs for cable TV networks, music, zines, films, and art shows that confronted mainstream ideas about queerness. Similarly, in the current moment we could use queer thinking for imagining in practical terms alternatives to inadequate or harmful data objects and practices. Of course, a decision to boycott working with data altogether also could be understood as a timely stance in tune with ideas on the power of negative affects, as fleshed out in the work of Heather Love, Lauren Berlant, Jack Halberstam, Sianne Ngai, and Sara Ahmed.[8] And yet, as a practice-based researcher, I think that those of us who think critically about data-driven work have enormous potential for undoing some of the damage data has done to queer people so far. In my case, I turned to creative data work on eastern Europe because I noticed that a pacified data-driven representation of local queer people was rapidly replacing the past historical erasure of queer presence across this region. I found it insufficient to simply write about the flaws of such representation in our increasingly visual and data-driven milieu.

Since data work is inseparable from representation (data results in spreadsheets, dashboards, presentation decks, visualizations, websites, mobile applications, billboards, etc.), I want to acknowledge two internal contradictions of any project that claims to use representation for the benefit of queer communities. The first contradiction of queer representation framed in positive terms is that more examples of representation might not necessarily deliver "better" representational practices. As scholarship of trans visual studies reminds us, visibility can be a trap.[9] There is a rich body of scholarship by queer artists, art historians, film scholars, and media researchers who have argued that the mainstream culture expresses queerness through a narrow set of ideas. Widely circulating images with queer subjects show bodies that may easily pass as normative. Popular visual culture prioritizes portrayal of identities that better assimilate into dominant Western ideas of kinship, citizenship, and sexuality. Because of these patterns, it is important to critically reflect on the language we use to describe our work with any representational dimensions. For example, in this chapter I refer to my data-driven project "Queer Routes" as work that can "benefit" queer lives. I am aware of the binary logic underlying this statement (that representation neatly falls into positive or negative effects on queer lives). As a practice-based researcher, I constantly wrestle with the implications of this binary logic. Yet, I hope my discussion reflects on this ongoing struggle in ways that can engage both those who create representation and those trained to notice its flaws.

The second relevant contradiction of representation framed as positive for queer communities is that not all queers embrace social relations as universally good. This is the argument of scholars like Lee Edelman and Leo Bersani, who have coined what is known as the "antisocial thesis."[10] This line of thinking finds anonymous same-sex sexual encounters in urban environments antisocial and, therefore, the most transformative for subject formation. Yet queer of color critique has demonstrated that this thesis mostly accounts for the "cosmopolitan gay white male urban culture" and neglects to register different dimensions of intimacy, love, pleasure, and affect evident in rural, non-Western, or domestic environments.[11] In this body of scholarship, the idea of queer people coming together does not necessarily result in neat positive or negative effects on subject formation. Some contexts I describe in this chapter will question the value of the antisocial thesis for a region that made a leap from imposed communist collectivity to neoliberal individualism.

POSTSOCIALIST FRONTIERS

My interest in the history of queer lives across eastern Europe stems from my background as a queer migrant negotiating my roots in this region. I was born and grew up in Lithuania, a small eastern European country with a 2022 population of 2.8 million. Having emigrated in my early twenties, I used practice-based research to explore the history of queer lives in Vilnius, the city in which I had spent most of my life. This research has resulted in several interdisciplinary art projects that include a range of media, such as text, photography, film, projections, digital maps, archival materials, zines, artist books, and, lately, data.

The broad spectrum of media I have used to home in on Vilnius as a historically multiethnic city reflects the difficulty of merging local queer stories into one coherent whole. This task is difficult not only because local queers, both currently and historically, demonstrate a range of experiences in terms of gender expression, desire, intimacy, self-presentation, and self-preservation but because the heterogeneity of eastern Europe and the city of Vilnius further complicate attempts to summarize this part of the world.

Eastern Europe sits at the crossroads of religions, empires, and capitalist experiments.[12] It is an area known for linguistic diversity and shifting regional borders due to the membership of some countries in Western alliances like the European Union (EU) and the North Atlantic Treaty Organization (NATO). After the enlargement of the EU in 2004, the largest to date, the exodus of eastern Europeans to western European labor markets and, now, the impact of Brexit, make migration an urgent issue in local policies. Whereas in the past this multiethnic region was known as a home for millions of European Jews, today antisemitism, xenophobia, and racism thrive.

The country's capital, Vilnius, exemplifies many of the region's paradoxes.[13] For most of the city's history, which dates to 1323, Lithuanians were a minority group among its residents, with Polish and Jewish locals significantly outnumbering ethnic Lithuanians.[14] The Holocaust, the repercussions of the Soviet occupation, and tensions over the impact of EU policies on local governance dramatically changed the legacy of Vilnius as a place where different cultures and ethnicities coexisted. Since 2009, an annual nationalist march takes over Vilnius's main street. While slogans used in this march change, the main idea remains the same—to honor moments of Lithuania's history that promote the idea of its ethnic homogeneity. In 2020 and 2022, an additional procession was organized during which hundreds of people carrying tiki torches walked to several Vilnius landmarks dedicated to antisemitic historical figures. In addition to the rise of explicit antisemitism, the city also witnesses dispossession of local Roma people.[15] Anikó Imre has written that, across eastern Europe, the struggles of Roma people have become emblematic of what she terms "East European nations' unspoken insistence on their whiteness."[16] The Vilnius municipality actively displayed this insistence when, in the summer of 2020, it demolished the last remaining buildings located in the historically largest local Roma settlement. Families who lost their homes were forced to move, without substantial municipal support for resettlement.[17] These recent events might suggest that Vilnius's multiethnic fabric is only a thing of the past. Yet the city is rapidly changing due to immigration flows and the return of Lithuanians who were economic migrants and created families with non-Lithuanians during their time abroad. A telling example of these demographic changes was the July 2020 Black Lives Matter march in Vilnius. It was organized by a diverse and informal network of Generation Z locals: Nigerian students and local social media influencers from ethnically and racially mixed families.[18]

The particularities of current eastern European contexts that have to do with ethnicity, race, and local migration flows demand that we complicate the methodologies traditionally used to study this postsocialist region.[19] Scholars who use postcolonial, decolonial, and critical race perspectives to examine queer contexts of the postsocialist world argue that Western theoretical frameworks might not deliver a more nuanced account of the region. For example, decolonial scholar Katharina Wiedlack has written that recent global attention to human rights violations in Russia, especially attacks on local gay people, has resulted in analysis that amplifies the superiority of the West and its supposed progressivism over regressive non-Western regions like Russia.[20] As critical race scholar Darja Davydova argues, one productive way to depart from such binary thinking would be to "produc[e] studies that focus on the dynamic changeability, mobility, flexibility, and complexity of interaction between post-Soviet spaces and the West."[21]

The experiences of Lithuania's queer people and the nuances of local queer history offer multiple instances of such dynamic interactions. The political developments that followed the 2004 enlargement of the EU can easily convince us that the traffic between the West and the East has always been one way, with the progressive West bringing human rights, including LGBTQ+ rights, into the regressive East. Lithuania's membership in the EU since 2004 certainly expanded opportunities for local nonprofits to demand improvement of local LGBTQ+ people's lives. These opportunities include funding frameworks for nonprofit projects and legal frameworks for making official complaints to the EU institutions regarding Lithuania-based human rights violations. However, a number of local events have exemplified the inadequacy of these frameworks to support the most marginalized queer groups, especially youth, trans youth, and those queers who are unaffiliated with established nonprofits.

One such event was the 2020 Vilnius Pride march, organized by an informal group of queer-identified, nonbinary, and trans youth. This march, mostly attended by youth and with over a thousand participants, was strikingly different from the Baltic Pride march, the largest event in the region with a mission to celebrate LGBTQ+ community. The Baltic Pride event rotates across the Baltic capitals Vilnius, Riga, and Tallinn and, since 2010, has taken place in Vilnius three times. Over the past several years, corporations, political parties, and international organizations have widely supported the Baltic Pride events in Vilnius. Often, representatives of these groups can be seen in the front rows of the march, and they, rather than members of local queer communities, became the face of the Baltic Pride event.[22] Embassies also play a big role in facilitating programmed events and distributing supportive public statements.[23] Vilnius Pride in 2020 exuded a very different atmosphere, given its bottom-up organization. Its organizers stated that corporate and political advertising would be unwelcome at this march, which culminated in a public reading of a list of demands, such as better support for trans individuals, legalization of same-sex partnership and marriage, and repeal of a 2009 law that censors minors' access to information on homosexuality.[24] In spite of successful attendance and the active involvement of local LGBTQ+ student groups, Vilnius Pride 2020 demonstrates that Lithuania's well-established human rights organizations and foreign diplomats are out of touch with local grassroots organizing. No foreign embassy extended any signs of support toward the mostly youth-led Vilnius

Pride event.[25] When journalists asked the Lithuanian Gay League executive director Vladimir Simonko, organizer of the better-known Baltic Pride, if he knew who oversaw Vilnius Pride 2020, he could not provide an answer.[26]

Vilnius Pride 2020 provides only a glimpse of the multilayered postsocialist east European landscape against which queer lives unfold. Emerging broader issues that have to do with local intersecting axes of race, ethnicity, migration, and organizing demand inventive, modular, and reorienting research frameworks. Such frameworks might help us better engage with region-specific power struggles, identity formations, short-lived activist networks, and fluctuating transnational alliances. Creative data work can animate such engagement.

DATA PROMISES

My current creative work with eastern European queer data (and, more specifically, queer data relevant to my hometown of Vilnius) builds on my past practices to ensure an afterlife for various original materials currently in my personal collection: audio recordings, photographs of no longer extant places, notes, correspondence, archival video footage, and artifacts. The shift from the more traditional practices of collection, documentation, and archival labor to data work expresses my interest in asking, "What can queer data do?" I am also interested in speculating on what I can do as an independent practice-based researcher, queer organizer, and artist in what danah boyd and Kate Crawford term "the era of big data."[27]

Recent years have shown us that a promise of survival haunts data on queer lives. We are led to believe that, without such data, we may not comprehend how queer people live and that such data is necessary for knowing what we need for our well-being. In North America, a telling example of high expectations regarding queer data was the battle over the 2020 US Census and the inclusion of questions to help queer individuals self-identify as such. Ultimately, the only way for queer people to be seen in the 2020 Census data was if they identified as cohabiting with or married to a same-sex partner. This logic ignores the existence of the most vulnerable LGBTQ+ individuals—those who may not be in monogamous partnerships or living with partners because they are teenagers, single immigrants, or homeless individuals.

The recent case of the 2020 US Census supports scholarly arguments that standards for demographic data collection fail at representing the breadth of lived LGBTQ+ experiences. For example, Dean Spade and Rori Rohlfs have argued that queer data collection by the US-based Williams Institute systematically excludes Black and brown queer households.[28] This analysis resonates with broader skepticism about the possibility for data to represent queer lives. For instance, Bonnie Ruberg and Spencer Ruelos note that life changes may alter how individuals self-identify in terms of their sexuality or gender.[29] Standardized demographic questionnaires ignore the possibility of such changes. These are just some examples of the ways queer communities encounter what Anna Lauren Hoffmann has termed "data violence."[30] This violence is a version of multiple forms of violence queer communities experience across the globe because of racism, poverty, the prison industrial complex, imperialism, surveillance, gentrification, immigration policies, classism in higher education, bigotry in health-care systems, and now the pervasiveness of the data regime.

In Lithuania, interest in extraction and analysis of data on LGBTQ+ individuals as objective evidence of our realities overshadows critical interrogations of queer data. This data optimism may reflect historical circumstances that, to date, have obstructed regional collection of data on LGBTQ+ individuals and communities. Whereas the US-based researchers have extensively used Census Bureau data to discuss the lives of queer communities, data collected by Lithuania's Department of Statistics is not useful for research in local queer contexts.[31] The absence of legal same-sex partnership or marriage in Lithuania further complicates collection of structured quantitative data about the local LGBTQ+ community. For now, data collected by Lithuanian officials provides no documentation of the lives of queers with Lithuanian passports.[32]

Those who are interested in local data on LGBTQ+ individuals can use several available resources: surveys initiated by local nonprofits, scholarly research, and surveys by international organizations. However, these resources embody many problematic issues. For example, surveys conducted by local nonprofits overrepresent homosexual male-identified individuals, as is the case with the 2015 survey on homophobic bullying in Lithuanian schools.[33]

A record of data-driven scholarly research on local LGBTQ+ lives goes back to 2007. Datasets included in this body of work vary from a dozen semistructured interviews with male-identified individuals on various aspects of homosociality to online surveys of nearly five hundred respondents about LGBT (*sic*) identity formation.[34] One type of research that includes queer data and continues to expand is scholarship by local students. In some cases, surveys used by students have up to three hundred respondents. Examples of topics in students' scholarly work include mental health issues and views on homosexuality among college-age youth.[35] Overall, datasets included in students' research significantly overrepresent youth with college degrees.

In 2020, the European Union Agency for Fundamental Rights (FRA) published the results of a major survey that had the potential to significantly transform existing patterns of queer data extraction in Lithuania and the entire EU. A closer look at the methodology and analysis of this survey demonstrates that the EU institutions dismiss the ongoing criticism of data gathering aimed at LGBTQ+ individuals. In fact, this widely celebrated survey, which to this day includes the largest sample of Lithuania's LGBTQ+ population, perpetuates many past queer data inadequacies.

The FRA survey was conducted in 2019 and included responses from 133,000 LGBTI (*sic*) individuals from the twenty-seven EU member states, the United Kingdom, North Macedonia, and Serbia.[36] The FRA's website celebrates the project's scope as "by far the largest collection of empirical evidence on discrimination and hate crime against LGBTI people worldwide."[37] While the monumental survey does provide an impressive pool of data on LGBTI mental health and discrimination in housing, many survey questions focus on simple elements of identity expression. For instance, one question asks if respondents ever avoid holding hands in public with their same-sex partner (thus assuming that respondents have a long-term monogamous partner and that they are partnered with a same-sex person). This reductive question, rather than the heftier topics the survey examined, dominated the coverage of the survey results across international media networks. For example, the CNN headline about the survey stated the following: "6 in 10 LGBTI People Afraid to Hold Hands in Public, Europe-Wide Survey Finds."[38] Overall, the survey's section on violence and harassment included more questions than other thematic sections. Unsurprisingly, the focus on LGBTI people's negative experiences resulted in many answers on negative experiences. The FRA's press release summarized the findings as follows: "little progress [happened] over the past seven years."[39] The European media picked up the message and covered the survey as an account of oppression.[40]

A closer look at the FRA survey demonstrates a number of basic methodological issues that cast doubt on the benefits of queer data for queer communities. The FRA never claimed that the survey was representative, but the disparities are striking. At the time of the writing of this chapter, microdata had not yet been released, but some data were available on the FRA website. These data show that the average age of respondents was twenty-nine and only about 4 percent of respondents were fifty-five years or older. Overrepresentation of youth is likely because the survey was administered online and could have excluded less tech-savvy older respondents and those without regular access to the internet. Gay-identified men outnumber bisexual women and lesbians (42, 20, and 16 percent, respectively). Pools of respondents from discrete countries varied dramatically, with 20,180 respondents from Spain and 16,119 from Germany, though the population of Germany is twice the size of Spain.

Answers of Lithuania-based respondents provide a particularly bizarre dataset, though it is the most expansive dataset I have identified in relation to research on Lithuanian queer lives. The answers of 1,398 Lithuanian respondents present a grim picture. LGBTI individuals in Lithuania experience discrimination at higher rates than anywhere else and depression rates are highest, with 14 percent of respondents stating they are constantly depressed, while 51 percent of working individuals "hide being LGBTI" at their place of employment. This rate is higher than in any other surveyed country (the phrase is from the survey answer option).

A closer look at the demographic arrangement of respondents suggests the inadequacy of standardized questionnaires for reflecting the realities of queer respondents. For example, the number of respondents living in Lithuania's countryside was too small for their answers to be included in relation to some questions. Furthermore, my private correspondence with the FRA demonstrates that the average age of Lithuania-based respondents was twenty-one.[41] The prominence of Lithuania's youth among the respondents provided fertile ground for asking respondents about topics that better reflect the issues of youth, such as interactions with parents or educators. Unfortunately, the FRA survey did not engage with these topics.

I describe the FRA's publicly available dataset to demonstrate that currently available data provide very limited narratives about queer lives in Lithuania. In spite of ongoing data-driven research and its promises to improve queer lives, this dataset and others I summarize fall into the following narrow categories: overrepresentation of oppressive experiences, overrepresentation of individuals who identify as men or gay men, and overrepresentation of college-age youth.

CREATIVE DATA WORKERS

The issues discussed so far provide valid grounds for mistrust in queer data extraction. Historically, health-care professionals, the criminal justice system, and academic researchers have extensively harmed queer communities through data collection and analysis. This volume provides multiple examples of scholarship focused on these issues, and, in many cases of current data extraction, technological advancement sets up the conditions for harming more queer lives than ever. This is evidenced by the 2018 Grindr data leak that impacted fifty million people and the recent scraping of thousands of personal photographs from dating websites for the purpose of facial recognition research at Stanford University.[42] Writing about the amplified role of data in queer lives due to the current reach of technology, data scientist Os Keyes has warned us that "data science is a profound threat to queer existences."[43]

There is no easy way to repair the damage data has inflicted upon queer communities. Yet, I want to propose that one way organizers, educators, and artists can confront this abusive legacy is by complementing critical work on data with creative data-driven work. After all, data science did not start with the big tech companies and their ongoing misuse of data. As the twentieth century was witnessing the expansion of infrastructures for information organization, parallel to these developments a lot of creative data-driven work emerged. Often, representatives of historically excluded groups produced such work to illuminate the experiences of these groups. More than a century ago, the American sociologist W. E. B. Du Bois and his students from Atlanta University used "ink, gouache watercolor, graphite and photographic prints" on paper to create a series of sophisticated data visualizations on the experiences of Black Americans.[44] The 1900 Paris Exposition featured this pioneering work.[45] Around the same time, the journalist Ida B. Wells-Barnett effectively used lists with data to expose that, across the United States, large numbers of Black Americans were routinely being lynched.[46] In 1932, a black cartoonist named Elmer Simms Campbell created an aestheticized, data-rich map of Harlem's nightclubs. This map provides several nods to the appeal of Harlem's multiracial nightlife among queer patrons and, conversely, documents the problematic racial hierarchies of American society.[47] These are just some examples I identify as early creative data-driven work.

These cases from the beginning of the twentieth century rely on simple aesthetic tools: ink, paper, lists, and hand-drawn maps. Today, artists and journalists also use simple aesthetic forms for data presentation, and this work resonates with feminist and decolonial principles of data work, such as examination of power and contextualization of data.[48] Hand-drawn visualizations by the British data journalist Mona Chalabi provide insights from publicly available large-scale datasets on subjects such as homelessness or the COVID-19 pandemic.[49] One of the effects of Chalabi's visualizations is that they significantly differ from the widespread digital presentation of quantitative data through sophisticated interactive dashboards and websites. Yet these advanced digital tools, as Roopika Risam has argued, prioritize totalizing narratives and reduce discrete, complicated lived experiences to tiny dots on interactive maps.[50]

Another current approach to the use of simple aesthetic tools in data work is evident in the practice of the Nigerian-American artist Mimi Ọnụọha. She stages mixed-media installations to expose the amount of important information missing in publicly available datasets. For example, Ọnụọha's 2016 installation *The Library of Missing Datasets* includes a standard filing cabinet with opened drawers in which labeled file organizers indicate types of publicly unavailable information, such as "Cause of June 2015 black church fires" and "Public list of citizens on domestic surveillance lists."[51] Ọnụọha's focus on missing data shows that the availability of data across privately owned online platforms is not synonymous with the availability of data that serves the public good.

These examples of low-tech approaches to data presentation help us reimagine the stakes of creative work with data and reconsider what counts as data labor. In terms of queer data, the experiences of individuals who specialize in queer history, its preservation, and outreach provide multiple examples of creative data-driven practices. At first glance, the methods of librarians, archivists, and educators might have little to do with aesthetics. Conceptually, however, creativity has been a crucial component of their labor.

A number of examples from libraries, archives, and artist networks demonstrate ongoing imaginative engagement with queer data. US-based librarians organized during the gay liberation movement of the 1970s and used the system of public libraries to help queer people access affirming information before such resources became more publicly available.[52] Anthropologist Shannon Mattern has even argued that librarians are the prototypical data scientists, since they have extensive experience in the establishment of complex systems that help the public access and navigate information.[53] Archivists who work with materials on multiple expressions of sexuality and gender have extensive knowledge of information design. For example, K. J. Rawson, the co-founder of the Transgender Digital Archive, has argued that "definitional and epistemological" questions are a major concern in the archiving of materials on the history of transgender individuals.[54] In the case of the Transgender Digital Archive, a specific section of the website summarizes discrete examples of terms used across the globe to describe gender diversity. The archive's information architecture separates those terms from the Anglo-American word *transgender*. In addition to librarians and archivists, artists and educators regularly and extensively work with data to amplify queer experiences. Queer artists' mindmaps, sketchbooks, and personal archives can be understood as compelling unstructured datasets. For educators, curation of syllabi requires labor that in many cases comes down to cleaning, coding, and organizing of information so students get clear insights from teaching materials. The process of sifting through dozens of readings in search of meaningful connections (something educators do on a regular basis) involves methodologies that share similarities with the responsibilities expected from professionals who gather, code, clean, and present data. In other words, comfort with large amounts of data, analytical ability, and critical thinking— these skills can be attributed not only to data scientists but also to educators, archivists, librarians, and artists.[55]

"QUEER ROUTES"

Something that has pushed me to think about the use of creative data work for thinking about queer communities is a digital mapping project I started in 2012. "Queer Routes" provides an audiovisual interpretation of historical data on a number of locations in Vilnius that local queer people identified as significant to their lives. Initially, the project was launched as a bilingual website (in Lithuanian and English) with a map of Vilnius and interactive location markers dispersed on the map. These location markers provided metadata: photographs of locations, ambient sounds from these locations, relevant digitalized archival materials, and oral histories I recorded. I created the original map with the help of the visual artist Laura Varžgalytė, who assisted me in setting up the website.

Initially, the project was inspired by critical insights from debates about queer representation. Specifically, it engaged with ideas about aesthetic forms that provide an alternative to the increasing visibility of queer people in the mainstream media. To confront the diluted representation of queerness, media practitioners and artists explore a range of questions about the broader relationship between images and queerness. How can visual media capture open-ended, shifting, and fluid ways of expressing sexuality and embodying gender? What can images teach us about the limitations of visual representation? How can we confront Western reliance on visual culture with other forms of media, such as sound? These questions informed the genesis of "Queer Routes."

As a documentary project, "Queer Routes" was designed to respond to these questions through the use of blurry photographs and oral testimonies presented without a clarifying voice-over. I juxtaposed clippings from the local gay press and misleading articles from the mainstream press to contrast pursuit of self-affirmation and the role of oppression in the formation of queer subjectivity. To the best of my knowledge, "Queer Routes" is the first audiovisual project committed to historical research on Lithuania's queer past. Funded by a grant of several hundred US dollars from the US Embassy in Lithuania, the digital map was available online for a year. Financial difficulties paused the project, and the original website is no longer available.

In 2019, several things led me to return to the project. Some individuals I interviewed had been diagnosed with terminal illnesses, and I wanted to preserve their voices. In addition, while the number of Lithuanian nonprofits committed to LGBTQ+ advocacy was growing, there was still no archive dedicated to Vilnius's queer past. Last but not least, I realized I had accumulated an unstructured dataset of substantial size with a lot of information that would be meaningful for the preservation of local queer history. I had identified thirty locations, which varied from places of worship to defunct women-owned bars known for their lesbian clientele. Field recordings, oral testimonies, and found footage together constituted over fifteen hours of aural information. There were dozens of emails documenting my correspondence with individuals whose testimonies I recorded. Additionally, I had personal photographs, numerous newspaper clippings, and documentation of defunct websites used in the past by nonprofits that primarily served gay and lesbian populations.

These data differ from previously described, better-known datasets on queer people in Lithuania. The data at my disposal highlight experiences of collective self-affirmation rather than accounts of individual plights. My queer data centers local activist struggles rather than signs of allyship.[56] These struggles include tensions between local lesbian and gay organizers and the challenges of running small businesses dedicated to LGBTQ+ people. The unstructured and multilayered data I collected provide multiple pathways for exploring local queer lives.

At the time of the writing of this chapter, "Queer Routes" was scheduled for a relaunch in 2023 as a free web application. That year will mark the thirtieth anniversary of homosexuality's decriminalization in Lithuania. The revamped project is designed around a series of maps with geolocations that can be explored both on the move and from the comfort of one's home. A fusion of actual maps from past city guides, hand-drawn mental maps, and collages present collected data in a series of thematic routes that take users through the streets of Vilnius. One map is dedicated to local lesbian history, which has been neglected in several existing brief summaries of the local queer past. One route takes visitors through cultural spaces that helped amplify queer voices through regular parties, art events, and TV shows. The headquarters of the Lithuanian National Television network, newsstands known for selling local gay press, and one Catholic church in which a play on AIDS was staged in 2012 are some of the stops on this route. The application provides access to all archival materials used in the making of the project. "Queer Routes" also includes several lesson plans for educators interested in teaching queer history and queer data to students of different ages. Free access to these lesson plans and original archival materials provide concrete steps for ensuring that queer history is not confined to narrow academic and activist networks, a pattern I noticed in Lithuania while conducting my research.

Ultimately, and almost a decade after the creation of the first interactive map, "Queer Routes" remains faithful to its initial ethos. The project creates a way for experiencing the city through the richness and particularities of local queer lives. The multiple routes presented in this cartographic data-driven work also demonstrate how engagement with queer history intersects with additional topics. These include gender dynamics, urban development, capital distribution, and ongoing privatization of public spaces under the current neoliberal regime. For example, "Queer Routes" presents images and field recordings from several public parks that the municipality of Vilnius severely reduced in size as part of urban renewal.

My labor on "Queer Routes" has taught me several lessons about the potential of creative work with queer data. I end this chapter with a summary of these practical lessons.

DATA LESSONS

Begin with Data Inventory

Data often starts as a spreadsheet, but we do not have to stick to standard tools to appreciate the richness of data at our disposal. One way to unleash our creativity is to conduct what Catherine D'Ignazio terms "data biographies."[57] These are inventories that help us account for the sources of our data so we acknowledge the labor carried out in the collection, analysis, and presentation of data. In the context of queer data inventories, they help document the labor that has been systemically disregarded, underpaid, or uncredited. For example, recent interest in the history of Black and brown trans organizing exemplifies how the labor of the most vulnerable queer populations has been subjected to historical erasure.[58]

The inventory of queer data may begin with several questions. What was your journey to the dataset at your disposal and what makes this data significant to you? Could you draw a mental map of your data journey? Did your data collection and analysis include any setbacks? Do you recall any details relevant to your labor? For instance, do the locations in which you collected your data still exist? Is there something you regret neglecting to ask? As we design our data inventories, we need to ask daring questions that may be left out in standard data science because they are subjective, trivial, or distracting.

Labor Is Important Data

Having completed the inventory of our data, we may discover that our projects entail a lot of previously neglected labor. Various aspects of this labor can provide meaningful insights about queer communities. Who conducts manual labor, such as the sorting of archival materials? Who advances their careers because of their work with data? Who provides emotional support when our projects get stuck? These are some questions that illuminate material aspects of working with data. As data science increasingly relies on automated labor conducted by machines, more attention to labor done by humans can provide important interventions into the future of data science.

Even compelling data-rich projects on queer history neglect to find ways for the presentation of the amount of labor alongside the volume of data examined. For example, Jen Jack Gieseking has created a series of data-rich maps with places in New York City mentioned in erstwhile lesbian and queer publications.[59] The breadth of information included in Gieseking's maps by 2020 is astounding—382 New York City–based organizations that existed between 1983 and 2008 and 1,500 addresses that, among other categories, include bars, locations known for specific events, and places used for political organizing. Gieseking acknowledges that contemporary statistical measures would define this dataset as insignificant—"a mere 789 KB worth of data."[60] However, the dataset is valuable, Gieseking argues, because it explores a historically neglected social group. Interestingly, the enormous labor involved in the making of this data-driven project does not become part of the visualization. In a journal article documenting the project's history, several details are provided: commuting to the archive ("multiple trips per week in just over a year, followed by multiple return trips over the following five years"), manual sorting of used publications, and the recruitment of research assistants.[61]

As work with data gets increasingly automated and described in opaque terms (e.g., "deep learning," "scaling," "modeling"), emphasis on the materiality of our data praxis might provide a refreshing alternative to the current direction of data science. The latter promotes classic capitalist values: accumulation, speed, exploitation. In the case of Gieseking's data-rich maps on New York's queer and lesbian places, it is possible to raise multiple illuminating questions on labor. Who enters the data into the system? How is the labor of research assistants distributed across axes of gender and race? Who builds skills that help ensure lasting careers? Attention to the materialist aspects of data labor might demonstrate that our datasets are big enough to raise multiple urgent questions about queer communities and questions that may be queer. For example, the struggle to collect data may produce a trail of unanswered emails or voicemails that never received replies. These difficulties may be adopted as data points about time spent waiting, pausing, feeling unheard, and so on.

Embrace Low-Tech Tools

Lately, scholars have expressed optimism about the expanding availability of tools for data analysis and presentation, with some researchers counting over five hundred such tools in 2018.[62] This growth suggests important shifts toward equity and access in data science, a field with a record of striking disparities in terms of gender and race.[63] As the number of tools for data analysis and presentation increases and suggests the democratization of data science, a closer look at these tools paints a different picture. To this day, data analysis and presentation tools are easier to use for those with specialized training in STEM, a field known for historical exclusion of demographics other than white cisgender men.[64] Many of these emerging data analysis and presentation tools are free or open source, but the speed at which some previously celebrated services disappear is alarming. Instead of promoting wider data access to the public, various services use their landing pages to prioritize display of paid customer plans, with free options barely visible.

In thinking about the future of data analysis and presentation, it is worthwhile to recall Audre Lorde's classic emancipatory call for action—"the master's tools will never dismantle the master's house."[65] So, what alternative tools of data analysis and presentation can be used today for meaningful labor on historically neglected topics, such as queer lives?

Data workshops are gaining traction as one possible approach to horizontal engagement with data and the democratization of data.[66] But workshops reinforce hierarchies, since they rely on educators who engage with a community of learners. We still need to see widespread use of workshops in which community members educate data scientists. Data workshops at art institutions may exclude demographics that historically have been less welcome in museums and galleries, such as disabled art patrons or visitors who may not have access to public transportation.

In my teaching experience, simple aesthetic techniques for data exploration have provided effective and horizontal means for demystifying data to a nonspecialist audience. For example, in my classes at a small private liberal arts college in western New York State, students used data visualization templates to reflect on their learning process. For this task, I provided students with postcard-size data visualization templates designed to help students note patterns of their learning experience in a classroom setting, such as discrete moments when they were curious, tired, or confused.[67] For some students, the project helped them note that their feelings of anxiety intensified when they used electronic devices. A number of students noted that the project inspired them to practice better self-care (e.g., snack before class, dedicate more time to rest, etc.). Overall, students were enthusiastic about observing how minor daily experiences become data points.

Use Maps to Enrich Storytelling

Researchers working on queer geography have argued that written text dominates accounts of queer history. Meanwhile, use of visual media, such as maps, is negligible.[68] As a scholar of visual culture, I find this argument reductive because television, cinema, art history, print culture, and internet culture provide a range of visual examples that document queer history. Yet maps (both analog and digital ones) can animate how queer history is told and taught. Maps that center queer lives tap into a rich artistic tradition of decolonial cartographic imagination that can subvert "regional and global flows of power systems, monopolies and administrative networks."[69]

"Queer Routes" demonstrates some subversive possibilities of maps. The initial interactive map from 2012 added queer spaces and voices to the map of

Vilnius to confront exclusion of such spaces and voices in the history of this city and of Lithuania. The map made queer lives present, tangible, and integral to local history. In its revamped iteration, "Queer Routes" evolves into a series of maps and routes, thus quantifying queer footprints. These multiple maps not only identify locations significant to queer people but also transform spaces, both past and present. For example, photography and sound are integrated to pay tribute to several locations that no longer exist or were gentrified, such as an area in the heart of Vilnius where there was a park known for cruising.

In addition to the subversion of local geography, "Queer Routes" responds to the domination of Western locations in digital mapping projects on queer history.[70] Even when the scope of such projects is global, little data is presented on locations outside of Western urban centers. One example of this pattern is the celebrated project "Queering the Map," which began in 2017 as a collaborative tribute to queer memories pertinent to Montreal, Canada. By 2020, the map had expanded to include multiple user-generated geotagged locations across the world. However, this map clearly shows a predominance of Western urban locations and the majority of memories expressed are in English, thus enhancing the map's imperialist logic that queerness primarily thrives in the West. Future digital projects on queer history will need to invent new media forms so they depart from past totalizing accounts of sexuality and gender expression.

Prepare for Digital Preservation

Digital technology has transformed the work of archivists, preservationists, and artists. While digital culture can expand and expedite access to information, our reliance on digital technology comes with a number of caveats relevant to data preservation. Digital storage is a booming industry with a growing impact on climate change, but individual artists, educators, and activists with less access to institutional support constantly battle digital preservation issues.[71] Lack of access to financial resources threatens the longevity of projects that are available only online. Additionally, websites keep disappearing due to rapidly changing technological infrastructures. Researchers call this phenomenon "link rot."[72] Data degradation, known as "bit rot," is a regular concern for those who work extensively with older visual media files.[73] Tech companies that provide cloud storage treat customers as "digital tenants," and users have increasingly limited agency in owning software packages, work files, personal memorabilia, and forms of entertainment.[74] The digital future may have little room for information hoarders with limited material means.

The most economically precarious creators of queer content face the biggest risk of losing their work, especially if such work is stored online with no alternative backups. Sudden loss of income can result in expiration of previously owned websites or cancellation of cloud storage plans. As social media users, we are giving away not only our psychographics (the data indicating what we enjoy or dislike) but also our copyright to the content we generate. For example, Facebook, which also owns Instagram, can use our images without our consent.[75] Cultural workers and activists who plan on creating digital content on queer lives should familiarize themselves with key concerns pertinent to digital preservation.

Rethink Collaboration

The history of data abuses makes it imperative to ensure that queer individuals can be active agents in data projects. Educators, artists, and activists consistently face the challenge of ensuring that collaboration with community members is a rewarding and lasting experience to those community members. For example, digital projects may offer internet users the ability to contribute data, but contributions may come from only a narrow set of individuals who may have easier access to a particular project. A number of collaborative online projects demonstrate that internet culture perpetuates past disparities. For example, only 1 percent of Wikipedia users create its content, and these contributions are mostly the result of the labor of white cisgender men from the Global North.[76]

In projects that go beyond digital environments, workshops may successfully incorporate community collaboration. But does data from queer communities stay with these communities? After all, workshops can easily become another form of data extraction, since workshop facilitators can use documentation of these events for career purposes. To invent productive forms of collaboration, critical data studies could benefit from insights made by scholars in media studies and art history. For instance, media studies provide a rich body of scholarship on the failed promises of participatory culture that emerged with the rise of internet use.[77] The art critic Claire Bishop has argued that when artists offer their audiences a chance to take part in the creation of performances or exhibitions, these opportunities romanticize the idea of community and idealize collaboration. Collaboration and participation in what Bishop calls "artificial hells" can reduce our ability to notice tensions within and between social groups.[78]

In creative work with data, several alternative directions could help reinvent collaboration with queer communities. To ensure the lasting effects of our projects, serial programming could replace singular events. Budgets of events could include lines for labor done by queer community members and especially youth, since they are the most financially precarious class in our current neoliberal regime. Various ways for exchanging resources could also be incorporated. For example, "Queer Routes" includes lesson plans for students of various ages so youth have tools for thinking about data, history, and queer storytelling.

Experiment with Translation

For queer individuals who belong to multiple cultures and navigate multiple languages, translation of their practice-based research is a challenging task. By saying "translation," I am thinking not only about the translation of something from one language into another. I also use this term to address how we make the objects we create resonate with people from cultures other than our own.

In my practice, I create work about people whose language is spoken by only three million people. Economic hardships define my region of origin. Creators who come from similar backgrounds often negotiate complex repercussions of translation or its absence. Our labor, if left untranslated, might stay in perpetuity within the more obscure networks of activism, scholarship, and art. Translation may be something we are required to produce when financial support of our labor comes from Western foundations, embassies, and grant networks. Translation might help artists connect with each other across the world and get various forms of support for our future labor. We may also withhold translation for various reasons. We may avoid translation because we do not have the resources to provide it. We may avoid translation because audiences with no stake in our histories may not appreciate the richness of contexts from which our stories and our experiences come.

In the context of queer history that speaks across different cultures, translation is an ongoing experiment. For example, my mother tongue provides no precise equivalents to the term "queer." In my native language, the project "Queer Routes" is called "Linkmės" (Directions). I used to think that erasure of the word *queer* from the title in my native language indicated my retreat from the project's initial commitment to the elevation of queer voices. But Linkmės, a rather archaic word that is rarely used in contemporary conversations, contains additional meanings. It refers to destinations, evolutions, ideological beliefs, bends. And there is one more, less common meaning, that opens up a surprisingly capacious world. In one part of Lithuania, it refers to a wet meadow, which is a very fertile ecosystem known for biodiversity. And so, through the act of translation, I leave my home and I come home, which turns out to be surprisingly queer.

CONCLUSION

In this chapter, I shared practical data lessons relevant to practice-based researchers, media creators, and artists who have access to smaller datasets pertinent to historically excluded social groups. While I discuss how data has been used to perpetuate violence on queer communities, I also recognize that, across the world, artists, educators, and community organizers actively work to ensure that data can stand for something other than extraction, surveillance, misuse, and, quite simply, evil. Emerging creative practices rethink what data can do in the hands of those whose toolkits prioritize critical perspectives on data and representation over "how-to" videos explaining the particularities of popular analytics tools. Because data is such a defining component of our lives, it is worth exploring what happens when we embrace some queer approaches for messing with our data.

NOTES

ACKNOWLEDGMENTS: The research described in this essay was supported by the University of Rochester's Susan B. Anthony Institute for Gender, Sexuality, and Women's Studies and the US Department of State. I am also grateful to Milda Ališauskienė, Lara Lempert, and Rasa Navickaitė for helping me refine my arguments.

1. My research on creative data work is indebted to Catherine D'Ignazio's concept of "creative data literacy." D'Ignazio and her colleagues at MIT's Data + Feminism Lab use this term to refer to various pedagogical settings that prepare individuals from nontechnical fields to use data for civic engagement and community empowerment. These pedagogical settings include workshops, data mural projects, and web-based projects. See D'Ignazio, "Creative Data Literacy." The projects of the Data + Feminism Lab can be accessed at https://dataplusfeminism.mit.edu/.

2. A note on terms: I use the acronyms LGBT and LGBTI if they were employed in research works other than my own. In this chapter, I use the acronym LGBTQ+ to refer to the broader landscape of experiences and forms of self-identification that do not fit within the traditional Western cisheteronormative constellation. I use the term "queer"

synonymously with this acronym and with an understanding that "queer" is not the same as LGBTQ+, since it can erase the particularities of sexual and gender expressions. I also want to note that in postsocialist contexts the term "queer" is inadequate as a summary of various local nonheterosexual contexts, practices, and embodiments simply because of the term's roots in Anglo-American cultures. That said, "queer" has been widely adopted and appropriated across the broader postsocialist region by activists, artists, and writers. In Polish contexts, the term is frequently inflected: (*solidarność queerowa* [queer solidarity]), *queerowe życie* [queer life]). In Russian-language contexts, квир (pronounced "kveer") is widely used as a Russian-language adaptation of "queer." In Lithuania, academics have actively explored possibilities for Lithuanian language equivalents of the term, but young local community organizers (teenagers, students) widely use the English "queer" without translation. See Kreivytė and Žigelytė, "Vertimas kaip vertinimas."

3. Ahmed, *Living a Feminist Life*, 251.

4. boyd and Crawford, "Critical Questions for Big Data."

5. The term "data industrial complex" gained traction especially after the 2016 US presidential election, because the outcome of the election has been widely attributed to the unprecedented use of voters' data for targeted social media marketing. For some early instances of the term's usage, see Peleschuk, "Germany Is Taking on Facebook's Data Industrial Complex"; and Albright, "How Trump's Campaign Used the New Data-Industrial Complex to Win the Election."

6. Sedgwick, "Paranoid Reading and Reparative Reading."

7. For early examples of this work, see the documentary film *Tongues Untied*, directed by Marlon Riggs (1989); and Bad Object Choices, *How Do I Look?*

8. See Love, *Feeling Backward*; Berlant, *Cruel Optimism*; Halberstam, *Queer Art of Failure*; Ngai, *Ugly Feelings*; and Ahmed, *Promise of Happiness*.

9. Tourmaline, Stanley, and Burton, *Trap Door*.

10. Caserio et al., "Antisocial Thesis in Queer Theory"; Bersani, "Is the Rectum a Grave?"

11. Rodríguez, "Queer Sociality and Other Sexual Fantasies," 333.

12. On postcolonial analysis of the postsocialist region, see the volume Annus, *Soviet Postcolonial Studies*. For a discussion of Lithuanian contexts from postcolonial perspectives, see Kelertas, "Perceptions of Self and the Other in Lithuanian Postcolonial Fiction." On Lithuania's religious heterogeneity, see Ališauskienė, "What and Where Is Religious Pluralism in Lithuania?"; and Račius, "Lithuania."

13. For a succinct account of the city's historical diversity, see Briedis, *Vilnius*.

14. For an account of Vilnius's Jewish history, see Sirutavičius, Staliūnas, and Šiaučiūnaitė-Verbickienė, *History of Jews in Lithuania*. For the history of Jewish Vilnius before the Holocaust, see the classic 1943 work by Israel Cohen, *Vilna*.

15. Žigelytė, "In Parubanka, Roma People Say History Is Repeating Itself."

16. Imre, "Whiteness in Post-Socialist Eastern Europe," 82.

17. NARA, "Palikti namus."

18. The protest provides a compelling example of eastern Europe's postsocialist racialized atmosphere. During the march, the police arrested one of the organizers, a nonwhite minor who is a Lithuanian citizen but grew up in a mixed Lithuanian-Caribbean family. The arrest was the culmination of a verbal confrontation between this young man and counterprotesters with racist, pro-Trump, and conspiracy theory–themed posters. Following the arrest, police held this BLM march organizer in custody for three hours—without charges or a chance to speak to a lawyer. See NARA, "Tūkstantis 'Ne' rasizmui."

19. This chapter was written before the Russian Federation invaded Ukraine on 24 February 2022. This invasion laid bare the limitations of Western activists, intellectuals, and academics to account for the legacy of Russian colonialism and imperialism across eastern and central Europe. During the first weeks of this war, Ukrainian authors actively discussed this topic to rally Western support of Ukrainian resistance. See Artiukh, "US-Plaining Is Not Enough."

20. Wiedlack, "Gays vs. Russia."

21. Davydova, "Between Heteropatriarchy and Homonationalism," 52.

22. At the 2013 Baltic Pride event in Vilnius, I marched with a group of antifascist queers under a banner stating "Queers against fascism." We were some of the last groups in the procession. Meanwhile, the front row of the procession carried a banner stating "Baltic Pride Vilnius 2013: For Equality!" and primarily consisted of local politicians and foreign representatives of international organizations.

23. For example, Baltic Pride, which in 2020 was expected to take place in Estonia's capital Tallinn but got canceled due to the COVID pandemic, received a letter of support from over twenty embassies, representing mostly Western countries. See US Embassy in Estonia, "Common Declaration in Support of Baltic Pride 2020."

24. Balčiūnaitė, "Vilnius Pride 2020," 14.

25. Vilnius Pride 2020 organizing committee, personal message to author, 31 January 2021.

26. Gudavičiūtė, "V. Simonko įvertino šeštadienį įvyksiančias 'Vilnius pride' eitynes, organizatorių vardai nežinomi."

27. boyd and Crawford, "Critical Questions for Big Data," 663.

28. Spade and Rohlfs, "Legal Equality, Gay Numbers and the (After?)Math of Eugenics."

29. Ruberg and Ruelos, "Data for Queer Lives."

30. Hoffmann, "Data Violence and How Bad Engineering Choices Can Damage Society."

31. Data on unmarried same-sex couples from the 1990 US Census is used in For-syth, "'Out' in the Valley." I have found the work of Zachary Adriaenssens helpful for identifying past use of Census Bureau data in research on LGBTQ+ communities. See Adriaenssens, "Mapping the Lesbian, Gay, Bisexual and Transgender Community in Atlanta."

32. While Foucauldian analysis shows that legal documents leave room for tracing the existence of various sexual practices and desires in repressive regimes, this line of argument in relation to contemporary Lithuania is outside of the scope of my chapter.

33. This survey was conducted by the Lithuanian Gay League, the longest-lived local organization focusing specifically on LGBTQ+ advocacy. The Lithuanian Gay League publishes the results of various surveys on its website, the Lithuanian Gay League / National LGBT Rights Organization, https://www.lgl.lt/en/.

34. Čičelis, "Reading between the Lines"; Zdanevičius, Reingardė, and Samuolytė, "Lesbiečių, gėjų, biseksualų ir transseksualų (LGBT) teisių apsauga ir socialinės at-skirties tyrimas."

35. Kriaučionytė, "Relationship between Well-Being and Self Assessment of Health of Homosexuals in the Context of Social Environment"; Jakštaitė, "Students' Views about Homosexuality."

36. For the survey report, see European Union Agency for Fundamental Rights, "Long Way to Go for LGBTI Equality."

37. European Union Agency for Fundamental Rights, "Does Hope or Fear Prevail among Europe's LGBTI People?"

38. Picheta, "6 in 10 LGBTI People Afraid to Hold Hands in Public, Europe-Wide Survey Finds."

39. European Union Agency for Fundamental Rights, "Does Hope or Fear Prevail among Europe's LGBTI People?"

40. Examples of media coverage that highlighted the survey's findings on the nega-tive experiences of LGBTI individuals include Halam, "European LGBT+ Equality Sur-vey Shows East-West Divide"; and Euronews, "High Levels of Discrimination against LGBTI People in EU, Survey Finds."

41. European Union Agency for Fundamental Rights, email to author, 4 August 2020.

42. Burns, "Report Says Grindr Exposed Millions of Users' Private Data, Messages, Locations"; Levis, "'I Was Shocked It Was So Easy.'"

43. Keyes, "Counting the Countless."

44. Mansky, "W. E. B. Du Bois' Visionary Infographics Come Together for the First Time in Full Color."

45. Battle-Baptiste and Russert, *W. E. B. Du Bois's Data Portraits*.

46. Wells-Barnett, *On Lynchings*.

47. Ataide, "Queer Spaces in 'A Night-Club Map of Harlem.'"

48. For a survey of feminist perspectives on work with data, see D'Ignazio and Klein, *Data Feminism*. The principles of decolonial theories for data research are discussed in Couldry and Mejias, "Decolonial Turn in Data and Technology Research."

49. Examples of these visualizations are available on the artist's website, https:// monachalabi.com/.

50. Risam, "Beyond the Migrant 'Problem.'"

51. Documentation of Ọnụọha's installation is available on the artist's website, http://mimionuoha.com/the-library-of-missing-datasets.

52. In the United States, librarians were the first group to form a professional national organization aimed at support of gays and lesbians: the American Library Association's Gay Task Force. On the history of this organization, see Gittings, "Gays in Libraryland."

53. Mattern, "Public In/Formation."

54. Rawson, "Introduction: 'An Inevitably Political Craft,'" 544.

55. Artists have been especially active in demystifying data visualization through transnational networks, such as the Data Visualization Society, https://www.datavisual izationsociety.org/.

56. One telling local project on LGBTQ+ allyship was launched in 2012, when Vilnius-based gay filmmaker Romas Zabarauskas reached out to local entertainment venues that wanted to be publicly known as friendly to LGBT (*sic*) people. By 2019, this initiative, known as "LGBT Friendly Vilnius," had grown to include more than fifty bars, restaurants, and cafés. These venues were presented on a map, available in print and on a dedicated website. The website stopped operating in 2020 because of a lack of resources to continue this project. However, the initiative is documented on a Facebook page, "LGBT Friendly Vilnius," https://www.facebook.com/lgbtfriendlyvilnius/.

57. D'Ignazio, "Creative Data Literacy," 9.

58. In the United States, there is a growing interest in the legacy of Sylvia Rivera (1951–2002) and Marsha P. Johnson (1945–1992), who were pioneering figures in the organizing of sex workers and homeless youth of color in New York. See Tourmaline, Stanley, and Burton, *Trap Door*. In Canada, queer organizers of color also are getting overdue acknowledgment of their labor. See Haritaworn, Moussa, and Ware, *Marvellous Grounds*.

59. Gieseking, "The Maps."

60. Gieseking, "Size Matters to Lesbians, Too," 151.

61. Gieseking, "Size Matters to Lesbians, Too," 153.

62. D'Ignazio and Bhargava, "Cultivating a Data Mindset in the Arts and Humanities."

63. Bayern, "Why Only 18% of Data Scientists Are Women."

64. Chang, *Brotopia*.

65. That phrase is the title of Lorde's chapter in Cherríe L. Moraga and Gloria E. Anzaldúa's *This Bridge Called My Back*, published in 1983.

66. D'Ignazio, "Creative Data Literacy," 8.

67. This low-tech data exploration was inspired by an award-winning data visualization project, "Dear Data," a collaboration between visual artists Giorgia Lupi and Stefanie Posavec. See Lupi and Posavec, *Dear Data*.

68. Brown and Knopp, "Queering the Map."

69. Mesquita, "Counter-Cartographies," 26.

70. Some examples of digital mapping projects that center Western geographies include the projects "Homosexual Activity," https://www.equaldex.com; "Pride of Place: England's LGBTQ Heritage," https://historicengland.org.uk/research/inclusive-heritage /lgbtq-heritage-project/your-contributions/; "Queer Maps," https://queermaps.org/; and "Queering the Map," https://www.queeringthemap.com/.

71. Natural Resources Defense Council, "America's Data Centers Are Wasting Huge Amounts of Energy."

72. Leslie, "Link Rot Infests Internet," 1799.

73. Gibbs, "What Is 'Bit Rot' and Is Vint Cerf Right to Be Worried?"

74. Tufekci, "We Are Tenants on Our Own Devices."

75. Friedman, "Stop Falling for This Facebook Scam."

76. Oberhaus, "Nearly All of Wikipedia Is Written by Just 1 Percent of Its Editors."

77. Jenkins, *Fans, Bloggers, and Gamers.*

78. Bishop, *Artificial Hells.*

BIBLIOGRAPHY

Adriaenssens, Zachary. "Mapping the Lesbian, Gay, Bisexual and Transgender Community in Atlanta." Unpublished manuscript, 2011. https://smartech.gatech.edu /bitstream/handle/1853/40805/ZacharyAdriaenssens_Mapping%20the%20LLGBT %20Community%20in%20Atlanta.pdf.

Ahmed, Sara. *Living a Feminist Life.* Durham, NC: Duke University Press, 2017.

——— . *The Promise of Happiness.* Durham, NC: Duke University Press, 2012.

Albright, Jonathan. "How Trump's Campaign Used the New Data-Industrial Complex to Win the Election" (blog post). London School of Economics Phelan US Centre, 26 November 2016. https://blogs.lse.ac.uk/usappblog/2016/11/26/how-trumps -campaign-used-the-new-data-industrial-complex-to-win-the-election/#Author.

Ališauskienė, Milda. "What and Where Is Religious Pluralism in Lithuania?" In *Religious Pluralism: A Resource Book*, edited by Aurélia Bardon, Maria Birnbaum, Lois Lee, and Kristina Stoeckl, 34–39. Florence: European University Institute, 2015.

Annus, Epp. *Soviet Postcolonial Studies: A View from the Western Borderlands*. New York: Routledge, 2019.

Artiukh, Volodymyr. "US-Plaining Is Not Enough: To the Western Left, on Your and Our Mistakes." Commons, 1 March 2022. https://commons.com.ua/en/us-plaining-not-enough-on-your-and-our-mistakes.

Ataide, Jesse. "Queer Spaces in 'A Night-Club Map of Harlem.'" *Queer Modernisms* (blog), 6 May 2016. https://queermodernisms.wordpress.com/2016/05/06/iotd-queer-spaces-in-a-night-club-map-of-harlem/.

Bad Object Choices, ed. *How Do I Look? Queer Film and Video*. Seattle: Bay Press, 1991.

Balčiūnaitė, Ada. "Vilnius Pride 2020." *Kreivės*, September 2020, 14–16.

Battle-Baptiste, Whitney, and Britt Russert, eds. *W. E. B. Du Bois's Data Portraits: Visualizing Black America*. New York: Princeton Architectural Press, 2018.

Bayern, Macy. "Why Only 18% of Data Scientists Are Women." *TechRepublic*, 20 May 2019. https://www.techrepublic.com/article/why-only-18-of-data-scientists-are-women/.

Berlant, Lauren. *Cruel Optimism*. Durham, NC: Duke University Press, 2011.

Bersani, Leo. "Is the Rectum a Grave?" *October* 43 (Winter 1987): 197–222.

Bishop, Claire. *Artificial Hells: Participatory Art and the Politics of Spectatorship*. London: Verso, 2012.

boyd, danah, and Kate Crawford. "Critical Questions for Big Data: Provocations for a Cultural, Technological, and Scholarly Phenomenon." *Information, Communication and Society* 15, no. 5 (June 2012): 673–75.

Briedis, Laimonas. *Vilnius: City of Strangers*. Budapest: Central European University Press, 2009.

Brown, Michael, and Larry Knopp. "Queering the Map: The Productive Tensions of Colliding Epistemologies." *Annals of the Association of American Geographers* 98, no. 1 (March 2008): 40–58.

Burns, Janet. "Report Says Grindr Exposed Millions of Users' Private Data, Messages, Locations." *Forbes*, 29 March 2018. https://www.forbes.com/sites/janetwburns/2018/03/29/report-says-grindr-exposed-millions-of-users-private-data-messages-locations/#3d60fa445c4c.

Caserio, Robert L., Lee Edelman, Judith Halberstam, José Esteban Muñoz, and Tim Dean. "The Antisocial Thesis in Queer Theory." *PMLA* 121, no. 3 (May 2006): 819–28.

Chang, Emily. *Brotopia: Breaking Up the Boys' Club of Silicon Valley*. New York: Portfolio/Penguin, 2018.

Čičelis, Augustas. "Reading between the Lines: Spatial Communities of Men with Same-Sex Attractions in Late 20th Century Lithuania." MA thesis, Central European University, 2011.

Cohen, Israel. *Vilna*. Philadelphia: Jewish Publication Society, 1943.

Couldry, Nick, and Ulises Ali Mejias. "The Decolonial Turn in Data and Technology

Research: What Is at Stake and Where Is It Heading?" *Information, Communication and Society* ahead-of-print (2021): 1–17. https://doi.org/10.1080/1369118X.2021 .1986102.

D'Ignazio, Catherine. "Creative Data Literacy: Bridging the Gap between the Data-Haves and Data-Have Nots." *Information Design Journal* 23, no. 1 (2017): 6–18.

D'Ignazio, Catherine, and Rahul Bhargava. "Cultivating a Data Mindset in the Arts and Humanities." *Digital Engagements; or, The Virtual Gets Real* 4, no. 2 (2018). https:// public.imaginingamerica.org/blog/article/cultivating-a-data-mindset-in-the-arts -and-humanities/.

D'Ignazio, Catherine, and Lauren F. Klein. *Data Feminism*. Cambridge, MA: MIT Press, 2020.

Davydova, Darja. "Between Heteropatriarchy and Homonationalism: Codes of Gender, Sexuality, and Race/Ethnicity in Putin's Russia." PhD diss., York University, 2019.

Euronews. "High Levels of Discrimination against LGBTI People in EU, Survey Finds." *Euronews*, 17 May 2020. https://www.euronews.com/2020/05/17/high-levels-of -discrimination-against-lgbti-people-in-eu-survey-finds.

European Union Agency for Fundamental Rights. "Does Hope or Fear Prevail among Europe's LGBTI People?" Press release, 14 May 2020. https://fra.europa.eu/en/news /2020/does-hope-or-fear-prevail-among-europes-lgbti-people.

——— . "A Long Way to Go for LGBTI Equality." Accessed December 15, 2022. https:// fra.europa.eu/en/publication/2020/eu-lgbti-survey-results.

Forsyth, Ann. "'Out' in the Valley." *International Journal of Urban and Regional Research* 21, no. 1 (1997): 36–60.

Friedman, Zack. "Stop Falling for This Facebook Scam." *Forbes*, 19 August 2019. https://www.forbes.com/sites/zackfriedman/2019/08/19/facebook-scam /#19855b09a4cf.

Gibbs, Samuel. "What Is 'Bit Rot' and Is Vint Cerf Right to Be Worried?" *The Guardian*, 13 February 2015. https://www.theguardian.com/technology/2015/feb/13/what -is-bit-rot-and-is-vint-cerf-right-to-be-worried.

Gieseking, Jen Jack. "The Maps." An Everyday Queer New York: Companion Site for *A Queer New York*, the Book. Accessed 15 December 2022. http://jgieseking.org /AQNY/the-maps/.

——— . "Size Matters to Lesbians, Too: Queer Feminist Interventions into the Scale of Big Data." *Professional Geographer* 70, no. 1 (2018): 150–56.

Gittings, Barbara. "Gays in Libraryland: The Gay and Lesbian Task Force of the American Library Association: The First Sixteen Years." *WLW Journal* 14, no. 3 (Spring 1991): 7–13.

Gudavičiūtė, Dalia. "V. Simonko įvertino šeštadienį įvyksiančias 'Vilnius pride'

eitynes, organizatorių vardai nežinomi." Lyrtas.lt, 10 July 2020. https://www.lrytas.lt
/lietuvosdiena/aktualijos/2020/07/10/news/v-simonko-ivertino-sestadieni-ivyksian
cias-vilnius-pride-eitynes-organizatoriu-vardai-nezinomi-15564942/.

Halam, Mark. "European LGBT+ Equality Survey Shows East-West Divide." *Deutsche
Welle*, 14 May 2020. https://www.dw.com/en/european-lgbt-equality-survey
-shows-east-west-divide/a-53436285.

Halberstam, Jack. *The Queer Art of Failure*. Durham, NC: Duke University Press, 2011.

Haritaworn, Jin, Ghaida Moussa, and Syrus Marcus Ware, eds. *Marvellous Grounds:
Queer of Colour Histories of Toronto*. Toronto: Between the Lines, 2018.

Hoffmann, Anna Lauren. "Data Violence and How Bad Engineering Choices Can Damage Society." *Medium*, 30 April 2018. https://medium.com/s/story/data-violence
-and-how-bad-engineering-choices-can-damage-society-39e44150e1d4.

Imre, Anikó. "Whiteness in Post-Socialist Eastern Europe: The Time of the Gypsies;
The End of Race." In *Postcolonial Whiteness: A Critical Reader on Race and Empire*,
edited by Alfred J. Lopéz, 79–102. Albany: State University of New York Press, 2005.

Jakštaitė, Aistė. "Students' Views about Homosexuality: Tolerance or Homophobia."
BA thesis, Vilnius University, 2008.

Jenkins, Henry. *Fans, Bloggers, and Gamers: Exploring Participatory Culture*. New York:
New York University Press, 2006.

Kelertas, Violeta. "Perceptions of Self and the Other in Lithuanian Postcolonial
Fiction." In *Baltic Postcolonialism*, edited by Violeta Kelertas, 251–69. Amsterdam:
Rodopi, 2006.

Keyes, Os. "Counting the Countless." 24 March 2019. https://ironholds.org/counting
-writeup/.

Kreivytė, Laima, and Lina Žigelytė. "Vertimas kaip vertinimas: Arba 'Queer,' teorija
lietuviškai." *7 meno dienos*, no. 993 (25), 22 June 2012. http://archyvas.7md.lt/lt/2012
-06-22/tarp_disciplinu/vertimas_kaip_vertinimas.html.

Kriaučionytė, Dalia. "The Relationship between Well-Being and Self Assessment of
Health of Homosexuals in the Context of Social Environment." MA thesis, Lithuanian University of Health Sciences, 2014.

Leslie, Mitch. "Link Rot Infests Internet." *Science* 295, no. 5561 (8 March 2002): 1799.

Levis, Paul. "'I Was Shocked It Was So Easy': Meet the Professor Who Says Facial Recognition Can Tell If You're Gay." *The Guardian*, 7 July 2018. https://www.theguardian
.com/technology/2018/jul/07/artificial-intelligence-can-tell-your-sexuality-politics
-surveillance-paul-lewis.

"LGBT Friendly Vilnius." Accessed on Facebook, 15 December 2022. https://www
.facebook.com/lgbtfriendlyvilnius/.

Lorde, Audre. "The Master's Tools Will Never Dismantle the Master's House." In

This Bridge Called My Back: Writings by Radical Women of Color, edited by Cherríe L. Moraga and Gloria E. Anzaldúa, 98–101. 3rd ed. New York: Kitchen Table, 1983.

Love, Heather. *Feeling Backward: Loss and the Politics of Queer History*. Cambridge, MA: Harvard University Press, 2007.

Lupi, Giorgia, and Stefanie Posavec. *Dear Data*. New York: Princeton Architectural Press, 2016.

Mansky, Jackie. "W. E. B. Du Bois' Visionary Infographics Come Together for the First Time in Full Color." *Smithsonian Magazine*, 15 November, 2018. https://www .smithsonianmag.com/history/first-time-together-and-color-book-displays-web -du-bois-visionary-infographics-180970826/.

Mattern, Shannon. "Public In/Formation." *Places Journal*, November 2016. https:// placesjournal.org/article/public-information/?cn-reloaded=1.

Mesquita, André. "Counter-Cartographies: The Insurrection of Maps." In *This Is Not an Atlas*, edited by Kollektiv Orangotango+, 26–30. Bielefeld, Germany: Transcript Verlag, 2018.

NARA. "Palikti namus: Nugriauto taboro šeimų istorijos." 4 December 2020. https:// nara.lt/lt/articles-lt/palikti-namus-nugriauto-taboro-seimu-istorijos.

——— . "Tūkstantis 'Ne' rasizmui." 12 June 2020. https://nara.lt/lt/articles-lt/tukstantis -ne-rasizmui.

Natural Resources Defense Council. "America's Data Centers Are Wasting Huge Amounts of Energy." NRDC Issue Brief, August 2014.

Ngai, Sianne. *Ugly Feelings*. Cambridge, MA: Harvard University Press, 2005.

Oberhaus, Daniel. "Nearly All of Wikipedia Is Written by Just 1 Percent of Its Editors." *Vice*, 7 November 2017. https://www.vice.com/en/article/7x47bb/wikipedia-editors -elite-diversity-foundation.

Peleschuk, Dan. "Germany Is Taking on Facebook's Data Industrial Complex." *The World*, 13 March 2016. https://www.pri.org/stories/2016-03-13/germany-taking -facebook-s-data-industrial-complex.

Picheta, Rob. "6 in 10 LGBTI People Afraid to Hold Hands in Public, Europe-Wide Survey Finds." CNN, 14 May 2020. https://www.cnn.com/2020/05/14/europe /lgbti-eu-discrimination-survey-intl/index.html.

Račius, Egdūnas. "Lithuania: The Predicament of the Segregation of Religions." In *Routledge Handbook on the Governance of Religious Diversity*, edited by Anna Triandafyllidou and Tina Magazzini, 111–20. Oxon, UK: Routledge, 2021.

Rawson, K. J. "Introduction: 'An Inevitably Political Craft.'" *TSQ: Transgender Studies Quarterly* 2, no. 4 (November 2015): 544–52.

Risam, Roopika. "Beyond the Migrant 'Problem': Visualizing Global Migration." *Television and New Media* 20, no. 6 (2019): 566–80.

Rodríguez, Juana María. "Queer Sociality and Other Sexual Fantasies." *GLQ: A Journal of Lesbian and Gay Studies* 17, no. 2–3 (2011): 331–48.

Ruberg, Bonnie, and Spencer Ruelos. "Data for Queer Lives: How LGBTQ Gender and Sexuality Identities Challenge Norms of Demographics." *Big Data and Society* 7, no. 1 (2020): 1–12.

Sedgwick, Eve Kosofsky. "Paranoid Reading and Reparative Reading, or, You're So Paranoid, You Probably Think This Essay Is about You." *Touching Feeling: Affect, Pedagogy, Performativity*, 123–51. Durham, NC: Duke University Press, 2003.

Sirutavičius, Vladas, Darius Staliūnas, and Jurgita Šiaučiūnaitė-Verbickienė. *The History of Jews in Lithuania: From the Middle Ages to the 1990s*. Boston: Brill, 2020.

Spade, Dean, and Rori Rohlfs. "Legal Equality, Gay Numbers and the (After?)Math of Eugenics." *Scholar and Feminist Online* 13, no. 2 (Spring 2016). https://sfonline.barnard.edu/dean-spade-rori-rohlfs-legal-equality-gay-numbers-and-the-aftermath-of-eugenics/.

Tourmaline, Eric A. Stanley, and Johanna Burton. *Trap Door: Trans Cultural Production and the Politics of Visibility*. Cambridge, MA: MIT Press, 2017.

Tufekci, Zeynep. "We Are Tenants on Our Own Devices." *Wired*, 20 May 2019. https://www.wired.com/story/right-to-repair-tenants-on-our-own-devices/.

US Embassy in Estonia. "Common Declaration in Support of Baltic Pride 2020." Press release, 22 June 2020. https://ee.usembassy.gov/2020-06-22-3/.

Wells-Barnett, Ida B. *On Lynchings*. Introduction by Patricia Hill Collins. Amherst, MA: Humanity Books, 2002.

Wiedlack, M. Katharina. "Gays vs. Russia: Media Representations, Vulnerable Bodies and the Construction of a (Post)modern West." *European Journal of English Studies* 21, no. 3 (2017): 241–57.

Zdanevičius, Arnoldas, Jolanta Reingardė, and Jolanta Samuolytė. "Lesbiečių, gėjų, biseksualų ir transseksualų (LGBT) teisių apsauga ir socialinės atskirties tyrimas." Report from the Office of Equal Opportunities Ombudsperson, Vilnius, 2007.

Žigelytė, Lina. "In Parubanka, Roma People Say History Is Repeating Itself." *Defending History*, 13 September 2013. https://defendinghistory.com/in-parubanka-roma-people-say-history-is-repeating-itself/59042.

MATHEW GAGNÉ

8 Reciprocating Sexy Information *Reflections on Studying the Data of Gay Sex in Beirut*

IN JUNE 2013, I arrived in Beirut, Lebanon—a city I had visited only handful of times before, while living in Damascus, Syria, in 2010—to begin ethnographic research into the digitally mediated intimate lives of queer Beiruti men. My plan was simple: I would arrive, obtain a local SIM card, and start chatting with men online, gradually forming relationships with people who might become interlocutors. I (re)constructed my profiles on Grindr, Scruff, Hornet, Tinder, OkCupid, Manhunt, and GROWLr (often updating them as I learned locally popular words, aesthetics, and rules for using sex apps in Beirut).[1] After a bit of fuss getting a Lebanese SIM card, I quickly connected with men, who asked me about my origins, what I was doing in the city, what I was looking for, whether I stayed alone (meaning if I had access to a private space), and for face and body pictures.[2]

A network of men quickly congealed around me through a patchwork of encounters that overlapped with those of others. Random chats gradually formed into this network of friends, lovers, enemies, acquaintances, former boyfriends, casual chatters, and profile browsers. Even those self-identified discreet men who fastidiously avoid Beiruti queer spaces and social networks insinuate themselves into these less visible networks. Sometimes Beirut feels exceedingly queer, as if the city hosts an infinite number of queer men. Other times, the network extends beyond Beirut when men find each other in various regional cities or even places around the globe. Across thousands of messages and hundreds of conversations spanning twenty months of fieldwork, I came to know many men who knew each other, connected by the information we shared about ourselves and others.

Queerness is not always equated with information networks. Their regularity and protocols preclude the kinds of connections that, in queerness's sense of the non-normative, might happen outside of or challenge these networks.[3] Yet queerness runs through networks, pushing and expanding them into new social realms, especially given information's principle of interoperability, whereby, in rhizomatic fashion, information creates feedback loops as it connects and disconnects within networks.[4] Anthropologist Shaka McGlotten calls such connections virtual intimacies that "describe a range of contacts and encounters, from the ephemeral to the enduring, made possible by digital and networked means."[5] Writing at a time when emerging digital intimacies were moralized as weak and inauthentic, McGlotten makes a case for legitimizing these digital intimacies as rife with queer meaning and the potentiality for experiencing sexual encounters against marginalizing heteronormative intimacies.[6]

Nadir, a close interlocutor with whom friendship began as a sexual encounter, often reminded me that sex creates social networks. One day, we discovered that we had both had sex with one of his neighbors. It was surprising to me but normal to him. He said of overlapping sexual connections that "it is easier to have sex than build up an alternative [to love or friendship] type of a network or relationship with that person. There is [sic] a lot of people who do have sex with each other. They maintain a connection with each other later on." Life in the network, McGlotten argues, "feels more like a mess of tangled yarn" where intimacies multiply between and at connections with others.[7] "We are," McGlotten states, "all threaded through by the yarning of the networks that are the ordinary stuff of life today."[8] Extending McGlotten's characterization, I examine life within the network through the informational practices necessary for the network's continued existence. Familiar to men are gatherings of friends casually browsing sex apps and keeping up with their online conversations while telling their friends about them, asking if they know so and so to see if they can gather further information about them. Within these networks, men pass along information that gathers personal experiences into social formations where intimacies are both personal and social, constituting collective feelings and knowledge.

Amid Beirut's social and political homophobias, the circulation of men's sexual information among vast, impersonal networks of gay sex app users risked a fraught publicness. Behind the screen could be anyone—a cousin, a neighbor, a coworker. Sharing one's personal information meant risking becoming known as a queer person, yet participation in sex apps necessitates the sharing of information to generate sexual possibilities. I explore how I situated myself between the necessity to be part of the circulation of information as part of these networks while mitigating the risks that such participation creates.

Participating in men's digitally mediated sex lives created an ethical and methodological terrain permeated by questions about how I engaged with their information. Full participation in these networks meant that I, as the researcher, increasingly couldn't maintain the subjective distance upon which ideals of ethics are based in a research context where queer men come to know so much more about others just through the circulation of our "sexy information." This raised questions about how the circulation of information was shifting, shrinking the distance between me and others. For instance, one day, a new friend, Charbel, told me over lunch that his friend had recently asked Charbel if he knew the "Canadian researcher in Beirut" doing research about Grindr. Charbel told me that his friend had stopped responding to me on Grindr because he was concerned with how I would use our conversation as data. To this day, Charbel's friend remains anonymous to me.

My contribution to *Queer Data Studies* is to explore pressing questions of how to ethnographically engage with other people's data.[9] I explore ethical questions concerning how to participate in the circulation of people's information while researching within their socio-sexual networks. Specifically, I argue that such emerging ethical quandaries in the digital age require a new kind of reflexivity that rethinks our engagement with the information of others as we negotiate our place not just within the sex lives of others but within networks made of many others.

But I begin by saying something about gay sex in Beirut and how the local socio-political conditions create a certain kind of need for sexual reflexivity related to taking on a shared vulnerability concerning sex and information.

SEXY INFORMATION: CREATING SEXUAL POSSIBILITIES

Men talk a lot about sex over sex apps. As Nadir once told me, "Sex is highly negotiable. People go into details of what they want to do and what they expect, where to cum, how to fuck, what position, do you want to do it on the floor, or on the bed, they go into so many details about sexual pleasure. They want to make sure that what they expect or the pleasure they are gonna get out of it is guaranteed." The sociality of sex apps is, like in Clifford Geertz's analysis of the bazaar economy in Morocco, the search for information about the quality of possibilities through communication networks.[10]

Queer-themed websites and apps have long been credited with having contributed to a sort of queer emergence in Beirut. They connected people like never before and made knowledge about local queer haunts and cruising spaces easier to obtain. Much of this usage centered on sex. In fact, Beiruti queer activist Ghassan Makarem wrote that much of men's early internet usage was to make "acquaintances for sex and sometimes politics."[11] In *Queer Beirut*, anthropologist Sofian Merabet notes that chatrooms were, around 2002, part of an emerging socio-sexual queer male terrain (along with internet pornography) that spurred different kinds of "erotic imaginations."[12] Merabet transcribes a brief chatroom conversation between two men trying to arrange sex. After sharing their name, age, and area of residence, they immediately tell each other whether they live alone and therefore can host a sex encounter, what they are looking for (one says sex with a bottom guy and the other says the same, although he later clarifies that he is a bottom looking for sex). What follows is a series of questions about sex and bodies: penis size and thickness, degree of hirsuteness, preferred sexual acts, where they like to orgasm—which is asked several times about specific locations on the body—whether to use a condom, and if he fucks mild or hard. At the end, one says he may have a free place in the evening if the other would like to meet. The conversation ends unpropitiously with the problem of a lack of place.[13]

Over the course of my fieldwork, I learned the words and images that were conventionally acceptable, the unspoken rules for chatting over apps, how men talked about sex. I learned the cultural meaning behind the information, such as the words and visual elements men used to signal class and normative masculinity. I learned how to feel sex through words and images, through the content of the message, like sexually affirming words, the speed of a response, and the indirect sexual euphemisms and suggestions. A symbolic world of embodied sex gradually appeared to me as I became further immersed in the culture of gay sex in Beirut.

In contrast to cruising in meatspace where men communicate through non-verbal gesture and one's position in space, gay sex in the digital age involves disembodied communication that relies more on words, images, and videos to create those feelings of sexual arousal.[14] Sex apps and their predecessors have digitalized sex into words and images that resignify bodies, masculinity, race, class desires, dislikes, and so on as information that comes to matter differently in cruising.[15] Sex apps establish a series of standardized categories and responses from which users choose when communicating their sexual desires and pleasures, in turn instructing men on what information is most important in determining their sex lives.

These are what I call "sexy information": the individual pieces of information that generate the affects and embodiments of sex, such as knowing one's height, weight, and body type as distinct information that can be combined to create an arousing abstraction of an individual's body. This information derives its sexiness from its capacity to affect another, that is, to arouse sexual feelings. These pieces of information gathered into the digital interface create an environment that defines the probabilistic outcomes from the actual to the likely to the improbable.[16] Kane Race calls this arrangement of information the "infrastructure of the sexual encounter" to frame how these apps shape gay sex, as well as what comes of sexual negotiations.[17] Men share and collect information about others to imagine and calculate the possibility of having good, fulfilling sex.

Sexy information is the result of the relationship between technology and affect theory, which challenges the separation of mind over matter, or in this case the abstract information over embodied experience. Information, as Patrick Keilty notes, acts upon and within the body as sensation.[18] The affordances and informational categories of the apps' interfaces give social, and therefore meaningful, life to sex's ineffable affects—perhaps also known in Brian Massumi's terms as those presocial intensities that play on and within the body—as textual and visual categories, cues, and norms.[19]

Sex has long been connected to talk, such as the sexual script theory that focuses on the role of meaning and symbols in the production of sexual feelings.[20] In the digital age, sex talk is networked, circulated, repeated, and standardized within digital interfaces. Sex apps hold onto profiles, conversations, and images—the materials that make up intimate histories—as digital objects. The messaging system does some of the memory work: tracking message histories, storing a backup of one's conversation history, enabling users to gather and share multiple photos in a digital album, and giving users control over tracking others through their profiles. Screenshots of dick pics, insults, befuddling conversations, salacious images, funny moments, and awkward texts are culled from the time and place of their exchange and recirculated as artifacts that make and remake socio-sexual networks.

The difference of the digital age I wish to point to is that sexual desires and affects are given social life with new "regimes of circulation" that involve practices of moving these pieces of information among users.[21] Kane Race calls this "speculative pragmatism," which "is concerned not only with what happens, but also what might happen, the possible—that is, what might come into being."[22] This brand of speculation frames interactions as realizations of possibilities that are co-created, not predetermined.[23] I think of speculation as the process of gathering information to calculate the possible outcomes that are most desired. The information men share contains a range of desires and pleasures discretized into individual units of language, codes, visuals, and data that can be arranged into alternative, possibilistic states.[24] Sexual and intimate possibilities are imaginable and actualizable from the meaning already imbued in information.

My ethnographic collection of men's sexy information garners ethical scrutiny for the greater moral judgment and risk of personal harm that can supposedly come from its public circulation, according to puritanical readings of data, which has led to greater control of sexy data through government legislation and closures of websites for sex workers and tech company community standards.[25] Information regarding sex and bodies is ontologically constructed as always about to violate something, whether personal privacy, laws, or standards, given the powerful social values of sex as private and, should it become too public, immoral. The risk of something being violate in the circulation of sexual information and images is neither absolute nor given. Rather, the social terrain of risk—and pleasure and possibility for that matter—is, as I'll show, co-constructed by the very ways that people in a network share the information of others.

THE RISKY CIRCULATION OF INFORMATION: A SHARED VULNERABILITY

In queer anthropology, gay sex is often shrouded in silence, where the act of sex is done without speaking of it more broadly, to uphold heteronormative expectations.[26] In Beirut, queer men generally act with discretion in their sex lives due to risk of unemployment, social abandonment, and arrest under Article 534 of the penal code, which criminalizes sex deemed against nature.[27] The risks associated with the circulation of men's information are not inherent but produced by the contextual conditions. As Ryan Conrad and Susanna Paasonen and Jenny Sundén show in their chapters of this volume, notions of risk and vulnerability attached to people's sexual information are shaped by the corporate business model, content policies, and community standards. In Beirut, while sex apps have slightly eased the conditions that make queer men vulnerable by moving gay sex lives online and away from cruising places, public sex, and queer bars embedded within heteronormative space and time, they have created a new kind of shared vulnerability: the risk that their private information might circulate widely within and beyond socio-sexual networks.

The conundrum of discretion in the digital age is that men have access to more information about each other but less control over its circulation and consumption. Participation in sex apps requires men to share information among one another to generate sexual possibilities, yet that very act of sharing creates risky conditions whereby their sexy information might be shared among semianonymous, faceless users who could be a cousin, boss, neighbor, family friend, classmate, or sibling.

Men acknowledge the shared vulnerability of being queerly visible in Beirut, negotiating how they control their own information. Some men create strict rules for how they share their information, like their face pictures, name, or place of residence. Discretion is written into the technologies: obscured, pixelated images, partial faces, and pulverized, fragmented bodies. Men declare themselves as discreet and demand discretion from others. Other lean into it. As Jamil once said to me, "People ask for sex pics with others, but only if their face is not shown. I respect people's discretion, but we still also talk about it [people's sexy information]. [The risk of circulating one's pictures and personal details is] part of the life we have chosen to live. The reality we are in."

Digital media have long remediated binaries of public and private, online and offline, having made private life public in new ways within a wider network of users that spans online and offline time and space.[28] Part of the labor of information sharing is the management of one's public sexual self within the circulations among the wider socio-sexual networks. It is the threat of being "widely gay to the world," as one young man put it to me. Men attempt to manage the circulation of their information to avoid being further integrated into queer networks, like not showing their face in body pictures, or by obscuring identifying markers like tattoos, or by not including their face in naked pictures.

Given the risks of sharing information, there is, I argue, a shared (although often broken) responsibility among men in the network to respect one's desire for discretion and to ethically manage one's use of another's information. As a foreign researcher, I was relatively less vulnerable, but my visibility as a queer man was part of their vulnerability via my own participation in queer socio-sexual networks. I had to adapt to this shared vulnerability by developing practices for engaging ethically with the information of others.

FULL IMMERSION: SEX AND OBJECTIVITY

Studying queer life within these networks meant availing myself of all that they do, expect, create, and limit. At first, I attempted to maintain sexual distance so as to not violate any ethical precepts or to overrepresent my desires within my data. However, my attempt was invalidated by the conventional terms of participation: sex is part of communicating over sex apps, which men often reinforced when I tried to speak in sexually vague terms. Sex became a condition of possibility for creating a social milieu I inhabited with my interlocutors. It brings people together in mutual pleasure, or an opening onto something more, a possible human flourishing. I had all kinds of sexual interactions: I talked about sex, met men for one-night stands, had ongoing sexual partners and threesomes, dated men, and fell for some. I became invested in all that sex does to share with others something insightful about the world that was deliberately nonobjectifying.

This research was approved by the University of Toronto Research Ethics Board (REB) with minimal concern. I made clear in my REB application that sex would be part of my fieldwork and that such sex was illegal in Lebanon. The REB agreed that my research did not increase illegal behaviors since it did not ask men to engage in illegal activities men were not already engaging in. Rather, the REB requested that I develop robust data security to ensure protection of my interlocutors' personal details given the illegality of gay sex in Lebanon. Of course, ethics in ethnography is more than this. I undertook several strategies for constantly taking stock of my relationships with others and my role in affecting them.

In anthropology's normative canon, sex in the field stands out from other kinds of intimacies like friendship and social kinship, with arguments that it risks awkward relationships, or violating local mores, or fears of exploitation based on asymmetric power relations.[29] Friendship and social kinship may involve an exchange of intimacy for information, whereas sex cannot, lest it be exploitative. Sex, as basic Euro-American social norms go, ought to be motivated purely by physical desire and love that is free from transactional exchange. Sexual motivations must ideologically exclude economic and material desires, yet anthropologists have come to theorize sex as complexly transactional, showing how exchange is part of intimacy.[30] Ethnographers, however, remain anxious about inserting these lessons into our dominant notions of fieldwork. What can be said of sex in the field can be said of many kinds of intimacies: our desires, and those of others, bring us toward and away from people regardless if it is friendship, social kinship, or exchanging goods for our interlocutors' time.

Ethnographic methodologies and ethics concerning how to act in the field have historically formed around the model of Western ethnographers who, although encouraged to be fully immersed, maintain a degree of social and subjective distance between themselves and others for the sake of objectivity. Such ethnographers are modeled off a Bronislaw Malinowski–type fantasy of the field as a far-off place containing a bounded, nameable culture to which ethnographers come and go, always remaining somewhat external, which Akhil Gupta and James Ferguson have dispelled as fantasy.[31] In fact, Esther Newton has argued that anthropology has modeled the ethnographer as a heterosexual male whose wife accompanies him to the field, separating his private life from his public research life.[32] Newton's critique insinuates that this ethnographer can objectify desire and sexual passions while reserving his own for the privacy of his married life. It means relegating sex to the realm of heterosexual domesticity as a private, personal space separate from life in the field. It also means ignoring the insights of queer theory and anthropology that sex is a rather public thing, central to the production of social life. Anthropology has a long history of studying the sex lives of others but with a feeling of distant objectification, or a scientific gaze.

Sex in the field risks enfolding the ethnographer into the otherness of the interlocutor through bonds of romantic love and feelings of being intimately at home with the other. Sex threatens the distance between home and field, private and professional life, and anthropologist and the other. In other words, sex is either problematized as exploitative because it is based on asymmetric power and exchange, or, if it is based purely on emotions, it threatens the conditions of difference embedded within anthropological knowledge production. This problematization of sex sees it as one-on-one encounters within a collection of relationships with individuals, rather than as part of the intersubjective nature of fieldwork where ethnographers negotiate their various positions in relation to many others through desire, pleasure, and possibility.

As in other studies of gay sex, sex meant positioning myself not just as a participant but as a co-creator alongside my interlocutors in the very socio-sexual worlds I studied.[33] As the center of my own decentralized network, my field is the result of my very immersion into the many relationships and practices that constituted shared networks with others. I created my own flows between myself and others, consuming their information, granting it desire and pleasure, passing it along to others. My field was a result of the intersubjective negotiations of my socio-sexual relationships with others.

Emerging feminist and queer methods insist upon the importance of acknowledging sex and sexuality as part of the ongoing intersubjective negotiation of social relations within the field.[34] In fact, feminist anthropology argues that sex is unavoidably part of fieldwork, especially as the involuntary sexualization of ethnographers, making it so that they cannot always control their own sexual positionality.[35]

What does it mean for ethnography to center (gay) sex within the intersubjective making of my field? It means acknowledging the role of the body in the production of knowledge. Feminist and queer methodologies encourage using the body to negotiate contextual practices and meaning, while sidestepping sensations, or "sensual immersion," as "bodily and emotional immersion."[36] Sexual interactions in the field were a form of body-sensorial knowledge production with my interlocutors.[37] Such critiques extend embodiment beyond a moment toward using a full range of sensations and feelings to learn through the constant negotiation of one's position in the field toward others.

This requires sexual reflexivity as methodology, especially as a matter of reciprocating emotions and intimacy within our relations and an ethic of care and emotional management.[38] Under this model, one must account for the forms of desire that permeate our relationships with others, like the desire to be their friend or lover, to never speak to them, or to interview them. Desire in the field is multifaceted, a force for the intersubjective negotiation of our relationships, or even our practices of co-implication with others.

Fully participating in men's sexual lives meant I had to be aware of how my own desire was shaping my data and how I was affecting others. I did not want my own practices to make people feel bad or excluded. I had to learn how to mitigate the effects of my desire as a compass toward and away from men within my data, while devising ways for me to reflect on and learn from moments when my methodological practices were less than perfect. I developed ways of talking to men while attempting to manage how I was affecting them, of letting them down gently, or not insulting them, or treating their information as undesirable. I also had to learn how to manage my own emotions and negative feelings. There is a lot of personal injury and woundedness on sex apps, my own and those of others, to which I learned to become sensitive. This reflexivity takes seriously the personal experiences of the ethnographer as a route to insight, therefore making it somewhat autoethnographic. Such reflexivity, as Tony Adams and Stacy Holman Jones point out, must account for the awkwardness and tensions of relationships that are never quite tied up, as well as personal stories as data that necessarily contain ambiguity, gaps, mistakes, openness.[39] It requires a vulnerability, as subjects of our ethnographic tales are usually absent because framing ourselves in relation to others is difficult.[40] Take away all the theorization, and this is just about the ways that we negotiate our attachments in the field. Affect, as Catherine Lutz points out, is about understanding how things and relationships come to matter.[41]

MANAGING MY POSITION WITHIN POSSIBILITIES: ETHICS OF RECIPROCITY

Within these networks, I was interpolated as many things: researcher, Canadian, white, object of desire, friend, conversationalist, potential and former lover, enemy, object of nondesire, and so on. To others, I became part of the terrain of negotiated possibilities filtered through many positionalities. It wasn't just about learning how to manage my relationships in the field between these many positions but about how to participate in the negotiation of possibilities through an ethics of reciprocation that addresses the moral challenges ethnographers face in building relationships with others.[42]

If we demystify the separation between professional (i.e., labor) and private (i.e., leisurely) life while in the field, then we can begin to see our relationships in the field as inhering norms of social exchange guided by post-Maussian theories of reciprocity as part of the maintenance of social life.[43] I was asking men to share with me their sexual energies and information, which required that I share mine as part of developing bonds of trust and openness. Anthropologist Jafari Allen came to a similar conclusion about the ethical need for reciprocity vis-à-vis intimate details.[44] Keeping part of myself outside of sex went against the terms of participation within these networks. I could not treat men's sexual experiences and emotions as objects to be collected while I painted myself as the privileged researcher without any of those things, as being beyond the fray of messy sexual feelings. Reciprocating, by exchanging my information with them, became a means of jointly navigating the shared vulnerability of information's circulation.

In many ways, the circulation of information acts like a gift economy in which there is an expectation that not only information will be shared but sexual emotions and feelings of sexual possibility as well, like telling a guy his pictures are hot or that he is desirable. Even a message of rejection is appreciated over a nonresponse. Nonreciprocation by way of silence or nothingness is often worse than being rejected outright.

Reciprocity, however, is a difficult ethical task given the limitations in giving back everything everyone gives. The central dilemma of participating fully in these networks is that I invariably became part of people's desires and possibilities, leaving me open to the ethical conundrum of causing bad feelings by not living up to their expectations toward me. Exchange creates dynamics of power through obligation, in which negative feelings of being unfairly repaid arise.

Reciprocity involves a different set of ethical questions that acknowledge the conditions of living each relationship on its own terms rather than through a set of proscribed institutionalized filters: how to be a good app user, friend, lover, respectful of people's emotions, and responsible for how I inevitably affected them. Reciprocity in the field, however, is not a utilitarian urge for trading relationships for information but is instead invested with affective attachments to our interlocutors, who often enrich and balance our time in the field.

This perspective eschews a researcher positionality as static and controlled in favor of one that places the researcher in a social milieu of constant negotiation of different social relations, whereby the ethical question becomes not one of acting toward others but reacting with them, to give back (at some level) that which they give.[45]

A story: in August 2014 I met a young man named Daoud. After some days of convivial chat spliced with his invitation for wine and a massage at my place, we took a drive one night. I was unsure about my sexual feelings for him, but I wanted to become acquainted. I enjoyed his company. Afraid that sexual rejection would negate our budding friendship, I spoke in equivocations about my degree of sexual interest. From my apartment in Tabaris in the east of Beirut, we drove to Ramlat al-Bayda, where we walked along Beirut's last public beach. He was nice, gregarious, engaging, and I felt a connection with him, a potentiality. In the shadows near a rock to the side of the beach, our bodies got closer and we began kissing and touching. It lasted until we noticed two men milling about nearby. Upon returning to my home, I gently dissuaded his request to come up, expressing my honest discomfort with hosting someone for sex while living with three straight, foreign men (although they wouldn't have cared). Once Daoud got home, he tried to engage me in some sexting while he masturbated. Now, after some exploratory kissing, I was sure I did not want a sexual relationship with him and again equivocated until he stopped.

In the following days, our texting was fun and friendly but still with Daoud's persistent suggestion for wine and a massage at my place—his way of insinuating sex. We met again for lunch. Still intent on creating a friendship with him, I was anxious about rebuffing his sexual advances, which I had encouraged with my early ambivalence or uncertainty toward him. A few days later, I texted him to confirm our plans for that night, asking what he wanted to do. Again, he suggested wine and a massage. This time, I stopped equivocating and told him I only wanted to be friends. He was confused: to him we were friends, a category that could include sex. I, however, excluded sex from friendship (I've learned otherwise since then). Upset, he called me out on my behavior the first time we met, to which I apologized, explaining that my feelings had changed. After some conversation, we agreed a friendship was unlikely since he made it contingent upon sex, whereas I did not want that. For months, we awkwardly crossed paths in bars and parties or community events, places where online connections spark anew when strangers come to say things like "hey, I saw you on Grindr before." Daoud and I never acknowledged one another. I wanted to, but I had an ethical practice of not being the first to acknowledge people offline without eye contact and body language that suggested it was okay lest I violate their discretion. Months later, he unexpectedly and graciously apologized over WhatsApp for his actions, while I reiterated my own apology for my ambiguous acts.

An ethics of reciprocity is not a practice of commensurate exchange between the ethnographer and others. I could not reciprocate Daoud's sexual desires. It is a far more intersubjective exchange between two individuals, one in which we interpolated each other as certain kinds of beings or possibilities with limits, sometimes beyond our control. Reciprocation is an act of reacting with others, of determining what they want from me, what I am willing to give, and how to reciprocate within those limits. It is an intersubjective field where I had to reflect on my sense of self in relation to their image or expectations of me and, through flexibility and reflexivity, figure out how to relate to them through these interpolations and the degree of reciprocation I could provide without shutting them out based on a strict self-image but with having to negotiate myself in relation to them.

Reciprocation is not always commensurate. In this intersubjective negotiation of sex and pleasure where there is always potential for awkwardness and bad feelings, I have the ethical responsibility to react with more clarity and honesty toward men than they have toward me. As a researcher, it is my responsibility more than theirs to be aware of and react with clarity and honesty, to be discerning of how I was affecting others. Ethically, I had the greater duty to manage people's feelings without expecting others to reciprocate in managing my own feelings.

I had to be aware of the kinds of erotic power I had as a white, cis, normatively gendered gay man affiliated with a top university in a Western country. In Beirut, my whiteness places me within a system of social stratification that assigns me erotic and social value as someone outside of social and familial relations that constrained queer visibility in a culture of discretion; immediate access to private spaces for sex; and the assumption that as a Westerner I was sexually liberated. As a native English speaker, my whiteness was also indicative of a classed hierarchy that intersects with language, which both created and foreclosed opportunities in the field.

REMAKING THE NETWORK OVER AND OVER

Men know so much more about one another by the circulation of information beyond the confines of one-on-one conversations within sex apps. Their socio-sexual networks are designed to never cease in connecting strangers through the sexual information they share. Take, for instance, an afternoon spent sipping coffee on a patio with Abid, Shadi, and Mahir. (I met Mahir through Abid and Shadi one night at Posh, a popular queer dance club. Months later, he and I reconnected on Grindr and ended up having sex after I interviewed him.) Across the street, we spotted a young man we all recognized from his Grindr profile. It was not the first time any of us had seen him in person; he often attended gay clubs or parties. We all noted how his profile image of his bare torso accompanied by text that he was looking for friends and something serious seemed contradictory. And, that he often started conversations by asking for dick pics or sexual desires. Shadi, who was looking for a relationship, told us the story of a date he had with him and how all he talked about was sex and gossip about other men. Men see each other over and over, often noticing one another offline just by their profile or past conversations. Across the city, men tell stories, share information, and establish connections between others. In moments like this, the networks are remade as our shared connections are made evident. As a participant, I felt obliged to do my part in making and remaking these networks, lest I awkwardly remain partially external to the networks I was researching.

It is easy for men to know each other simply by repeatedly seeing one another's profiles. Sex apps arrange users based on their location in physical space, and in Beirut, where the density of users is low, my interface of three hundred profiles extended to four kilometers. I often saw the same profiles as I moved around the city, becoming familiar with others only by their rarely updated profile information. There is a sort of unintentional voyeurism to sex apps.

One of the most difficult questions when it came to reciprocity was how it exists in tension with an ethical imperative toward anonymity. As part of these networks, I couldn't help participating in the constant flows of information. It is how these networks formed, and I had a sometimes unwanted role in circulating men's information to others, often inadvertently and sometimes awkwardly (re)connecting them to others.

Another story will animate the tense social fields where a single user has a history with all three friends but refuses to acknowledge these histories when they meet. This example of the formation of these networks involves Murad, a young man I initially met over Hornet. One Friday night, we were at an art show. Near the end of the event, Murad and I decided to return to my apartment. I invited Michael, Mano, and James to join us. To me, they were all strangers except for James and Murad, who, I had found out a few days earlier, had been casually chatting over Scruff. I mentioned that James would be there. He laughed and said that the encounter might be awkward but that he could handle it.

Murad asked who else was going. I mentioned their names. "Wait," he interjected, "what are their Grindr names?" I mentioned their names. "Nooooo," he cried. "I never thought I would see them again." He had met Michael a few years earlier. It was pleasant, with no sex, and they continued texting. But one day he decided to stop responding. With Mano, they too had met once or twice but for sex. Again, he just decided to stop engaging one day for no concrete reason.

He began to rethink his decision to join us, fearing the repercussions of his previous actions. I advised him to just acknowledge the past upon introduction, but he hesitated. He eventually realized he needed to face these awkward network connections. When the others arrived, I went to the door to grab them, whispering that there was someone here they may not want to see. Michael immediately recognized Murad and amicably said hello. James introduced himself as if their recent online interaction had no bearing on the immediate introduction, a typical reaction since it was their first in-person meeting. Michael and Mano followed me into the kitchen, mouthing, "What they hell? Oh my god!" Mano was upset that Murad did not acknowledge him, given that there was sex involved, especially since Mano, a self-professed femme top, bottomed for him. He had done for Murad something he rarely does for anyone and was peeved when Murad feigned recognition. Michael, however, was less upset by the slight of their sexual past going unacknowledged.

I was filled with tension that night, feeling as if I had overstepped an ethical duty toward minimizing the degree to which my association with men became known among the network. I waded through this ethical conundrum by developing a sensitivity to understanding how men maintain discretion and managing my own discretion among them in various ways. Sometimes I withheld tales, other times I indulged or acknowledged my acquaintanceship with those in the stories of others.

MANAGING MY QUEER VISIBILITY

This convergence of one's sex life within a wider network is what plenty of discreet men seek to avoid. As a foreign ethnographer whose presence was tied to the social lives of others, I had to be mindful of my place within this culture of discretion. Being with me, an out, visibly queer man, could threaten their discretion or lead to invasive questions from their friends and family about the nature of our association. Given that my ethnographic participation in these networks meant I had to be part of their formation and reformation by moving around information, I had an ethical and methodological imperative to learn the social and informational cues indicating when and how to connect men to others through me.

I managed my own discretion by obscuring my research subject to nonparticipants. I went along with fabrications about how interlocutors and I met when we were with their friends and families. Sometimes I helped others devise stories about how we met, sometimes narratives more complex than simply having mutual friends but incorporating minute details of their lives so that the story would seem more plausible. I had to be careful of my own bodily movements, my own masculine performance so that my own sexuality was not brought into question. On the street, I was careful not to say hello to people I casually knew, in case my greeting was an unwelcomed interpolation leading those around them to ask who I was and how we knew each other. I managed my speech and body language in social situations where being tied to me could out an interlocutor. When necessary, I obfuscated the nature of my research with others in order to protect interlocutors from being outed. Working with queer men in a country where gay sex is illegal, I had to be careful about my engagements with authorities like the police and border control, lest they search my phone (a common but illegal practice in Lebanon) and entrap interlocutors through their contact information. Reacting ethically in these moments means knowing how specific conditions congeal into various degrees of homophobic threat, as well as how to conceal those visibilities of gayness that are largely displayed on the body (gait, gestures, voice, utterances, accoutrements).

Take, for instance, a weekend trip with Wahid—with whom I had a budding intimacy—to his hometown in the south of Lebanon. We spent the first day on a boat with four others: an old friend of Wahid and his girlfriend (to whom Wahid was out) and a new friend of Wahid and a girl he was courting (to whom he was not out). To avoid making our intimacy visible to the two of them, we policed our behaviors, avoiding touch and too much eye contact. Things were said beyond earshot. Distance was kept. Men have a cultural knowledge of how to manage these scenes, a knowledge I had to acquire.

After wandering amid the warm sea breeze that night, just he and I, we spent the second day at a seaside restaurant with direct access to the water for anyone who wanted a swim. We were with a group Wahid had become close to that summer as beach buddies, to whom he was not out. Again, he asked me to avoid gestures and information that threatened his discretion. When questions arose about our connection, we told them we met through friends in Beirut. Fortunately, my presence among them made sense under the precepts of Lebanese hospitality, where it is acceptable for people to play tour guide for foreigners. When the question of the reason I am in Lebanon comes up, I tell them I am doing doctoral research into the youth culture around social media. Excited, one woman offers to introduce me to a faculty member at a local university also interested in my fabricated topic. Nervous, I graciously sidestep her invitation, to avoid any further questions.

In a hush, Wahid pointed to another queer man among us who was afraid that I, as the Westerner unfamiliar with the trials of discreet life, would haphazardly blurt out something that would incriminate us all. Soon, his boyfriend arrived. They are intimate, appearing like children who are inseparably close, almost with their own language. Wahid whispered that he overheard others questioning their relationship, suspecting their homosexuality. The scene is tense with traveling knowledge, questions, and unspoken but shared understanding of how to act in these scenarios. I notice one woman, who from my brief observation seemed prone to catty gossip, glaring at the two of them as they talk, leading me to assume she is interrogating their camaraderie. Often, in these moments, men try to deflect and distract possible questions with lies about female lovers, jokes and comments thrown in to perform a feigned heterosexuality, like when Wahid made a tactless sex joke to an engaged women. The moment produced a bit of tension, which Wahid cut by noting that her fiancé wouldn't mind that joke since they were friends. Being within queer networks evokes a tapestry of cues for knowing when and how to make secrets socially obvious, as part of my participation in practices of information circulation, and when to conceal them.

METHODS AND ETHICS OF STUDYING QUEER DATA

The politics of data within queer life entails the possibilities and limits of information upon sex's ineffabilities, specifically how men use data infrastructures and networks to stir up the possibility for new intimacies within their use of information. Queer data does not exist in the world. It is made in everyday moments, shrouded under layers of so many things, emergent from the encounters with others. Most important, it is the result of an ethically reflective and reciprocated imbrication of my life in the field with the lives of others, without the burden of striving for subjective and sexual distance when it is impossible. I learned early that trying to maintain that distance was futile and would have directed my energies away from the more grounded ethical work. I began to see it through practices of co-implication within its circulation and production in everyday life. I was a participant in sex apps before I was a researcher of sex apps, while with others in the field and even before ever conceiving of this project. I was always already embedded within the flows of sexy information throughout digitally mediated networks. It was through developing my own practices of information, new forms of ethical engagement with others, that

I became able to understand the complexity of queer life within socio-sexual networks. Learning the codes and cues for how to circulate information among networks in ways that make it meaningful gave my data its queerness.

NOTES

1. Although such technologies are known by many names, I call them sex apps because that is how my interlocutors primarily used them.

2. My plan was to unobtrusively recruit research participants through casual chatting, talking to them about my project, which would develop into their agreeing to participate. I generally spoke to men in English but sometimes in Arabic or French. I put a face picture and my status as a foreigner, along with a few lines about things I like. While I did not directly include the nature of my research, I wrote my status as a PhD student in my profile and would tell anyone of my project in conversation. From my experience with chatting, I knew that putting my project in my profile would have made men nervous and cagey. Being a researcher studying sex apps made my participation more than personal but slightly public. And some men thought I could be straight. This was, to me, an ethical violation against doing harm, since my digital presence might have created negative feelings among some men. Many men offered to be directly involved, while others stopped talking to me, which I interpreted as nonconsent.

3. Galloway and Thacker, *The Exploit*, 23–102.

4. Terranova, *Network Culture*, 42.

5. McGlotten, *Virtual Intimacies*, 7.

6. McGlotten, *Virtual Intimacies*, 7.

7. McGlotten, "Life in the Network," 166.

8. McGlotten, "Life in the Network," 166.

9. The Association of Internet Researchers has a document outlining ethical guidelines based on a general agreement that there is a rightful expectation on the part of the individual that any information people put in their dating profiles is private and therefore should be aggregated and anonymized in research and reporting. For more information, see franzke et al., *Internet Research*.

10. Geertz, "Bazaar Economy," 30.

11. Makarem, "Story of HELEM," 102.

12. Merabet, *Queer Beirut*, 56.

13. Merabet, *Queer Beirut*, 57–59.

14. Humphreys, *Tearoom Trade*, 59–65; Delany, *Times Square Red, Times Square Blue*, 118–19; Tikkanen and Ross, "Technological Tearoom Trade," 122–23; Race, "Speculative Pragmatism and Intimate Arrangements," 506; Race, *Gay Science*, 172–73.

15. Raj, "Grindring Bodies," 1–4; Roth, "Locating the 'Scruff Guy,'" 2120–21.

16. Terranova, *Network Culture*, 21.

17. Race, "'Party and Play,'" 254.

18. Keilty, "Embodied Engagements with Online Pornography," 68.

19. Massumi, *Parables for the Virtual*, 24–27.

20. Gagnon and Simon, *Sexual Conduct*, 66.

21. Cody, "Daily Wires and Daily Blossoms," 287.

22. Race, "Speculative Pragmatism and Intimate Arrangements," 500.

23. Race, "Speculative Pragmatism and Intimate Arrangements," 500.

24. Massumi, *Parables for the Virtual*, 137–38.

25. On puritanical readings and tech company community standards, see chapter 4 in this volume. On greater control of sex data through government legislation and closures of websites for sex workers, see chapter 6 in this volume.

26. Boellstorff, "Between Religion and Desire," 575–76.

27. This prohibition is a vestige of colonial law implemented during the French mandate from 1920 until 1946, when Lebanon gained independence.

28. Lange, "Publicly Private and Privately Public," 364–65; Gray, *Out in the Country*, 92–93.

29. Kulick and Willson, *Taboo*, 3–6; Irwin, "Into the Dark Heart of Ethnography," 157–60.

30. Cole and Thomas, "Introduction: Thinking through Love in Africa," 9, 21; Zelizer, *Purchase of Intimacy*, 32.

31. Gupta and Ferguson, "Discipline and Practice," 6–15.

32. Newton, "My Best Informant's Dress," 4.

33. Orne, *Boystown*, 12–13; Langarita Adiego, "On Sex in Fieldwork," 1256.

34. Irwin, "Dark Heart," 158–59; Kaspar and Landolt, "Flirting in the Field," 108–9.

35. De Craene, "Fucking Geographers!," 454–56.

36. Irwin, "Dark Heart," 157.

37. Gagné, "Studying Gay Sex in Beirut," 33.

38. Orne, *Boystown*, 51–61; Irwin, "Dark Heart," 158–59; De Craene, "Fucking Geographers!," 451–52.

39. Adams and Jones, "Telling Stories," 113–14.

40. Adams and Jones, "Telling Stories," 112–13.

41. Lutz, "What Matters," 181–82.

42. Wax, "Research Reciprocity Rather than Informed Consent in Fieldwork," 34–35.

43. Peebles, "Anthropology of Credit and Debt," 226–27; Befu, "Social Exchange," 255; Gosovic, "Gifts, Reciprocity and Ethically Sound Ethnographic Research," 71–72.

44. Allen, ¡*Venceremos?*, 8.

45. Irwin, "Dark Heart," 159–60.

BIBLIOGRAPHY

Adams, Tony E., and Stacy Holman Jones. "Telling Stories: Reflexivity, Queer Theory, and Autoethnography." *Cultural Studies ↔ Critical Methodologies* 11, no. 2 (2011): 108–16.

Allen, Jafari S. *¡Venceremos? The Erotics of Black Self-Making in Cuba*. Durham, NC: Duke University Press, 2011.

Befu, Harumi. "Social Exchange." *Annual Review of Anthropology* 6 (1977): 255–81.

Boellstorff, Tom. "Between Religion and Desire: Being Muslim and Gay in Indonesia." *American Anthropologist* 107, no. 4 (2005): 575–85.

Cody, Francis. "Daily Wires and Daily Blossoms: Cultivating Regimes of Circulation in Tamil India's Newspaper Revolution." *Journal of Linguistic Anthropology* 19, no. 2 (2009): 286–309.

Cole, Jennifer, and Lynn M. Thomas. "Introduction: Thinking through Love in Africa." In *Love in Africa*, edited by Jennifer Cole and Lynn M. Thomas, 1–30. Chicago: University of Chicago Press, 2009.

De Craene, Valerie. "Fucking Geographers! Or the Epistemological Consequences of Neglecting the Lusty Researcher's Body." *Gender, Place and Culture* 24, no. 3 (2017): 449–64.

Delany, Samuel R. *Times Square Red, Times Square Blue*. New York: New York University Press, 1999.

franzke, aline shakti, Anja Bechmann, Michael Zimmer, Charles Ess, and the Association of Internet Researchers. *Internet Research: Ethical Guidelines 3.0*. 2020. https://aoir.org/reports/ethics3.pdf.

Gagné, Mathew. "Studying Gay Sex in Beirut: The Lascivious Suture of Home/Field." In *Home: Ethnographic Encounters*, edited by Farhan Samanani and Johannes Lenhard, 31–44. New York: Bloomsbury, 2019.

Gagnon, John H., and William Simon. *Sexual Conduct: The Social Sources of Human Sexuality*. Chicago: Aldine, 1973.

Galloway, Alexander R., and Eugene Thacker. *The Exploit: A Theory of Networks*. Minneapolis: University of Minnesota Press, 2007.

Geertz, Clifford. "The Bazaar Economy: Information and Search in Peasant Marketing." *American Economic Review* 68, no. 2 (1978): 28–32.

Gray, Mary L. *Out in the Country: Youth, Media, and Queer Visibility in Rural America*. New York: New York University Press, 2009.

Gosovic, Anna Kirkebæk Johansson. "Gifts, Reciprocity and Ethically Sound Ethnographic Research: A Reflexive Framework." *Journal of Organizational Ethnography* 9, no. 1 (2020): 66–79.

Gupta, Akhil, and James Ferguson. "Discipline and Practice: 'The Field' as Site,

Method, and Location in Anthropology." In *Anthropological Location: Boundaries and Grounds of a Field Science*, edited by Akhil Gupta and James Ferguson, 1–29. Berkeley: University of California Press, 1997.

Humphreys, Laud. *Tearoom Trade: Impersonal Sex in Public Places*. Chicago: Aldine, 1975.

Irwin, Katherine. "Into the Dark Heart of Ethnography: The Lived Ethics and Inequality of Intimate Field Relationships." *Qualitative Sociology* 29, no. 2 (2006): 155–75.

Kaspar, Heidi, and Sara Landolt. "Flirting in the Field: Shifting Positionalities and Power Relations in Innocuous Sexualisations of Research Encounters." *Gender, Place and Culture* 23, no. 1 (2016): 107–19.

Keilty, Patrick. "Embodied Engagements with Online Pornography." *Information Society* 32, no. 1 (2016): 64–73.

Kulick, Don, and Margaret Willson, eds. *Taboo: Sex, Identity and Erotic Subjectivity in Anthropological Fieldwork*. New York: Routledge, 1995.

Langarita Adiego, Jose Antonio. "On Sex in Fieldwork: Notes on the Methodology Involved in the Ethnographic Study of Anonymous Sex." *Sexualities* 22, no. 7–8 (2019): 1253–67.

Lange, Patricia G. "Publicly Private and Privately Public: Social Networking on YouTube." *Journal of Computer-Mediated Communication* 13, no. 1 (2007): 361–80.

Lutz, Catherine. "What Matters." *Cultural Anthropology* 32, no. 2 (2017): 181–91.

Makarem, Ghassan. "The Story of HELEM." *Journal of Middle East Women's Studies* 7, no. 3 (2011): 98–112.

Massumi, Brian. *Parables for the Virtual: Movement, Affect, Sensation*. Durham, NC: Duke University Press, 2002.

McGlotten, Shaka. "Life in the Network." *Women and Performance: A Journal of Feminist Theory* 28, no. 2 (2018): 161–69.

———. *Virtual Intimacies: Media, Affect, and Queer Sociality*. Albany: State University of New York Press, 2013.

Merabet, Sofian. *Queer Beirut*. Austin: University of Texas Press, 2014.

Newton, Esther. "My Best Informant's Dress: The Erotic Equation in Fieldwork." *Cultural Anthropology* 8, no. 1 (1993): 3–23.

Orne, Jason. *Boystown: Sex and Community in Chicago*. Chicago: University of Chicago Press, 2017.

Peebles, Gustav. "The Anthropology of Credit and Debt." *Annual Review of Anthropology* 39 (2010): 225–40.

Race, Kane. *The Gay Science: Intimate Experiments with the Problem of HIV*. New York: Routledge, 2017.

———. "'Party and Play': Online Hook-Up Devices and the Emergence of PNP Practices among Gay Men." *Sexualities* 18, no. 3 (2015): 253–75.

———. "Speculative Pragmatism and Intimate Arrangements: Online Hook-Up Devices in Gay Life." *Culture, Health & Sexuality* 17, no. 4 (2014): 496–511.

Raj, Senthorun. "Grindring Bodies: Racial and Affective Economies of Online Queer Desire." *Critical Race and Whiteness Studies* 7, no. 2 (2011): 1–12.

Roth, Yoel. "Locating the 'Scruff Guy': Theorizing Body and Space in Gay Geosocial Media." *International Journal of Communication* 8 (2014): 2113–33.

Terranova, Tiziana. *Network Culture: Politics for the Information Age.* Ann Arbor, MI: Pluto, 2004.

Tikkanen, Ronny, and Michael W. Ross. "Technological Tearoom Trade: Characteristics of Swedish Men Visiting Gay Internet Chat Rooms." *AIDS Education and Prevention* 15, no. 2 (2003): 122–32.

Wax, Murrey L. "Research Reciprocity Rather than Informed Consent in Fieldwork." In *The Ethics of Social Research,* edited by Joan E. Sieber, 33–48. New York: Springer, 1982.

Zelizer, Viviana A. *The Purchase of Intimacy.* Princeton: Princeton University Press, 2005.

HARRIS KORNSTEIN

9 Homobiles *Queering Data through Ephemerality and Intimacy*

ON A SUMMER AFTERNOON IN 2010, I was dancing on the patio at El Rio, a neighborhood queer bar in San Francisco, when Lynn Breedlove handed me a flyer. Breedlove explained in his typical style, "Hey queen, need a ride somewhere? We're starting up this new thing, Homobiles! Getting girls to their gigs, the club, dates, doctor's appointments, whatever, you name it. You know: 'Moes Getting Hoes Where They Needz 2 Goes.'" A version of that last line was printed on the flyer, along with a studly image of Breedlove himself and promises of "cheap rides for expensive babes." Breedlove is certainly a character: a queer and trans writer and musician, he was known as the lead singer of the 1990s queercore band Tribe 8.[1] I pocketed the flyer with a polite-but-skeptical "thank you"; at the time, Silicon Valley's innovation bubble was intensifying, and there was often—even among queers—an entrepreneurial ethos toward big ideas that failed to pan out. Yet, I soon started using Homobiles regularly, and so did many others. For about five years, it operated as a robust community transportation service across the San Francisco Bay Area, packing queers of all kinds into cars. At its peak, it engaged a fleet of about twenty drivers, and operated twenty-four hours a day, seven days a week. That is, until Uber and Lyft cornered the market, dramatically disrupting taxi industries and contributing to broader restructurings of labor and transportation systems in the United States. Still, as of this writing, Homobiles continues to operate in a limited capacity via grant funding, especially in supporting trans people to access health care.

In this chapter, I present Homobiles as a case study of a low-tech service by and for queer and trans people that demonstrates strategies for queering popular technologies and their collection, storage, and use of data. I contrast it with app-based ride-hailing services like Uber and Lyft, given that both also began their on-the-ground operations in San Francisco in the early 2010s.[2] There is also both speculation and evidence that Homobiles directly inspired its competitors. For example, Sunil Paul, founder of the now-defunct service Sidecar, framed his company as "a scalable, technology-enabled version of [H]omobiles."[3] Breedlove reasonably suspects that Lyft's "your friend with a car" motto and early pink mustaches were nods to the queer service, as he wrote in a Facebook post: "the original pink mustache on the bumper, in our humble opinion, was the risqué 'mustache ride' answer to the sexual innuendo of [H]omobiles."[4]

As such, Homobiles occupies an ambiguous and ambivalent position in the history of ride hailing: on the one hand, Homobiles contributed to the normalization of precarious "gig" labor, specifically through a moral positioning as a community-driven social service; on the other hand, Homobiles differed significantly from Silicon Valley's values in not seeking venture capital, competing to corner global markets, or aggressively fighting local taxi regulations and driver classifications.[5] Further, as I focus on in this chapter, Homobiles also diverged in its queer use of data, refusing business models rooted in forms of data-driven surveillance that scholars variously refer to as "dataveillance," "automated surveillance," and "surveillance capitalism."[6] In this way, Homobiles serves as an example of what Benjamin Nicoll refers to as a "minor platform" in both offering a unique form of affective engagement with digital and human platforms as well as complicating teleological understandings of success and failure (which I return to at the end of this chapter).[7] Homobiles suffered its own shortcomings, perhaps most notably a lack of financial sustainability and a shifting of risks and costs onto drivers (though with greater attempts to mitigate that issue than many of its competitors).[8] Nevertheless, I argue that Homobiles contributes a small but significant case explaining how fundamental shifts in digital technologies, surveillance, and labor might have been—and still might be—routed through a framework of social and economic justice.

In what follows, I begin with a brief recounting of the founding of Homobiles, situating it within queer and trans digital media studies, as well as legacies of mutual aid, queer separatism, and punk. I then focus on specific queer values and technical strategies that Homobiles engaged: in particular, a small-scale and ephemeral approach to data use, as well as an intimate approach to ensuring trust and safety. Throughout, I draw on a dozen ethnographic interviews with riders, drivers, and organizers (sourced through my own social networks and Breedlove's recommendations), as well as analysis of social media posts, and post-hoc reflections on my own experiences using the service. Given that several years have passed since most riders have used the service, I cautiously note the nostalgia that inflects some of these accounts (including my own). Despite my best attempts, it was nearly impossible to find people to be interviewed who had negative things to say about the service. While this may suggest a form of sampling or acquiescence bias, I speculate that these affective attachments are also indicative of often-dubious forms of romanticizing the notion of "community" that, like many queer/trans San Francisco art and activist projects, were key to Homobiles both becoming a beacon and also quickly burning out.[9]

"EVERYBODY GETS HOME SAFE":
MAPPING QUEER DESIGN, VALUES, AND CARE

The beginnings of Homobiles are embedded in Breedlove's unique personal circumstances, as well as the social and technological landscapes of the Bay Area at the end of the aughts. In recounting its founding, Breedlove explained that it began with him returning home from a performance tour after his mother experienced a stroke, which left him with access to her car—a prized possession for a queer punk. The seed of an idea first came to him while driving trans, femme, and stripper friends around town, highlighting the need for safe transportation options as well as sparking his inclination toward a chivalrous form of community service. The idea solidified at a party, when a fellow queer punk casually suggested that Breedlove create an app-based ride service that could be called Homobiles. Breedlove scoffed, "I don't know anything about apps!" But the idea took off a few months later when another friend called from the annual Femme Conference in Oakland, suggesting Breedlove give rides to attendees. By his telling, he "rolled up [to the conference] . . . blasting Le Tigre . . . and all these ladies . . . way more than the legal amount, femmes with big hair and, you know, cleavage and everything, climbed into the car, packed in, just babes poking out of all the windows."[10] After that first night, Breedlove created a flyer using his mom's printer and began advertising at queer events. The service was offered for a suggested donation of $1 per minute with a policy of no one turned away for lack of funds. Homobiles quickly expanded to multiple drivers, eventually became a registered nonprofit, and unsuccessfully attempted to build its own mobile app.[11] Still, that original flyer cemented the queer politics and policies of Homobiles.

Beyond the demographics of its leadership and ridership, Homobiles demonstrates queerness in its function, design, and use. Specifically, Homobiles might be situated within Kara Keeling and others' framing of "Queer OS," which, following Wendy Hui Kyong Chun, positions queerness "and/as technology" and articulates how computational operations might be queered through non-normative functions.[12] In this vein, Bo Ruberg's formulation of "playing queer" suggests the ways in which digital platforms (games or otherwise) might be queered not merely via inclusive representation but through non-normative mechanics, values, and modes of engagement.[13] Similarly, Sara Ahmed's work on "queer use" stresses the queerness in users interacting with systems in unintended ways, by unexpected users, or in refusing to use them at all, thereby "releasing a potentiality that already resides in things."[14] Finally, in a more practical sense, Homobiles might serve as an example of design justice as defined by Sasha Costanza-Chock, given its rootedness in community needs, nonprofessional design approaches, and professed values of access and safety.[15]

Building from these theoretical frameworks, I situate the Homobiles community-centered logic of care as rooted in the interrelated, if often contradictory, historical legacies of punk, separatism, and mutual aid. I develop these further in an in-progress book/project but offer brief notes here. Perhaps most directly, Breedlove and several of the early Homobiles volunteers emerged from queer and trans punk music scenes, infusing the project with what Jayna Brown, Patrick Deer, and Tavia Nyong'o describe as the "punk spirit of misbehavior, improvisation, disobedience, and deviance."[16] Equally important, the DIY approach of Homobiles also reflects punk's traditions of building anticorporate communication and information infrastructures, such as small record labels and zine distribution. Additionally, viewed through the lens of historical lesbian and gay separatist commitments to economic sustainability—via collective publishing or agricultural projects—Homobiles further offered a means for queer and trans people to earn an income by keeping dollars within a local, queer economy (though this promise did not always pan out in ways that benefited drivers).[17]

The leaders, drivers, and riders of Homobiles also tended to characterize the organization's work through discourses of "service" and "safety," terms that resonate with historical legacies and recent theorizations of mutual aid. For example, Homobiles met several defining benchmarks as outlined by Dean

Spade, including making commitments to provide material support for unmet needs, focusing on the most marginalized members of the community (with expressed commitments to riders who were trans and BIPOC), and "building new social relations that are more survivable."[18] Similarly, Homobiles might be understood through Ren-yo Hwang's decarceral and queer-of-color framework of "deviant care," encouraging understandings of interdependent aid that deviate not only from social norms but also from colonial and philanthropic power dynamics of subject and object.[19]

Within this context, Homobiles positioned itself as providing reliable and safe transportation at a time when San Francisco's public transportation and taxis were perceived to be unreliable and often unsafe, particularly for queer and trans people and communities of color.[20] Many of the people I interviewed recounted instances of taxi or Lyft and Uber drivers canceling rides or driving by once they saw their appearance, and many also shared personal or friends' stories of offensive comments, sexual assault, or concerns about drivers knowing where they lived.[21] In response, the stated mission of Homobiles was "to provid[e] secure and reliable transit to the SF Bay Area LGBTIQQ community and its allies."[22] It was, in short, what drag queen Persia summarized simply as "to get the queers home safe."[23] In this way, though not directly cited as inspiration, Homobiles might also be seen as part of a global legacy of both community-oriented and public-health driven "safe ride" programs, generally organized around safety for women or to prevent drunk driving.[24]

However, the Homobiles discourses of identity and safety also echoed some of the historical exclusions of punk, separatism, and mutual aid, perhaps inadvertently contributing to the very neoliberal discourses and effects that it otherwise emphatically countered. For example, though the Homobiles leadership offered nuanced social analyses rooted in intersectionality, its critiques of taxi drivers were often taken up by media and regulatory agencies in ways that inaccurately pitted a predominantly immigrant workforce against LGBTQ riders.[25] Particularly with the emergence of Lyft and Uber, such discourse often took an exceptionalist tone, with assumptions that these drivers did not live in San Francisco proper and, whether they were from the suburbs or abroad, brought ideas that did not mesh with the city's perceived liberal values.[26]

Interestingly, this emphasis on safety was also taken up directly by regulators. The California Public Utilities Commission (CPUC) "applauded the founders of Homobiles for establishing a non-profit 501(c)(3) volunteer organization that caters to the underserved communities of San Francisco," noting its commitment to LGBTQ riders who had faced discrimination. However, in a somewhat ironic twist of logic, the CPUC also used Homobiles as an example of how such social purposes could be achieved without explicit regulation (and indeed, it classified Uber and Lyft as less-regulated "Transportation Network Companies," or TNCs, rather than taxis), writing that "while some parties argue that TNCs such as Lyft, UberX, and SideCar must be regulated either as taxi cabs or limousines in order to ensure nondiscrimination and public safety, Homobiles was formed to meet the needs of consumers whose transportation needs are not being adequately met by either taxi cabs or limousines."[27] Thus, while the CPUC suggested that these much larger corporations *should* address concerns of diversity and discrimination, it offered no specific enforcement mechanism nor did it give any serious consideration to differences in scale, social purpose, or actual safety measures between Homobiles and its for-profit counterparts. Thus, as much as Homobiles operated with a drastically different set of values and practices than its Silicon Valley counterparts, its mere existence was used uncritically by policy makers to further deregulate app-based transportation services.

Additionally, Homobiles offered a mixed bag of economic opportunity and challenges, reflecting existing critiques of ride hailing and gig work in other contexts.[28] Though most of the drivers and dispatchers positioned their work as a form of volunteerism (and some had well-paying jobs outside of Homobiles), for many, the pay-what-you-can donations they received from riders provided a lifeline in a context in which they were unable to secure good jobs elsewhere due to transphobia, racism, and/or ableism. Still, the donation-based model also left many in the red, particularly given the mileage and wear they put on their often-aging vehicles (another aspect of a punk service), resulting in frequent driver turnover. As a community-based organization, Homobiles attempted to mitigate these precarities. In particular, though it was not a formal co-op, the organization was flexible with the cut that the organization requested from drivers, especially when a driver was having a difficult time, and several reported informal mutual aid moments of "passing the hat" to support drivers with unexpected needs. Additionally, Homobiles worked with a queer-owned mechanic who had a record of working with taxi drivers to provide discounts and timely repairs, ensuring drivers could get back on the road more quickly. Though far from perfect, such commitments nonetheless differ significantly from Uber and Lyft, which largely discourage drivers from communicating (let alone organizing), and most interactions are facilitated through the driver "hubs" or "portals" of their corporate apps.

QUEERING DATA: "BACKWARDS, IN HIGH HEELS, AND WITH LOVE"

I now consider several of the ways that Homobiles operated queerly in its data practices, that is, how it deviated from the standard values of services like Lyft and Uber. In particular, I focus on two areas: first, how its operations bring together queer and media theories of refusal through strategic ignorance and ephemerality, and, second, how it foregrounded intimacy and small-scale-ness. For both, I offer concrete examples for how abstract theories might be enacted on the ground (and indeed already are). I am especially keen to contrast these with Silicon Valley's opaque approaches to data collection, storage, and processing, including the extraction of vast amounts of data for purposes that do not directly serve their customers, the construction of behavioral profiles for advertising and beyond, and the use of algorithmic models to influence the behavior of both users and paid workers.[29]

Though I stress that Homobiles was not a technology company, it nonetheless made creative use of existing communication technologies. And while its low-tech approach was partially due to the organization's limited expertise and resources, as theories of non-use by media and STS scholars indicate, the reasons for refusing technologies (and their attendant ideologies) are often complex, reflecting questions of access, non-interest, cultural values, and public perceptions.[30] In this vein, the political and punk commitment of Homobiles to being low-tech was a notable source of pride, as Breedlove once commented on Facebook: "Homobiles has been doing since the git—with a phone, a dispatcher, and a handful of drivers—what the big guys do—with radios, an app, and 1000 drivers—backwards, in high heels, and with love."[31] Moving beyond a simple low-tech versus high-tech dichotomy, I note the different material circumstances and orientation of Homobiles toward technology and business, while still positioning it as worthy of comparison to its competitors.

Need to Know Data: Ignorance and Ephemerality

Using a simple but profound practice, Homobiles collected and utilized data on a "need to know" basis, which particularly resonates with queer theories and histories of selectively disclosing information across a range of social and sexual contexts. In his work on queer failure, Jack Halberstam notes the political value in strategically embracing ignorance, stupidity, and naïveté, theorized not as limited innate intelligence but rather as a tactical "refusal of mastery" and an acknowledgment of "the limits of certain forms of knowing."[32] C. Riley Snorton also theorizes ignorance, specifically from queer and Black vernaculars, describing it as a "performance of not knowing," often feigned as limited knowledge in order to get away with socially unacceptable behavior.[33] In this case, the Homobiles organization's choice not to seek out particular information offers an alternative to logics of surveillance capitalism that seek omniscience and profit through extracting and hoarding data.[34] Indeed, such strategic orientations to ignorance might resist the drive to omniscience, countering Silicon Valley's version of what Donna Haraway refers to as an epistemological "god trick" or, in this case, Uber's eerily named "God View" interface that allowed its executives to track users in real time.[35]

Without a digital app, Homobiles implemented a tacit policy of ignorance, collecting only the information needed to offer rides. Homobiles offered its services primarily using text messages (with occasional phone calls), alongside paper-based notes and calendars, modeling a centralized dispatch system used by bike messengers (based on Breedlove's own past professional experience) and traditional taxi companies. From a user experience perspective, the system was quite simple. Passengers would send a text message requesting a ride, indicating their name, the number in their party, any special requests, pick-up and drop-off locations, and a time frame (immediate or a prebooking).[36] A Homobiles dispatcher would manually find an appropriate driver—utilizing what Breedlove described as a "free call system" in which dispatch would broadcast requests to drivers, allowing them to accept rides as they were able—and text back to confirm an estimated time of arrival and the vehicle to look for (which the passenger could also decline, depending on their time line and needs). Passengers also paid in cash based on the suggested donation, a practice that not only promoted a punk form of "no one turned away" accessibility but also was rooted in less formalized economies of nightlife in which the service operated. And though, at the time, mobile payment apps like Venmo were still not common among friends in the United States, this cash-based system certainly represented a reluctance toward a Silicon Valley ethos of incorporating all elements into a singular app.[37]

Without an app, there was no log of users' locations in the background, no records of rides or financial transactions, and no integrations with social media APIs or users' contacts that might be used to build out advertising profiles. Additionally, there was little need for users to directly obfuscate their own information or identities: with no logins or credit cards, riders did not need to use their legal names, an important consideration for trans people and drag performers, who often face challenges based on seeming discrepancies in corporate databases—furthering a sense of trust among riders, drivers, and organizers.[38] That is, there was little need for riders to mask themselves or otherwise render themselves opaque in the ways that Shaka McGlotten suggests (chapter 1, this volume) as a tactic for protecting oneself from the harms of observation; instead, the incommensurability of opacity that Gary Kafer theorizes (also in this volume, chapter 3) was in many ways already built into the procedures of Homobiles, allowing for provisional and relational presentations of self to suffice.

In addition to not collecting significant data in the first place, Homobiles also opted not to store much data about its users or operations, precluding the possibility of optimization or targeted advertising based on data analysis—though, as I will discuss, it did maintain some records. As José Esteban Muñoz's work on "ephemera as evidence" demonstrates, this resonates with queer experiences that disavow traditional archives in favor of ephemeral performances and anecdotes that follow the "traces, glimmers, residues, and specks of things."[39] Similarly, Halberstam also calls for strategic forgetting as a means to resist memorialization.[40] In a more tactical spirit, Benjamin Haber notes the shortcomings of privacy frameworks rooted in visibility, arguing that ephemeral practices on social media platforms like Snapchat allow for public intimacy in the present through a forgetting of the past, reflecting the more nuanced assessments of risk and reward that are common to queer lives.[41] In its practices, Homobiles demonstrates how these theories might be implemented tactically across systems (rather than at the level of individual users), as a reminder that platforms need not retain significant amounts of user data, even to provide highly customized experiences.

That said, Homobiles did in fact store a limited amount of data about riders, opening itself to some vulnerabilities. Notably, Homobiles used a third-party Android app called MightyText, which enabled texting from the same number across multiple devices. The dispatchers also used MightyText's address book as an informal database, including shorthand symbols to note particular riders to prioritize, such as a "T" for trans passengers or "G" for drag and nightlife performers deemed to be "glitterati." Still, as dispatcher Mitch Perez informed me, there was little consideration given at the time to the data usage policies of MightyText itself—an oversight that could have exposed users to data collection outside of its operations. Moreover, there was no explicit internal data retention or destruction policy, adding to the informality of the system in which participants had little recourse should things go awry. Interestingly, Breedlove informed me that early on, Lyft approached him about sharing the Homobiles client list, which he refused on the grounds that it would be a breach of community trust, commenting, "I'm an old punk, [so] I care about surveillance and shit." In practice, this limited use and retention of data stands in contrast to Uber and Lyft, which use data for all sorts of questionable purposes—including when customers are not using the apps—such as setting (and "surging") ride prices, analyzing traffic to optimize routes, sharing traffic patterns with local governments, selling data to advertising brokers, and developing self-driving vehicle technologies—to name but a handful.[42]

Building Trust: Intimacy and Small Data

In addition to its limited data collection, storage, and use, Homobiles also generated a sense of intimacy at a scale that engendered trust in its service, further precluding the need for dubious forms of data-driven governance and algorithmic accountability. It thus served as one model of a queer "infrastructure of intimacy" (to borrow a phrase from Ara Wilson), in which various forms of intimacy—for example, the proximity of riding in someone else's car, the trust in sharing personal information, the sense of belonging to a larger community—both shaped and were shaped by its practices.[43] More specifically, its small-scale service model ensured that trust and safety were not merely affective but also shaped real practices of accountability outside of formalized systems. Here we might consider Jack Gieseking's provocation of "small data" that conveys the complexity of queer experiences and relationships, rather than obsessions with big data's scale.[44]

A sense of familiarity and shared community with fellow riders, drivers, and organizers—even if indirectly—was one of the primary reasons that Homobiles riders felt safe, despite little in the way of formal safety policies like background checks. As many noted, there was a general understanding that gendered, sexualized, and racialized precarities were implicitly understood. As rider JB described, "I felt really seen and . . . understood without being bombarded with questions, just simply accepted . . . which is refreshing." Additionally, riders could request particular drivers (a feature that remains unavailable in ride-hailing apps that dispatch based on location) or request not to be paired with others (based on poor riding experiences or unrelated personal histories). And because Homobiles volunteers were friendly with riders, they were often able to personalize their services, such as prioritizing pick-ups to ensure performers got to work on time. Homobiles might even proactively send messages to regulars, particularly around busy times like Pride, to ensure they could access the service. To riders, such communications felt personal, friendly, and based on appropriately intimate information, rather than the apps' cryptic notifications indicating a new driver or algorithmically generated deals or "nudges" to encourage use.[45]

Because of these intimate relationships, Homobiles was also able to offer more direct forms of care tailored to its riders' needs. As a basic policy, drivers waited for passengers to be inside their homes before the car would leave. Several riders also noted times when drivers assisted them in particularly dangerous situations, referring to the service as "guardian angels," "a rescue," and "knight[s] in shining armor." Drag performer Lola Rabbitt explained to me that, at a time when she was struggling with drug addiction, Homobiles was often the only way she got home safely, even when she could not pay or remember the details. She warmly recalled the lack of judgment on the part of the drivers, speculating that some may have shared similar life experiences that allowed them to empathize—a sentiment several drivers confirmed. Another rider, Peter, recounted an incident in which his drink at a bar was drugged, leaving him incapacitated: he was able to contact Homobiles because it was one of the few numbers saved in his phone, and since they had his address saved, they were able to get him home and into his apartment.

In such a way, though Homobiles did not necessarily meet legal benchmarks for accessibility, it practiced an approach to access with a spirit akin to disability justice or "access intimacy," understood as ongoing, solidarity-driven processes based on shared resources, decision-making, and improvisation.[46] That is, while Homobiles rarely (if ever) had ADA-compliant vans among its fleet of private vehicles—an unfortunate reality given its stated values of inclusion—rather than ask for a one-size-fits-all approach, its riders could make specific requests, such as asking for a driver with trunk space for a wheelchair or suitcase. In an implicit nod to the intersections of crip and queer intimacy practices, one interviewee further compared the Homobiles communication process to negotiating a BDSM scene, implying this to be a unique skill set that, in its ideal form, enables parties to meet their mutual needs through clear communication and boundary setting. (Still, there are likely examples in which such improvisational techniques also failed disabled riders, though I was not able to identify such instances through my interviews.)

This spirit of familiarity also made Homobiles fun. As Elijah Adiv Edelman notes in his work on "trans vitalities," community-based care work can also contribute to a collective affect, "that which makes lives worth living."[47] Many riders and drivers alike noted that Homobiles was often seen as a way of keeping the night's party going, either en route to the next one or simply by virtue of the gossip, sing-alongs, or shenanigans in the car itself. As Lola Rabbitt mentioned, drivers would sometimes ask her about the number she was performing that night and play her CD so she could practice (and they could have a private sneak preview). Some drivers would also take breaks to participate in the nightlife themselves. Phatima Rude, who was also a drag performer, would take breaks from driving to perform "drive-by drag" at various shows, then go back to taking people home—a practice that, for those in the know, made this legendary performer even more so. Some noted a lax enforcement of rules within certain cars, such as squeezing in too many passengers without seatbelts or looking the other way when passengers would smoke or consume club drugs, though Homobiles had clear rules that drivers remain sober and refrain from flirting with customers while working. While some of these behaviors might be problematic (and some riders I spoke to expressed frustration at fellow riders and lax drivers), I suggest that the Homobiles approach be understood within a framework of harm reduction, in which its open communication style encouraged collective assessment of boundaries and interventions to ensure safety outside of formal regulations. As Edelman's work also suggests, "safety is a phenomenological experience," often tied not to institutions or regulations but to relationships and the intimacy of shared space.[48]

Even if riders and drivers did not know each other personally, their degrees of social separation were minimal, ensuring a sense of accountability that exceeded Lyft's and Uber's rating and reporting systems. Homobiles had a minimal vetting process for riders or drivers, which primarily operated by word-of-mouth reputations. Still, that was enough for riders to get in strangers' cars, as interviewee Deven described: "I knew I was getting into a vehicle with somebody who was from my community. . . . I didn't know the person, but they knew somebody I knew. . . . [It was as if] my friend said you'll give me a ride home and I'm okay with that." Though none of my interviewees recounted times in which they needed to offer direct complaints, most confidently believed that they could have easily reported incidents directly to the Homobiles leadership. Organizers confirmed that some drivers and riders were eighty-sixed due to problematic behavior and documented in a "no-ride" book, without further incident. Indeed, here is one area in which my own experience with Homobiles offers a clear example, as I once experienced an incident in which a particular Homobiles driver awkwardly accused me of impersonating my own drag persona, despite my insistence otherwise. After the ride, I sent a message to Breedlove, explaining that I felt bad critiquing a driver but that the situation felt uncomfortable and a bit unsafe, and he offered to talk to the driver and not pair me with them again, which I accepted as a reasonable outcome. Still, though I was not able to identify further examples of negative experiences in my interviews and outreach, I wish to be careful not to romanticize such procedures, as these informal processes also constitute the implicit dangers of ephemerality and intimacy: that when exploited, they can in fact enable problematic behaviors and a lack of recourse, disproportionately impacting those who already lack social and political power.

Nonetheless, such a system based on existing social relations (even distant ones) stands in stark contrast to Uber's and Lyft's ratings systems, which operate using what Arun Sundararajan describes as "digital trust infrastructure" to account for semianonymous transactions in which authenticity and safety may be questionable.[49] Five-star-type rating systems require both riders and drivers to anonymously score each other, with limited evaluative feedback. Several riders accurately reported these systems as biased against already marginalized groups and felt that their own (or friends') ratings had been negatively impacted due to their identities. Additionally, as Alex Rosenblat and Luke Stark highlight, such rating systems force "passengers to perform a type of managerial assessment," structuring the terms of drivers' labor (including their affective labor).[50] And, within these larger systems of information asymmetry, both drivers and riders are often unaware of the minimum rating needed to remain active in the service. Still, many riders agreed that some sort of reviews mechanism might be necessary for safety at larger scales but expressed discomfort in their power over people's livelihoods and that numeric ratings offered little practical information for their safety purposes. Some even suggested that more narrative evaluations might better protect users from particular kinds of incidents or biases, perhaps as a way to formalize the direct or word-of-mouth reviews that Homobiles afforded.

The ability of Homobiles to operate with such high-touch communication was an effective strategy because it operated on a relatively small and localized scale—though, as Gieseking might remind us, a scale generally "big enough" for its purposes.[51] In such a way, Homobiles further refuses what Alex Hanna and Tina M. Park refer to as "scale thinking," or a drive toward growth through efficiency that ignores a heterogeneity of users' needs and uses and forecloses possibilities for social change.[52] Similarly, in his work on platform cooperativism, Trebor Scholz challenges fixations on growth, commenting that services "don't always have to scale up."[53] For its part, Homobiles frequently struggled to bring on new drivers to serve more riders. However, it also playfully worked to keep its offerings "in the family," balancing its inclusivity with explicit commitments to queer and trans riders. Breedlove often posted half-joking Facebook missives like "every time we take a straight guy to the [M]arina there's 3 drag queens standing on a corner crying."[54] There were also frequent anecdotes documenting moments that directly benefited low-income or multiply marginalized community members. Still, some riders noted that even the limited growth of Homobiles within its years of operation posed challenges, often straining the service and at times stretching its capacities, which itself further prevented scaling in a typical Silicon Valley fashion.

When I asked riders what it might look like if Homobiles was to grow, several suggested that it would work best if adapted to local contexts in a networked model. Indeed, Breedlove publicly expressed interest not in scaling but in franchising Homobiles and expressed mixed feelings about not expanding, saying, "I wish that I had cared more about money and realized that money actually does make shit happen. . . . I realized that if you had a pile of money, you could get a pile of tech, and then you could be of more service. . . . It's like, we're not doing zines anymore, we're doing social media, dude, so . . . change or die." Several interviewees also suggested ways to build an app while still maintaining its values and community ties, such as Persia's suggestion to integrate events (like some queer hook-up apps already do) or interviewee Crystal Why's suggestion to offer Patreon-like subscription plans to promote sustainability and offer incentives to consistent riders.

CONCLUSION

Homobiles produced more than just an alternative transportation service: it asserted a spirit of queerness not as identity or aesthetic but, in the words of bell hooks, as a practice "at odds with everything around it and [that] has to invent and create and find a place to speak and to thrive and to live."[55] In its queer approach to data collection, retention, and use, Homobiles stood in stark contrast to Silicon Valley corporate practices, not in order to be oppositional but because its leaders were rooted in queer, trans, and punk communities with their own existing legacies of entrepreneurship and mutual aid. That is, though I have described many of the contributions of Homobiles specifically in contrast to the practices of Uber and Lyft, it is important to reiterate that Homobiles was not a reactive but rather a proactive project designed to serve queer, trans, and communities of color. In this way, it might be seen less as in opposition (or even relation) to Uber and Lyft and more as a present-day instantiation of Melville's infamously unbothered character Bartleby, whom Jacob Gaboury describes as embodying "not a politics of resistance but a refusal of the very terms of engagement."[56] Further, in its seemingly quaint commitment to a transparent business model, aesthetic and technological minimalism, and community-based forms of trust-building, Homobiles might also be understood along the lines of Jessa Lingel's analysis of platforms that are "ungentrified," representing less of a repudiation of Silicon Valley and more of an anterior alternative to it.[57]

Still, in its refusal, Homobiles evoked a spirit of glamorous defiance in reclaiming ownership over a local cultural geography that was increasingly overrun by the capital (and values) of its neighboring tech giants. As rider Peter explained to me, "The queer community I was involved in . . . [we] were like, 'no, this city is ours.' . . . Homobiles was definitely a puzzle piece of a larger picture of activism. . . . It was a part of that 'we're fags, we're queers, we're dykes, we're trans, and we want a bigger part of this pie.'" Similarly, its leaders took pride in foregrounding its anticorporate and DIY structures, selling the service as charmingly scrappy, asking riders to forgive its shortcomings, and inviting them to join in the process of making something work—often against the rules and all odds. However, the difficult reality is that Homobiles largely failed not only by the standards of Silicon Valley (in which success is measured in maximizing scale, longevity, and valuation) but also in not being able to sustain its full range of services within the community as Uber's and Lyft's perceived convenience, reliability, and ubiquity ultimately resulted in most riders joining these mainstream services (though, as mentioned above, Homobiles continues to operate on a smaller, mission-driven scale as of this writing). In such a way, Homobiles serves as yet another case within, in Halberstam's terms, a "queer art of failure," albeit one with very different material stakes than more aesthetic examples might imply, suggesting the limits of romanticizing failure: that while queerness may offer imaginative possibilities for critiquing neoliberal visions of success, failure alone cannot provide conditions for community care.

At the same time, Homobiles demonstrates that certain types of queer failure can be strategic, especially as I have outlined above: a failure to collect and use data comprehensively and a failure to grow at all costs. Given the rumblings of a popular backlash against surveillance capitalism, I maintain some hope that the dominant trajectory may not hold and that queer tactics embodied in platforms like Homobiles may indeed have more lasting power than today's monopolistic platforms, that strategic ignorance and ephemerality may become more desirable than omniscience, or that intimacy and smallness may win out over unrelenting scalability. (And yet, I also fear that, as with many queer projects, these current modes of refusal may soon be co-opted or integrated into technologies in even more nefarious ways.) Already, within queer and trans communities, digital projects have emerged that critically remediate earlier formats or invent new approaches with a commitment to alternative values. These include digital platforms such as the queer dating app Lex, which draws on the simple and descriptive text-based nature of newspaper personal ads rather than a database or algorithmic model.[58] Another example is the Ottawa Independent Companions, which Ryan Conrad discusses in chapter 6 (this volume). Such projects engage both similar and different approaches to queering data, including ignorance and intimacy, but also additional practices like community moderation and curation of content relevant to their respective audiences.

One of the themes that surprised me most in interviewing Breedlove was that, though he criticized aspects of Lyft's and Uber's business practices, he was also eager to claim their successes as part of the Homobiles legacy of ensuring safe rides. As he explained to me, rather than trying to fight these companies, he eventually chose to take pride in knowing that his idea had helped lead to more safe transportation options, asking of his competitors, "Are my queens getting home safe?" While this might serve as a form of assimilation of queer identities into a dominant platform, I would argue that Breedlove's insistence on situating Homobiles as part of the broader story of safe transportation reinserts friction into an otherwise teleological narrative, refusing to let large companies disingenuously claim inherent inclusivity or innovation. Instead, Breedlove calls attention to the historic and ongoing failures of these services themselves while still holding the door open for alternative models. In this way, we might consider this expansion of safety less as assimilation and more as a mode of queering technology and gig platforms in a viral manner: injecting queer values into mainstream platforms, enabling the Homobiles mission of safely transporting queer and trans people to exceed its own operations—while not letting the big companies entirely off the hook.

Finally, the failures and small victories of Homobiles not only gesture toward historic alternatives but also invite a reimagination of how things might still be done differently, in both the present and the future.[59] As Nicoll argues, "Minor platforms always imply the possibility that history could be otherwise, even in questionable, undesirable, or potentially disconcerting ways." Furthermore, he states, "an intervention in the past has a reverberating effect—it can refresh our awareness of the present and help us find paths into the future that can be different."[60] And while I wish I could have written an account of a punk queer car service that started off as "two daggers . . . [with] dead-mom cars, driving drag queens around" (as Breedlove once described it) and ended up restructuring Silicon Valley toward queer and anticapitalist collective care, I remain cautiously (if perhaps cruelly) optimistic.[61] As a project that outlived many of its venture-funded peers, Homobiles offers a roadmap for how things might be done differently, making clear that it is simply not necessary to surveil or algorithmically exploit users. As such, the legacy of Homobiles buys time and creates space for new examples of queer enchantment that may still be on the horizon. As Sara Ahmed writes, the potential in "not being selected is to have more room to roam, to vary, to deviate; to proliferate . . . the variations that are possible when you are not selected and rewarded for going the right way."[62] Indeed, what better vehicle than an imagined vintage pink convertible to help us figure out just where we need to go next?

NOTES

1. Several scholars write about Breedlove's performance; see, for example, Cvetkovich, *Archive of Feelings*, 83; Halberstam, *In a Queer Time and Place*; and Breedlove, *45 Thought Crimes*.

2. I avoid uncritically using terms like "ridesharing" or "sharing economy" throughout this chapter, given their disingenuous use among Silicon Valley companies and tech journalists. I tend toward more descriptive terms like "ride-hailing" service. See Harnett, "Words Matter"; and Oei, "Trouble with Gig Talk."

3. Paul, "Untold Story."

4. Breedlove, "I Know This Looks Like It's about Lyft."

5. Malin and Chandler, "Free to Work Anxiously"; Collier, Dubal, and Carter, "Disrupting Regulation, Regulating Disruption."

6. Raley, "Dataveillance and Countervailance"; Van Dijck, "Datafication, Dataism and Dataveillance"; Andrejevic, "Automating Surveillance"; Zuboff, *Age of Surveillance Capitalism*.

7. Nicoll, *Minor Platforms in Videogame History*.

8. See Dubal, "Drive to Precarity."

9. As Miranda Joseph smartly notes, "Fetishizing community only makes us blind to the ways we might intervene in the enactment of domination and exploitation." Joseph, *Against the Romance of Community*, ix.

10. These quotations are from personal interviews; for a public account, see Nelson and Silva, "Making of the Homobile."

11. Though Homobiles began as a low-tech project, there were later attempts to develop a mobile app via community fundraising and hackathons led by queer and trans developers. However, given that the mobile app was never fully implemented, I do not focus on it here.

12. Keeling, "Queer OS," 156; Barnett et al., "QueerOS: A User's Manual"; Chun, "Race and/as Technology"; Gaboury, "Becoming NULL."

13. Ruberg, *Video Games Have Always Been Queer*.

14. Ahmed, *What's the Use?*, 200.

15. Costanza-Chock, *Design Justice*.

16. Brown, Deer, and Nyong'o, "Punk and Its Afterlives," 2.

17. Enszer, "'How to Stop Choking to Death'"; Vider, "'Ultimate Extension of Gay Community.'"

18. Spade, "Solidarity Not Charity," 136.

19. Hwang, "Deviant Care for Deviant Futures," 570.

20. However, as to the historical unreliability of public transit, Veena Dubal's historic account of chauffeur work in San Francisco over the past century indicates that taxis' limited availability more accurately reflects decades of shifts in industry regulation, taxi ownership, and driver organizing that left a once financially sustainable line of work in a precarious position. Dubal, "Drive to Precarity."

21. There is empirical evidence about the mistreatment of LGBTQ and Black riders via app-based services; see Mejia and Parker, "When Transparency Fails." Additionally, in 2017 a group of San Francisco drag queens sued Lyft for discrimination; see Lang, "Lyft Adopts New Policies."

22. "Homobiles," accessed 30 August 2020 (website no longer active), https://web.archive.org/web/20221204190323/https://www.homobiles.org/.

23. Interview participants were invited to be credited by name or pseudonym or to remain anonymous.

24. See, for example, RightRides, accessed 30 August 2020, http://www.rightrides

.org/about/; and Dunckel-Graglia, "Women-Only Transportation." Many thanks to Lina Žigelytė for alerting me to a queer transportation project in St. Petersburg, Russia, associated with the club 3L.

25. See views expressed in news articles like Smith, "Homobiles, SF's Queer Ride Service, Is the Anti-Uber"; and Gross, "Homobiles Is San Francisco's Queer and Community-Based Answer to Uber."

26. For analyses of race, class, and citizenship hierarchies across taxi and ride-sharing industries, see Hua and Ray, "Beyond the Precariat"; and Schor, "Does the Sharing Economy Increase Inequality within the Eighty Percent?"

27. California Public Utilities Commission, *Decision Adopting Rules and Regulations to Protect Public Safety While Allowing New Entrants to the Transportation Industry.*

28. Schor, *After the Gig*; Ravenelle, *Hustle and Gig.*

29. Tufekci, "Engineering the Public"; Noble, *Algorithms of Oppression.*

30. Wyatt, "Non-Users Also Matter"; Portwood-Stacer, "Media Refusal and Conspicuous Non-Consumption"; Benjamin, "Informed Refusal."

31. Nonpublic post to the Homobiles Facebook page, 2014, quoted with permission. I have added punctuation for readability.

32. Halberstam, *Queer Art of Failure*, 11, 12.

33. Snorton, *Nobody Is Supposed to Know*, 91.

34. For refusals of datafication, see Cifor et al., "Feminist Data Manifest-No."

35. Haraway, "Situated Knowledges," 581; Hill, "'God View.'"

36. Homobiles introduced prebooking within its first months, a feature Lyft and Uber did not add until years later, in 2016. For apps, this might pose an operational or programming challenge, which was mitigated by the analog approach Homobiles used.

37. For more on digital payments, see Swartz, *New Money.*

38. I have written about identity, names, and obfuscation; see Hot Mess, "Selfies and Side-Eye"; and Kornstein, "Under Her Eye."

39. Muñoz, "Ephemera as Evidence," 10.

40. Halberstam, *Queer Art of Failure.*

41. Haber, "Digital Ephemeral Turn."

42. For example, see Calo and Rosenblat, "Taking Economy"; Cici et al., "Assessing the Potential of Ride-Sharing"; Gandhi, Sucahyo, and Ruldeviyani, "Investigating the Protection of Customers' Personal Data in the Ridesharing Applications"; Korosec, "Lyft Is Using Data from Its Rideshare Drivers to Develop Self-Driving Cars"; and Vaccaro, "Highly Touted Boston-Uber Partnership Has Not Lived Up to Hype So Far."

43. Wilson, "Infrastructure of Intimacy."

44. Gieseking, "Size Matters," 150.

45. On nudges, see Yeung, "'Hypernudge.'"

46. Mingus, "Access Intimacy"; Piepzna-Samarasinha, *Care Work.*

47. Edelman, "Beyond Resilience," 109.

48. Edelman, "Beyond Resilience," 124.

49. Sundararajan, *Sharing Economy*, 60.

50. Rosenblat and Stark, "Algorithmic Labor and Information Asymmetries," 3771.

51. Gieseking, "Size Matters to Lesbians, Too," 154.

52. Hanna and Park, "Against Scale."

53. Scholz, "Platform Cooperativism," 25.

54. As with many Homobiles Facebook posts, the privacy settings were not public but widely available to riders.

55. hooks, *Are You Still a Slave?*

56. Gaboury, "Becoming NULL," 149.

57. Lingel, *Internet for the People*, 1.

58. Specter, "Queer Dating App Lex." I thank Cait McKinney for suggesting this connection.

59. Muñoz, *Cruising Utopia*.

60. Nicoll, *Minor Platforms in Videogame History*, 36.

61. Berlant, *Cruel Optimism*.

62. Ahmed, *What's the Use?*, 219.

BIBLIOGRAPHY

Ahmed, Sara. *What's the Use? On the Uses of Use*. Durham, NC: Duke University Press, 2019.

Andrejevic, Mark. "Automating Surveillance." *Surveillance and Society* 17, no. 1–2 (31 March 2019): 7–13. https://doi.org/10.24908/ss.v17i1/2.12930.

Barnett, Fiona, Zach Blas, micha cárdenas, Jacob Gaboury, Jessica Marie Johnson, and Margaret Rhee. "QueerOS: A User's Manual." In *Debates in the Digital Humanities 2016*, edited by Matthew K. Gold and Lauren F. Klein. Minneapolis: University of Minnesota Press, 2016. http://dhdebates.gc.cuny.edu/debates/text/56.

Benjamin, Ruha. "Informed Refusal: Toward a Justice-Based Bioethics." *Science, Technology, and Human Values* 41, no. 6 (1 November 2016): 967–90. https://doi.org/10.1177/0162243916656059.

Berlant, Lauren. *Cruel Optimism*. Durham, NC: Duke University Press, 2011.

Breedlove, Lynn. *45 Thought Crimes: New Writing*. San Francisco: Manic D Press, 2019.

——— . "I Know This Looks Like It's about Lyft." Facebook, 5 April 2019. https://www.facebook.com/lynnbreedlove/posts/10156377217203460.

Brown, Jayna, Patrick Deer, and Tavia Nyong'o. "Punk and Its Afterlives: Introduction." *Social Text* 31, no. 3 (116) (1 September 2013): 1–11. https://doi.org/10.1215/01642472-2152900.

California Public Utilities Commission. *Decision Adopting Rules and Regulations to Protect Public Safety While Allowing New Entrants to the Transportation Industry.* Decision 13-09-045, Rulemaking 12-12-011 COM/MP1/avs (2013). https://docs.cpuc .ca.gov/PublishedDocs/Published/G000/M077/K192/77192335.PDF.

Calo, Ryan, and Alex Rosenblat. "The Taking Economy: Uber, Information, and Power Essay." *Columbia Law Review* 117, no. 6 (2017): [i]–1690.

Chun, Wendy Hui Kyong. "Race and/as Technology or How to Do Things to Race." In *Race after the Internet*, edited by Lisa Nakamura and Peter Chow-White, 38–60. New York: Routledge, 2011.

Cici, Blerim, Athina Markopoulou, Enrique Frías-Martínez, and Nikolaos Laoutaris. "Assessing the Potential of Ride-Sharing Using Mobile and Social Data: A Tale of Four Cities." In *Proceedings of the 2014 ACM International Joint Conference on Pervasive and Ubiquitous Computing*, 201–11. UbiComp '14. New York: Association for Computing Machinery, 2014. https://doi.org/10.1145/2632048.2632055.

Cifor, Marika, Patricia Garcia, T. L. Cowan, Jasmine Rault, Tonia Sutherland, Anita Say Chan, Jennifer Rode, Anna Lauren Hoffman, Niloufar Salehi, and Lisa Nakamura. "Feminist Data Manifest-No." 2019. https://www.manifestno.com.

Collier, Ruth Berins, V. B. Dubal, and Christopher L. Carter. "Disrupting Regulation, Regulating Disruption: The Politics of Uber in the United States." *Perspectives on Politics* 16, no. 4 (December 2018): 919–37. https://doi.org/10.1017/S1537592718001093.

Costanza-Chock, Sasha. *Design Justice: Community-Led Practices to Build the Worlds We Need.* Cambridge, MA: MIT Press, 2020.

Cvetkovich, Ann. *An Archive of Feelings: Trauma, Sexuality, and Lesbian Public Cultures.* Durham, NC: Duke University Press, 2003.

Dubal, Veena. "The Drive to Precarity: A Political History of Work, Regulation, and Labor Advocacy in San Francisco's Taxi and Uber Economies." *Berkeley Journal of Employment and Labor Law* 38 (1 January 2017): 73–135.

Dunckel-Graglia, Amy. "Women-Only Transportation: How 'Pink' Public Transportation Changes Public Perception of Women's Mobility." *Journal of Public Transportation* 16, no. 2 (1 June 2013). https://doi.org/10.5038/2375-0901.16.2.5.

Edelman, Elijah Adiv. "Beyond Resilience: Trans Coalitional Activism as Radical Self-Care." *Social Text* 38, no. 1 (142) (1 March 2020): 109–30. https://doi.org/10.1215 /01642472-7971127.

Enszer, Julie R. "'How to Stop Choking to Death': Rethinking Lesbian Separatism as a Vibrant Political Theory and Feminist Practice." *Journal of Lesbian Studies* 20, no. 2 (2 April 2016): 180–96. https://doi.org/10.1080/10894160.2015.1083815.

Gaboury, Jacob. "Becoming NULL: Queer Relations in the Excluded Middle." *Women and Performance: A Journal of Feminist Theory* 28, no. 2 (4 May 2018): 143–58. https://doi.org/10.1080/0740770X.2018.1473986.

Gandhi, Arfive, Yudho Giri Sucahyo, and Yova Ruldeviyani. "Investigating the Protection of Customers' Personal Data in the Ridesharing Applications: A Desk Research in Indonesia." In *2018 15th International Conference on Electrical Engineering/Electronics, Computer, Telecommunications and Information Technology* (*ECTI-CON*), 118–21, Chiang Rai, Thailand, 2018. https://doi.org/10.1109/ECTICon.2018.8619912.

Gieseking, Jen Jack. "Size Matters to Lesbians, Too: Queer Feminist Interventions into the Scale of Big Data." *Professional Geographer* 70, no. 1 (2 January 2018): 150–56. https://doi.org/10.1080/00330124.2017.1326084.

Gross, Anisse. "Homobiles Is San Francisco's Queer and Community-Based Answer to Uber." BuzzFeed, 21 February 2014. https://www.buzzfeed.com/anissegross /homobiles-is-san-franciscos-queer-and-community-based-answer.

Haber, Benjamin. "The Digital Ephemeral Turn: Queer Theory, Privacy, and the Temporality of Risk." *Media, Culture and Society* 41, no. 8 (March 11, 2019): 1–18.

Halberstam, Jack. *In a Queer Time and Place: Transgender Bodies, Subcultural Lives.* New York: New York University Press, 2005.

———. *The Queer Art of Failure.* Durham, NC: Duke University Press, 2011.

Hanna, Alex, and Tina M. Park. "Against Scale: Provocations and Resistances to Scale Thinking." *arXiv* (Cornell University), 17 October 2020. https://arxiv.org/abs/2010 .08850v2.

Haraway, Donna. "Situated Knowledges: The Science Question in Feminism and the Privilege of Partial Perspective." *Feminist Studies* 14, no. 3 (1988): 575–99. https:// doi.org/10.2307/3178066.

Harnett, Sam. "Words Matter: How Tech Media Helped Write Gig Companies into Existence." SSRN Scholarly Paper. Social Science Research Network, 7 August 2020. https://papers.ssrn.com/abstract=3668606.

Hill, Kashmir. "'God View': Uber Allegedly Stalked Users for Party-Goers' Viewing Pleasure." *Forbes*, 3 October 2014. https://www.forbes.com/sites/kashmirhill/2014 /10/03/god-view-uber-allegedly-stalked-users-for-party-goers-viewing-pleasure/.

hooks, bell. *Are You Still a Slave? Liberating the Black Female Body.* Recorded conversation at The New School, 2014. https://www.youtube.com/watch?v=rJkohNROvzs.

Hot Mess, Lil Miss. "Selfies and Side-Eye: Drag Queens Take on Facebook." *Studies in Gender and Sexuality* 16, no. 2 (3 April 2015): 144–46. https://doi.org/10.1080 /15240657.2015.1038202.

Hua, Julietta, and Kasturi Ray. "Beyond the Precariat: Race, Gender, and Labor in the Taxi and Uber Economy." *Social Identities* 24, no. 2 (4 March 2018): 271–89. https:// doi.org/10.1080/13504630.2017.1321721.

Hwang, Ren-yo. "Deviant Care for Deviant Futures: QTBIPoC Radical Relationalism as Mutual Aid against Carceral Care." *TSQ: Transgender Studies Quarterly* 6, no. 4 (1 November 2019): 559–78. https://doi.org/10.1215/23289252-7771723.

Joseph, Miranda. *Against the Romance of Community*. Minneapolis: University of Minnesota Press, 2002.

Keeling, Kara. "Queer OS." *Cinema Journal* 53, no. 2 (Winter 2014): 152–57.

Kornstein, Harris. "Under Her Eye: Digital Drag as Obfuscation and Countersurveillance." *Surveillance and Society* 17, no. 5 (10 December 2019): 681–98. https://doi.org/10.24908/ss.v17i5.12957.

Korosec, Kirsten. "Lyft Is Using Data from Its Rideshare Drivers to Develop Self-Driving Cars." *TechCrunch* (blog), 23 June 2020. https://social.techcrunch.com/2020/06/23/lyft-is-using-data-from-its-ride-share-drivers-to-develop-self-driving-cars/.

Lang, Nico. "Lyft Adopts New Policies after Drag Queens Refused Rides." *The Advocate*, 2 August 2019. https://www.advocate.com/news/2019/8/02/lyft-adopts-new-policies-after-drag-queens-refused-rides.

Lingel, Jessa. *An Internet for the People: The Politics and Promise of Craigslist*. Princeton: Princeton University Press, 2020.

Malin, Brenton J., and Curry Chandler. "Free to Work Anxiously: Splintering Precarity among Drivers for Uber and Lyft." *Communication, Culture and Critique* 10, no. 2 (1 June 2017): 382–400. https://doi.org/10.1111/cccr.12157.

Mejia, Jorge, and Chris Parker. "When Transparency Fails: Bias and Financial Incentives in Ridesharing Platforms." *Management Science* 67, no. 1 (5 May 2020). https://doi.org/10.1287/mnsc.2019.3525.

Mingus, Mia. "Access Intimacy: The Missing Link." *Leaving Evidence* (blog), 5 May 2011. https://leavingevidence.wordpress.com/2011/05/05/access-intimacy-the-missing-link/.

Muñoz, José Esteban. *Cruising Utopia: The Then and There of Queer Futurity*. New York: New York University Press, 2009.

——— . "Ephemera as Evidence: Introductory Notes to Queer Acts." *Women and Performance: A Journal of Feminist Theory* 8, no. 2 (1 January 1996): 5–16. https://doi.org/10.1080/07407709608571228.

Nelson, Davia, and Nikki Silva. "The Making of the Homobile: A Story of Transportation, Civil Rights, and Glitter." *The Kitchen Sisters* (podcast), 2 July 2014. Available at https://soundcloud.com/fugitivewaves/the-making-ofthe-homobile.

Nicoll, Benjamin. *Minor Platforms in Videogame History*. Amsterdam: Amsterdam University Press, 2019. eBook.

Noble, Safiya. *Algorithms of Oppression: How Search Engines Reinforce Racism*. New York: New York University Press, 2018.

Oei, Shu-Yi. "The Trouble with Gig Talk: Choice of Narrative and the Worker Classification Fights Altruism, Community, and Markets." *Law and Contemporary Problems* 81, no. 3 (2018): 107–36.

Paul, Sunil. "The Untold Story of Ridesharing—Part III: The Birth of Sidecar and

Ridesharing." Medium, 10 September 2017. https://medium.com/@SunilPaul/the
-untold-story-of-ridesharing-part-iii-the-birth-of-sidecar-and-ridesharing-9f6e6
c706d8d.

Piepzna-Samarasinha, Leah Lakshmi. *Care Work: Dreaming Disability Justice*. Vancouver, BC: Arsenal Pulp Press, 2018.

Portwood-Stacer, Laura. "Media Refusal and Conspicuous Non-Consumption: The Performative and Political Dimensions of Facebook Abstention." *New Media and Society*
15, no. 7 (1 November 2013): 1041–57. https://doi.org/10.1177/1461444812465139.

Raley, Rita. "Dataveillance and Countervailance." In *"Raw Data" Is an Oxymoron*,
edited by Lisa Gitelman, 121–45. Cambridge, MA: MIT Press, 2013.

Ravenelle, Alexandrea J. *Hustle and Gig: Struggling and Surviving in the Sharing Economy*. Oakland: University of California Press, 2019.

Rosenblat, Alex, and Luke Stark. "Algorithmic Labor and Information Asymmetries: A
Case Study of Uber's Drivers." *International Journal of Communication* 10 (27 July
2016). https://ijoc.org/index.php/ijoc/article/view/4892/1739.

Ruberg, Bo. *Video Games Have Always Been Queer*. New York: New York University
Press, 2019.

Scholz, Trebor. "Platform Cooperativism: Challenging the Corporate Sharing Economy." Rosa Luxemburg Stiftung, January 2016. https://rosalux.nyc/wp-content
/uploads/2020/11/RLS-NYC_platformcoop.pdf.

Schor, Juliet B. *After the Gig: How the Sharing Economy Got Hijacked and How to Win
It Back*. Oakland: University of California Press, 2021.

———. "Does the Sharing Economy Increase Inequality within the Eighty Percent?
Findings from a Qualitative Study of Platform Providers." *Cambridge Journal of
Regions, Economy and Society* 10, no. 2 (1 July 2017): 263–79. https://doi.org/10.1093
/cjres/rsw047.

Smith, Heather. "Homobiles, SF's Queer Ride Service, Is the Anti-Uber." *Grist* (blog), 6
March 2015. https://grist.org/cities/homobiles-sfs-queer-ride-service-is-the-anti-uber/.

Snorton, C. Riley. *Nobody Is Supposed to Know: Black Sexuality on the Down Low*.
Minneapolis: University of Minnesota Press, 2014.

Spade, Dean. "Solidarity Not Charity: Mutual Aid for Mobilization and Survival."
Social Text 38, no. 1 (142) (1 March 2020): 131–51. https://doi.org/10.1215/01642472
-7971139.

Specter, Emma. "Queer Dating App Lex Is All About Words, Not Pictures." *Vogue*, 22
November 2019. https://www.vogue.com/article/lex-queer-dating-app.

Sundararajan, Arun. *The Sharing Economy: The End of Employment and the Rise of
Crowd-Based Capitalism*. Cambridge, MA: MIT Press, 2016.

Swartz, Lana. *New Money: How Payment Became Social Media*. Illustrated ed. New
Haven: Yale University Press, 2020.

Tufekci, Zeynep. "Engineering the Public: Big Data, Surveillance and Computational Politics." *First Monday* 19, no. 7 (2 July 2014). https://doi.org/10.5210/fm.v19i7.4901.

Vaccaro, Adam. "Highly Touted Boston-Uber Partnership Has Not Lived Up to Hype So Far." Boston.com, 16 June 2016. https://www.boston.com/news/business/2016/06/16/bostons-uber-partnership-has-not-lived-up-to-promise.

van Dijck, José. "Datafication, Dataism and Dataveillance: Big Data between Scientific Paradigm and Ideology." *Surveillance and Society* 12, no. 2 (9 May 2014): 197–208. https://doi.org/10.24908/ss.v12i2.4776.

Vider, Stephen. "'The Ultimate Extension of Gay Community': Communal Living and Gay Liberation in the 1970s." *Gender and History* 27, no. 3 (2015): 865–81. https://doi.org/10.1111/1468-0424.12167.

Wilson, Ara. "The Infrastructure of Intimacy." *Signs: Journal of Women in Culture and Society* 41, no. 2 (9 December 2015): 247–80. https://doi.org/10.1086/682919.

Wyatt, Sally. "Non-Users Also Matter: The Construction of Users and Non-Users of the Internet." In *How Users Matter: The Co-Construction of Users and Technology*, edited by Nelly Oudshoorn and Trevor Pinch, 67–79. Cambridge, MA: MIT Press, 2005.

Yeung, Karen. "'Hypernudge': Big Data as a Mode of Regulation by Design." *Information, Communication and Society* 20, no. 1 (2 January 2017): 118–36. https://doi.org/10.1080/1369118X.2016.1186713.

Zuboff, Shoshana. *The Age of Surveillance Capitalism: The Fight for a Human Future at the New Frontier of Power*. New York: PublicAffairs, 2019.

10 Situated Indications *Queer STS Experiments on Global Datafication*

THE DATA GAP

In 2017, a headline on the World Bank blog made this pronouncement: "to fight discrimination, we need to fill the LGBTI data gap."[1] Reading this statement, you might be wondering what exactly this data gap might be. In the post, SOGI experts discussed how quantitative data on LGBTI people is crucial to tackling discrimination and inclusion as international development issues and how such data "remains scarce especially in developing countries."[2] The identified gap exists between research (to collect data) and action (to fight discrimination), making quantitative data a precursor to policy changes. The second and implicit gap lies between the availability of such data in developed and developing countries, prompting international organizations' calls for "investing in a research revolution for LGBTI inclusion."[3] In other words, we are witnessing a global (albeit uneven) datafication of LGBTI inclusion, or the representation of LGBTI inclusion through numbers and the conversion of its qualitative aspects into quantified data.[4]

Consider the proposed "LGBTI inclusion index," which would enable you to appraise a country's performance on LGBTI inclusion based on numeric measurements.[5] You could scroll through forty-nine indicators that assess the status of LGBTI people in five key domains: education, health, personal safety and violence, economic well-being, and political and civic participation. You could track changes within a country over a given period, compare the degree of inclusion across countries, and weigh these geographic differences and temporal changes against a benchmark.[6] As an imagined product of global datafication, the index promises a global-level commensurability to compare across time and space. But to operationalize it, we'd face the arduous task of filling the gap of national-level data for the constituent indicators.

Undergirding the talk of a "data gap" is an imaginary fused with data optimism, "that such data is necessary for knowing what we need for our well-being."[7] We might pause and reflect whether quantified data is so dispensable as to be prioritized by advocates or its appeal is a form of cruel optimism ultimately detrimental to queer flourishing and worldmaking.[8] As I unpack in this chapter, the dichotomy between global index and national data is not just based on fictive scales but often is inconducive for advocacy efforts. While focusing on the empirical case of datafying LGBTI inclusion, I invite you (who have picked up this book and I presume shared our collective concerns about queer and/or data) to dwell on a capacious question: how could we imagine queer relations with data and datafication beyond optimist frames affixed to hegemonic scales?

Data agnosticism? Many queer critics would likely repudiate approaching inclusion within a positivist premise.[9] Data skepticism? Minoritized groups, including LGBTI people, have been skeptical of data collection and extraction because of its complicity in historically inflicted harm.[10] Data pragmatism? Activists and activist-scholars might recognize the practical role of quantitative evidence in advocacy work and the necessity to be "postmodernist in the street but positivist in the spreadsheets."[11] These sentiments are diffuse in queer responses to data and datafication. Rather than an attempt at reconciliation or adjudication, this chapter calls for expanding our toolbox when approaching data as a queer object. I submit that we turn to feminist science and technology studies (STS) to cultivate a non-innocent sensibility and an experimentational mode of engagement.

Feminist Non-Innocence, Queer Experiments

I deploy the term "non-innocence" as a sensibility elaborated by feminist STS scholarship. As Donna Haraway puts it, "the standpoints of the subjugated are not 'innocent' positions."[12] A non-innocent critique, as Michelle Murphy argues, must attend to the convergences and complicities between any (inter) disciplinary enterprise and its objects.[13] For example, when addressing the analytic-empirical conjuncture of ethnography and global health, Ramah McKay points out that ethnographers usually treat global health facts as external objects to be destabilized while ignoring the co-constitution and adjacency between social science and global health projects.[14] Similarly, a non-innocent queer critique of global datafication needs to recognize that queer theory emerged as a racially and geopolitically unconscious field in North American universities. We'd be exercising the antinormative urge to "queer" datafication at our own peril if we do not consider the continuing call to decolonize queerness itself.[15]

My analysis puts experimentation—an expansive yet long-standing theme in STS—to queer uses.[16] Experiments create scenarios for STS investigation that bring technoscience and the public into intimate interactions.[17] In this chapter, I pivot on two artifacts produced as experts and advocates experiment on datafying LGBTI inclusion: (1) an index and a map that seek to objectively represent LGBTI acceptance worldwide yet may end up reinforcing polarization, and (2) a supposedly feasible-to-measure conversion therapy indicator nevertheless rendered as indeterminate in China by competing activist and public narratives. Combining discursive, visual, ethnographic, and speculative sources, I analyze how the social worlds of development experts, researchers (myself included), activists (often lay experts), and the public intersect around these two artifacts.[18] Rather than supplying an exhaustive account of a global index or Chinese LGBTI activism, I utilize the two artifacts to excavate and problematize a premise found in both cases: the dichotomy between *global index* and *national data*.

Experiments have also served as an instrument of intervention for STS researchers that "does not operate from a detached scholarly position . . . (or) aim at implementing a pre-set normative agenda."[19] Echoing this ethos, my analytic starting point is neither an "objective" assessment nor a "paranoid" debunking of index efficacy but the question of engagements: what has been done *about* datafication and what is to be done *with* datafication? Writing is the immediate tool at my disposal for experimental interventions. My performative experiments on data visceralization and narration in the next two sections were composed with the purposes of "rethinking form to expose content . . . and creating new ways of seeing and understanding."[20] I use argumentation and exposition to anatomize the representational forms of my data artifacts, as well as emplotment and elicitation to surface the theoretical, conceptual, and practical problems being provoked. In each section, I engage with a classic feminist STS theory-method—situated vision and ontological multiplicity—to reconsider the dichotomous formation of collecting national data for a global index. At the end, I put forth "situated indications" as an alternative paradigm to analyze and practice datafication queerly and offer a set of metaphors for your use.

> EXPERIMENT ON DATA VISCERALIZATION. Originally developed in visceral design for digital interaction, data visceralization seeks "to help make abstract information have a meaningful visceral impact on users."[21] To repurpose it from the original context of designing for usership to my context of writing for readership, I compose my prose in a purposefully dialogical and elicitory manner to model the interactional experiences with a visceral object and let out the embedded and sometimes concealed affective intensities in an LGBTI index and map.

GLOBAL INDEX OR SITUATED DATAFICATION

Seeing Like an Index

Go to https://bit.ly/global-datafication. What do you see? A world map, perhaps the most tangible rendition of "globality." This map was an interim result from development experts' experiment on quantifying and visualizing inclusion. The map was based on the "Global Acceptance Index" (GAI), a precursor to the more exhaustive "LGBTI Inclusion Index" mentioned at the beginning of this chapter.[22] As the comprehensive Inclusion Index still lacks source data for most indicators, GAI is chosen here as our best available artifact since it bears sufficient analytical similarities. A country's GAI score is calculated according to national and regional surveys that contain information on social attitudes and public opinion toward homosexuality (and, in some cases, transgender people). However, as a case of "formal representations," GAI is "not tied to a particular situation or set of empirical data but, rather, . . . a synthesis of data and a presentation of rules for combining and acting."[23] To illustrate cartographically how this happens, I will spend some time here walking you through the map's "aesthetics," which Saida Hodžić usefully defines as "formal qualities of authoritative knowledge."[24] Take a close look. I'll be your guide.

The LGBT Global Acceptance map is gradationally colored. I'm seeing country names, although not all of them. There are small and large chunks of land that are gray—data voids.[25] The gray areas exist out there, without borderlines or country specifications. Gray, empty, and with a sense of nothingness (wait, why am I sounding like a colonial explorer?).[26] Actually, here is a quiz: could you name the countries in gray and without data? Let me try: North Korea,

Mongolia, Burma, Laos, Cambodia, Nepal, Bhutan (am I spelling it right?), Cuba, Papua New Guinea (among the many Pacific Island countries), and Somalia, as well as a significant part of sub-Saharan Africa. I feel ashamed for lumping African countries together as a continent. How about you? Do you experience vicarious ignorance and shame? Or perhaps you feel none of these sentiments because, to be fair, the lack of specification for these regions is by the map's design.

Moving on, I see blue countries. The bluer, the higher the GAI score is. The bluest countries are Australia, New Zealand, and countries in western Europe, as well as Argentina and Canada. Wait a second, I wonder to what extent this map overlaps with the GDP per capita map (do I remind you of a modernization theorist?). I also see that most in-between countries are assigned from blue to light green. But some countries are colored yellow, which contrasts with blue and even the neighboring light green. This contrast seems to be intentional, as the map is an accompaniment to a policy paper titled "polarized progress."[27] Among the most homophobic countries in yellow are two from the Middle East and Northern Africa (MENA, an acronym that may only be understood by those familiar with US area studies parlance): Egypt and Saudi Arabia. Wait, Bangladesh is also in yellow. What do these countries have in common? (Queer theorists might want to cite Jasbir Puar here.) Okay, before you accuse me of bullshitting or lacking rigor, I shall stop my paranoid stream-of-consciousness map-reading voice-over. Let's shift to a more analytic and argumentative register.

What I attempt to lay bare above are the affective circuits undergirding numeric commensurability.[28] As historians of science have demonstrated, novel techniques of visualization precipitate configurations of objectivity; the epistemic imperatives to represent the world often prefigure a desire to intervene in what is represented.[29] Behind the talk of the LGBTI data gap and the efforts to enumerate inclusion is a similar desire to intervene in the problem of inclusion globally. If anything, global humanitarian knowledge production does not shy away from its goal of generating actionable evidence.[30] In fact, the desire to enumerate, measure, and quantify is by no means specific to the LGBTI policy domain but has been internal to international governance since its inception and is particularly tangible around gender, reproduction, and development.[31] In this map based on GAI, the seemingly dispassionate schematic index is in fact charged with affective aspirations, especially through its cartographic elements: seeing the red inverted triangle denoting the retrogression of LGBT acceptance, do you feel a sense of alertness and urgency, a need for action, and a will to work toward improvement?

Feeling Like a Queer Theorist

If ways of seeing are built on circuits of affect, how are you feeling now? You might notice that the term "global datafication of LGBTI inclusion" almost readily invites queer interventions. After all, inclusion is perhaps *the* most fraught term and the prototypical problem space in which queer studies coheres as a field. With the liberal agendas of inclusion and assimilation into marriage and market institutions dominating Western gay and lesbian politics, queer critics have mobilized concepts such as homonormativity to unpack novel forms of normativity and vulnerability emerging from the logic of respectability and domesticity.[32] Queer of color critique, by examining intersectional processes involving racialization, gendering, and sexualization, has cautioned that the kind of freedom promised by gay liberalism is conditional at best and complicit in inflicting violence.[33] In a time of homonationalism, formal inclusion could turn into an alibi, if not an outright legitimating apparatus, for state-sanctioned violence against other marginalized populations.[34] Queer critics working in the transnational contexts of the Global South/East have long been concerned with the alleged universality of a rights-based approach where inclusion is gauged as *the* exceptional window to understanding lived realities.[35] The light of visibility-based rights may as well be a "shadow of Stonewall" that flattens the complex processes of hybridization and legacies of colonialism trafficked under the sign of globalization.[36]

Based on these critical insights on inclusion, how are you feeling when you become capable of seeing "LGBT global acceptance" through this map, or rather when this map invites you to see (or demands that you see) "LGBT global acceptance"? When my queer-theory trained eyes encounter this map for the first time, some immediate criticisms come to mind. Is the index going to democratize how we represent LGBTI inclusion globally, with enumerative comprehensiveness and precision, or is it just a persisting orientalist gaze inciting datafied discourses around homophobia? Is the quantified inclusion benchmark an effective policy tool, or is it in aid of revamping the colonial-era civilizational hierarchy into a global inclusion hierarchy?[37] What is counted in and out of the metrics, and who are the beneficiaries of such enumerative practices? Perhaps unsurprisingly, you will likely find traces of Western centrism, as the Western legal equality approach leads the parameters of "inclusion." (More on this in discussions on the case of conversion therapy, up next).[38]

Critical readers like you might also ask, so what? What are the author's politics anyway? Is he going to defend or subvert (i.e., "queer") the said global indexes? Is he an ally of the people subjected to the data gaze or a sympathizer with the metrics experts? I list this litany of questions not to defend my authorial integrity (I will, however, directly address my "politics" toward the end of this chapter) but to remind us again of the non-innocent terrain in which we are situated and engaged. Within queer studies, there have been reflections on the field's analytic habitus of antinormative "queering," which features an affective attachment to marginality over everyday banality.[39] In the scenario of global datafication, it's the very old wine of universality versus specificity in the new bottle of global index versus local reality (to be collected as data). The antinormative desire could lead queer analysts to readily identify with an imagined, subjugated position in the face of a monolithic global data gaze. Such a queer romance with grassroots resistance could quickly turn into a nightmare of scholarly narcissism and analytic reductionism, thereby characterizing all international development experts as neocolonialists and denying outright any utility of quantification due to some intrinsic epistemic violence. The question then is, how could we "de-idealize," as Kadji Amin would put it, the always already queered object of global datafication?[40]

Imagining Countertopographies

A map has a worldview. The LGBT Global Acceptance map, made based on a paper titled "Polarized Progress," pictures a topography of segregated countries, separate struggles, linear progress, flat comparisons, and data voids. But whose view is it?

Feminist epistemology's insistence on specifying the unmarked knowing subject position is instructive here.[41] Who is the actively knowing subject, and who are the passive objects to be known? Who is the subject of the index? Per Banu Subramaniam and her coauthors, "scientific knowledge does not equally benefit everyone."[42] In the hierarchized contours of gender, race, sexuality, and coloniality, some bodies are seen as possessing the faculty of reasoned judgment; other bodies are treated as "the objects of scientific inquiry but also the raw materials."[43] Under the acronym of LGBTI, datafication's logic of enumerability operates by counting individually transparent subjects into aggregately visible populations.[44] It renders unintelligible the kinds of felt and sensorial forms of knowledge and opaque and tacit forms of subjectivities that are deployed and embodied in everyday navigation and survival.[45] As Lina Žigelytė asks elsewhere in this volume (chapter 7), are there really "not enough meaningful data"? Or perhaps we should ask who guards the gate of meaningfulness and data worthiness. Flipping the view, could we see data voids as a form of refusal instead of an epistemic lack?

Yes, we could and should. The promise of potentiality and alterity is commonly invested in queer gestures toward alternative worldmaking. Per Angela Davis's motto, "you have to act *as if* it were possible to radically transform the world."[46] Yet the challenge sometimes lies in not so much the normative question of *whether* as in the tactical one of *how* to see otherwise—what Donna Haraway describes as the task of holding together the inherent contradictions between "the power to see" and "the violence implicit in our visualizing practices."[47]

Engaged scholars and activists have been undertaking what I dub *situated datafication*, a work of analysis and practice that locates, surfaces, and embeds the historical, social, political, and value contexts of the knowing agents—be they human, machinic, or cybernetic—into the representational and operational processes of datafication.[48] Many have begun the work of peering into the black box of datafication: exposing the encoded, automated, and unmarked biases in sociotechnical systems and building value-responsive and justice-oriented ones.[49] Insofar as it is relevant to our topic of discussion, situated datafication brings up a scenario in which actors guided by positioned collective concerns seize the means of datafication and repurpose the same instruments to gain new perspectives and make countertopographies.

A countertopography is generated through "a situated, but at the same time scale-jumping and geography-crossing, political response."[50] According to Cindi Katz, the construction of countertopographies involves imagining "a politics that maintains the distinctness of a place while recognizing that it is connected analytically to other places along contour lines that represent not elevation but particular relations to a process."[51] If an index has a way of seeing the world and creates a topography of polarized progress, could we use similar means to imagine a politics and countertopography based on what Chandra Mohanty calls "common contexts of struggles"?[52] Following thinkers of transnational and intersectional feminisms, might we quantify and visualize the afterlife of colonialism and imperialism trafficked under the banner of LGBTI or queerness? Is it possible to have an index answering to cross-border solidarity and transversal intersectionality?[53] This is an open invitation extended to you. I end this section with an example from the US heartland to bring the countertopographic possibility into view.[54]

"What if Black America was a country unto itself?" In 2008, the Black AIDS Institute (BAI) opened the report *Left Behind: Black America: A Neglected Priority in the Global AIDS Epidemic* with that question, echoing Black nationalism from decades ago.[55] The purpose of the report is to shift the US government's zeal from leading global health diplomacy to fighting the actually existing yet neglected epidemic at home. By the first decade of the twenty-first century, if one were to look at US statistics, AIDS rates had been contained nationwide. Domestic funding for AIDS in the United States plunged, with resources and attention increasingly being invested in global health interventions, especially in Africa. However, the national amelioration of AIDS in the United States should be more appropriately described as AIDS being contained *within* the Black population, among whom AIDS continued its growth and became the leading cause of death in some age categories. In the early 2000s, the prevalence rate in the US Black population was even higher than in many African countries, a situation in which US global humanitarianism became an alibi for its domestic racial inequality.[56] To expose the ironies (or hypocrisies) in the "U.S. government's failure to take AIDS in Black America seriously," the report implored readers to consider that question: what if Black America were a country unto itself?[57]

Go to https://bit.ly/situated-datafication. You see the maps of Côte d'Ivoire, South Africa, and the northeast US region, which are spread through the report. Why? As the captions under each map explain, each of those places is the equivalent of the size of Black America's AIDS epidemic, economy, and population. The African countries and provincialized US region constitute the representational proxies for the hypothetical nation of "Black America." In these cases of curated datafication, commensurability is established across rather disproportionate scales of subpopulation AIDS rate, country GDP and AIDS rate, and subregional population size. These illustrations defy default units of comparison and instantiate a countertopographic imagination, jumping across infranational, national, and supranational geographies and triangulate interscalar relations in the racialized political economy of the global AIDS response. Compared to the Global LGBT Acceptance map presented earlier, what makes these data commensurate is not a disembodied set of rules of calculation such as an index, or preset national borders, but a standpoint epistemology exemplified by the Black AIDS Institute's slogan "Our People, Our Problem,

Our Solutions": the analysis and problematization grounded in the structural locations Black Americans occupy and the resultant public health urgency and political agency articulated through a Black nationalist imaginary.[58] In a nutshell, a countertopography produced by situated datafication.[59]

EXPERIMENT ON DATA NARRATION. My ethnographic storytelling next is informed by the importance of narratives in making sense of data because "data do not speak for themselves . . . (and) must be narrated—put to work in particular contexts, sunk into narratives that give them shape and meaning, and mobilized as part of broader processes of interpretation and meaning-making."[60] You will follow my odyssey into a pluriverse where actors on the grounds of datafication attempted to ascertain and measure the value of an indicator and, as a result, rendered it simultaneously true and false. Expect puzzlement and dazzlement (but also the reveal!).

NATIONAL DATA OR INDICATION MULTIPLE

A Self-Contradictory Fact?

You are looking at a table extracted from the document proposing the LGBTI inclusion index (table 10.1).[61] It presents the technical specifications of one of forty-nine constituent indicators. This indicator is simply named "conversion therapy," which helps measure one aspect of inclusion called "bodily, physical, and psychological integrity" in the lesbian, gay, bisexual, and transgender populations. The other indicator for this aspect concerns legal protections against "normalizing medical interventions" in the intersex population. This subset of indicators is further nested in the parent category "personal safety and violence," which comprises indicators from hate crime legislation and violence monitoring, to asylum protections. The "conversion therapy" indicator falls under the second tier of feasibility, meaning "data already exist in some sense (such as a law or policy either exists or not), but resources would be necessary to collect the data."[62] Measuring indicators in the third feasibility tier would require population-based survey data, which is still scarce. By comparison, the data needed to measure the conversion therapy indicator is more readily accessible since we only need to establish *whether or not* the related policy exists. It is arguably the simplest form of data: a dummy variable coded as 1 (yes, presence of policy) or 0 (no, absence of policy).

TABLE 10.1 Conversion therapy indicator

Dimension of the LGBTI inclusion index	Personal safety and violence
Aspect of inclusion	Bodily, physical, and psychological integrity
Name of indicator	5.2 "Conversion therapy"
Indicator	Laws, regulations, judicial decisions, and policies prohibiting/banning/protecting against sexual orientation and gender identity "conversion therapy"
Feasibility tier	2
Potential sources of data	May be collected from reports from LGBTI human rights organizations. Likely to involve qualitative data from a small number of countries.

Source: Adapted from M. V. Lee Badgett and Randall Sell, "A Set of Proposed Indicators for the LGBTI Inclusion Index," United Nations Development Program, 2018.

As procedurally uncomplicated as the measurement of this indicator sounds, I encountered competing data regarding this simple yes-or-no fact in my ethnographic fieldwork in China. One of the basic facts about LGBTI inclusion turned out to be quite difficult to establish. As the popular historical account of LGBTI rights in China goes, activists in the 1990s made concerted efforts to lobby psychiatrists to depathologize homosexuality. The third revision of the Chinese Classification of Mental Disorders (CCMD-3), published in 2001, is the watershed event and document that declassified homosexuality as a mental illness and made news in mainstream Western media such as the *New York Times*.[63] Ever since I came out and started consuming Chinese LGBTI media in 2013, activists, community members, and interested observers have mentioned that year and the document in a matter-of-fact way, as if it were just an item in the litany of LGBTI rights milestones and another box China had checked. It seemed like a plain fact and banal common sense that China depathologized homosexuality in 2001. The answer to this indicator would then be a yes, indicating that there indeed exists the required regulatory policy (CCMD-3) preventing the use of conversion therapy.

Yet activists since the 2010s have strived to prove otherwise to the global public and suggest that homosexuality (and, less frequently mentioned, transgender individuals) continues to be pathologized by psychiatrists and mental health practitioners and that conversion therapy does not just exist but abounds. Domestic and international NGOs have been trying to gather data and assess the current state of conversion therapy in China.[64] The Beijing LGBT Center, in a series of published reports on LGBT mental health, surveyed community members and mental health practitioners to pinpoint the percentage of respondents who reported having undergone conversion therapy or offered such services.[65] In these efforts to document conversion therapy through datafication, quantitative evidence of harm is frequently presented alongside a human victim figure. Exposing conversion therapy, one might say, has been among the dominant agendas of LGBTI advocacy in mainland China since the 2010s, making many international headlines and resulting in an entry for "conversion therapy in China" in the *Global Encyclopedia of Lesbian, Gay, Bisexual, Transgender, and Queer (LGBTQ) History.*[66]

One might reasonably infer, as I did, that advocacy efforts exposing conversion therapy should have debunked the narrative that homosexuality was depathologized in 2001 through CCMD-3. The answer to the conversion therapy indicator would therefore change from a yes (i.e., there exists CCMD-3 as a regulatory policy) to a no (i.e., conversion therapy in practice is not effectively prohibited at all). Well, it turned out to be my wishful thinking. Tuning in on public discourses during this time period, you'd hear media—Chinese or Western, state-controlled newspaper or community social media—repeatedly cite the document CCMD-3 and 2001 as the watershed moment of depathologization. You would thus often encounter proclamations, sometimes from the same source, that in China the depathologization of homosexuality happened (per community celebration of CCMD-3) *but also* did not happen (per community condemnation of conversion therapy). For a long time, I couldn't fathom how such self-contradictory claims could coexist so frictionlessly on a supposedly easy-to-falsify fact and feasible-to-measure indicator.

Was it a matter of empirical inaccuracy? I began with some simple fact-checking efforts. If CCMD-3 was indeed the watershed document, I wanted to find out what exactly changed compared to its predecessor. In comparing CCMD-3 and its predecessor, CCMD-2-R, one could see that homosexuality, along with its parent diagnosis of "sexual orientation disorders," was retained in CCMD-3 based on the existence of prospective conversion-seeking patients "anxious, depressed, or agonized" (i.e., "ego-dystonic," diagnostically speaking) by their sexual orientation. However, the entry in CCMD-3 did contain an affirmative caveat that "(homosexuality and bisexuality) is not necessarily abnormal (as long as it is ego-syntonic)."[67] It seemed that the matter of contradiction was settled through empirical specification: depathologization of ego-syntonic homosexuality happened, but depathologization of ego-dystonic homosexuality did not happen. Both popular accounts were in part wrong because depathologization happened in 2001 but only in partial and incomplete ways.[68] If I were the scorer for the conversion therapy indicator, I'd complain that a dichotomous variable is not enough because China's situation is neither a 1 nor a 0, but a 0.5. But should I have to choose, I'd probably go for a 0, given that China's underregulated psychotherapeutic market makes it hard to enforce standards such as CCMD-3 yet easy for opportunistic profiteers to offer conversion therapy.[69]

Into the Pluriverse!

I was probably not wrong, as far as the scoring part went. But the puzzle persisted. While I understood the differences between what psychiatrists wrote in CCMD-2-R and CCMD-3, I still didn't have a plausible explanation for the contradictions within public narratives that I encountered. If it were merely a matter of empirical accuracy that the depathologization in 2001 was not complete, why did so many people remain so *attached* to and ready to restate an empirically inaccurate claim on homosexuality's officially depathologized status, even after knowing that conversion therapy exists widely? If the CCMD-3 did depathologize ego-syntonic homosexuality, why was there more public attention paid to conversion therapy after the CCMD3 than before, when conversion therapy was supposedly more sanctioned by diagnostic standards?[70] The more I learned, the more indeterminate the indicator became. Either nobody cared about "the truth," or . . .

I was following the rules of a rigged game. And the game is indeed rigged. A simple dummy variable, the conversion therapy indicator is nevertheless encoded with the assumption that conversion therapy would be attempted everywhere and thus require a "ban" (a term inflected with legal equality approach), which could then be measured as an indicator for "personal safety and violence."[71] This assumed reality is composed of a story line better known as Western history—from the very definitions of safety and violence to the supposed historical trajectories and means of redress.[72] In other words, knowledge practices such as the conversion therapy indicator are performative: they "generate not only representations of reality, but also the realities those representations depict."[73] If my puzzlement is with contradictions within public narratives about an indicator, I should perhaps listen more carefully to what the public concern themselves with instead of what the indicator designates as relevant. Instead of treating them as the "raw" materials to produce a measurable result *for* an indicator, why not treat the public narratives as data meaningful *in* themselves and *indicative* of realities? What if we live not in a universe but in a pluriverse—"a world where many worlds fit" and where "worlds can be part of each other and radically different at the same time"?[74]

Here I am guided by Annemarie Mol's idea of ontological politics: "that reality does not precede the mundane practices in which we interact with it, but is rather shaped within these practices."[75] Echoing her constituent view of politics, some scholars working across STS and scientometrics have argued that indicators have both "representative value" and "organizing capacity," which "engage and include or exclude actors."[76] The processes of designing and interpreting an indicator in practice open an interface "between measurement and participation."[77] Mol's ontological multiplicity further posits that reality/realities are more-than-one, as they are enacted by multiple practices, but also less-than-many, as these sometimes contradictory enactments are coordinated to maintain a workable stability.[78] To understand data ontology as similarly multiple, we need to first expand our definitional purview of datafication and reconsider what kinds of practices and enactments are analytically relevant. Paul Dourish and Edgar Gómez Cruz alert us to everyday narrative practices and imaginative work that "underlie coming to thinking of something as 'data' in the first place."[79] In other words, datafication involves not just the technical domain of operational specification but also the semiotic domain of narrational signification.

What if we understand the self-contradictory statements on depathologization and conversion therapy as narrational acts and everyday practices of *indications*? We could then shift gears from a singular and nominal indicator as *representative of* a fictive reality (of which the indicator is constituent) to multiple indications as *participatory in* actually existing realities. An indicator demands an answer to the question of "what nominal value an indicator *is*," the premise and parameter of which are preset. By contrast, indications invite participation in an open-ended provocation: "what realities and imagined futures do indicating practices enact?," which are open for experimentations by activists, the public, and lay experts.[80] Resembling Mol's praxiography (ethnography of practice) but with pointed attention to power, Lina Dencik suggests "a practice approach to datafication," a *process*-focused analysis" aiming to "*situate* data in a way that can illuminate its *relation* to dominant agendas and potentials for resistance."[81] With a pair of glasses called ontological multiplicity and a compass called situated relationality to traverse the pluriverse, let me take you to the year 1992, when . . .

A campaign called Love Knowledge Action was launched first by Wan Yan-hai, a former public health official turned AIDS and gay activist. Wan leveraged the epistemic authority of international standards such as the World Health Organization's International Classification of Disease (ICD-10) to urge Chinese psychiatrists to declassify homosexuality as a mental disorder. As the campaign name advertises, he followed a consciously "nonpolitical" strategy that framed international standards as scientific, objective, and therefore superior.[82] The insistence on scientific neutrality successfully concealed activist aims against the Cold War–inflected, state-sanctioned ideological framing of sexual matters (e.g., AIDS, pornography, homosexuality) as symptoms of Western moral decadence and threats to socialist moral hygiene. The underlying scientific internationalism also usefully converged with Chinese psychiatrists' plan to come up with a dual diagnostic system meeting international standards while also preserving Chinese characteristics. Psychiatrists speculated that "the two systems will merge, and nationwide and worldwide standardization will be achieved."[83] This internationalist imaginary enabled a partial alliance between psychiatrists and activists to depathologize homosexuality; however, for gay activists and communities, depathologization carried another layer of meaning, which is the afforded cosmopolitan belonging of sexual citizenship.[84] As internationalist aspirations of science and sexuality became intertwined, the local gay communities and Western media willfully claimed (or wishfully misinterpreted, if you will) CCMD-3's one-sentence caveat as evidence of homosexuality's official depathologization in China.

For psychiatrists, depathologization indicated their compliance, albeit partial, with international professional standards, enacting their aspirations of gaining membership in the international scientific community. For the Chinese gay and lesbian community and the sympathetic global civil society, depathologization indicated that gay identity in China had been normalized, enacting their cosmopolitan sexual belonging sanctioned by the global scientific standard.[85] Activists like Wan skillfully coordinated between the two indications and their partially aligned, imagined futures by camouflaging the claims to sexual cosmopolitanism with triumphant scientific internationalism.[86] It is the affective attachments and values of belonging and citizenship that have driven community narratives, time and again, to assert CCMD-3's watershed role and reaffirm homosexuality's depathologized status, making it what Joshua Hubbard calls an "invulnerable fact."[87] Such an empirically inaccurate fact has persisted not because it is true but because it has been willfully rendered as real and invulnerable.[88] However, the discursive inscription of the depathologized status has also served to obscure actual malpractices such as conversion therapy and clinical harm, which a younger generation of activists have worked to expose.

While activists in the Love Knowledge Action campaign lobbied psychiatrists with handouts containing Chinese translations of international standards, after almost thirty years . . .

~~Oxymoronic~~ Data

. . . in the summer of 2019, *Lovers Action*, a mobile installation art project protesting against conversion therapy, appeared in my social media feed.[89]

What changed after three decades? Most notably, the name. The subject of action shifted from science to people, and the object of love shifted from knowledge to another person. In the age of gay rights as human rights, conversion therapy activism in China has centered on surfacing a human figure, be it a plaintiff seeking redress in court or a victim of clinical malpractice and violence. In *Lovers Action*, the figure of innocent lovers was invoked to contrast with the image of coerced patients treated because of who they love. The aesthetic form of *Lovers Action* featured visual theatricality compared to the formal textuality in Love Knowledge Action. It borrowed ideas from the Hollywood blockbuster *Three Billboards outside Ebbing, Missouri* (2017), in which the protagonist uses billboard slogans as tools of protest. The organizing artist and volunteers printed three protest slogans on three trucks and then drove them to medical facilities and city landmarks, where photos and videos were taken, posted, and went viral on social media. The ephemeral and mobile characteristics echoed the feminist art-based pop-up activism of the same time.[90] This tactic emerged in response to the state crackdown on advocacy NGOs and foreign nonprofit agencies, as the activists maneuvered to escape surveillance and scrutiny and maximize space for action in an increasingly repressive environment.

Peng Yanhui is one of the leading activists against conversion therapy in

China. He coordinated efforts to win lawsuits against clinics practicing conversion therapy and textbook publishers wrongly labeling homosexuality as a disease. When I asked how he would assess homosexuality's depathologization status in China, I heard an oxymoron: "Sometimes, we say homosexuality is depathologized in China. Sometimes, we say it has not been depathologized."[91] Peng spoke candidly about the strategic and realistic rationales for doing so. While he was keenly aware of the partial nature of depathologization and how misleading a celebratory or triumphant narrative about CCMD-3 could be, he sometimes still cited CCMD-3 as an authority when endeavoring to educate the general public that homosexuality is not a disease. Part of the reason is that advocacy in the 1990s was limited, and necessarily so, to a select group of psychiatrists, especially the CCMD-3 revision working group. Depathologization is far from an accepted consensus and therefore needs to be restated, sometimes through litigation, among textbook writers, teachers, and the public. Here, activists' proclamation about homosexuality's depathologized status is an indication of its legitimacy, enacting a yet-to-be-fulfilled citizenship.[92]

In other circumstances, Peng would shift to a different narrative, that homosexuality is *not* depathologized. He noted that Western observers tend to examine LGBT issues elsewhere according to their own histories and readily identify certain signs, such as CCMD-3 or an exposed conversion therapy clinic, in a dichotomous framework of Western liberalism versus authoritarian repression, along with a linear timeline of progress.[93] Yet, in recent years, the Chinese propaganda apparatus has become adept at discursively appropriating this framework based on Western (gay) liberalism and formal inclusion. In the state-sponsored *Global Times* and *People's Daily*, Chinese commentators have cited the depathologized status of homosexuality and made empty promises about tolerance, inclusion, and rights as indications of China's progress and progressiveness to sometimes brush off criticism about its human rights record, enacting China's membership and the party-state's legitimacy in an international order still dominated by Western values.[94]

Might we call this an authoritarian homonationalism? Whatever we call it, activists not only face an increasingly adversarial institutional environment for organizing advocacy work on the ground but also have to come up with novel ways to expose the party-state's hypocrisy and push for substantial policy changes (recall how US presidential candidate Hillary Clinton shamed Xi Jinping as a hypocrite on Twitter in September 2015 when he spoke about women's rights at the United Nations; Chinese activists under constant scrutiny cannot always afford to do so). It is in this triply compromised institutional and discursive environment of domestic authoritarianism, Western gay liberalism, and authoritarian homonationalism that anticonversion therapy activism unfolds under the declaration that homosexuality has not been depathologized in China. In other words, activist insistence on the not-yet-depathologized status and the efforts to expose conversion therapy indicate the Chinese state's inaction with respect to this clinical violence, enacting a limited resistance by seeking accountability in a compromised situation.

Facts pronounced over depathologization are necessarily self-contradictory, and the generated data are oxymoronic because the realities activists face are full of contradictions. Judged from the epistemic rules of an indicator, such an oxymoron is a liability because we cannot arrive at a measurable outcome, not even a simple answer of yes or no. However, if we shift our focus from the definite value of an indicator to the dynamic process of indications, we might see that the contradictions arise from the multiplicity of activist "relations to dominant agendas" and tactics for resistance.[95] What's at stake is not data feasibility but actionability.[96] Seen in this light, the empirical ambiguity and indeterminacy—"sometimes depathologized, sometimes not"—is a form of strategic opacity and political maneuvering.

GAP SUCKS, INDICATIONS BOUNCE

Writing before the LGBTI inclusion index was proposed, geographer Kath Browne and colleagues noted that the relative absence of a global standard "could offer a welcome opportunity to work with LGBTIQ people across different contexts and cultures to create our own measures and analyses." As we witness the datafication of LGBTI lives unfold, this chapter has argued for a non-innocent and experimental sensibility to involve ourselves in the business of turning matters (of inclusion or otherwise) into numbers and data. My unsaid politics is that abstraction through datafication is not antithetical to but combinative with abstraction through theorization. What's queer is not to be found within the apparatuses and tools (for enumeration or interpretation) but in their multiple, unintended, perverse, and thus queer uses. For your use, this chapter has exemplified "situated datafication" and "indication multiple" as feminist STS inspired theory-method with which to diagnose locations/relations of power and appreciate multiplicity and contradictions in data practices. I now return to my opening question: how could we imagine queer relations with datafication

TABLE 10.2. Properties of two datafication paradigms

Properties/paradigms	Global index	Situated indications
Metaphors	Gap, suck	Situations, bounce
Trajectories	Preset, singular, linear, definitive	Participatory, multiple, recursive, contingent
Scales	Fixed, nation-state	Flexible, interscalar
Purposes	Represent, compare	Diffract, triangulate
Origins	International governance	Actions on the ground
Subjects of knowledge	Experts	Activists, open to stake-holders
Placement of value	Encoded	Responsive
Principles of evaluation	Feasibility	Actionability

beyond optimist frames affixed to hegemonic scales? I end this chapter with a discussion on metaphors (table 10.2).

When it comes to globalization, we often resort to "flat" metaphors, ones that obscure power differentials and uneven topographies. For example, James Ferguson says "flow" is a bad metaphor for analogizing the movements of global capital. Instead, he offers the metaphor of "hop" to capture the constitutive territorial unevenness of global capitalism. Capital is "globe-hopping": it "does not 'flow' from New York to Angola's oil fields, or from London to Ghana's gold mines; it hops, neatly skipping over most of what lies in between."[97] Flows cover, engulf, and irrigate. Hops select, segregate, and discriminate. Just like "flow" and "hop" evoke drastically different political outlooks, metaphors afford imagination and "shift the grounds, waters, skies of our scholarship" (and experimentation).[98]

Returning to the talk of "filling the LGBTI data gap," I contend that "gap" is a bad, flat metaphor and brings forth a set of flattening metaphors. Imagine the LGBTI lived experiences as differently positioned in a diverse terrain, with some on a hill, some on a lowland, some on a plateau. In the enumerative design of global indexes, filling a gap means bringing what exists on this terrain on par with a preset benchmark specified by an index irrespective of its topography and preexisting disparity. The abstraction of information moves according to a singular designated directionality of extraction. In queer parlance, a gap sucks. However, any reader who ever wrote a literature review would know that a "gap" does not naturally exist to be filled but must be enunciated and pronounced into existence. This means that we can choose to do away with metaphors infused with colonial logics of extraction. I propose "situated indications"—data and narrative practices that bounce between situations in an uneven topography to elevate positioned LGBTI experiences and find common contexts of struggles—as a paradigm to analyze and practice datafication queerly and offer "bounce" as the spatial and operational metaphor at work.

NOTES

ACKNOWLEDGMENTS: I am grateful to Colin Garon, Stephen Macekura, Patrick Keilty, Darius Longarino, and the anonymous referees for their gifts given in the form of formative provocations, constructive feedback, and editorial work. I received funding for this research from the Tobias Center for Innovation in International Development and the Institute of Digital Arts and Humanities, both at Indiana University.

1. Ijjasz-Vasquez and Cortez, "To Fight Discrimination, We Need to Fill the LGBTI Data Gap."

2. LGBTI stands for lesbian, gay, bisexual, transgender, and intersex; SOGI refers to sexual orientation and gender identity. For identity-indicating terms such as SOGI or LGBTI, I follow the parlance used by the subjects in question for self-description or representation. I use "queer" in an analytic vein or when I address queer theories and studies as a field of research and practice.

3. Badgett and Crehan, "Investing in a Research Revolution for LGBTI Inclusion."

4. My use of the concepts *quantification* and *datafication* in this chapter is based on the work of Martha Lampland and Susan Leigh Star, who define quantification as "the representation of some action, being, or model through numbers," and Minna Ruckenstein and Natasha Dow Schüll, who define datafication as "the conversion of qualitative aspects of life into quantified data." Lampland and Star, *Standards and Their Stories*, 9; Ruckenstein and Schüll, "Datafication of Health," 261.

5. Badgett and Sell, "Set of Proposed Indicators for the LGBTI Inclusion Index."

6. Badgett and Sell, "Set of Proposed Indicators for the LGBTI Inclusion Index." 5.

7. Žigelytė, "Not Enough Meaningful Data?" (chapter 7, this volume).

8. Lauren Berlant offers an analysis of optimism as "an affective form" inherent in all attachments. The term "cruel optimism" is intended as "an explanation of our sense of *our endurance in the object* [of attachment]" even when the object or its conditions

of possibility prove to be "compromised . . . *im*possible, sheer fantasy, or *too* possible, and toxic." The emphasis on form is key, as "whatever the *content* of the attachment is, the continuity of its form provides something of . . . continuity." Berlant, *Cruel Optimism*, 23–34 (original emphasis). Cultural critics have made productive uses on the affective forms of woundedness, marginality, and disappointment in making sense of certain persisting yet problematic attachments in feminist and queer projects. See Brown, "Wounded Attachments"; Amin, *Disturbing Attachments*; and Chu, "Impossibility of Feminism." STS analysts have similarly turned to concepts such as techno-optimism/solutionism to understand the unintended consequence of aspirational imaginaries we persistently attach to certain technoscientific objects/projects. Quinlan, "Rape Kit's Promise"; Ames, *Charisma Machine*, 18–26. Taking clues from both strands of scholarship, this chapter applies an affective analytic for understanding our relations of attachments to queer and/or data.

9. See Love, *Underdogs*, for an analogous reappraisal of deviance studies as an unremembered positivist project in (North American) queer theory's field formation.

10. See Nikita Shepard's and Stephen Molldrem's chapters (2 and 5, respectively) in this volume. Shepard describes the relationship between minorities and data collection as a double bind: "while *not* being counted meant invisibility and denial of social recognition and urgently needed services, *being* counted without protections against discrimination could be life-threatening."

11. Fugard, "Should Trans People Be Postmodernist in the Streets but Positivist in the Spreadsheets?"; Grundy and Smith, "Activist Knowledges in Queer Politics."

12. Haraway, *Simians, Cyborgs, and Women*, 191.

13. Murphy, "Unsettling Care."

14. McKay, "Critical Convergences."

15. Arondekar and Patel, "Area Impossible"; Eng, Halberstam, and Muñoz, "Introduction: What's Queer about Queer Studies Now."

16. In this chapter, I invoke queer STS and bring queer and STS into relation based on Sara Ahmed's idea of use and queer uses. Scholarly work under the banner queer STS have critically interrogated the oftentimes oversized role that scientific practices and medical institutions played in constructing gender and sexuality as objects of knowledge and thereby shaping them as categories of lived experiences. Here, I try to invert this technoscientific overdetermination and loosen its grip on subjects by turning to the idea of "use". According to Ahmed, use points to "activities in which subjects are occupied in tasks that require they have a hold of things." A relation of use could exist between queer and STS as practical problems emerge outside the conventionally recognized objects of study in each field. "Use can be queer…things can be used in ways other than how they were intended to be used or by those other than for whom they were intended." The purview of queer STS is too often designated by boundaries

of technoscience. However, just like queer as a subjectless critique, queer STS might just be queer uses of STS, regardless of whether sex, sexuality, or gender is involved or not. Ahmed, *What's the Use*, 5, 44. For commentaries on queer STS, see Cipolla, Gupta, and Rubin, *Queer Feminist Science Studies*; Molldrem and Thakor, "Genealogies and Futures of Queer STS"; and Fishman, Mamo, and Grzanka, "Sex, Gender, and Sexuality in Biomedicine."

17. Lezaun, Marres, and Tironi, "Experiments in Participation."

18. Clarke and Star, "Social Worlds Framework."

19. Zuiderent-Jerak, *Situated Intervention*, 5.

20. Fischer, *Anthropology in the Meantime*, 39.

21. Stark, "Come on Feel the Data (and Smell It)." See also Wernimont, "Pandemic Death Counts Are Numbing. There's Another Way to Process." For similar uses of multimodal senses in qualitative data collection and discussions on the role of emotions in everyday engagements with data visualization, see D. Harper, "Talking about Pictures"; and Kennedy and Hill, "Feeling of Numbers."

22. Flores and Park, "Polarized Progress." There have been several updates to GAI datasets with more comprehensive country coverage and added interactive features to the GAI visualization. Readers can consult the "Global Acceptance Index" project on Williams Institute's website, https://williamsinstitute.law.ucla.edu/projects/gai/.

23. Lampland and Star, *Standards and Their Stories*, 9.

24. Hodžić, "Ascertaining Deadly Harms," 90.

25. The term "data voids," here used to describe the results of globally uneven research and statistical infrastructure, is borrowed from a discussion originally in the context of search engine results and the subsequent vulnerabilities for manipulation. See boyd and Golebiewski, "Data Voids."

26. Harding, *Postcolonial Science and Technology Studies Reader*.

27. Flores and Park, "Polarized Progress."

28. Espeland and Stevens, "Commensuration as a Social Process."

29. Haraway, *Modest_Witness@Second_Millennium.FemaleMan_Meets_OncoMouse*; Daston and Galison, "Image of Objectivity"; Hacking, *Representing and Intervening*.

30. Hodžić, *Twilight of Cutting*; Biruk, *Cooking Data*.

31. Macekura, *Mismeasure of Progress*; Merry, *Seductions of Quantification*; Murphy, *Economization of Life*; Data against Feminicide, accessed 9 December 2022, https://datoscontrafeminicidio.net/en/home-2/.

32. Duggan, "New Homonormativity."

33. Reddy, *Freedom with Violence*.

34. Puar, *Terrorist Assemblages*.

35. Chang, "Postcolonial Problem for Global Gay Rights."

36. Martin et al., *AsiaPacifiQueer*; Manalansan, "In the Shadows of Stonewall."

37. Bleys, *Geography of Perversion*.

38. Spade and Rohlfs, "Legal Equality, Gay Numbers and the (After?)Math of Eugenics"; Browne et al., "Limits of Legislative Change."

39. Wiegman and Wilson, "Introduction: Antinormativity's Queer Conventions."

40. Amin, *Disturbing Attachments*.

41. Harding, *Sciences from Below*.

42. Subramaniam et al., "Feminism, Postcolonialism, Technoscience," 408.

43. Subramaniam et al., 411 (emphasis removed).

44. Geographer Kath Browne and colleagues articulated the following assumptions in efforts to base funding allocation decision-making upon LGBTI inclusion measures: "[i] that sexual and gender identities and related discriminations can be captured in the term 'Lesbian, Gay, Bisexual and Trans' and that these are useful and universal categories that are globally applicable; [ii] that all sexual and gender dissidents and relatedly sexual and gender freedoms are related to these categories; [iii] that measures of equality/human rights are rightly defined and aid decisions implemented by supra-national organizations such as the World Bank; and [iv] that these assumptions rely on a conceptualization of LGBTQI people as recipients, and a uniform mass, who share common agendas." Browne et al., "Intervention — Gay-Friendly or Homophobic?"

45. Decena, *Tacit Subjects*; De Villiers, *Opacity and the Closet*; P. Harper, "Evidence of Felt Intuition." See also Shaka McGlotten's essay on black data (chapter 2, this volume) and Gary Kafer's on queer opacity (chapter 3, this volume).

46. Angela Davis's quote is "from a lecture delivered at Southern Illinois University, Carbondale. February 13th, 2014," according to the Feminist Press website, accessed March 18, 2023, https://thefeministpress.tumblr.com/post/163104615517/you-have-to -act-as-if-it-were-possible-to.

47. Haraway, *Simians, Cyborgs, and Women*, 192.

48. This putative definition is owed to "situated knowledge," the inseparability between knowing and doing, and the important distinction between the representational (for communication with a human audience) and the operational (for machine-mediated processing) in datafication raised in the "situated data analysis." Haraway, "Situated Knowledges"; Barad, "Agential Realism"; Rettberg, "Situated Data Analysis."

49. See Benjamin, *Race after Technology*; and D'Ignazio and Klein, *Data Feminism*.

50. Katz, "On the Grounds of Globalization," 1216.

51. Katz, "On the Grounds of Globalization," 1229.

52. Mohanty, *Feminism without Borders*, 11.

53. Pryse, "Trans/Feminist Methodology"; Crenshaw, "Mapping the Margins."

54. While attempting to recenter the peripheral in the global system, I chose to end with a discussion about the disenfranchised in the center (the United States). I take

cues from the productive tensions between intersectional and transnational strands of feminist theories and practices, particularly those that critically interrogate the neglect of Black people in transnational and global discourses. See Falcón and Nash, "Shifting Analytics and Linking Theories"; and Coogan-Gehr, "Politics of Race in U.S. Feminist Scholarship."

55. Wilson, Wright, and Isbell, *Left Behind: Black America*.

56. Atanasoski, *Humanitarian Violence*.

57. Wilson, Wright, and Isbell, *Left Behind: Black America*, 5.

58. The analysis and call for action in the report echo a long tradition of Black American health activism and Black feminist politics of location. See Collins, *Black Feminist Thought*; and Nelson, *Body and Soul*.

59. Interestingly, the two countries selected as proxy representations of Black America are in Africa: South Africa, for its equivalent economy size, and Côte d'Ivoire, for the size of its AIDS epidemic. Some might object to the stereotypes of the developing/developed distinction and the popular epidemic imaginary of Africa at play here. The authors likely mobilized the popular perception of Africa as the center of the AIDS epidemic, which is tied to the rise of US global health science and intervention. As a rhetorical tactic, juxtaposing Black America and Africa could reveal the severity of the AIDS crisis of the former and the urgency for federal action. Going beyond the scope of the BAI report, we could push the analysis and extend the countertopographic imagination even further: why Africa, not elsewhere? As Katz relates, countertopographies aspire to reveal "the connectedness of vastly different places made artifactually discrete by virtue of history and geography but which also reproduce themselves differently amidst the common political-economic and sociocultural processes they experience." Katz, "On the Grounds of Globalization," 1229. What makes up the affinity between the Black American population and African countries? The affinity in the report is underpinned by a Black nationalist imaginary. We could perhaps situate this affinity or intimacy further in the anticolonial struggles in Africa and the Third World, which inspired Black nationalism in the first place. We might also follow the scholarly insight that the Atlantic slave trade and colonialism still haunt the living realities of Black people in the United States and worldwide. The AIDS crisis among Black Americans and in Africa then is not just a statistical or epidemiological coincidence but is enmeshed in shared colonial roots and neocolonial processes. But how to datafy and visualize such transatlantic connections without sacrificing the present contextual specificities? This is an open-ended invitation to you. On transatlantic slave trade and Black experience, see Hartman, *Lose Your Mother*; and Sharpe, *In the Wake*. On popular culture and the scientific construction of Africa and AIDS, see Crane, *Scrambling for Africa*; and Glick, *Infrahumanisms*.

60. Dourish and Gómez Cruz, "Datafication and Data Fiction," 1.

61. Badgett and Sell, "Set of Proposed Indicators for the LGBTI Inclusion Index," 24.

62. Badgett and Sell, "Set of Proposed Indicators for the LGBTI Inclusion Index." 7.

63. Associated Press, "Homosexuality Not an Illness, Chinese Say."

64. See, for example, Tcheng and Human Rights Watch, "'Have You Considered Your Parents' Happiness?'"

65. Beijing Tongzhi Zhongxin, *Jingshenweisheng yu xinlizixun congyerenyuan dui xingshaoshuqunti taidu diaochabaogao*; Beijing Tongzhi Zhongxin and Beijingdaxue shehuixuexi, *2017 Zhongguo Kuaxingbiequnti shengcunxianzhuang diaochabaogao.*

66. Bao, "Conversion Therapy in China."

67. Chen, *CCMD-3*, 76 (my translation). The terms "ego-dystonic" and "ego-syntonic" are only explicated in CCMD-2-R, not CCMD-3. However, the associated interpretive distinctions underpin the CCMD-3's diagnostic descriptions. For the history of the diagnostic categories of ego-dystonic homosexuality and ego-syntonic homosexuality, see Drescher, "Queer Diagnoses Revisited."

68. For a historical overview, see Kang, "Decriminalization and Depathologization of Homosexuality in China."

69. Longarino, "Converting the Converters."

70. To be sure, the regulation of conversion therapy overlaps with but does not equal the revision of diagnostic standards. For example, in the US context, conversion therapy, even after being outlawed by professional societies, has persisted in para-clinical or pseudo-scientific spaces. While not my focus here, China's booming and internally diverse psychotherapeutic market and the lack of clear professional jurisdiction and regulatory bodies might also help explain the gap between diagnostic standards and actual clinical practices. See Waidzunas, *Straight Line*; and Huang, "From Psychotherapy to Psycho-Boom."

71. I thank Colin Garon for pointing this out.

72. The narratives of progress could erase contextual understandings of not only how LGBTI people (from the Global South) "create 'friendly space' without affirmative legislation" but also "how discrimination, marginalization, and prejudices may continue to exist in nations and cities where legal protections are in place." Browne et al., "Intervention—Gay-Friendly or Homophobic?" As a case in point, antiviolence activisms dominating the US gay and transgender advocacy agendas have produced unexpected effects of racialization and marginalization within the community. Hanhardt, *Safe Space*; Westbrook, *Unlivable Lives.*

73. Law, "Seeing Like a Survey," 239; Barad, "Agential Realism."

74. Escobar, *Designs for the Pluriverse*, xvi, 216; Gahman, "Zapatismo."

75. Mol, "Ontological Politics," 75.

76. Marres and de Rijcke, "From Indicators to Indicating Interdisciplinarity," 1042. For discussions on constituent politics, see Papadopoulos, "Alter-Ontologies."

77. Marres and de Rijcke, "From Indicators to Indicating Interdisciplinarity," 1046.

78. Mol, *Body Multiple*.

79. Dourish and Gómez Cruz, "Datafication and Data Fiction," 2.

80. On the lay/expert and public/science interfaces, see Epstein, *Impure Science*; and Lezaun, Marres, and Tironi, "Experiments in Participation."

81. Dencik, "Situating Practices in Datafication," 245, 246 (original emphasis).

82. Wan, "Zhongguo tongxinglian zouxiangzhengchang."

83. Zhonghua Yixuehui Jingshenkexuehui and Nanjing Yikedaxue Naokeyiyuan, *CCMD-2-R*, 3.

84. Rofel, *Desiring China*.

85. For similar discussions and reflections on statistical citizenship in the Euro-American context, see Shepard, "'To Fight for an End to Intrusions into the Sex Lives of Americans'" (chapter 2, this volume); Currah and Stryker, "Making Transgender Count"; and Westbrook, Budnick, and Saperstein, "Dangerous Data."

86. See also Epstein, "Cultivated Co-Production."

87. Hubbard, "Invulnerable Facts." For discussion on similar dynamics in the legally unfounded yet popularly recited "decriminalization" of homosexuality in China, see Guo, "Zhongguo youguo tongxinglian de feizuihua ma?"

88. One might argue that willful/wishful proclamations are integral to advocacy efforts toward a desired future. Gay activists in the United States also pronounced 1973 as the watershed moment of depathologization despite the similar phrasing regarding ego-dystonic homosexuality in 1974's revised DSM II. I thank Darius Longarino for pointing this out.

89. Zheng, "Yige zhendui tongxing niuzhuanzhiliao."

90. Tan, "Digital Masquerading."

91. Personal correspondence, 23 March 2022.

92. On recent activist efforts of legal mobilization around these matters, particularly impact litigation on conversion therapy, see Zhu, "Straightjacket," 177–212.

93. Lalor and Browne, "Here versus There."

94. See for example, Yi, "Politicizing LGBTQI Issues in China Could Backfire on West"; People's Daily, "Homosexuality Debate Shows Progress in Society."

95. Dencik, "Situating Practices in Datafication," 246.

96. Alvarado Garcia, Young, and Dombrowski, "On Making Data Actionable"; Hanssmann, "Epidemiological Rage"; Guyan, *Queer Data*.

97. Ferguson, *Global Shadows*, 38.

98. Cowan and Rault, "Introduction: Metaphors as Meaning and Method in Technoculture," 7.

BIBLIOGRAPHY

Ahmed, Sara. *What's the Use? On the Uses of Use*. Durham, NC: Duke University Press, 2019.

Alvarado Garcia, Adriana, Alyson L. Young, and Lynn Dombrowski. "On Making Data Actionable: How Activists Use Imperfect Data to Foster Social Change for Human Rights Violations in Mexico." *Proceedings of the ACM on Human-Computer Interaction* 1, no. CSCW (2017): 19:1–19:19.

Ames, Morgan G. *The Charisma Machine: The Life, Death, and Legacy of One Laptop per Child*. Cambridge, MA: MIT Press, 2019.

Amin, Kadji. *Disturbing Attachments: Genet, Modern Pederasty, and Queer History*. Durham, NC: Duke University Press, 2017.

Arondekar, Anjali, and Geeta Patel. "Area Impossible: Notes toward an Introduction." *GLQ: A Journal of Lesbian and Gay Studies* 22, no. 2 (2016): 151–71.

Associated Press. "Homosexuality Not an Illness, Chinese Say." *New York Times*, 8 March 2001, sec. Health.

Atanasoski, Neda. *Humanitarian Violence: The U.S. Deployment of Diversity*. Minneapolis: University of Minnesota Press, 2013.

Badgett, M. V. Lee, and Phil Crehan. "Investing in a Research Revolution for LGBTI Inclusion." World Bank Group and United Nations Development Program, 2016.

Badgett, M. V. Lee, and Randall Sell. "A Set of Proposed Indicators for the LGBTI Inclusion Index." United Nations Development Program, 2018.

Bao, Hongwei. "Conversion Therapy in China." In *Global Encyclopedia of Lesbian, Gay, Bisexual, Transgender, and Queer (LGBTQ) History*, edited by Howard Chiang, 418–22. Farmington Hills, MI: Gale, 2019.

Barad, Karen. "Agential Realism: Feminist Interventions in Understanding Scientific Practices." In *The Science Studies Reader*, edited by Mario Biagioli, 1–11. New York: Routledge, 1999.

Beijing Tongzhi Zhongxin. *Jingshenweisheng yu xinlizixun congyerenyuan dui xingshaoshuqunti taidu diaochabaogao* [A survey report on psychiatric and mental health practitioners' attitudes toward sexual minorities]. Beijing: Beijing Tongzhi Zhongxin, 2017.

Beijing Tongzhi Zhongxin and Beijingdaxue shehuixuexi. *2017 Zhongguo Kuaxingbiequnti shengcunxianzhuang diaochabaogao* [A survey report on the living conditions of transgender people in China]. Beijing: Beijing Tongzhi Zhongxin, 2017.

Benjamin, Ruha. *Race after Technology: Abolitionist Tools for the New Jim Code*. Medford, MA: Polity, 2019.

Berlant, Lauren. *Cruel Optimism*. Durham, NC: Duke University Press, 2011.

Biruk, Crystal. *Cooking Data: Culture and Politics in an African Research World.* Durham, NC: Duke University Press, 2018.

Bleys, Rudi. *The Geography of Perversion: Male-to-Male Sexual Behaviour outside the West and the Ethnographic Imagination, 1750–1918.* New York: New York University Press, 1995.

boyd, danah, and Michael Golebiewski. "Data Voids: Where Missing Data Can Easily Be Exploited." *Data and Society,* 29 October 2019. https://datasociety.net/library/data-voids/.

Brown, Wendy. "Wounded Attachments." *Political Theory* 21, no. 3 (1993): 390–410.

Browne, Kath, Niharika Banerjea, Leela Bakshi, and Nick McGlynn. "Intervention—Gay-Friendly or Homophobic? The Absence and Problems of Global Standards." *Antipode Online* (blog), 11 May 2015. https://antipodeonline.org/2015/05/11/gay-friendly-or-homophobic/.

Browne, Kath, Niharika Banerjea, Nick McGlynn, Leela Bakshi, Sumita Beethi, and Ranjita Biswas. "The Limits of Legislative Change: Moving beyond Inclusion/Exclusion to Create 'a Life Worth Living.'" *Environment and Planning C: Politics and Space* 39, no. 1 (1 February 2021): 30–52. https://doi.org/10.1177/2399654419845910.

Chang, Stewart. "The Postcolonial Problem for Global Gay Rights." *Boston University International Law Journal* 32, no. 2 (2014): 309–54.

Chen Yanfang. *CCMD-3 Zhongguo jingshenzhangai fenlei ji zhenduanbiaozhun (han yingwen mingcheng)* [Chinese classification of mental disorders, including English nomenclature]. 2001. http://www.jhak.com/uploads/soft/201410/2_05151719.pdf.

Chu, Andrea Long. "The Impossibility of Feminism." *Differences* 30, no. 1 (2019): 63–81.

Cipolla, Cyd, Kristina Gupta, and David A. Rubin, eds. *Queer Feminist Science Studies: A Reader.* Seattle: University of Washington Press, 2018.

Clarke, Adele, and Susan Leigh Star. "The Social Worlds Framework: A Theory/Method Package." In *The Handbook of Science and Technology Studies,* edited by Edward J. Hackett, Olga Amsterdamska, Michael Lynch, and Judy Wajcman, 113–37. 3rd ed. Cambridge, MA: MIT Press, published in cooperation with the Society for Social Studies of Science, 2008.

Collins, Patricia Hill. *Black Feminist Thought: Knowledge, Consciousness, and the Politics of Empowerment.* Rev. 10th anniversary ed. New York: Routledge, 2000.

Coogan-Gehr, Kelly. "The Politics of Race in U.S. Feminist Scholarship: An Archaeology." *Signs: Journal of Women in Culture and Society* 37, no. 1 (2011): 83–107.

Cowan, T. L., and Jasmine Rault. "Introduction: Metaphors as Meaning and Method in Technoculture." *Catalyst: Feminism, Theory, Technoscience* 8, no. 2 (7 November 2022). https://doi.org/10.28968/cftt.v8i2.39036.

Crane, Johanna Tayloe. *Scrambling for Africa: AIDS, Expertise, and the Rise of American Global Health Science.* Ithaca: Cornell University Press, 2013.

Crenshaw, Kimberle. "Mapping the Margins: Intersectionality, Identity Politics, and Violence against Women of Color." *Stanford Law Review* 43, no. 6 (1991): 1241–99.

Currah, Paisley, and Susan Stryker, eds. "Making Transgender Count." *TSQ: Transgender Studies Quarterly*, special issue, 2, no. 1 (2015).

Daston, Lorraine, and Peter Galison. "The Image of Objectivity." *Representations*, no. 40 (1992): 81–128.

Decena, Carlos Ulises. *Tacit Subjects: Belonging and Same-Sex Desire among Dominican Immigrant Men*. Durham, NC: Duke University Press, 2011.

Dencik, Lina. "Situating Practices in Datafication—from Above and Below." In *Citizen Media and Practice: Currents, Connections, Challenges*, edited by Hilde C. Stephensen and Emiliano Treré, 243–55. London: Routledge, 2020.

de Villiers, Nicholas. *Opacity and the Closet: Queer Tactics in Foucault, Barthes, and Warhol*. Minneapolis: University of Minnesota Press, 2012.

D'Ignazio, Catherine, and Lauren F. Klein. *Data Feminism*. Cambridge, MA: MIT Press, 2020.

Dourish, Paul, and Edgar Gómez Cruz. "Datafication and Data Fiction: Narrating Data and Narrating with Data." *Big Data and Society* 5, no. 2 (2018): 1–10.

Drescher, Jack. "Queer Diagnoses Revisited: The Past and Future of Homosexuality and Gender Diagnoses in DSM and ICD." *International Review of Psychiatry* 27, no. 5 (2015): 386–95.

Duggan, Lisa. "The New Homonormativity: The Sexual Politics of Neoliberalism." In *Materializing Democracy: Toward a Revitalized Cultural Politics*, edited by Russ Castronovo and Dana D. Nelson, 175–94. Durham, NC: Duke University Press, 2002.

Eng, David L., Judith Halberstam, and José Esteban Muñoz. "Introduction: What's Queer about Queer Studies Now." *Social Text* 23, no. 3–4 (2005): 1–17.

Epstein, Steven. "Cultivated Co-Production: Sexual Health, Human Rights, and the Revision of the ICD." *Social Studies of Science* 51, no. 5 (2021): 657–82.

——— . *Impure Science: AIDS, Activism, and the Politics of Knowledge*. Berkeley: University of California Press, 1996.

Escobar, Arturo. *Designs for the Pluriverse: Radical Interdependence, Autonomy, and the Making of Worlds*. Durham, NC: Duke University Press, 2018.

Espeland, Wendy Nelson, and Mitchell L. Stevens. "Commensuration as a Social Process." *Annual Review of Sociology* 24, no. 1 (1998): 313–43.

Falcón, Sylvanna M., and Jennifer C. Nash. "Shifting Analytics and Linking Theories: A Conversation about the 'Meaning-Making' of Intersectionality and Transnational Feminism." *Women's Studies International Forum* 50 (May–June 2015): 1–10.

Ferguson, James. *Global Shadows: Africa in the Neoliberal World Order*. Durham, NC: Duke University Press, 2006.

Fischer, Michael M. J. *Anthropology in the Meantime: Experimental Ethnography,*

Theory, and Method for the Twenty-First Century. Durham, NC: Duke University Press, 2018.

Fishman, Jennifer R., Laura Mamo, and Patrick R. Grzanka. "Sex, Gender, and Sexuality in Biomedicine." In *The Handbook of Science and Technology Studies,* edited by Ulrike Felt, 379–405. 4th ed. Cambridge, MA: MIT Press, 2017.

Flores, Andrew R., and Andrew Park. "Polarized Progress: Social Acceptance of LGBT People in 141 Countries, 1981 to 2014." Williams Institute at UCLA School of Law, 1 March 2018. https://williamsinstitute.law.ucla.edu/wp-content/uploads/Polarized -Progress-GAI-Mar-2018.pdf.

Fugard, Andi. "Should Trans People Be Postmodernist in the Streets but Positivist in the Spreadsheets? A Reply to Sullivan." *International Journal of Social Research Methodology* 23, no. 5 (2020): 525–31.

Gahman, Levi. "Zapatismo." *Global Social Theory* (blog), n.d. Accessed 11 December 2022. https://globalsocialtheory.org/topics/zapatismo/.

Glick, Megan H. *Infrahumanisms: Science, Culture, and the Making of Modern Non/ Personhood.* Durham, NC: Duke University Press, 2018.

Grundy, John, and Miriam Smith. "Activist Knowledges in Queer Politics." *Economy and Society* 36, no. 2 (2007): 294–317.

Guo Xiaofei. "Zhongguo youguo tongxinglian de feizuihua ma?" [Did China ever decriminalize homosexuality?] *Fazhi yu shehuifazhen* [Law and social development], no. 4 (2007): 51–65.

Guyan, Kevin. *Queer Data: Using Gender, Sex and Sexuality Data for Action.* London: Bloomsbury, 2022.

Hacking, Ian. *Representing and Intervening: Introductory Topics in the Philosophy of Natural Science.* Cambridge: Cambridge University Press, 1983.

Hanhardt, Christina B. *Safe Space: Gay Neighborhood History and the Politics of Violence.* Durham, NC: Duke University Press, 2013.

Hanssmann, Christoph. "Epidemiological Rage: Population, Biography, and State Responsibility in Trans-Health Activism." *Social Science and Medicine* 247 (2020): 1–11.

Haraway, Donna. *Modest_Witness@Second_Millennium.FemaleMan_Meets_Onco- Mouse: Feminism and Technoscience.* 2nd ed. New York: Routledge, 2018.

——— . *Simians, Cyborgs, and Women: The Reinvention of Nature.* New York: Routledge, 1991.

——— . "Situated Knowledges: The Science Question in Feminism and the Privilege of Partial Perspective." *Feminist Studies* 14, no. 3 (1988): 575–99.

Harding, Sandra G., ed. *The Postcolonial Science and Technology Studies Reader.* Durham, NC: Duke University Press, 2011.

——— . *Sciences from Below: Feminisms, Postcolonialities, and Modernities.* Durham, NC: Duke University Press, 2008.

Harper, Douglas. "Talking about Pictures: A Case for Photo Elicitation." *Visual Studies* 17, no. 1 (2002): 13–26. https://doi.org/10.1080/14725860220137345.

Harper, Phillip Brian. "The Evidence of Felt Intuition: Minority Experience, Everyday Life, and Critical Speculative Knowledge." *GLQ: A Journal of Lesbian and Gay Studies* 6, no. 4 (2000): 641–57.

Hartman, Saidiya V. *Lose Your Mother: A Journey along the Atlantic Slave Route.* New York: Farrar, Straus & Giroux, 2008.

Hodžić, Saida. "Ascertaining Deadly Harms: Aesthetics and Politics of Global Evidence." *Cultural Anthropology* 28, no. 1 (2013): 86–109.

——— . *The Twilight of Cutting: African Activism and Life after NGOs.* Oakland: University of California Press, 2017.

Huang, Hsuan-Ying. "From Psychotherapy to Psycho-Boom: A Historical Review of Psychotherapy in China." *Psychoanalysis and Psychotherapy in China* 1, no. 1 (2015): 1–30.

Hubbard, Joshua A. "Invulnerable Facts: Infant Mortality and Development in Nationalist Gansu." *East Asian Science, Technology and Society: An International Journal* 14, no. 4 (2020): 623–45.

Ijjasz-Vasquez, Ede, and Clifton Cortez. "To Fight Discrimination, We Need to Fill the LGBTI Data Gap." *Voices* (World Bank blog), 1 March 2017. https://blogs.worldbank.org/voices/fight-discrimination-we-need-fill-lgbti-data-gap.

Kang, Wenqing. "The Decriminalization and Depathologization of Homosexuality in China." In *China in and beyond the Headlines,* edited by Timothy B. Weston and Lionel M. Jensen, 231–48. Lanham, MD: Rowman & Littlefield, 2012.

Katz, Cindi. "On the Grounds of Globalization: A Topography for Feminist Political Engagement." *Signs: Journal of Women in Culture and Society* 26, no. 4 (2001): 1213–34.

Kennedy, Helen, and Rosemary Lucy Hill. "The Feeling of Numbers: Emotions in Everyday Engagements with Data and Their Visualisation." *Sociology* 52, no. 4 (2018): 830–48.

Lalor, Kay, and Katherine Browne. "Here versus There: Creating British Sexual Politics Elsewhere." *Feminist Legal Studies* 26, no. 2 (2018): 205–13.

Lampland, Martha, and Susan Leigh Star, eds. *Standards and Their Stories: How Quantifying, Classifying, and Formalizing Practices Shape Everyday Life.* Ithaca: Cornell University Press, 2009.

Law, John. "Seeing Like a Survey." *Cultural Sociology* 3, no. 2 (2009): 239–56.

Lezaun, Javier, Noortje Marres, and Manuel Tironi. "Experiments in Participation." In *The Handbook of Science and Technology Studies,* edited by Ulrike Felt, 195–221. 4th ed. Cambridge, MA: MIT Press, 2017.

Longarino, Darius. "Converting the Converters: Advocates in China Make the Case for

LGBT-Affirming Mental Health Care." ChinaFile, 18 October 2019. http://www
.chinafile.com/reporting-opinion/viewpoint/converting-converters.

Love, Heather. *Underdogs: Social Deviance and Queer Theory*. Chicago: University of
Chicago Press, 2021.

Macekura, Stephen J. *The Mismeasure of Progress: Economic Growth and Its Critics*.
Chicago: University of Chicago Press, 2020.

Manalansan, Martin F. "In the Shadows of Stonewall: Examining Gay Transnational
Politics and the Diasporic Dilemma." *GLQ: A Journal of Lesbian and Gay Studies* 2,
no. 4 (1995): 425–38.

Marres, Noortje, and Sarah de Rijcke. "From Indicators to Indicating Interdisciplinarity: A Participatory Mapping Methodology for Research Communities in-the-Mak-
ing." *Quantitative Science Studies* 1, no. 3 (2020): 1041–55.

Martin, Fran, Peter A. Jackson, Mark J. McLelland, and Audrey Yue, eds.
AsiaPacifiQueer: Rethinking Genders and Sexualities. Urbana: University of Illinois
Press, 2008.

McKay, Ramah. "Critical Convergences: Social Science Research as Global Health
Technology?" *Medicine Anthropology Theory* 6, no. 2 (2019): 181–92.

Merry, Sally Engle. *The Seductions of Quantification: Measuring Human Rights, Gender
Violence, and Sex Trafficking*. Chicago: University of Chicago Press, 2016.

Mohanty, Chandra Talpade. *Feminism without Borders: Decolonizing Theory, Practicing
Solidarity*. Durham, NC: Duke University Press, 2003.

Mol, Annemarie. *The Body Multiple: Ontology in Medical Practice*. Durham, NC: Duke
University Press, 2002.

——— . "Ontological Politics: A Word and Some Questions." *Sociological Review* 47,
no. S1 (1999): 74–89.

Molldrem, Stephen, and Mitali Thakor. "Genealogies and Futures of Queer STS: Issues
in Theory, Method, and Institutionalization." *Catalyst: Feminism, Theory, Technoscience* 3, no. 1 (2017): 1–15.

Murphy, Michelle. *The Economization of Life*. Durham, NC: Duke University Press, 2017.

——— . "Unsettling Care: Troubling Transnational Itineraries of Care in Feminist
Health Practices." *Social Studies of Science* 45, no. 5 (2015): 717–37.

Nelson, Alondra. *Body and Soul: The Black Panther Party and the Fight against Medical
Discrimination*. Minneapolis: University of Minnesota Press, 2011.

Papadopoulos, Dimitris. "Alter-Ontologies: Towards a Constituent Politics in Technoscience." *Social Studies of Science* 41, no. 2 (2011): 177–201.

People's Daily. "Homosexuality Debate Shows Progress in Society." Published in *Global
Times*, 17 April 2018. https://www.globaltimes.cn/page/201804/1098396.shtml.

Pryse, Marjorie. "Trans/Feminist Methodology: Bridges to Interdisciplinary Thinking."
NWSA Journal 12, no. 2 (2000): 105–18.

Puar, Jasbir K. *Terrorist Assemblages: Homonationalism in Queer Times*. Durham, NC: Duke University Press, 2007.

Quinlan, Andrea. "The Rape Kit's Promise: Techno-Optimism in the Fight against the Backlog." *Science as Culture* 30, no. 3 (2021): 440–64.

Reddy, Chandan. *Freedom with Violence: Race, Sexuality, and the US State*. Durham, NC: Duke University Press, 2011.

Rettberg, Jill Walker. "Situated Data Analysis: A New Method for Analysing Encoded Power Relationships in Social Media Platforms and Apps." *Humanities and Social Sciences Communications* 7, no. 1 (2020): 1–13.

Rofel, Lisa. *Desiring China: Experiments in Neoliberalism, Sexuality, and Public Culture*. Durham, NC: Duke University Press, 2007.

Ruckenstein, Minna, and Natasha Dow Schüll. "The Datafication of Health." *Annual Review of Anthropology* 46, no. 1 (2017): 261–78.

Sharpe, Christina Elizabeth. *In the Wake: On Blackness and Being*. Durham, NC: Duke University Press, 2016.

Spade, Dean, and Rori Rohlfs. "Legal Equality, Gay Numbers and the (After?)Math of Eugenics." *Scholar and Feminist Online* 12, no. 2 (2016).

Stark, Luke. "Come on Feel the Data (and Smell It)." *The Atlantic*, 19 May 2014. https://www.theatlantic.com/technology/archive/2014/05/data-visceralization/370899/.

Subramaniam, Banu, Laura Foster, Sandra Harding, Deboleena Roy, and Kim TallBear. "Feminism, Postcolonialism, Technoscience." In *The Handbook of Science and Technology Studies*, edited by Ulrike Felt, Rayvon Fouché, Clark A. Miller, and Laurel Smith-Doerr, 407–33. 4th ed. Cambridge, MA: MIT Press, 2017.

Tan, Jia. "Digital Masquerading: Feminist Media Activism in China." *Crime, Media, Culture* 13, no. 2 (1 August 2017): 171–86. https://doi.org/10.1177/1741659017710063.

Tcheng, Jonathan, and Human Rights Watch. "'Have You Considered Your Parents' Happiness?' Conversion Therapy against LGBT People in China." Human Rights Watch, 15 November 2017. https://www.hrw.org/report/2017/11/15/have-you-considered-your-parents-happiness/conversion-therapy-against-lgbt-people.

Waidzunas, Tom. *The Straight Line: How the Fringe Science of Ex-Gay Therapy Reoriented Sexuality*. Minneapolis: University of Minnesota Press, 2015.

Wan Yanhai. "Zhongguo tongxinglian zouxiangzhengchang" [Homosexuality in China marches toward normalization]. In *Tongxinglian feibinglihua yiji xiangguanwenjian* [Depathologization of homosexuality and related documents], 2–15. Beijing: Beijing Aizhixing Yanjiusuo.

Wernimont, Jacqueline. "Pandemic Death Counts Are Numbing: There's Another Way to Process." *Wired*, 21 July 2022 https://www.wired.com/story/covid19-data-visceralization-death-statistics/.

Westbrook, Laurel. *Unlivable Lives: Violence and Identity in Transgender Activism*. Oakland: University of California Press, 2021.

Westbrook, Laurel, Jamie Budnick, and Aliya Saperstein. "Dangerous Data: Seeing Social Surveys through the Sexuality Prism." *Sexualities* 25, no. 5–6 (2022): 717–49.

Wiegman, Robyn, and Elizabeth A. Wilson. "Introduction: Antinormativity's Queer Conventions." *Differences* 26, no. 1 (2015): 1–25.

Wilson, Phill, Kai Wright, and Michael T. Isbell. *Left Behind: Black America; A Neglected Priority in the Global AIDS Epidemic*. Los Angeles: Black AIDS Institute, 2008.

Yi Zhi. "Politicizing LGBTQI Issues in China Could Backfire on West." *Global Times*, 2 December 2021. https://www.globaltimes.cn/page/202112/1240533.shtml.

Zheng Hongbing. "Yige zhendui tongxing niuzhuanzhiliao de kangyijihua" [A protest action plan against gay conversion therapy]. *Matters*, accessed 26 January 2023. https://matters.news/@hobinz/4137-一个针对同性扭转-治疗-的抗议计划-zdpuB1352QwyKevWyLdNKSbHuqTWF9rpRH9YPG57HEWF6UZUd.

Zhonghua Yixuehui Jingshenkexuehui and Nanjing Yikedaxue Naokeyiyuan, eds. *CCMD-2-R Zhongguo jingshenjibing fenleifangan yu zhenduanbiaozhun* [Chinese classification of mental disorders and diagnostic criteria]. Nanjing: Dongnan Daxue Chubanshe, 1995.

Zhu, Jingshu. "Straightjacket: Same-Sex Orientation under Chinese Family Law—Marriage, Parenthood, Eldercare." PhD diss., Leiden University, 2018.

Zuiderent-Jerak, Teun. *Situated Intervention: Sociological Experiment in Health Care*. Cambridge, MA: MIT Press, 2015.

CONTRIBUTORS

RYAN CONRAD is an adjunct research professor at the Feminist Institute of Social Transformation at Carleton University in Ottawa, Ontario. His writing, which is archived online at faggotz.org, has appeared in journals such as *Jump Cut, Scholar and Feminist, Women Studies Quarterly*, and in edited volumes, including *Between Certain Death and a Possible Future: Queer Writing on Growing Up with the AIDS Crisis; Queer and Trans Migrations: Dynamics of Detention, Deportation, and Illegalization*; and *Decolonizing Sexualities: Transnational Perspectives and Critical Interventions*.

MATHEW GAGNÉ is an assistant professor in the Department of Sociology and Social Anthropology at Dalhousie University in Halifax, Nova Scotia. His research examines the impacts of digital media within the intimate lives of queer Beiruti men. His research is published in the *Journal of Middle East Women's Studies, Middle East Journal of Culture and Communication*, and Jadaliyya.com, as well as a chapter in *Home: Ethnographic Encounters*.

GARY KAFER is a teaching fellow in the Department of Cinema and Media Studies and in the College at the University of Chicago. His research interests include surveillance, media materialisms, biopolitics, and theories of race, gender, and sexuality. His work has appeared in numerous journals and books, including *Surveillance and Society, qui parle, Contemporaneity, Jump Cut, Digital Culture and Society*, and the edited volume *From Self-Portrait to Selfie: Representing the Self in the Moving Image* (Peter Lang, 2019). He is also the coeditor of a special "Queer Surveillance" issue of *Surveillance and Society*.

PATRICK KEILTY is associate professor in the Faculty of Information and the Cinema Studies Institute at the University of Toronto. His research interests include the politics of digital infrastructures in the sex industries and the materiality of sexual media. He has published variously on embodiment and technology, data science, the history of information retrieval, archives, design and experience, graphic design, temporality, and sexual taxonomies. His writing has appeared in *Feminist Media Studies*, *Information Society*, *Porn Studies*, *Catalyst: Feminism, Theory, Technoscience*, *Uncertain Archives* (MIT Press, 2021), and elsewhere. His other editorial work includes serving as co-lead editor of *Catalyst: Feminism, Theory, Technoscience* (2017–19); coeditor of *Feminist and Queer Information Studies Reader* (Litwin Books, 2013); the special "Traversing Technology" issue of *Scholar and Feminist Online*; the special "Reconfiguring Race, Gender, and Sexuality" issue of *Library Trends*; and the forthcoming *Handbook of Adult Film and Media* (Intellect).

HARRIS KORNSTEIN is a scholar and artist whose research and art practice focuses on surveillance, data and algorithms, media art/activism, and queer studies. Their research has been published in *Surveillance and Society*, *Curriculum Inquiry*, and *Studies in Gender and Sexuality*; their popular writing on digital culture has appeared in *The Guardian*, *Wired*, and *Salon*; and as a media artist, curator, and drag queen, they have presented work at the San Francisco Museum of Modern Art, Institute for Contemporary Art in Los Angeles, and *ONE* Archives. Harris is currently an assistant professor in the Department of Public and Applied Humanities at the University of Arizona, in Tucson.

SHAKA MCGLOTTEN is professor of media studies and anthropology at Purchase College–SUNY. Their work stages encounters between Black study, queer theory, media, and art. They have written and lectured widely on networked intimacies and messy computational entanglements as they interface with qtpoc lifeworlds. They are the author of *Virtual Intimacies: Media, Affect, and Queer Sociality*, published by SUNY Press in 2013. They are also the coeditor of two edited collections, *Black Genders and Sexualities* (with Dána-Ain Davis) and *Zombies and Sexuality* (with Steve Jones). Their book *Dragging: Or, in the Drag of a Queer Life* and their current project, *Black Data*, have been supported by Data & Society, the Alexander von Humboldt Foundation, Akademie Schloss Solitude, and Creative Capital | The Andy Warhol Foundation.

STEPHEN MOLLDREM is an assistant professor at the University of Texas Medical Branch at Galveston in the Institute for Bioethics and Health Humanities. He is an ethnographer and qualitative researcher situated at the intersection of sexuality studies, public health ethics, policy studies, and science and technology studies (STS). His research on HIV surveillance and prevention programs in the United States has focused on transformations related to the digitization of public health data systems, the emergence of HIV treatment-as-prevention as a public health strategy, and the incorporation of HIV molecular epidemiology into routine public health practice.

SUSANNA PAASONEN is professor of media studies at University of Turku in Finland. With an interest in studies of sexuality, media, and affect, she is the principal investigator of the Intimacy in Data-Driven Culture consortium, funded by the Strategic Research Council at the Academy of Finland (2019–25) and author of, for example, *Carnal Resonance: Affect and Online Pornography* (MIT Press, 2011), *Many Splendored Things: Thinking Sex and Play* (Goldsmiths Press, 2018), *NSFW: Sex, Humor, and Risk in Social Media* (MIT Press, 2019, with Kylie Jarrett and Ben Light), *Objectification: On the Difference between Sex and Sexism* (Routledge, 2020, with Feona Attwood, Alan McKee, John Mercer, and Clarissa Smith), *Who's Laughing Now? Feminist Tactics in Social Media* (MIT Press, 2020, with Jenny Sundén), *Dependent, Distracted, Bored: Affective Formations in Networked Media* (MIT Press, 2021), and *Technopharmacology* (Minnesota/Meson 2022, with Joshua Neves, Aleena Chia, and Ravi Sundaram).

NIKITA SHEPARD studies, teaches, and writes about LGBTQ communities, sexuality and gender, and social movements. They are a PhD candidate in history at Columbia University in New York, where they led the Data, Algorithms, and Social Justice Working Group at the Center for the Study of Social Difference and serve as a graduate affiliate of the Columbia Research Initiative on the Global History of Sexualities. Their dissertation explores the history of public bathrooms and political struggles around them in the modern United States. They received the 2022 Gregory Sprague Prize from the American Historical Association's Committee on LGBT History for the chapter included in this volume.

JENNY SUNDÉN is professor of gender studies at Södertörn University in Sweden. Her work is situated in the intersection of digital media studies and gender and sexuality studies. She is currently working on questions of technological brokenness, disruption, and delay, as well as on feminist uses of humor in social media as forms of resistance. She is the author of *Who's Laughing Now? Feminist Tactics in Social Media* (MIT Press, forthcoming, with Susanna

Paasonen) and *Gender and Sexuality in Online Game Cultures: Passionate Play* (Routledge, 2012, with Malin Sveningsson).

SUISUI WANG is a PhD candidate in gender studies at Indiana University Bloomington. He is broadly interested in feminist and queer studies, science and technology studies, and the transnational and intersectional imbrications within and between these fields. His research has examined conversion therapy and crisis hotlines as sites and devices for activist mobilizations in health, law, and technoscience. He is currently working on his dissertation, titled "Answering the Call(s): Women's and LGBT Hotlines, Interface Politics, and the Infrastructuralization of Crisis."

LINA ŽIGELYTĖ is a researcher, educator, curator, and audiovisual artist. She was born in Vilnius, Lithuania, and is now based in western New York. Her scholarly work explores the relationships between transnational media history and sexuality studies. Her writing has been published in *Another Gaze: A Feminist Film Journal*, *Open Democracy*, *Kreivės Magazine*, and *Flaherty Stories: Voices from the Robert Flaherty Film Seminar*, edited by Patricia R. Zimmermann and Scott MacDonald (Indiana University Press, 2021). She served as a faculty member at Hobart and William Smith Colleges and the University of Rochester. She works in the tech industry and helps create digital technologies for cancer research, health care, education, and community organizing.

INDEX

black ops, 7, 33, 37–38
Black people, 17–29, 86; AIDS, 261–62; civil rights movement, 53; data visualization, 183, 261–62; exclusion from queer data collection, 180; invisibility and hypervisibility, 19, 87; maps, 261–62; online life, 21; police killing of, 18, 23; police profiling of, 29; "racist algorithms" and, 98. *See also* Black Lives Matter
Black Quantum Futurism Collective, 20
Black queer studies, 22, 23–24, 38
Black Twitter, 20, 21
Blas, Zach, 30–32, 51, 85, 86
Boellstorff, Tom, 145
Boise, Idaho: homosexual scandal of 1955, 57–58
Boston Marathon bombing: biometrics and, 29–30
Bowers v. Hardwick, 70, 71, 81n78
breasts, female, 119; nipples, 116–18, 119–20, 122; in social media, 114–15
Breedlove, Lynn, 228–31, 234, 235, 237, 240, 242–44
Bregler, Christoph, 29–30
Brock, André, 19–20
Brooks, Daphne, 27, 102n19
Brown, Jayna, 231
Browne, Kath, 270, 275n44, 276n59
Browne, Simone, 18–19, 30, 88, 104n48

California Public Utilities Commission (CPUC), 232–33
California Supreme Court, 60
Camera Surveillance, 54–55, 58
Cameron, Andy, 109
Cameron, Bruce, 59
Campbell, Elmer Simms, 183
Canada v. Bedford, 165

Canadian Organization of the Rights of Prostitutes (CORP), 168
Captivating Technology (Benjamin), 20
The Case against Colonel Sutton (Cameron), 59
Census, US, 49–50, 179, 180
Centers for Disease Control (CDC), 131, 132
Chalabi, Mona, 183–84
Chen, Mel, 23
Chicago Gay Alliance, 65
China: conversion therapy, 255, 263–65, 268–70, 277n70; depathologization of homosexuality, 263–65, 267–70; social media, 109
Chinese Classification of Mental Disorders, 3rd revision (CCMD-3), 263, 264–65, 268, 269
Chow-White, Peter, 40n24
Chun, Wendy, 30, 83, 231
Clinton, Chelsea, 50
Clinton, Hillary, 269
Cloudflare, 160, 161, 162
Cockerline, Danny, 168
Cohen, Cathy, 136
Cohn, Roy, 129
Cold War, 53, 56, 96, 267
Coleman, Beth, 40n24
collaborative projects, 191, 192–93
commensurability. *See* (in)commensurability
community standards, 107, 108, 111, 113
computer vision-based pornography filtering (CVPF), 115
Conrad, Kathryn, 72
Conrad, Ryan, 112–13
consent, 1–2, 51; HIV data collection and, 131, 132; social media content, 112–13, 122, 192; third-party advertising, 162

facial recognition systems, 17, 30–32, 73, 98

"Facial Weaponization Suite" (Blas), 30–32

Fag Face Mask (Blas), 30–32

Fairchild, William, 57–58

Fair Employment Committee, 61–62

Fairey, Shepard: "Yes We Scan" alteration, 25, 26

Faust, Gretchen, 120

FBI, 53, 54, 56, 57, 67, 68; myRedBook raid, 157

female breasts, 114–15, 119; nipples, 116–18, 119–20, 122

feminism: epistemology, 259; feminist anthropology, 214; "non-innocence," 254; social media filtering and, 122

Ferguson, James, 271

Fidelifacts, 57, 62, 63, 64

Fight Online Sex Trafficking Act—Stop Enabling Sex Traffickers Act, 163

fingerprints, 32

Fischel, Joseph, 122

Florida, Richard, 34

Foucault, Michael, 128, 133, 135, 145

Fourth Amendment, 60

Free the Nipple movement, 117–20

French, Martin, 134, 137

Fritsch, Kelly, 11

Gaboury, Jacob, 84, 242

Galloway, Alexander, 28

Gay Activists Alliance (GAA), 52, 61–65, 67–68, 80n74

gay bathhouse raids, 167

gaydar, 29

gay men: AIDS and, 128–29; escort services, 155–62, 164, 165; overrepresentation in surveys, 180; sex work, 155, 158

Gehl, Robert W., 115

gender nonconforming people, 55, 57, 59, 98, 116, 135–36

gentrification, 33, 34, 35, 36–37

Gieseking, Jen Jack, 188–89, 237, 240

Gillen, Vincent, 64, 79n56

Glissant, Édouard, 27, 84, 85, 86, 94–96, 99–100; "penetrability," 87, 88; Simek on, 102n16

The Golden Girls, 129

Gómez Cruz, Edgar, 266

Goodell, Charles, 63

Google buses, 35

"Google Google, Apps Apps" (Black Glitter Collective), 33–38

government employees' rights, 62

Grindr, 205, 207, 217, 218, 219; 2018 data leak, 183

Griswold v. Connecticut, 70, 81n76

Guibert, Hervé, 128–29

Guyan, Kevin, 11

Haber, Benjamin, 236

Halberstam, Jack, 37, 51, 101, 175, 234–35, 236, 242

Halperin, David M., 135

Hamraie, Amy, 11

Hanna, Alex, 240–41

Haraway, Donna, 235, 254, 260

Hartman, Saidiya, 4

Hein, Vain, 36, *36*

heterosexism, 116, 117, 118

Highsmith, Patricia, 59

HIV/AIDS, 22, 70–71; Black people, 261–62, 276n59; hierarchies of disclosure, 137; HIV genetic sequence data, 138–39; "malicious infectors," 142–43; new sex hierarchy, 141–43, 144; treatment as prevention, 130–40;

viral load tests, 130, 132, 137, 138, 140, 141

HIV Care Continuum, 138

Hodžić, Saida, 256

Hoffman, Anna Lauren: "data violence," 180

Homobiles: accessibility, 238; beginnings of, 230–31; and data, 234–36; and intimacy, 237; and service and safety, 231–32, 237–38, 239; volunteers, 231, 232, 233, 237, 241; and word of mouth, 239. *See also* "safe ride" program

homophobia, 158, 221, 258; eastern Europe, 180, 181; Middle East, 206, 221, 257

homosexuality, depathologization of, 263–65, 267–70, 278n88

hooks, bell, 241

Hornet, 205, 219

housing, 56; European survey, 181

Howard, Clayton, 56

How to Be Black (Online) (Thurston), 21

Human Rights Campaign, 50

Humphreys, Laud, 1–2, 51

Hurant, Jeffrey, 155–56, 157

Hwang, Ren-yo, 232

hypervisibility: black bloc, 42n53; Black invisibility and, 87; Black women, 19; performative, 27

identification, biometric. *See* biometrics

ignorance, political value of, 234–35, 236, 243

Igo, Sarah, 73

Imre, Anikó, 177

(in)commensurability, 85, 86–87, 88, 89

Indy Companion, 164, 167

"infrastructure of intimacy" (Wilson), 237

Instagram, 109, 111, 115, 116, 121

intersectionality, 19, 136

intuition, 25

iris scans, 32

Jacobs, Julia, 117

Jennings, Dale, 60

job screening. *See* employee screening and employment discrimination

Jones, Stacy Holman, 215

Joseph, Miranda, 245n9

Joseph, Steven, 70

Kafer, Gary, 20, 75, 111

Katz, Cindi, 260, 276n59

Keeling, Kara, 97, 100, 231

Keilty, Patrick, 209

Keyes, Os, 183

Kingsley, Jeff, 161

Kornstein, Harris, 89

Kushner, Tony, 129

Lambda Legal, 50

"Lavender Scare," 53–58

Lawrence v. Texas, 71

Lefebvre, Nathalie, 163–65, 166, 167

Left Behind: Black America: A Neglected Priority in the Global AIDS Epidemic, 261

lesbians, 69–70; *The Ladder*, 57; right to privacy, 60–61

LGBTQ Global Acceptance map, 256–62

LGBTQ people: antiqueer legislation, 12; assimilation, 175, 243, 258; bathhouse raids, 167; China, 263–65, 267–70; conversion therapy, 255, 262–65, 268–70, 277n70; depathologization, 263–65, 267–70, 278n88; "inclusion index," 253–54, 255; "Lavender Scare" repression, 53–58; marriage, 72, 178, 257; US census, 179, 180; violence against, 177. *See also* gaydar; gay men; homophobia; lesbians; queers of color

FEMINIST TECHNOSCIENCES

Rebecca Herzig and Banu Subramaniam, Series Editors

Figuring the Population Bomb: Gender and Demography in the Mid-Twentieth Century, by Carole R. McCann

Risky Bodies and Techno-Intimacy: Reflections on Sexuality, Media, Science, Finance, by Geeta Patel

Reinventing Hoodia: Peoples, Plants, and Patents in South Africa, by Laura A. Foster

Queer Feminist Science Studies: A Reader, edited by Cyd Cipolla, Kristina Gupta, David A. Rubin, and Angela Willey

Gender before Birth: Sex Selection in a Transnational Context, by Rajani Bhatia

Molecular Feminisms: Biology, Becomings, and Life in the Lab, by Deboleena Roy

Holy Science: The Biopolitics of Hindu Nationalism, by Banu Subramaniam

Bad Dog: Pit Bull Politics and Multispecies Justice, by Harlan Weaver

Underflows: Queer Trans Ecologies and River Justice, by Cleo Wölfle Hazard

Hacking the Underground: Disability, Infrastructure, and London's Public Transport System, by Raquel Velho

Queer Data Studies, edited by Patrick Keilty